FOLLOWING IN HIS STEPS

THE EVANGELICAL LUTHERAN GOOD SAMARITAN SOCIETY 1922 - 1997

By Lynwood E. Oyos

Ex Machina Publishing Company
for The Evangelical Lutheran
Good Samaritan Society

FOLLOWING IN HIS STEPS

The Evangelical Lutheran
Good Samaritan Society
1922-1997
By Lynwood E. Oyos

Copyright © 1998 by The Evangelical Lutheran Good
Samaritan Society.

Published by Ex Machina Publishing Company
Sioux Falls, South Dakota
for The Evangelical Lutheran Good Samaritan Society

Second Printing, 2005

Dustjacket photo of author courtesy of Augustana College

Photo page 244 © 1995 by Sioux Falls *Argus Leader*, used by
permission

Library of Congress Catalog Card Number: 97-77440

ISBN 0-944287-19-0

FOREWORD

The genesis for this history came in the spring of 1994 at a luncheon meeting with Dr. Mark Jerstad, president of the Good Samaritan Society, and Dr. Elliot Thoreson, a member of the Society's Board of Directors. Doctor Jerstad asked if I would be willing to prepare a history of the Good Samaritan Society for the occasion of its seventy-fifth anniversary in 1997. The account which follows indicates my response.

The real beginning of this story, of course, was with a young Lutheran pastor who volunteered to serve "wherever no one else wants to go." After 14 years of serving parishes in North Dakota, Reverend August Hoeger, Sr., was led by faith to found the Good Samaritan Society. What followed involves two stories.

The two stories — that of two families, the Hoegers and the Jerstads, and that of the Good Samaritan Society — are woven in this book, as in reality, into a single narrative from in September 1922 to the present. The telling of this story has required the tools of both history and biography; the effort to illuminate the qualities of Dad Hoeger, his sons, Augie and John, and his grandson, Mark Jerstad, has demanded occasional departures from chronology. Yet, the spine of this work is narrative.

There is a quality to the history of the Good Samaritan Society which can be conveyed only through narrative — the commitment of its leaders and employees to Christ-centered, quality care for the handicapped, disadvantaged young people, and foremost, the elderly. Guided by this conviction and bolstered by their unwavering faith in God and his son, Jesus Christ, the Society's leaders and their fellow workers moved together, sometimes through painful adversities, toward undreamed-of achievements. Seventy-five years after its humble beginning in the rural community of Arthur, North Dakota, the Good Samaritan Society has become the largest, nonprofit, long-term care corporation in the United States. Throughout this time of achievement, innovation, and growth, the Society's foremost concern has always been its commitment to its Christian mission. — ***Lynwood E. Oyos***

ACKNOWLEDGMENTS

Every historian depends absolutely on available archives. In this case, I am indebted to Augie and Betty Hoeger, who between 1987 and 1989 organized the current archives of the Good Samaritan Society.

A very special thank you is due those people who shared their experiences, memories, and ideas through personal interviews with me. They gave of their time and their memories because of their great love for and belief in the Good Samaritan Society.

My wife, Bedia, has been at my side through all my writing. She shared in the research and shaping of the story, helped me to articulate the larger themes, and spent much time editing the manuscript.

It was a joy to work at the national headquarters of the Good Samaritan Society. The personnel were extremely helpful and hospitable; their spirit exemplifies the spirit of the Society.

The pages that follow were written with great humility toward the task and with affection for the people and circumstances dealt with. — *L.E.O.*

CONTENTS

August John Hoeger with his mother, Maria Hoeflinger Hoeger.

Chapter One
AS THE TWIG IS BENT

*"Honor your father and mother,
that it may be well with you and that
you may live long on the earth."
—Ephesians 6:2-3.*

The shaping of the man who would found the Good Samaritan Society began in the farm country near Sterling, Nebraska. Following the completion of elementary school, August John Hoeger began working on the farm of a widow, Tjade Ehmen, located approximately thirty-five miles southeast of Lincoln, Nebraska. He wanted to repay a $300 loan made to his mother, Maria Hoeflinger Hoeger, by her close friend, Mrs. Ehmen. Maria had invested the money in a variety store in Sterling.[1] Having repaid the loan, August rented land and machinery in the winter of 1902. He had determined to be a farmer. He loved to till the soil, to plant seed and to watch it grow. As spring approached, he made plans to buy a team of horses and to plant a crop.

The solitude of his rural environment enabled the 18-year-old Hoeger to carry on his prayer life and to reflect on his existence, on social needs, and on his relationship with God. He prayed for guidance. As the snow melted across Nebraska's countryside, a dramatic change took place in the teenager's thinking. He decided that the Lord wanted him to become a minister. He would cast seeds, but they would be the seeds of the Word. Within two decades after he made this fateful decision, August J. Hoeger would establish The Evangelical Lutheran Good Samaritan Society upon Christian principles of faith and service that have endured for 75 years.

His decision to enter the ministry was also shaped by his home life. His mother and his father were part of the missionary movement that emanated from the small Bavarian village of Neuendettelsau, Germany, in the latter half of the 19th century. Residing in Neuendettelsau was Reverend Wilhelm Loehe, the Director of Foreign and Inner Missions for the German Lutheran Church. Loehe played a key role in sending mission people to the United States to work among the settlers and the Indians.

August's father, John Jacob Hoeger, came to the United States as a lay missionary to the Indians and to assist in the development of the Lutheran Church on the northern Prairie Plains. In 1857, he became the house father and farm manager of Wartburg Seminary at St. Sebald, Iowa, near Strawberry Point.[2] John Jacob Hoeger was married twice. He and his first wife, Amelia Oppermann Hoeger, had two children. Augusta Christina was born on October 26, 1862. Johann Michael Siegmund Hoeger was born on February 10, 1864. Three years later, on February 25, 1867, Amelia died after the birth of a stillborn child.[3]

John Jacob wrote to Reverend Loehe, requesting the assistance of a young woman to care for and to provide spiritual training for his two young children. Twenty-nine-year-old Sister Maria Hoeflinger of Nordlingen, Bavaria, responded to his call. Maria had been trained as a deaconess at the Augsburg Deaconess Training School. With her five years of nursing experience, she had served in the war against Prussia (1866), caring for the sick and wounded of the Bavarian Army. Using a passport dated May 16, 1868, the brown-haired Maria traveled from Nordlingen to Bremen, where she boarded a sailing ship, the *Johannes*, for the two month voyage to North America. During the ocean voyage, Maria recorded that the weather was stormy, and the meals were very poor.[4]

Arriving at Wartburg Seminary, she was introduced to Hoeger and to a Reverend J. M. Schueller, who was the founder and superintendent of an orphanage at Andrew, Iowa. A reluctant Maria accepted Schueller's invitation to go to Andrew to serve as an administrator. Accompanying her were Hoeger's two small children, Augusta and Siegmund.

Maria experienced great difficulties at the orphanage. She found it difficult to communicate with her young charges as they spoke English and she spoke German. An orphan herself since age three, she reported that the orphanage was dirty, the boys were undisciplined, and Pastor Schueller was corrupt. Later on, his nefarious activities were revealed, and with a warrant issued for his arrest, he fled to Europe.[5]

For five years, Maria endured adverse conditions at the orphanage. In the meantime, Wartburg Seminary had been transferred from St. Sebald to Mendota, Illinois. John Jacob Hoeger was offered a promotion at the Seminary, but he said he would fill the position only if he had a wife. He journeyed to Andrew and asked Maria to be his bride. Although he was 15 years her senior, she said that esteem and respect kept her from saying no. She, with the two children and an 18-month-old orphan named Karl, accompanied Hoeger to St. Sebald. John Jacob and Maria were married at St. Sebald Church on November 5, 1873. A few months later, they moved to Mendota, where she became housemother to the seminarians. The Hoeger family, along with the students, resided in the seminary building. For a time, they experienced a hand-to-mouth existence. John Jacob Hoeger would hitch up the horses to a wagon and travel to neighboring farms, literally begging for food. When sufficient cabbage, beans and potatoes had been secured, he would hurry back to the Seminary, and Maria would quickly prepare the produce for the hungry students.[6] While at Mendota, Maria gave birth to five sons, the last being the farm boy turned seminarian, August John Hoeger, on July 12, 1885. Four years later, the Hoeger family relocated to Dubuque, Iowa, the new site of the well-traveled Seminary.

August's father died of stomach cancer on October 27, 1892. Maria, a middle-aged widow with no property or pension, searched for a way to support her children. While residing in Mendota, she and John Jacob had become good friends with William and Tjade Ehmen. William Ehmen graduated from the Seminary and accepted a call to western Nebraska. Despite being separated by distance, Maria and Tjade continued to communicate with one another. At this time of crisis, her old friend, Mrs. Ehmen, also a widow by this time, encouraged Maria to come to Sterling, Nebraska, and loaned her the $300 to open a variety store, from which Maria sold stationery, notions, toys and other miscellaneous items.[7]

Maria's influence on young August is reflected through the many letters she wrote to him during his youth and until her death on December 12, 1912. She was a deeply Christian woman, a faithful and understanding parent. Maria constantly guided, polished, and improved August's ways. She admonished him lovingly, reminded him of his goals and encouraged him.[8]

In returning to the academic world, August Hoeger faced the first of several major challenges during his long and productive life. The pattern for his life, however, had been set. If this was what the Lord wanted, he would do it. In his later years, he remarked that he had decided to "Let go and let God." August was inadequately prepared for seminary training. Thus, he spent the first two years at Wartburg College, Waverly, Iowa, taking general preparatory courses. He had difficulty writing essays as he lacked proper training in grammar and spelling. He also had difficulty in pronouncing many words.

His mother was his strongest supporter. In her letters, she encouraged him to stay the course. His writing skills did improve, and one of his grade sheets indicated that he received a 94 in his composition class. The same academic record noted that August was above the middle of his class.[9] Maria Hoeger also provided financial help, and August received free room and board because he resided in Waverly with his brother, Henry, who owned a local newspaper, *The Democrat*.

August's academic difficulties continued as he moved on to Wartburg Seminary, Dubuque, Iowa, where the textbooks were in German, and the instructors spoke German in the classroom. The academic disciplines were taught in two sections. The Practical Section was designed for students who were somewhat older and who had not had the advantage of a complete college education. They did not have to take Hebrew; they took just enough Greek to understand the gist. The Theoretical Section followed the old humanistic curriculum in Germany, requiring Hebrew, Greek and Latin.[10] August was enrolled in the Practical Section. Hoeger appreciated theological discussions, but he often had difficulty grasping the complexities of the doctrines under consideration. He received tutorial help from Professors Fritschel and Rue. Professor Conrad S. Fritschel, the father of Dr. Erwin Fritschel, a founder of the Bonell Nursing Home, the Good Samaritan facility at Greeley, Colorado, was also equipped to teach courses in English. Many of the seminary students were required to preach in either English or German following their graduation from Wartburg Seminary. Hoeger's commitment to service is found in a paper he wrote while at the Seminary. In the "The Value of Education," he wrote, "No man is truly educated until his relation to his fellow men and his desire to serve them fill a large place in his thoughts."[11]

At the seminary, Reverend William Kraushaar and Hoeger lived in an old wooden building with brick facing. Once when there was a fire on the second floor, August was a part of the "bucket brigade" which put it out. He served as a janitor and fired the furnace for two years, which meant that he had to get up earlier than the other students. Kraushaar reported that they and the 60-70 other seminarians led a disciplined life. The students had to get up at 6:00 a.m. and go to a study room for a half hour of private devotions. At 7:00 a.m. one of the students conducted a group devotion before they went to breakfast.

There were diversions from the classroom. August loved music and played the violin in the Seminary orchestra from 1905 to 1908. He played the piano, as well, and he developed a lifelong love of listening to grand opera. He and his fellow students took long walks. On one occasion, they hiked 28 miles to a monastery. They started at 4:00 A.M. and returned to the Seminary at 10:00 p.m. Dead tired after walking 56 miles, they reported that everyone was silent at the monastery except for a designated spokesman.[12]

Firmly convinced that the ministry would be the best way for him to do Kingdom work, and with dogged determination, August prevailed. Although it took him four years, rather than the normal three, he graduated from Wartburg Seminary with 12 other men on June 25, 1908.[13] He was ordained into the Lutheran ministry at Waverly three days later. When asked by Church officials where he would like to serve, he replied, "Wherever no one else wants to go."[14]

Hoeger was assigned to an area where few pastors wanted to go, south-central North Dakota. The region was ripe for mission work. For several years, thousands of Germans from Russia had come to this area via the Northern Pacific Railroad. Debarking at Jamestown or Bismarck, the immigrants claimed homesteads in the region between the two cities and south into northern South Dakota. The topography was much like the Russian steppe from which they came. The land was a rolling plain, almost devoid of trees and subject to bitter cold and fierce winter blizzards.

Reverend Hoeger was accompanied to Arena, North Dakota, by his 69-year-old mother, Maria. She had sold the store in Sterling, Nebraska, to help her son plant the seed of the Word in the hearts of these hearty sod busters and their children. There was no parsonage so their first residence was a two-story dwelling on a 160-acre homestead which August acquired near Tuttle in western Kidder County.[15] It was a primitive area judged by modern day standards. There were no roads, only prairie trails. There were no fences and the cattle ran loose. Most people traveled by horse and buggy, including Reverend Hoeger. Cow chips were used for fuel. Construction lumber could be obtained at Goodrich, 25 miles to the north. For several years, many of the settlers lived in sod houses.[16] Within their small dwelling, the Hoegers heard the wind and coyotes howling during the night.

Undaunted by these conditions, Reverend Hoeger began immediately to display the energy and vision that characterized his life. At first, he used schools for places of worship. He gratefully recalled, "The services were so crowded, we'd have more standing outside, looking in, than in, looking out."[17] A year after his arrival, the Zion Langedahl congregation, southwest of Tuttle, had its own house of worship. The church, constructed under Hoeger's supervision, was dedicated on October 24, 1909. The structure had a large pot-bellied stove in the middle of the nave. During worship services, the women sat on one side, the men on the other and the children in front. Early in 1916, German-speaking Lutherans in Tuttle organized their own congregation. Under Pastor Hoeger's direction, they began building a church, St. Paul Lutheran, which was completed and dedicated in 1918.[18]

Maria Hoeger spent only one year with her son in North Dakota. She moved to Mendota, Illinois, to live with another of her sons, Adolph, following August's marriage to Amelia Aden on June 24, 1909, at Gothenburg, Nebraska.[19] He had met Amelia while conducting a Summer Bible School at Gothenburg during his seminary training. Their first conversation followed Amelia's running into him while she was roller skating, knocking August's hat off. He often walked her home after she finished work at her brother's store in Gothenburg. He was welcomed into the Aden home, and he entered into lively conversations with her parents. Amelia helped the courtship along. When she received a letter from August stating that he was unable to afford a trip to Gothenburg because of his meagre salary, 18-year-old Amelia, who had been doing odd jobs around the community, offered to pay his way. She told August that the only other people who would know about her offer were her parents.

His marriage to Amelia followed a two-year engagement. August brought his 19-year-old bride to North Dakota by train, via Minneapolis. With the help of parishioners, he built a seven room house on the homestead, near a small lake. Amelia's father had given the newlyweds $500 with which to furnish their new home. August used the money to buy a buggy and a pair of trotters. Later on, he made up for this mistake by promising Amelia that she could have any piece of furniture she desired.[20] At first, Amelia had difficulty communicating with the settlers as she spoke a different German dialect. She soon received instructions from some of the housewives for the preparation and preservation of foodstuffs. Beef was canned, crocks were filled with sauerkraut, other meats were fried in lard (for preservation), and eggs were placed in a preservative.[21] The congregations often gave the young couple food, particularly pork, and extended frequent invitations to dinner following worship services.[22]

The Hoegers kept busy at the homestead and in parish work. They cared for a garden, chickens, one or two cows and a couple of horses. One source indicated that August rented out his farm land and that threshers came to the home during the harvest season. Amelia would go out to the pasture, picking up cow chips and carrying them in a sack over her shoulder back to the house, where she used the chips as fuel in the kitchen range. August was constantly moving across the countryside to conduct services in his multi-point parish, with services at Arena and Langedahl in the morning and another service at Tuttle on Sunday afternoon. At Arena he conducted a Summer Vacation Bible School, following the conclusion of public school in May. During these six weeks of day-long confirmation instruction, the students learned how to read and write German.[23] There was a blanket on the classroom wall with the admonition, *auf Deutsch*, — "Children, here we speak German."[24] For his pastoral endeavors, Reverend Hoeger received $500 per year.[25]

His disdain of personal materialism was displayed early in his ministry. On one occasion, Amelia gave August money to buy new shoes, but he found someone who needed the money more than he did and he gave it away.[26] When he was not involved in parish work, Reverend Hoeger was always reading, making plans, or helping to build the community. Hoeger ordered many books from Germany, including texts that described working with the handicapped at the Bethel Institute in Bielefeld, Germany. Ideas were being planted in his mind that would be realized a few years later at Arthur, North Dakota.

He wanted more people to settle in Burleigh and Kidder counties. To this end, he founded the Lutheran Colonization Society of Arena, North Dakota. August placed an ad in the Church paper, inviting people to come and see the land. When this effort failed, he turned to improving the quality of life for farm families in the area. His interest in farming never diminished. He loved the smell of moistened earth ready for the seeder. In his efforts to bring quality farming to his parishioners, Hoeger traveled to Fargo, North Dakota, and purchased a pure-blooded registered Holstein cow, named Selma, Sian the Brightest, for $100. At first the bemused farmers smiled at this, but they soon discovered that such cattle adapted well to the severe winters and that they gave more milk. The dynamic and perceptive pastor-farmer brought with him Leghorn chickens, as well, which soon proved to be the best layers of any chickens in the region.

Reverend Hoeger was disturbed by the prevalence of "ethnic gopher holes" on the Prairie Plains. The various nationalities such as German, Norwegian, and Danish tended to associate only with their own ethnic group. In a lengthy article directed at the entire Lutheran church, Hoeger provided an exhaustive survey of Inner Mission work in America. Inner Mission referred to the institutions and social services related to the Christian Church in contrast with secular institutions. He criticized the ethnic separations mentioned above and the policy of having homes for German Lutherans, homes for Norwegian Lutherans, *etc.* What was needed, he wrote, were Lutheran Christian homes for all people who needed help as the children of God. He went on to state what constituted proper Christian homes. The qualities he associated with these homes became the guiding principles for the Good Samaritan Society. He argued that secular organizations were primarily concerned with the external welfare of humans while Christian homes saved souls for the Lord. Hoeger wrote:

> But we must not say that we do not need Christian homes when so many others are at work, because there is a big difference between Inner Mission and the so-called social services. Those engaged in social services want mainly to improve the external welfare of their fellow men. All workers of the Inner Mission, however, see the main purpose of their work as saving souls for the Lord. To improve the external well-being is only a secondary purpose because a person is only helped if he or she lives in peace with God. The Lord said to the paralytic: "Your sins are forgiven." And then after that, "Take up your bed and walk." What good comes of it for the people if they are relieved of all misery and can live in a beautiful state institution with all the modern comfortable furnishings but have no peace and rest in their hearts. Therefore, it must be the main purpose of all Inner Mission institutions to lead the souls to the Lord.[27]

Hoeger's reading also included works on foreign missions. Realizing that the Iowa Synod had no definite mission field of its own, he proposed the organization of a foreign mission society. To realize his vision, he worked with a few other pastors on the northern Prairie Plains, including Reverend Martin Wiederaenders at nearby Goodrich, North Dakota. Reverend Hoeger wrote an article for *Die Kirchlich Zeitsschrift*, a pastors' magazine, suggesting ways by which congregations would become interested in foreign missions. Despite economic hardships, people responded and agreed to subsidize a mission field in New Guinea.[28] The New Guinea mission was orphaned during World War I as communications with mission headquarters in Neuendettelsau, Germany, were cut off. After the war, through the efforts of an Australian Lutheran pastor, the group led by Hoeger and Wiederaenders renewed support for the New Guinea mission. Across the Prairie Plains the faithful gathered in tents for mission festivals. To sustain the interest in foreign missions, Hoeger and Wiederaenders published a monthly mission magazine, *Die Mission Stunde*.[29] August mortgaged his homestead for $2,000 to start the publication. The periodical was later renamed *The Lutheran Missionary*, and it was published nationwide by the American Lutheran Church until 1970. The Mission Auxiliary which August Hoeger organized in the old Iowa Synod in 1915, the *Mission Huelfs Verein*, was the forerunner of the Board of World Missions of the first American Lutheran Church. Several of the Synod's leaders had first opposed the idea of a mission society.[30]

Reverend Hoeger honed his fund-raising skills in support of the mission in New Guinea. He printed pamphlets directed to women's clubs of the ALC. For example, the mission station in New Guinea needed a saw mill to prepare lumber for the construction of houses. Using photographs and a logical narrative, he compared the output of 20 men using hand saws, sawing 2,500 board feet in 28 days with the same output using a motor saw in half-a-day. He appealed for $2,000 to $3,000 to purchase the power saw and construct a saw mill.[31] After 1922, Hoeger effectively used publications to raise monies for the Good Samaritan Society.[32]

The United States entered World War I on April 6, 1917. The next year, the pastor at Arthur, North Dakota, Reverend J. H. Groth, joined the U.S. Navy as a chaplain. Reverend August J. Hoeger accepted the call to be Groth's successor. His ten years of

Kingdom work in south-central North Dakota had been productive and fruitful. The Word of God had been conveyed to many hearty prairie folk, congregations formed, churches constructed, confirmands trained and a foreign mission program established. These were formative years for the young farmer- turned-pastor. Several of his visions had become realities, and he had been able to develop his Christian entrepreneurial skills. After a two day drive from Arena in their Model T Ford, purchased in 1914, Reverend and Mrs. Hoeger and their three daughters – Agnes, Ruth and Cecelia – arrived in Arthur on a May evening in 1918. They were unaware of the dramatic changes that were to take place in their lives in the next decade.

Chapter Two
AN INSTRUMENT
IN GOD'S HANDS
1918-1925

"...You shall love the Lord your God
with all your heart, and with all your
soul, and with all your strength, and
with all your mind. And you must love
your neighbor just as much as you
love yourself." —Luke 10:27.

Within six months of accepting the call to Arthur, Reverend August Hoeger had revolutionized the St. John's parish. The quiet and energetic pastor possessed a certain charisma when he spoke from the pulpit.[1] While his sermons were not scholarly, they reflected his deep faith. He used simple language that rural people understood and liked, and he exuded enthusiasm as he wove biblical citations and personal experiences into his message. He became a popular speaker at the annual summer Bible Camp held at a 4-H retreat center south of Leonard, North Dakota. Pastor Hoeger loved young people, and they, in turn, wanted him to conduct Bible Studies because he could relate biblical events in a language they could understand.[2]

Area pastors wanted him to speak to their congregations when Mission Festival Sunday was held each summer. Customarily, this event was held in the community's park with services in the morning and afternoon, interrupted by a potluck picnic at noon. Hoeger's impact as a fund raiser was felt during his first summer at his two-point parish in Arthur and Amenia. The prior summer, the offering for the combined congregations in a Missionfest at Amenia was $65.00. In his first summer at Arthur, Reverend Hoeger held Missionfests at both sites; at Amenia, the offering was over $200.00 and at Arthur it totaled $300.00.[3]

During the 1920s, Hoeger was invited to preach to mission festival audiences in other states. For three consecutive years, he spoke to one of his former Wartburg Seminary classmate's congregation. The congregation had never given over $50.00 for the missions' cause. After Pastor Hoeger's first presentation, the congregation gave $75.00; the second year they gave over $300.00 and after his third presentation, the offering plates contained over $500.00. The president of the congregation told his pastor — "Don't get Hoeger to speak again or we will all be in the poor house."[4]

St. John's Lutheran Church at Arthur was a former schoolhouse which had been purchased and furnished for $400.00. The unattractive building accommodated only a small number of people. Capitalizing on the economic prosperity that immediately followed the end of World War I in 1918, Pastor Hoeger headed up a drive to build a new church. At a meeting in January 1919, he suggested that the 30-family congregation build a new red brick church. After several people made known their opposition to the building proposal, Hoeger announced in his sermon on the Sunday before construction was to start, "Tomorrow morning we are going to start digging for the church. I am going to be here with my spade. If any of the rest of you show up, all right, and if you don't, I will just keep on digging myself." Everybody showed up.[5]

At a cost of $12,000, the 30-by-60-foot structure was dedicated on June 27, 1920. Members of the congregation made individual contributions, and the Ladies' Society raised $1,500 for interior decorations, including the art glass windows. The Youth Club paid for the pipe organ, using funds earned through helping harvest the fall potato crop.[6] Nevertheless, as they moved into their new house of worship, the congregation still had a debt of several thousand dollars.[7]

St. Martin's congregation, a country church six miles from Arthur, was added to Pastor Hoeger's responsibilities.[8] He commuted to St. Martin's in his old Model-T Ford with open side curtains. During the winter months, Hoeger would put a quilt or blanket over the radiator and hood of the car when he arrived at the church. If the roads were blocked by snow drifts, he would rent a horse and sleigh to make the six-mile journey. There was no foundation under the church, and the pot-bellied stove hardly warmed the interior during the bitterly cold Dakota winters. Often Hoeger had to keep his coat on during the service. The congregation finally made an agreement with him that if the temperature dropped below -10 degrees, there would be no church service.[9] In lieu of money, Reverend Hoeger was often given farm produce for his pastoral services. After confirming their children, the parents gave him grain or corn to feed his cow.[10] Eggs, cream and slabs of pork also showed up at the parsonage.

August Hoeger became the victim of the anti-German hysteria that pervaded the United States during the final year of World War I. Howard Pueppke, a confirmation student, recalled what happened when Pastor Hoeger was conducting catechism, writing and songs in German during the summer of 1918. Eighteen to 20 carloads of anti-German zealots appeared at the schoolhouse, the front car displaying a large American flag. The extremists interrupted the confirmation class and confronted Hoeger, insisting that he use only English in his teaching. He replied that "I am teaching the Bible in German. I'm teaching God's Word and what is wrong with that?" The bigots retorted, "This is the United States and there is a war going on, and we are at war with Germany, and you should teach English." Hoeger insisted that he was not talking against the United States government. He never displayed any undue excitement as he debated with these self-appointed super-patriots. After they drove away, he told the confirmands that he would talk to the church council about using English for confirmation instruction. The irony of it all was that the support of many German-Americans for the war effort, via the purchase of Liberty Bonds, was far greater than those people who opposed all but the use of the English tongue.[11] Reverend Hoeger involved himself in post-war rehabilitation programs, helped find and create jobs for returning servicemen, and organized drives to gather funds for relief of the war-ravaged European countries.

The children of immigrants, no matter what their nationality, began using English during the 1920s. At St. John's, by the middle of the decade, Hoeger conducted a German worship service in the morning and one in English in the afternoon. All Sunday School and confirmation classes were in English as well as Luther League programs on Sunday evenings.[12]

While ministering to his congregations, Pastor Hoeger continued his support of foreign missions. The Mission Auxiliary operated on a sound financial basis. The money gathered at Missionfests, and through special offerings, was sent to the Neuendettelsau Mission in New Guinea. Although some officials of the Iowa Synod objected to sending monies overseas, the Synod, at a general meeting in Dubuque, Iowa, in 1925, voted to establish a

Board of Foreign Missions. August Hoeger, as a founder of the Mission Auxiliary, was selected to serve on the Board. He resigned from the Mission Board in 1930 to devote his time to the Good Samaritan Society.

He continued to be very interested in inner mission work. To this end, he encouraged a friend, the Reverend Carl Schaffnit, to begin inner mission work and a Bible School in Minneapolis. Hoeger believed that Christians of all denominations should come together to do works of charity in the United States and that there should be Christian homes for the disabled, the disadvantaged and the aged. These were needed inner mission programs, he believed, and with this vision in mind, he would open the first Good Samaritan Society home at Arthur on March 1, 1923.

Poliomyelitis was a prevalent disease among children until 1956 when Jonas E. Salk developed a vaccine for injection to prevent the disease. One of polio's victims in the early 1920s was Christian Wuerth, the son of a pastor at Upham, North Dakota. Knowing of a doctor in Kansas City, Missouri, who could help Christian, a national appeal for financial assistance was placed in the *Kirchen-Blatt*, an ALC publication. Readers were asked to contribute two pennies for Chris. The response was overwhelming and $2,000 more than was needed was received. August Hoeger believed that the surplus should be used to establish a local non-profit institute for the physically handicapped. Since in 1922, there were no welfare organizations and no social service agencies available in the area, he wrote to officials at the orphan's home at Waverly, Iowa, suggesting that they should provide a building for crippled children. They said no, stating that they had their hands full with orphans. Hoeger received a similar reply when he appealed to another orphanage at Muscatine, Iowa.[13]

Pastor Hoeger, who had inherited his mother's love for children, would not be denied. At one time, he had applied to manage an orphanage, but he had not received the position. Now he had another opportunity to carry out an inner mission project for people in need on the northern Prairie Plains. A Conference of the Laity was held at Arthur on June 27, 1922, to discuss the establishment of "a Home for Cripples and Feeble Minded." At the conference, Hoeger spoke of the large number of physically and mentally handicapped in the Synod for whom nothing was being done. Noting that they were put in state institutions, he said that our Christian love demands that we take care of them. State institutions cared only for the body and not the soul. The chairman, Reverend H. Elster, appointed a seven man committee, including Hoeger, to provide a definite plan for a home. During the afternoon of June 27, the assembly decided on a name for the proposed institution. Reverend Hoeger had suggested they call it the Good Shepherd Society. Because a Doctor Raker had founded a Good Shepherd Home for crippled children at Allentown, Pennsylvania, circa 1908, the suggestion was rejected.[14] Reverend Walter Keller's recommendation that they name the new organization The Evangelical Lutheran Good Samaritan Society was accepted. The conferees also decided that members of the Society should all be Lutherans in good standing. A seven-person Board of Directors, three ministers and four laymen — to be elected out of the Ohio, Iowa, and Norwegian Synods — was instructed to draw up a constitution and to have the Society incorporated. This momentous meeting concluded with the election of officers. They included: Reverend August J. Hoeger, President; Reverend Walter Keller, Vice President; Reverend Herman Lechner, Secretary; and F. J. Koehn, Treasurer.[15]

At a subsequent meeting at Casselton, North Dakota, a constitution was drafted. On September 29, 1922, the State of North Dakota issued a Certificate of Incorporation to Reverend August Hoeger, Reverend W. W. A. Keller and F. J. Koehn. The Articles of Incorporation stated that the purpose of The Evangelical Lutheran Good Samaritan Society "shall be to open and maintain Christian homes for epileptics, cripples and other defectives, and to engage in other work of charity and benevolence."[16] The Articles further stated that the membership of the Society should be confirmed members of the Lutheran faith, who contributed at least 50 cents annually. The Board of Trustees was increased to nine members; each person to be elected for a term of three years. The Board was to meet four times per year with the annual meeting to be held in May.[17]

Making up the nine-member Board were: Reverend August J. Hoeger, Arthur, Reverend W. W. A. Keller, Jamestown, and F. J. Koehn, a Jamestown businessman for a three year term; Reverend N. J. Lohre, Mayville, Secretary of the Norwegian Lutheran Church of America, W. A. Geerdes, a Davenport farmer and O. Kinitz, a Buffalo businessman, for a two year term; P. O. Sathre, Finley, a states attorney, Reverend A. H. Berger, Fort

Ransom, and Reverend J. A. Johanson, Jamestown, for a one year term.

Upon hearing of this new institution in North Dakota, Professor H. J. Arnold of Waverly, Iowa, wrote Reverend Hoeger the following note:

> I was surprised to hear that you have launched a new enterprise. I thought you had all the work you could do at the present time; on the other hand, I know that there is a great need of a home for cripples, etc., and someone has to make a start. I hope God will give you strength to complete the work you have started to do.[18]

August Hoeger believed in institutional work. He recognized that institutions made society work. Once again, he had been influenced by his parents, who had worked in institutions for much of their lives. Hoeger's reading of work done by German institutions contributed to his vision of what could be accomplished on the Prairie Plains. He had read three volumes on the wonderful work of Dr. Wilhelm Loehe at Neuendettelsau. August had also read of Father Friedrich von Bodelschwingh's creation of a city of epileptics at Bethel, a community within the city of Bielefeld in Westphalia. It was not Hoeger's intent to build a new Bethel on the Plains. He drew inspiration from reading Bodelschwingh's words, but his faith and actions were his own.

Prior to the Good Samaritan Society's incorporation, Hoeger wrote an article for the *Kirchen-Blatt*. In it he said:

> In the spirit of Christ we must begin to take care of our own cripples, epileptics and other unfortunates and for that we need an institution.... We must see to it that every father and mother who has such an unfortunate child may die without worry knowing that his Lutheran brethren will help care for his child because of their love for Christ.
>
> Hasn't it always puzzled us when we heard how the priest and the Levite passed by on the other side? They surely knew God's will. What a sur-

prise when the half-heathen Samaritan took care
of the maimed and robbed. Do we also want to
pass by on the other side and let the half-heathen
state do what we ought to be doing or do we just
look on while non-Christians do that work?[19]

Pastor Hoeger went on to say that the newly organized Good
Samaritan Society would begin small and that a small house
would be rented for the care of the Society's first residents. Meeting at Casselton on October 30, the Board of Directors decided to
open a building in the spring of 1923 or earlier if necessary.
Hoeger recruited two women from his parish, Augusta Priewe
and Lena Gebhardt, and sent them to the Bethphage Mission,
Axtell, Nebraska, where the Augustana Synod (Swedish) had a
home for epileptics and mentally handicapped children. The two
women spent three months at Axtell, learning how to care for
their future charges. Stressing that the projected home must be
a Christian home with Christian workers, Reverend Hoeger proposed to follow a German practice that the two women should be
deaconesses, a part of a sisterhood. They should be willing to dedicate their lives to serving God through this kind of work.
Although some of the first workers in the Society's home at
Arthur were addressed as Sisters, Hoeger found this Germanic
concept impractical in the United States, and the idea of a special sisterhood was abandoned.

Stepping out in faith, Reverend Hoeger, on March 1, 1923,
rented a small, six-room house for $20 per month at Arthur,
North Dakota. Sisters Priewe and Gebhardt became the first two
women on the Good Samaritan Society's payroll. When asked by
Hoeger to be the first employee in the little house, Augusta
Priewe said, "Sounds hard. I don't know if I can do it." He had
replied, "Oh, don't think like that — then you can't." It was an
early indication of the great possibilities he saw in certain people. A place now existed for some of God's forgotten people —
cripples, epileptics, blind, deaf mutes, feeble-minded, the aged,
and many others in need of care.

Sister Sena Hested, a parish worker with First Lutheran
Church in Fargo, brought the first homeless children to Arthur,
two boys and a girl. Within a month the house was full with an
illegitimate baby, her mentally retarded thirty-eight year old
mother, two teen-age brothers with muscular dystrophy, two
adult epileptic men, three mentally retarded children and the

youngsters brought by Sister Sena from Fargo. One of the epileptic men was the Reverend Paul Weiss, who once had a call in the eastern United States. Weiss was of great assistance to Hoeger, as he typed Hoeger's English and German letters and corrected the English grammar for articles and letters submitted for publication. He did all of the bookkeeping for the Society, working in Reverend Hoeger's office upstairs in the parsonage. Weiss would have an occasional epileptic seizure which was preceded by a piercing scream.

The small house became so crowded that one of the new workers, Minnie Hermina Hove, first slept on a bed in Hoeger's office in the parsonage. Later, Minnie shared a room with a mentally handicapped woman.[20] Pastor Hoeger found another four-room house to rent, and the Society took in more patients.[21]

Augusta Priewe, as the first matron of the Arthur Home, encountered many difficulties. Modern conveniences were lacking, laundry was washed in the garage as the kitchen was too small, and some of the water used was pumped from a cistern. An epileptic boy hung the wet clothes on outside clothes lines for drying or for freezing in the cold North Dakota winter. The stiff, frozen clothes would ultimately be brought into the Home for thawing and further drying. Residents received their Saturday night bath in a wash tub placed in the kitchen. Sister Augusta carried pail after pail of water to the tub from a ditch in back of the Home in the summer months. During the winter months, melted snow was a source of water. One one occasion, one of the epileptic residents had a seizure, falling against the tub. Water spilled in all directions, throughout much of the ground floor and into the basement. Fortunately, the house tilted slightly toward the front door and most of the water went in that direction.[22] Augusta and other workers slept in an upstairs room where the walls were covered with frost during the winter months. She kept the young infant from the Home in her bed.[23]

The workers had been promised $20 per month. Many times there was nothing. If wages were received, they were often used for necessities to keep the Home in operation. An economic depression had struck rural America in 1921. Grain prices, which had soared during World War I, dropped drastically in 1920 as foreign grain growers renewed production and the U. S. government ended its subsidies for domestic grain production. Many farmers were confronted with high mortgage payments and increased taxes. Hundreds of small-town banks in the Dakotas failed. With the decline in the rural economy, contributions to the Good Samaritan Society decreased.

Sister Augusta often prayed for food during the Arthur Home's first years. Usually, there were potatoes to cook but sometimes they, too, were in short supply. She would retire to the cellar to pray as it was the one place she could be alone. One day her brother brought smoked bacon, lettuce and cream when she had just begun to pray. Reverend Hoeger was the visionary, the inspiration, and the guiding force for the Good Samaritan Society but without the support of a committed group of women and men, the Society might have floundered in its early years. The heart was there, and when the heart was there, nothing else really mattered. Faith was there. God heard prayers and provided some kind of answer. Reverend Hoeger told Bertha Bosch Christian, *"Kind, wir mussen glauben."* ("Child, we must believe.") The workers' faith in Hoeger, and what he believed, seldom wavered.[24]

"Giving is more blessed than receiving" was the prevailing theme at the Christmas Eve celebrations at the Arthur Home. A Christmas tree lit with many colored electric bulbs stood in the dining room. Under the tree were presents for everyone and small bags filled with nuts, candy and popcorn balls. Residents participated in the festivities by singing songs and reciting pieces learned at an earlier time.[25]

With the troubled farm economy, few residents could pay for their own care. No help came from county governments. August Hoeger solicited financial support for the Society through letters to individual pastors and through *Sunshine* or *Freudenstrahlen* (Happy Beams), the organization's periodical, printed on a small printing press at Arthur. The Articles of Incorporation had called for the printing of *Sunshine*.

The prayers of the people in Arthur were answered when a letter arrived from Mrs. M. C. Trautman of Butler, Pennsylvania, who had read of the Good Samaritan Society's work in *Sunshine*. On November 12, 1923, she sent a cashier's check for $2,000 "to be used for ... work at the Lutheran Hospital." In her letter, she wrote, "We can give without loving, but we cannot love without giving."

The Arthur Home soon added to its responsibilities. An old man on crutches stepped off the train at Arthur and asked Pastor Hoeger if he would take in a crippled man. When it was discovered that the man could walk on his own, Hoeger realized that the man had feigned his infirmity in order to find a home.

Reverend Hoeger later stated, "That opened our eyes; we realized that something must be done for the elderly who had no place to go."[26] His recognition of the needs of the lonely aged soon set the Good Samaritan Society on a new course.

Contending with overcrowding, and with many applications pending, the Board of Directors decided to build a new residence in the fall of 1923. Forty acres were purchased at the north end of Arthur, and on this site, a building with cement walls, which were sunk two feet into the ground, and a cement roof was hastily constructed. By Christmas 1923, the new residence was furnished and dedicated. Unfortunately, an error was made in constructing the flat cement roof. The builders were told that if they added lime to the cement it would be waterproof. They soon discovered that the roof leaked like a sieve. In the spring, a second story of tile and brick was added to the building and a new and reliable roof was placed over the structure.[27] By this time, Hoeger had been named superintendent of the Good Samaritan Home and treasurer of the maintenance fund. He was also elected to a fund-raising committee that included Reverend Keller and Sister Sena Hestad. Construction costs for the new Home as of December 18, 1923, totaled $6,000. Pastor Hoeger was authorized to secure a loan of an amount necessary to take care of immediate and urgent bills.[28] Working on a shoestring budget, he began to face problems that would plague the Good Samaritan Society until the 1940s — unpaid bills, loans on which no principal could be paid, and bank overdrafts.

Yet, Hoeger pressed on. Firmly believing that God would provide, he persuaded the Board of Directors to construct two additional buildings at the Arthur site. His belief was "If the Lord would want us to have it ... we will have it." The first story of the Loehe Home was constructed in 1924. In the latter part of August, the Board resolved to campaign for funds to build a second story on the Loehe Home and to construct a special children's home for cripples. During the winter of 1924-1925, construction began on the second story. The estimated cost of the addition was $6,000. The Society had only $200 available in cash; no one knew where the remaining money would come from. Hoeger continued to proceed with certainty, stating that "But one thing we did know, and that is that the Father in Heaven, in whose name and to whose honor we are doing this work, has many ways to provide."[29] Reverend Hoeger trusted in the Lord, and the Board of Trustees (Directors) trusted in Hoeger. In 1925,

they authorized him to secure loans for the necessary maintenance of the Home.[30] The money did come in. An elderly man
gave his farm to the Home on condition the Society agree to keep
him for the rest of his life. A short time later, an interested
farmer paid the Good Samaritan Society $4,480 in cash for the
land.[31]

On July 7, 1925, in the midst of 40 of the Home's residents,
seated and standing in a cornfield, Reverend Carl Schaffnit of
Minneapolis gave an address. Following his talk, a former missionary to New Guinea, S. Lehner, dug out three spadefuls of dirt
in the name of the Father, the Son and the Holy Ghost. Thus, the
Society began, in the name of the Lord, the Lutheran Sunday
Schools' Cripple Home, designed to shelter 16 residents.[32]
Although the building was completed before the onset of winter,
the dedication of the Sunday School Home for Cripples was post-
poned until June 6, 1926. Several hundred people appeared for
the dedication despite a severe sandstorm, and they endured a
hot and closed building because of the high wind. Women of the
congregations at Arthur and Amenia served free lunches to people in the basement of the Arthur church. The church was packed
for the worship service and the annual business meeting. Chairs
were placed in the aisle, approximately 50 people stood in the
back of the church, and planks were secured from the lumber
yard to seat a part of the overflow crowd in the church basement.[33] This Home cost $8,000, of which $4,000 was paid by Sunday Schools of the Iowa Synod. It was hoped that the remaining
$4,000 could be paid by Christmas, 1926.[34]

The growing complex at Arthur had three buildings at the end
of 1925, one for females, one for males and one for crippled children.[35] At this time, the Society received a total of $300 per
month from all paying patients while salaries for workers
amounted to about $350 per month.[36] Given these circumstances,
how did Hoeger keep the Society operating? Through the *Sunshine* and personal letters, donations continued to flow in, some
residents willed their farms to the Society, and these farms were
either sold for current operating funds or to pay outstanding
bills. He continued to secure small loans at a reasonable rate of
interest and for as long a time as possible. Area farmers provided
provisions, including clothing, canned goods and sides of beef and
pork. Other donations came from Luther Leagues. The Home had
no cow and had to buy milk and butter. Pastor Hoeger posed the
question — "Why doesn't the Board buy a cow?" In answering his

own query, Hoeger said, "The reason is that our finances will not allow such a large outlay and Sears-Roebuck does not sell them on the installment plan."[37] Aware of the Home's plight, the Verona, North Dakota, Luther League gave the Home a cow which was gratefully named "Verona." When the pastor from Verona went through Enderlin on his way to Arthur, pulling "Verona" in a trailer behind his coupe, the pastor in Enderlin was challenged to do a similar act of charity. His Luther League bought a team of horses to be used on the Home's 40-acre farm.[38] By the fall of 1926, the Board of Directors saw the need for a barn at the Arthur Home. The farm had six good Holstein heifers and there were 18 well-fed hogs. Hoeger reported that "The family of pigs from the two sows are thriving well and we can already see the sausages that will be made this fall."[39] A shed would be built to get the livestock through the winter. The Home's garden had also been very productive: two hundred gallons of sauerkraut had been processed, there were nearly 500 bushels of potatoes and 50 bushels of carrots in the cellar, and the Home's workers had canned 200 quarts of corn.[40]

The Board of Directors, on November 18, 1925, authorized the purchase of 120 acres of land which adjoined the Society's 40-acre holding. It was purchased from Edmond H. Viestenz for $100 an acre. Much of the land was the rich and heavy soil of the Red River Valley. The Good Samaritan Society incurred a debt of $12,000 in making the purchase, but Hoeger, exuding faith and optimism, said "with good management and the Lord's blessing, we hope that the farm by and by will pay for itself."[41] For a time, the Society owned 480 acres near Arthur. All but 160 acres of this land was ultimately sold to meet the Home's debt load and for funding current operations. The farming operation provided several of the handicapped residents with meaningful jobs. With his vision and wisdom, Pastor Hoeger realized the value of work therapy. Regarding the farm, he said, "We have found that many people do not feel caged in when they are doing some sort of farm work." The farm contained a sand and gravel pit which caused the Arthur Home to build a tile factory in 1926. The factory sold bricks for foundations, warehouses and garages. The tile factory ceased operation in 1929 when the quality of the gravel declined.[42]

When Superintendent Hoeger, now receiving a monthly salary of $25.00, delivered his annual report on June 6, 1926, the Arthur Home had taken in 81 patients in little more than three years.

Included in this number were 31 cripples, 16 epileptics and 34 feeble-minded people. They were cared for by 12 workers under the supervision of Sister Etta Jensen, who arrived at Arthur in 1925.[43] The three-home complex at Arthur housed 52 residents in the summer of 1926.

Commenting on the Society's beginning, August Hoeger, Sr., at a later date, said:

> I, of course, like to think that the whole good Samaritan Society started in the heart of God, that it was His good will that His old people should have Christian care, and so He put into the hearts of men that they should go and do His good pleasure.[44]

As the reputation of the good work of the Good Samaritan Society began to spread, Hoeger and the Board of Directors had to decide whether to open homes in other communities or use Bodelschwingh's model of Bethel in Bielefeld, Germany, of concentrating all their care at one site.

Top: Haymaking was one of the activities on the Arthur, North Dakota, farm. *Middle:* Arthur Home Day in the mid-1930s. *Bottom:* Putting up silage.

Chapter Three
DOING AS THE LORD GUIDES
AND DIRECTS
1925 - 1933

"The days were not so dark because
we knew that God was with us, and
even in the greatest hours of trial, He
always found a way out."
— Rev. August Hoeger, Sr.

As a visionary, August Hoeger was never satisfied with the way things were, he always considered what they could become. At the depth of the Great Depression in 1932, he commented that the economic disaster which caused so much distress throughout the nation had opened many doors of opportunity, enabling the Good Samaritan Society to extend its work to many other states. There were days when the Society faced collectors and past due accounts without a cent. "However, behind the darkest clouds," said Reverend Hoeger, "God's sun is always shining and when the need is greatest, the Lord in his own wonderful way provides."[1]

Will Rogers, the cowboy humorist from Oklahoma, aptly described the rural economic crisis of the 1920s when he said, "Stock on the Exchange in Wall Street was never higher, stock on the ranch was never lower." The lack of government regulation and the ease with which stocks could be bought on margin caused speculation to run wild on the floor of the New York Stock Exchange. All of that came to an end with the collapse of the Stock Market on October 29, 1929, when 16 million shares of stock were sold. A universal Great Depression was under way.

Following the Wall Street crash, commodity prices fell faster and further than at any other period in the history of American agriculture. Hog prices stood at $11.36 per head in 1931, at $6.14 in 1932, and at $4.21 in 1933. The market price of a bushel of wheat sank from $1.03 in 1929 to a low of 24-28 cents per bushel in 1932. In the local general store, coffee was 10 cents a pound, and calico sold for 2.5 cents a yard. A person with a wry sense of humor related the story of the champion wrestler who broke his back attempting to lift 50 cents worth of oats.

By the early 1930s, the farmers of the Prairie Plains were once again reminded how dependent they were on the vicissitudes of nature. During World War I, farmers had overcropped the Plains as they produced millions of bushels of wheat and corn and fed not only America but many overseas nations. The overcropping caused the plowing up of thousands of acres of grassland. In prior decades, the limited amount of rain that fell on the sea of grass was trapped by the vegetation's tough roots, resulting in soil that was nourished and held in place. Then, in 1930, years of drought commenced. Summer sun baked the land; any rain that fell did not penetrate the soil. High winds, synonymous with the region, swept over the Plains. It picked up the parched, dry soil that had nothing to hold it down and blackened the sky with dust.

The dusters reached their intensity in 1933 and 1934. Hardest hit in the Plains' states were the counties located between the 98th and 100th meridians. Each storm reminded rural people of their own physical and economic mortality. Lois Phillips Hudson, who grew up west of Jamestown, North Dakota, wrote — "Dust storms are like that; no matter how many times you clean or how much you scrub and repaint and dig into crevices, you are always finding another niche the dust has found. And in the dust is the smell of mortality, of fertility swept away and spring vanished."[2]

As the drought and economic depression intensified, there was a general air of despair and hopelessness. Fields once covered with lush vegetation were now blown barren. Ditches and fence lines were filled with drifted dust. Tumbleweeds and thistles blew across prairie and roads until they came to rest against the side of a building or fence line. The forces of nature were relentless. One grizzled old Arthur farmer said he wished it would rain — not for his sake but for his son's benefit. The old farmer had *seen* rain.[3] The dry conditions provided an excellent environment for grasshoppers to lay their eggs and to multiply. Periodically, throughout the early 1930s, they struck at fields and orchards that contained some vegetation.

In this hostile economic and natural environment, August Hoeger described the plight of the Good Samaritan Society in a letter to Hattie Hoeger, Santa Monica, California, on November 12, 1932. He wrote:

We are just living from hand to mouth as I get my
salary from the Good Samaritan Society but the
Good Samaritan Society is in the dumps just now
— donations have fallen off practically to nothing. Where last year by this time we had nearly
$9,000 in donations, this year we have not
$3,000.[4]

He went on to say that he was not discouraged, and he opti-
mistically commented that it would take a year or two before
times got better. The Great Depression was a great burden,
Hoeger wrote Hattie, "But with God's help we are not going to
fight it through but go right ahead." He told her that the Good
Samaritan Society had taken over seven more institutions during the summer.[5]

Approximately 95 percent of the donations to the Society had
come from farmers. This source of income had almost dried up,
leading to an increased debt load for the Society. Because of the
many unpaid bills, the Home's relationship with the Arthur community was strained for several years. When Reverend Hoeger
kept acquiring Homes without paying debts owed to Arthur merchants, some people said, "Faith is all right, but don't expect the
Lord to do it all." [6]

Large amounts of money were owed to the Farmers Elevator
at Arthur for coal, electricity and feed. The elevator operated the
light plant from 1914 to 1962. Al Burgum, manager of the elevator, recognized Hoeger's dilemma.[7] Government entities were
unable to pay their bills. The various facilities of the Good
Samaritan Society were paid by governments for welfare
patients with IOU's. County governments had agreed to pay the
Society $30.00 a month for taking care of the poor. When money
became available, county officials promised to pay the IOU's with
interest.[8]

To pay bills, Pastor Hoeger drove 250 miles to Stanton, North
Dakota, where a friend who had cash bought the IOU's at 10 percent discount. With $5,000 to $10,000 on the Farmers Elevator's
books, Hoeger traded farms to Burgum to reduce the debt,
including one farm in Texas and another in northwestern North
Dakota.[9] It was not until 1942 that the Good Samaritan Society
emerged from its considerable debt load.

Reverend Hoeger believed that the Society had to become self-
sufficient to survive. Produce from the farm and the large garden

played a major role in the survival of the Arthur Home during the 1930s. The Red River Valley did not experience the severe drought conditions that struck the Plains only a few miles further west. Many acres of potatoes and other root crops were planted and subsequently harvested. Several of the male residents helped to build a new barn in 1927; others were out in the field putting up the first cutting of alfalfa.[10] By 1929, the Society had 45 head of cattle. The registered Holsteins averaged 318 pounds of butterfat. There was always adequate tame hay and silage (corn husks and stalks) to provide sustenance for the herd.[11] Feed was secured from the elevator to feed the registered Poland China hogs. Thus, garden produce, beef, pork, poultry, eggs, and milk were the staples during this critical period in the history of the Good Samaritan Society and the Prairie Plains.

By December 1932, the Armour and Swift packing companies offered the Good Samaritan Society only two cents per pound for hogs. Hoeger was undaunted. The Society started its own slaughter house in Aberdeen. In his December 1932 newsletter to Society workers, he wrote:

> Where there is a will there is a way. So instead of letting Armour or Swift and Co. make a big profit, we started a slaughter-house in Aberdeen and are selling our hogs, instead of in their black or red dress, in a nice white gown, and we received five cents a pound for them.[12]

In the same newsletter, he announced that a "fine second-hand" bakery was being purchased in Fargo. His ministerial colleagues were collecting flour for the bakery. The bread, produced at low cost, would be sent to Arthur, Aberdeen and Valley City, resulting, he hoped, in the saving of thousands of dollars.[13]

The several services of the Society actually made a little money. Included in these services were the tile factory at Arthur, the bakery in Fargo, printing and shoe repair shops, a business college in Fargo, two Bible colleges, one in Fargo and the other in Waterloo, Iowa, and two crippled children's schools in Fargo and Hot Springs, South Dakota.[14] Crippled children in the Art Department at the Good Samaritan Institute made baskets and shopping bags which were sold as Christmas gifts for 25 cents to $1.50.[15]

The Home at Arthur also relied on the good will of area congregations. In the fall of 1933, the Society received over 100 sacks of flour from friends in Linton, Wishek, and Ashley, North Dakota, and Eureka, Hosmer, and Bowdle, South Dakota. The Home used a sack of flour every day, baking 900 loaves of bread every week. Through the *Sunshine*, the Good Samaritan Society announced it had a truck and its willingness to drive 100-200 miles, as long as a truck-load of commodities resulted from the trip.[16] In reflecting back on the 1930s, Hoeger wrote, "The days were not so dark because we knew that God was with us and even in the greatest hours of trial, He always found a way out."

Pastor Hoeger's optimism was reflected in the appearance of the Good Samaritan Society's farm. Many farmers, in their despair, failed to maintain their farm buildings and grounds. This was not true at the Society's farm, where the lawns, gardens and fields were clean and orderly. Hoeger commented that "It was the only place that looked like people had hope for the future." He gave much credit to the home's matron, Sister Etta Janssen. He said she could carry her cross and the cross of others with a smile.[17]

Credit for survival must also be given to the committed staff and to others who labored long hours, knowing that their only compensation would be their room and board. Four people, who would devote their lives to the Society's work, Bertha Bosch Christian, Bertha Halverson Holstein, Viola Baugatz and Marie Schugann Bosch, began their association with the Good Samaritan Society and the Hoeger family between 1928 and 1937.[18] In living his Christianity, Hoeger always sought out other Christians. He always met new workers at the train depot in nearby Casselton, North Dakota, and transported them to the Home at Arthur. He viewed the workers as his own children.[19] Reverend Hoeger treasured the workers' support and dedication. He said, "You can give me all the money in the world but if I haven't got helpers I can't do anything. But if you give me helpers and very little money, I will get something done."[20]

Bertha Bosch Christian indicated that the workers were not paid for three years. She said that one day Reverend Hoeger brought a Sears-Roebuck catalog to the Home and said, "Here, look at this and dream." He was one with the workers, coming to the Arthur facility each day, often in striped overalls and with a pail to milk one cow at a time. He would work in the flower garden, conduct worship services and visit with residents. The staff

arose at 5 a.m. and carried on their duties until 9 p.m. In taking
care of the residents, they patched their clothes, cut their hair,
shaved the epileptic adult males and went after them when they
walked away from the grounds.[21]

Another key person at the Arthur Home was Reverend Ernst
H. Haacke from Minneapolis. Hoeger invited him to come to
Arthur for one year, but Haacke stayed at the Arthur facility for
almost seven years, during the lean years of the Great Depression. Haacke became the superintendent of the Home, managed
the farm, and served as the Home's chaplain, conducting morning and evening devotions. His management duties included
supervising the care of a growing dairy herd, 40-50 hogs, nearly
300 chickens and a 500-acre farm. It was Reverend Haacke who
presided over butchering, filling silo, milking time and the planting of a bountiful garden. He made frequent trips to Fargo, taking produce to the Good Samaritan Institute and returning to
Arthur with fresh baked bread. When an elevator burned at
nearby Erie, North Dakota, Haacke drove there with a trailer to
bring back scorched grain for feed. An almost daily occurrence
was going to downtown Arthur to return a resident who had
wandered away. It was his unpleasant task to take residents to
the dentist at Casselton and hold them down while the dentist
proceeded with whatever needed to be done to the unfortunate
patient.[22] As a consecrated worker, he knew no 8- or 12-hour day.
He spent many nights at the bedside of the sick and dying, com-
forting them with the Word of God. Quite often he left the house
in the morning before his children were awake, and he returned
at night after they were asleep. The children said that their
father had one week of vacation in seven years. They spent considerable time at the Home, and they recalled old grandmothers
making rugs and the elderly men playing dominoes in the
evening. The youngsters got to ring the bell at mealtime, and
they remembered the little green books used for singing a hymn
after breakfast and supper. The Christmas program in the
Home's dining room always featured a male quartet, their average age probably well past 75, rendering "*Au du frohliche.*"[23] In
1937, Reverend Haacke was called to be pastor at Steele, North
Dakota. In paying tribute to his service at the Arthur Home, Reverend Hoeger wrote, "The Good Samaritan Society has laid down
a rule that the first thing necessary to build God's kingdom is not
money, but real consecrated workers." Haacke was one of those
workers, offering the main support for the Society's work.[24]

There was no standing still and agonizing over economic and climactic difficulties at the Arthur Home. Additional land was acquired from farmers who entered the Home. In addition to the barn, a kitchen and dining room were constructed between two of the three buildings in the residential complex. The Duntile brick factory flourished for a period of time. A shoe repair shop, where some of the residents could learn a trade, and a print shop were located on the grounds. The print shop produced the *Sunshine* and its German language version, *Freudenstrahlen*, which were distributed to approximately 10,000 subscribers. Through all of these physical changes, however, the status of the residents remained foremost in Hoeger's mind. He told the Society's Board of Directors, "The patients must therefore be and remain the main object in all our reports. In other words, they take first place."[25]

Superintendent Hoeger's mind continually ground out ideas and pondered problems, but he was never overwhelmed by them. There was always evidence of feeling that "God will handle it."[26] One of the problems that perplexed him for a short while was the establishment of Society facilities in other communities. He had, from the beginning, thought of concentrating the Society's work only at Arthur. All of this changed in 1924 when he received letters from friends who recommended that he use a closed church academy building at Sterling, Nebraska. These friends argued that the Society should not have to engage in any more building when there was a building available.

After pondering the issue for some time, Hoeger decided "Well, God is probably guiding different than I was dreaming and if we were to go as God guides and directs, we cannot go and do what we want to do."[27] He told the Board of Directors on November 5, 1924, that the recently closed Lutheran college at Sterling would be a good home for feeble-minded children if the Iowa Synod would give or sell it for a reasonable price.[28]

The next year, the Iowa Synod sold the property to the Good Samaritan Society for $1,000. At a meeting in the library of the former Martin Luther Academy, the Martin Luther Home Society was founded on October 20, 1925. It would be a home of Christian charity for epileptic, feeble-minded, and partly crippled children. The founders of the Martin Luther Home were Dr. F. Richter, President of the Iowa Synod, Reverend August Hoeger, Reverend Richard Fruehling, William Ehmen, John Aden, and Reverend Moehl. Hoeger served as chairman of the Martin

Luther Home Society and its Executive Board from 1925 to circa 1930.[29]

Doctor Richter believed that every Home should be incorporated by itself. Thus, the Martin Luther Home was only managed by the Good Samaritan Society for several years. Sister Sena Hestad was named the matron of the Martin Luther Home. Hoeger sent a few children from Arthur to Sterling.[30] Using the Home Day practice begun at Arthur, an annual Martin Luther Day was held annually in Sterling. William Ehmen loaned his large tent, and seats made from planks accommodated the large crowds. Area bands furnished music for the day and songs were sung by the children who resided in the home.[31] The Good Samaritan Society gradually withdrew from the Sterling operation. In the late 1920s, there were only 15 or 16 patients at the Martin Luther Home. Later, the Home was moved from Sterling to Beatrice, Nebraska, where 6-7 times as many residents could be accommodated.

Although care of the handicapped continued in the 1930s, the main emphasis of the Good Samaritan Society switched to the care of the elderly. One of the great feats of August Hoeger and the Society was to remove the elderly poor from county poor farms and to give them respect and proper care in Society Homes for the elderly.

The Society opened an Old People's Home in late 1928 at Fargo. August Hoeger asked a reluctant Hermina "Minnie" Hove, who had worked at the Arthur Home for several years, to start the new home. He took her trunk to the house he had rented in Fargo, gave her a check book and a key, and told her to go ahead. The Home soon held 13 elderly residents and two workers.[32] With the Old People's Home and the Arthur Home filled, Pastor Hoeger quickly looked for another available house in Fargo. On March 6, 1929, the Board of Directors purchased a house and eight lots for $21,000.[33] Six months later, on September 15, the Society dedicated the Lutheran Home for Aged at Fargo. The Good Samaritan Society held its annual meeting in conjunction with the dedication. In the *Sunshine*, Pastor Hoeger continued to express his reservations concerning the Society's out-of-Arthur expansion. In his published remarks, he said:

> It has been our rule in life to do as the Lord
> guides and directs. If we were running things to
> our liking, we would have one large institution
> here at Arthur, for much can be said about cen-

tralizing in one place. But the Lord seems to direct us in other ways.[34]

By this time, the Good Samaritan Society had become involved in the Luther Home of Mercy at Williston, Ohio. It had been founded by one of Hoeger's seminary classmates, and a close friend, Reverend Max Schlecher, who was influenced by what he had heard about the Society's work at Arthur. Some of this information he gained from Hoeger upon the latter's visits to Ohio. Luther Home of Mercy was designed to be a haven for the afflicted who could not gain admittance to other homes. Similar to Arthur, it became a refuge for the blind, deaf, epileptics, physically disadvantaged and the mentally retarded. The first cottage for adults was completed in early 1929. By the spring of 1931, the Luther Home of Mercy was filled, and there were people waiting for admittance.[35]

At a meeting of the Barnes County Commissioners in Valley City, North Dakota, a welfare worker recommended that the commissioners ask the Good Samaritan Society to operate the county's so-called poor farm. The commissioners offered the Riverside Hospital on a 15-acre site along the Sheyenne River in Valley City as a residence for the indigent elderly. The Society's Board of Directors, on August 28, 1929, agreed to rent the hospital for $100 per month with the provision that the Society take care of the Barnes County poor at $25 per person per month.[36] The Society's third home for the aged was opened on September 1, 1929. The brick structure could accommodate 40 residents. Twenty people were to be brought immediately to the Valley City Home.[37]

The considerable growth of the Good Samaritan Society increased Superintendent Hoeger's responsibilities. The Society had 100 crippled, epileptics, and feeble-minded at Arthur, 30 elderly residents at Fargo, and another 40 people in the Valley City Home.[38] Believing that he must devote his considerable energy to the Society alone, Reverend Hoeger resigned his two-church parish at Arthur in 1930. He moved his family and the Society's headquarters to Fargo.[39] During his 12 years at Arthur, his family had increased from three to eight children. Agnes, Ruth, and Cecelia were joined by Laura, Amelia, John, August, Jr., and Gertrude.

Fargo was a communications hub for the region, and from North Dakota's largest city Superintendent Hoeger could board trains or busses to the communities where the Society would have homes in the next few years. He viewed the economic depression as a great opportunity for the Good Samaritan Society. There were hundreds of buildings — schools, hospitals and colleges — that stood empty and often were for sale with no money down and with a small monthly payment. Between August 1930 and December 1933, 14 additional facilities were either begun or managed by the Society. They were located in Colorado, Montana, Nebraska, North Dakota, and South Dakota. In the summer of 1932, Hoeger commented, "We are taking over institutions this summer oftener than we are printing our *Sunshine*."[40] Society Board Minutes for 1932 indicated the tenor of the times and the spirit of the Good Samaritan Society's leaders. The minutes stated:

> ... The great panic, which is causing so much distress throughout the nation, has opened many a door of opportunity enabling the Society to extend its work to many other states. That there is a shortage of funds and the organization's bank account frequently shows an overdraft, need hardly be mentioned.[41]

Unique among these new facilities were a hospital at Harvey, North Dakota and the sanatorium at Hot Springs, South Dakota. The 40-bed, fully equipped hospital at Harvey was secured for reasonable terms in 1931. Hoeger envisioned three uses for the hospital. First, 20 beds would be used for invalids. Second, all charity patients at other Society Homes would be brought to Harvey for treatment. Hospital bills for the Society often amounted to $2,000 to $3,000 per year. Third, the hospital could be used to train workers, having them work six months or a year in the hospital. Reverend Hoeger believed that workers could be best imbued with the Good Samaritan spirit if they were trained by the Society.[42]

The Society agreed to manage the Hot Springs sanatorium on November 6, 1931.[43] The Board of Directors emphasized that the Society should not incur any financial obligation and not a cent of charity money should be invested in the sanatorium. If the venture proved successful, the Good Samaritan Society might take possession of the Hot Springs facility.[44]

Donations to the Good Samaritan Society did not increase in proportion to the number of facilities acquired. The contributions to all locations for 1933 totaled $4,000. In earlier years, donations had totaled $10,000 to $12,000. Even though the Great Depression "bottomed-out" in 1932, it continued to take its toll. Searching desperately for operating funds, the Board of Directors, in a fund-raising effort, in October 1933, recommended that an appeal be sent to all American Lutheran Church (ALC) pastors and to every public school teacher in North Dakota.* The appeal to the pastors did bring a limited, favorable response. During the same month, the Board instructed each facility to remit 5 percent of its monthly income to the home office at Fargo.

In Fargo, the Good Samaritan Society rented office space over Leeby's grocery and delicatessen. At this site, Reverend Hoeger began a new enterprise, Augsburg Business College. In its three classrooms, students took courses in typing, shorthand, accounting, business methods and business law. The curriculum was designed to attract non-traditional students — those who were older, the physically handicapped, and people who had had no formal education beyond high school. Mrs. Alma Penheiter served as principal and a teacher at the college. One of Hoeger's former parishioners at Arthur — Wallace Franke, a victim of polio — believed that Reverend Hoeger began the college to help people with physical difficulties. During his matriculation, Franke did the bookkeeping and general work for the Society while Hoeger traveled on Society business.[45] As of 1931, Pastor Hoeger had a radio broadcast over WDAY-Fargo every Thursday evening at 7:15 p.m.. Often, he would dictate his remarks to Franke for transcribing but there were occasions when he spoke without notes. The devotional program consisted of Scripture reading, a sermonette, reading letters written to him and contributions from students at the Good Samaritan Institute in Fargo. The radio program went on for a year or two.[46] Franke completed his course work in 1934 and secured employment at Fort Peck, Montana, where the first of the major dams that would alter the Missouri River Basin was under construction.

One of Franke's instructors at Augsburg Business College was Frederick R. Knautz, who taught accounting and business law. Knautz was affiliated with the Good Samaritan Society for

* The Iowa, Ohio and Buffalo Synods merged on August 11, 1930, at Toledo, Ohio, to form the American Lutheran Church (ALC).

approximately ten years, from 1929 to 1938. A farm boy from
Washington State, Knautz had met his future wife, the former
Margaret Viestenz of Arthur, North Dakota, at a Salvation Army
booth at Fort Lewis, Washington, while he was in the Marines.
After their marriage in June 1921, Knautz decided on a career in
the Salvation Army. On their way to the eastern United States
for training, the newly married couple stopped at Arthur for a
visit. They heard August Hoeger appeal for mission workers for
New Guinea in one of his sermons. They went to Minneapolis for
special training for the mission field, and they were to spend the
next seven years in New Guinea. Knautz was the business manager for ten mission stations. Because of his health problems,
they returned to Arthur. Shortly thereafter, Superintendent
Hoeger appointed him the business manager for the Society. For
a few years, they worked well together. Both men were rural-ori-
ented, concerned with health care and the problems of the disabled and the handicapped. Both men, however, were strong-
willed and possessed different business philosophies. Knautz
stressed the "bottom line" in all transactions whereas Hoeger
wanted to proceed immediately with a project when he perceived
need, imbued with the firm belief that God would provide. In the
latter half of the 30s, their differences led to serious schism in
the Good Samaritan Society.

In his prayer life, August Hoeger always asked, "Lord, what do
you want of me today?" In response to his own question, he
looked to help those people that he saw had needs. As a board
member of the Inner Mission Society, Hoeger saw the need for a
haven for young farm girls working in Fargo. To fulfill this need,
he bought a large house in 1927 which became Luther Hall, a
kind of Lutheran YWCA. At Luther Hall, young women coming
to work in Fargo, or to go to school, could reside for about $3.65
per week. In 1929, Hoeger asked Margaret Knautz, who had
been a practical nurse and teacher, to be the matron of Luther
Hall. Some of the young women resented the supervised living
environment. They were required to be in by 10:30 p.m., and
table devotions preceded every evening meal. Eventually, Hoeger
turned Luther Hall over to a Lutheran welfare agency which
established a child placement bureau in the home.[47]

The Good Samaritan Society had weathered the leanest years
of the Great Depression. When most corporate endeavors were
retrenching, the Society had expanded from its base at Arthur
into four other states. Its debt load had increased but the needs

of more people were met. It was a time of transitions — Hoeger had moved the Society's headquarters and his family to Fargo. The Society shifted its emphasis to caring for the elderly, and many of them were extricated from sub-standard conditions on county poor farms. The Depression was a learning period for August Hoeger. He learned frugality. He learned that one must be willing to get along with small beginnings. He learned very early that charitable efforts must do business on a sound, above-board basis to avoid any opportunity for critics to raise questions.

In the midst of this time of change and trauma, Pastor Hoeger did not forget young people with physical handicaps. Always the visionary, he established the first school for the physically hand-icapped at Fargo in 1932. Except for a few schools given over to this type of endeavor in large cities in the eastern United States, the Good Samaritan Institute was the first school dedicated to educating physically handicapped young people, providing them with both academic learning and vocational skills.

"Among the trades that were taught at the Good Samaritan Institute were stenography, bookkeeping, typing, shoe and watch repairing, baking, sewing, and art. Crafts such as basket weaving, flower making, and wood working were also taught by the seven teachers in the various academic and vocational courses in 1937." **Above:** Basket weaving. **Below:** Manual arts.

Chapter Four
THE GOOD SAMARITAN INSTITUTE
1932-1940

"Thus, as you drop a grain of corn
into the ground, it grows and so also
the work that is being done for God
and with God grows and flourishes."
— Rev. August Hoeger, Sr.

August Hoeger, as early as 1923, had envisioned a special school for physically handicapped children with sound minds. He was two to three decades ahead of his time in this regard as little was being done for these children nationwide.[1] When Superintendent Hoeger was approached regarding the availability of three college campus buildings in the middle of a pleasant residential district in the southern part of Fargo, North Dakota, he quickly saw the possible fulfillment of another dream.

There was no money available, however, to make a down payment on the deserted Fargo College property. When he was assured that delayed payments could be arranged, Hoeger took action. A man not given to trivial or inconsequential talk, he had the determination and zeal to do, and he believed that time was short. His philosophy was "Do it now and don't wait." The seed that he sowed with the Good Samaritan Institute resulted in boarding school facilities for physically handicapped youngsters in many states of the Union. Activities on the Fargo campus terminated in 1940 because of opposing views and financial problems, but Hoeger "had the dream - the dreamer dies, but never dies the dream."[2]

Reverend Hoeger carried the offer of the buildings of the defunct Fargo College to the Good Samaritan Society Board of Directors on June 20, 1932. He said the property would be used for opening a school for physically handicapped children with normal mentalities.[3] Fargo College had been founded by the Congregational Church in 1888. The College buildings, Jones Memorial Hall, Dill Hall, and a Carnegie Library were constructed at that time.[4] The College discontinued operations in 1922. After lengthy negotiations with the trustees of Fargo College, financial terms were finalized on August 1, 1932. The Society agreed to purchase the College for $70,000, with the first interest payment due January 1, 1934, and the first payment on principal to begin on January 1, 1935.[5] It was a calculated risk, but Hoeger saw that Christian charity overruled a shortage of money. He realized that human needs were growing more and more. In the summer of 1932, he wrote, "We know that these are very hard and trying times for everyone and no doubt many will think that this is the wrong time to begin a work of this kind. But this is just the time when these crippled children are all the more neglected and thus need the help so badly." He was convinced that Christians would provide a helping hand for his new venture.

Reverend Hoeger decided to begin the school in the Library, the smallest of the buildings. It was a two story, brick building with a beautiful Spanish tile roof. The rooms were large and airy, admitting plenty of light and sunshine.[6] The building had to have bathrooms and a new heating plant installed. His initial intent was to have special teachers for the grade school subjects and vocational training for the older students. The latter group would have the opportunity to take bookkeeping, stenography, watch or shoe repairing and printing. He planned to move into the Library in October 1932.[7] When workers were secured to clean the building, Hoeger did not have enough money to make a deposit to have the utilities turned on. Hot water and lighting were needed for mopping floors and scrubbing the walls and windows. To secure kerosene for a two-burner kerosene stove and lanterns and to purchase soap, Pastor Hoeger appealed to his eldest son, John, to relinquish a quarter he had received for his birthday. Tears rolled down John's cheeks as he broke open his piggy bank to provide the money needed to purchase kerosene.[8] Nine year old John Hoeger was unaware at the time that he had made the first contribution toward the beginning of the hospital school concept or residential schools for severely handicapped children on the northern Prairie Plains. August Hoeger proved very persuasive in soliciting contributions for the school. He secured sufficient funds for installing a new heating plant, and he was able to obtain five pianos and a pipe organ for the school's projected music program.

The Good Samaritan Institute (GSI) officially opened in November 1932 in the Library Building. The first student to enroll was Wallace Franke of Arthur. A victim of infantile paralysis a year before his graduation from high school, Franke entered the school in a wheelchair. Arrangements were made for him to take business courses through Augsburg Business College. (Chapter 3).[9] Franke made remarkable progress. With the aid of braces, he discarded the wheelchair and learned to climb steps. Upon his graduation from the Institute, he took a civil service exam, passing with a record 120 words per minutes in shorthand and 60 words per minutes in typing.[10]

In the *Sunshine*, Hoeger announced that the Good Samaritan Institute would be open to any crippled or disabled person irrespective of race, color or creed. By the end of the first year, 16 students enrolled, a sufficient number to prove the need and value for a boarding school. Dorothea Olson, a graduate of North Dakota State College, Fargo, was the first teacher and matron.

Leland S. Burgum became the principal and business manager of the Institute. A graduate of the University of North Dakota in 1925, he had married Ruth Hoeger, a daughter of August and Amelia Hoeger. Burgum also taught music, commercial subjects and social studies.[11] Because it was the only school of its kind on the Prairie Plains, the Institute, for the most part, had to work out its own standards of admission. Other instructors at the Institute during its nine year existence included Anne Carlsen, Ruth Dike, Emma Eide, Ruth Erickson, Lenore Gulbranson, Delia Paulson, Vangeline Quam, and Judy Nord.

Three of the teachers were physically handicapped, Carlsen, Dike, and Erickson. Although some of the teachers joined the staff because there were no other jobs available when they graduated from college, they nevertheless became devoted to their charges. Wages were minimal but most of them were more interested in the outcome of their students and not personal income. Their obligations went beyond the classroom as they helped students dress and undress, bathe and shave. Some of them planned the meals and did the cooking until the Jorgensons, Olga and Clara, arrived. One of the Jorgenson sisters was a cook and the other was a nurse.[12]

Burgum had charge of all vocal music, which included a sextette of handicapped young women. The sextette, organized in the spring of 1936, was the Institute's Extension or Outreach Group. The women sang in area churches to promote the school, to acquaint the public with the abilities of the handicapped and to express the school's gratitude for the financial support it received from area congregations.[13] According to Lucille Greer Wedge, a member of the sextette, Burgum had the task of transporting the women to the various churches. It was no easy effort as two of the women were in wheelchairs and had to be carried, two could walk but had to be carried up steps and the other two could walk up steps but needed an arm to lean on. Burgum's successor, Reverend William Schoenbohm, could not do the same lifting because of a bad back. Thus, it became August Hoeger's job to take the Outreach Group to its various concerts. His strength was tested when they returned to the school late in the evening with no adult help available except for the matron. Reverend Hoeger was the driver for 18 programs during the spring of 1938. He gave brief talks at each of the concerts. The free will offering ranged from $11-$29 per night.[14]

Although he enjoyed working with children, Hoeger did no teaching at the Good Samaritan Institute. He did conduct regular worship services and confirmation classes at the school. Because he put on his clerical robe to conduct a service, Anne Carlsen felt it was more like a real church service.[15] Each day an hour was set aside for a chapel service with visiting pastors and missionaries often conducting devotions. There were occasional musical and patriotic programs. Usually, the hour was directed by teachers or workers with the assistance of students whenever possible.[16] Radio station WDAY-Fargo had morning devotions during the 1930s. Once in awhile, students from the Institute would either give the devotion or provide appropriate music for the occasion.[17]

Outside ramps provided access to the Library Building. Inside the structure, however, it was difficult for many of the handicapped students to move about because of the many steps. Superintendent Hoeger did not express the need for an elevator until the fall of 1939. Students who could not go to the dining room and kitchen in the basement had their meals brought to two tables in the lobby.[18]

Royal Sundet, an eighth grade student in 1936, provided the following description of an average day for a student at the Good Samaritan Institute:

> The bell rings at 6:30 in the morning. I rise at
> about quarter to seven and prepare for breakfast.
> After breakfast, I get ready for school and play in

the hall until the school bell rings at 8:30. The school day begins with opening exercises with songs or reading by the teacher. After that I have arithmetic and grammar and spelling, after which comes recess for fifteen minutes. At 10:45, the entire school gathers for chapel and devotional exercises. After chapel we have geography and then it is noon. I am in the eighth grade.

After I have my dinner in the dining room, I go to my room and lie on my bed for a forty-five minute rest period. Classes start at fifteen after two. Manual training class lasts until school is dismissed for the day at 3:15. After that I just play around until supper time, either in the hall or else I go outside on the porch. We have supper at 5:30. After supper I listen to the radio and play until study period at 7:30. I am through studying between 8:30 and 9:00 and play awhile before going to bed. I usually go to bed around 9:30.[19]

The Institute maintained fully accredited elementary and high school departments. Ruth Erickson, a member of the first graduating class of Good Samaritan Institute, said she learned "that you can do something even though you are handicapped." Ruth, who went on to college, said she worked harder at the Institute than she did in college.[20] The Institute stressed academic work with corrective physical care and treatments given only when necessary. The School provided learning opportunities for bright, young people that they could obtain nowhere else on the Prairie Plains. Fifty-two percent of the students were admitted because it was impossible or inconvenient for them to attend public school. Social maladjustment was a large factor in admitting students to GSI. Forty percent of the students came from inadequate and unsatisfactory homes.[21]

A form of behavior modification was used at the Good Samaritan Institute long before it was given that name. The children kept a report card in one of their pockets, and each evening, they received a mark as to whether their behavior had been good or bad during the day. At the end of the week, a tally was made. If the report was good, a student received some paper money with which he or she could buy candy, nuts, pencils, tablets, *etc.* at the school store.

By 1936-1937, there were a number of extracurricular activities for students. There were 16 members in the Institute's orchestra, a mix of horns, strings, and an accordion. Twenty-three people made up the mixed chorus, and there were students who participated in various vocal ensembles. There were regular meetings of the Luther League, and with their adviser, Emma Eide, League members witnessed for Christ through song and testimony in communities near Fargo.[22]

One of the significant components of the Good Samaritan Institute's curriculum was its vocational program. Superintendent Hoeger was a firm believer in work therapy. He believed that the students who came to the school must have something meaningful to do. Reverend Wilko Schoenbohm, principal of the Institute between 1938 and 1940, believed the vocational program at Fargo was modeled after programs at Bethel in Bielefeld, Germany, and other similar European facilities. Others believed that Hoeger had seen the therapy and usefulness of such programs on his own and that he emphasized training that would be most practical and useful for people with physical handicaps.[23]

Among the trades that were taught at the Good Samaritan Institute were stenography, bookkeeping, typing, shoe and watch repairing, baking, sewing, and art. Crafts such as basket weaving, flower making, and wood working were also taught by the seven teachers in the various academic and vocational courses in 1937. The school had its own print shop in the basement of the Library Building. The shop contained three presses, a paper cutter, embosser, and a stitcher. The older students, who were responsible for the print shop, printed publications for the Good Samaritan institutions and for other private concerns. Among the periodicals rolling off the Institute press in 1937 were *The Valley Lutheran*, *The Lutheran Missionary*, *Mission Stunde*, the *North Dakota Parent-Teacher*, *Sunshine*, and the *Freudenstrahlen*.[24]

The print shop produced the school annual and booklets designed to reach a particular group of readers. During the summer of 1937, the press issued a booklet, *Mother's Book*, which contained 40 meditations for expectant, young mothers. It sold for 35 cents at the Good Samaritan Bookstore in Fargo.[25] Hoeger used the print shop as well to solicit contributions for the school.

Some of the printed literature was directed at the area's Sunday School children. Offered for sale were prayer books for Christmas and a picture of Jesus blessing children. The description accompanying the advertisement for the picture, which could be purchased from the Institute for 25 cents, read "Some day we hope to send to you a large picture that you can hang up in your Sunday School room and you can tell your friends: `This is our school for crippled children.'" The same promotional material offered for sale baskets, door stops, and handbags that had been made by the children at the school.

Between November 1, 1932, and May 30, 1937, the Good Samaritan Institute rendered service to 117 physically handicapped children and disabled persons. Eighty-two young people enrolled in various educational departments for nine months or more. Sixty were enrolled in grades one through 12, while 22 received vocational training in various trades. Twenty-two students graduated from the Institute during the first five years. Despite the sick economy, 81 percent of the graduates found successful occupational employment.[26]

On April 2, 1934, Reverend Hoeger brought another innovative proposal to the Board of Directors. He believed that the Good Samaritan Society must train its own workers to take care of older people. Of primary concern, these prospective employees must learn the Word of God. Thus, he proposed to establish a Bible and Training School which would include courses in Bible study, practical nursing, hospital visitation, home economics, public speaking, and business training at Augsburg Business College.[27] Through theory and practice, enrollees in the Bible and Training School would become more efficient Christian workers. The new school became operative in 1934 with Hoeger as dean and Sister Sena Hestad as registrar and chief instructor.[28] In 1937, seven women were enrolled in the two year course of study; two of them graduated in the spring of 1937.[29]

The Bible and Training School's motto was "We would see Jesus." Superintendent Hoeger outlined the following purposes for his new endeavor:

1. To instill in young people the realization that the people they care for have an immortal soul and to teach them how to deal with the soul, to read for, and pray with the sick and dying, and at the same time care for the bodily needs in the best way possible.

2. To impart a direct and definite knowledge of the Word of God through a daily study of the Bible itself.

3. To give the students the necessary knowledge through study and practical work, to make them efficient workers, in caring for the sick.[30]

The Bible and Training School was relocated to Waterloo, Iowa, in late 1938. Earlier, August J. Hoeger had entered into discussions to take over the Allen Memorial Hospital in Waterloo. The hospital admitted its first patients on February 15, 1925. Financial reverses had followed with the onset of the Great Depression, and the hospital was placed in receivership on March 15, 1934.[31] Hoeger asked Reverend H. H. Diers, pastor of the First Evangelical Church, in Waterloo, to lead in forming the Allen Memorial Hospital Corporation.[32] After Waterloo citizens pledged $51,475 to remove the hospital from receivership, and the receiver made his final report, the Allen Memorial Hospital Corporation, a subsidiary of the Good Samaritan Society, took control under a deed from the Deaconess Society of the Evangelical Church. Reverend Hoeger served on the Memorial Hospital's board of directors and as business administrator for the convalescent home associated with the Hospital. Sister Sena Hestad became the Dean of the Bible and Training School and matron of the Home.[33]

The Nurses' Home at the Waterloo site had been converted to a convalescent home, accommodating 75-90 elderly people, with space set aside for the Bible and Training School. The function of the School was expanded to train women 18-21 years of age, not only for Lutheran institutions of mercy but also for state institutions. Five other women were consecrated as Good Samaritan sisters by Reverend Hoeger in Waterloo on July 2, 1939.[34] For three additional years, the Bible and Training School continued to thrive. With 18 students enrolled in the program, more room was needed in the spring of 1941. Plans were also made to enlarge the scope of training and staff for a larger school.[35] The involvement of the United States in World War II necessitated expansion of the training program for nurses to meet the needs of the American armed forces, and Allen Memorial Hospital needed the space occupied by the Bible and Training School to train additional nurses. As a result, the operations of the Good Samaritan Bible and Training School were suspended in mid-October 1944.[36] Proposals to reestablish the program after World

War II never materialized, but another seed for the future had been planted by Hoeger. Some of the objectives of the Bible and Training School would be found in the Good Samaritan Society's intern program introduced in late 1971. The latter program, designed to train nursing home administrators, included the Society's history and philosophy and practical experience under the supervision of a licensed administrator.[37]

Meanwhile, the Good Samaritan Institute in Fargo became a pawn in the growing rift among members of the Board of Directors. The foremost critic of Reverend Hoeger's leadership of the School, and the Good Samaritan Society, was Fred Knautz, the Society's business manager. In his reports to the Board, he said that the Library Building was a fire trap and that the Fargo fire department opposed having children in the structure. He also said that operating the Institute was too costly, and he recommended its closure.[38] Despite the attacks upon his management style, August Hoeger continued to make improvements at the Fargo facility. In the summer of 1936, a modern automatic sprinkler system was installed in the Library.[39] A physiotherapy room was equipped on the main floor in the summer of 1939. The various pieces of equipment included swirl baths, finger stretchers, and heat lamps.[40] A trained nurse had been in charge of the physiotherapy program since 1936. It was likewise in the summer of 1939 that Superintendent Hoeger began to formulate plans to raise funds for a much needed elevator in the Library.

A serious blow for the Good Samaritan Institute had occurred on November 8, 1937, when Leland Burgum announced his resignation as principal of the Institute.[41] He left for New York City in late December to engage in graduate study at Columbia University. He became one of the pioneers in special education after receiving an Ed. D. at Columbia. During the remainder of his professional career, Burgum taught special education at Southwest Texas University, San Marco, Texas. Shortly after his resignation, the North Dakota State Board of Administration asked three members of the Good Samaritan Society's Board of Directors to meet with them in Bismarck. Approximately four months later, the Institute was inspected by the State Board of Administration. Following the inspection, the State Board refused to issue a license for the Institute. This was a crippling blow because it meant no state aid was forthcoming.[42]

The Reverend Wilko Schoenbohm was called to be the new principal of the Institute on May 23, 1938. A graduate of Wartburg Seminary and a pastor at Bryant, South Dakota, at the time of his call, Schoenbohm's beginning salary was $1,500 per year, with his house rent to be paid out of his salary.[43] Schoenbohm quickly discovered that the Good Samaritan Institute lacked assets and that it had many liabilities. County commissioners provided vouchers for students at the School who originated from their respective jurisdictions. The vouchers bore interest and were redeemable at a future rate. Schoenbohm was able to eliminate much of the Institute's debt by selling a number of the vouchers to railroad companies for cash.[44] One of the teachers he recruited was Anne Carlsen, a recent graduate of Concordia College, Moorhead, Minnesota. She later gained national recognition as the director of the School for Crippled Children at Jamestown, North Dakota.[45]

In his reports to the Society's Board of Directors, Knautz was critical of the Good Samaritan Institute. He said that residents adjacent to the Fargo College campus did not want handicapped people in their front yards for the rest of their lives. The area residents believed that the School's presence reduced the valuation of their property. He told the Board that the community in and around Fargo did not like the Institute's way of doing business. In an indirect attack upon Hoeger, Knautz wrote the Board of Directors that people in Fargo "will get behind the school only if they can be convinced that we do things in a business-like manner and will build on a solid foundation."[46]

In an Executive Committee meeting of the Board of Directors, he said that the trustees of Fargo College wanted to know what the Good Samaritan Society intended to do regarding the School. The Society had operated the school for seven years and had made no payment on the purchase price.[47] If the Society could raise $20,000, the College property could probably be purchased for that price. The trustees and receivers of Fargo College wanted a definitive answer by July 1, 1939.[48] By this time, the Board had instructed Reverend Walter Keller to investigate the possibility and advisability of starting a Crippled Children's Hospital and School in the Lutheran Hospital at Jamestown, North Dakota.[49]

The schism in the Good Samaritan Society, which will be discussed fully in the next chapter, began officially on January 3, 1938, when the Lutheran Hospitals and Homes Society (LHHS) was incorporated.[50] Eleven months later, a group of Lutheran men and women met, and they agreed to form a corporation to take over the Good Samaritan Institute. On a motion by Reverend Keller, the Good Samaritan Society's Board of Directors voted to relinquish the Society's contract with the trustees of Fargo College and to turn the school over to the new corporation.[51] Henceforth, the institution would be known as the North Dakota School for Crippled Children.[52] The Executive Board of the LHHS quickly moved to negotiate with the new corporation relative to an affiliation of the North Dakota School for Crippled Children with the Lutheran Hospitals and Homes Society.

By this time, the Good Samaritan Institute and the Good Samaritan Society had come under the scrutiny of the Commission on Charities of the American Lutheran Church. On October 31, 1939, Dr. C. E. Krumbholz reported to the Commission on Charities that the Good Samaritan Institute was the only institution of its kind in North Dakota and that it received $10,000 annually from the State. Defaming the Institute, he said that political considerations made "welfare officials hesitant to close institutions with sub-standard facilities and administration."[53] Meeting again on December 12, 1939, the commission requested that Reverend C. F. Schaffnit write to the State Welfare Department of North Dakota asking its officials to survey Superintendent Hoeger's institutions at Arthur and Fargo. He was told to invite only F. R. Knautz and Reverend Keller to appear before the Commission to discuss the financial conditions of the institutions of the Good Samaritan Society, its outstanding notes, and its programs.[54] In issuing the invitation, the Commission on Charities pointedly ignored Reverend Hoeger, the founder of the Good Samaritan Society and the Good Samaritan Institute.

With Reverend Hoeger present, the Board of Directors of the LHHS, on April 9, 1940, acted to purchase the Good Samaritan Institute, and if it were advisable, move the school to Jamestown. It was a sad day for Hoeger. He lost one of his greatest dreams and discovered that men he had considered his friends no longer wanted to work with him. There were several resignations from the Board of Directors as several of his former associates shifted their exclusive allegiance from the Society's Board of Directors to the Board of the LHHS. Included among the resignations was that of Reverend Schoenbohm as principal of Good Samaritan Institute. A motion was made and approved for the Lutheran Hospital and Homes Society to purchase the equipment of the

Institute for a price not to exceed $3,000. The transfer of assets, including printing press equipment, was completed on August 9, 1940.[55] Superintendent Hoeger was told to transfer the Society's files and accounts from the office in Fargo to Arthur. At the same April 9 meeting, it was announced that Fred Knautz had been named general manager of the Lutheran Hospital and Homes Society.[56]

Reverend Keller, one of the strongest advocates for moving the Crippled Children's School to Jamestown, found a site for the school in that city adjacent to the James River. Following an inspection of the site by board members of the LHHS, construction began.[57] The School for Crippled Children at Jamestown was dedicated on September 21, 1941. Reverend Schoenbohm was named superintendent of the new school, and Reverend W. W. A. Keller served as president of the School's governing body.[58] Anne Carlsen followed Schoenbohm to Jamestown in 1941. During the 40s she took time off from her teaching obligations to continue her graduate studies, ultimately receiving a Ph.D. from the University of Minnesota. She succeeded Schoenbohm as superintendent of the Crippled Children's School in the summer of 1949.[59] Under her leadership, the School became a model for schools of its type, and in her honor, it was renamed The Anne Carlsen School.

John Hoeger stated that when his father lost the Good Samaritan Institute to Jamestown, there were tears coming from his eyes.[60] For August Hoeger, operating the School was more than a job, it was a mission. He felt that working for the disadvantaged and handicapped was his mission in life. He was a pioneer in this type of education, and he did much in the School with very limited funds.[61] The Institute was an amazing accomplishment, considering that he began the School when the Great Depression was at its worst. Reverend H. S. Froiland, one of the first board members of the GSS said that "...No one has ever done more good with as little money as Hoeger did."[62] Schoenbohm stated that the facility in Jamestown would not have existed if it had not been for the germ Hoeger sowed when he took over the old Fargo College building.[63] Hoeger, in his own humble way, confirmed this. In reference to the Institute, he said, "Thus, as you drop a grain of corn into the ground, it grows and so also the work that is being done for God and with God grows and flourishes."[64]

The loss of the School for Crippled Children was only one part of a very traumatic time for Reverend Hoeger and the Good Samaritan Society between 1938 and 1940. Men he had considered as colleagues in a common cause had allied against him. His relationship with Walter Keller was never the same after 1940. The reasons for the breakup of friendships and the Good Samaritan Society must be considered next.

Above: *The first rented home, 1922.*
Left: *"Dad" Hoeger standing in front of the first house.*
Below: *The Lutheran Home for the Aged in Sioux Falls, South Dakota.*

Chapter Five
DROUGHT, DOUBT, AND DIVISION
1936-1940

"I have put the best years of my life in it [the Good Samaritan Society] and also my reputation, and with God's help I intend to live up to the principles on which this work was founded."—Rev. August Hoeger, Sr., June 24, 1940.

Monetary gifts and loans had been of primary importance in carrying on the work of the Good Samaritan Society since its inception. Adequate rainfall had always been a necessity for farmers to survive economically on the Prairie Plains. During the 1930s, farmers looked longingly to the sky for rain clouds but these were years when little moisture fell to earth. It had been these same farmers who provided much of the financial support for the Society. Thus, as they wrestled with debt and lack of credit, so did the Good Samaritan Society.

One of the worst years for North Dakota farmers was 1936. In that year, the dust storms returned. The rainfall for the summer averaged a disastrous 8.8 inches. The heat was intense. On July 6, the temperature rose to 121 degrees at Steele, North Dakota, a community near Arena, where Reverend Hoeger had begun his ministry. The 1936 crop was almost a total failure with the average production of wheat across the state being five bushels per acre. In many counties, the average was zero. It was the worst crop in the history of North Dakota. The Reverend Peter Larson, a pastor in the Minot area, commented:

> Those were bad days for everybody; the spirits of the people were low. I spent most of my time assuring my people that things would get better and that God would answer their prayers. By

1936 it was hard to get them to believe either. I
had doubts myself.[1]

The drought and oppressive heat made their impact upon the
Society's home at Arthur. Several of the elderly patients passed
away in the summer heat wave. Their deaths increased the number of white crosses in the home's cemetery, established in 1925,
to 62. The facility's potato crop was almost a total failure, and
they were forced to buy potatoes at $1.50 per bushel. There were
few vegetables to can, and it was obvious that there would not be
enough to last the winter. The entire small grain crop did not provide flour for bread. Twenty-one acres of wheat netted between
one and two wagon loads. The yield from 105 acres of corn did not
produce enough silage to feed the cows. The dedicated workers at
the Arthur Home received board and room plus IOU's with the
pledge they would be redeemed later.[2]

Problems on the Prairie Plains were actually worse in 1938
than they were in 1932. The farm belt faced another economic
recession in 1937. Market prices fell and farmers received nine
cents per pound for hogs and six cents per pound for steers.
Because of the unprecedented drought coupled with a farm economy in shambles, many farmers turned to the Works Progress
Administration (WPA), a program that had not been designed to
aid farmers. In the winter of 1936-1937, almost 53,000 North
Dakotans found work on WPA projects. WPA workers earned
about $40 a month for working 100 hours.[3] The rural economy
recovered slowly from 1937 through 1939. As growing conditions
improved, crop production increased. In 1937, 8.2 bushels of
wheat were produced per acre. By 1939, wheat production averaged 10.5 bushels per acre with farmers receiving between 53
and 94 cents per bushel for their investment and labor.[4]

August Hoeger said that without its farm, despite the low production, the Arthur Home could never have made it financially.
During the record-breaking heat wave in the summer of 1936, he
continued to sound an optimistic note. He wrote: "Were it not for
our faith in God and our fellow Christians, we would be miser-
able indeed. But God lives. He has helped us in the past. He will
not forsake us now, nor in the future."[5]

In this new time of trial, members of the Good Samaritan
Society confronted a new problem, internal dissension. The man-
agement of the Society's finances came under scrutiny by its
Board of Directors. Hoeger had said that the activities of the

Good Samaritan Society would not be hampered by the Great Depression. Despite having days when the Society faced collectors and past due accounts without a cent of money, he believed that the "hard times" had opened the door of opportunity.[6] Reverend Hoeger admitted there were financial problems; he said, "We continually have them." With the Lord's help, he told the Board of Directors, "all financial troubles can be overcome."[7] With this frame of mind, he acquired nine new facilities in a ten-month period during the very depth of the Great Depression.

Different perspectives have been advanced for the growing differences within the Society by 1937. The growing rift has been attributed to financial exigencies, a clash of personalities, sharply different management styles, a Board in revolt against its president, led by the Society's general manager, and to a struggle for power. A study of the available documents and the words of several of the participants indicates that several of the foregoing factors played a role.

With the radical decline in income from gifts and government welfare payments because of the adverse climactic and economic conditions, the Society's debt load rapidly increased after 1935. Between 1935 and late 1937, the amount owed on loans for the Arthur Home alone increased from $60,000 to $85,000. On many of these notes, the Society was unable to pay interest that was long past due. The only way to make payments to needy note-holders was to make new loans. In addition, Reverend Hoeger shifted property received from patients at the Fargo Old People's Home to pay some of the debt of the Arthur facility.[8]

Throughout the first 15 years of the Society's existence, August Hoeger, Sr., worked quite independently. It was difficult for him to work through a Board of Directors because he felt that working through the Board consumed a lot of time and slowed progress. He wanted to move ahead and move now. The Board was a rubber stamp for some of his rather arbitrary decisions. He was reluctant to discuss or consult with Board members on certain matters, sometimes entirely ignoring the Board when acquiring another facility. In his mind, this was the way it was, and for those other strong-minded persons he dealt with, this policy did not go over very well.[9]

One of the strong-willed personalities that Superintendent Hoeger met on a day-to-day basis was Frederick R. Knautz, whom Hoeger had employed in 1929. In 1934, Knautz was appointed Field Manager for the Good Samaritan Society, and approximately a year later, on March 15, 1935, he was named the Business Manager for the Good Samaritan Society. A former instructor at Augsburg Business College, he was a practical accountant and businessman who fussed and fumed over budgets and payrolls in an attempt to make ends meet.[10]

As the business manager, Knautz had continuous communication with Board members. Reverend Hoeger, quite obviously, was not aware of the content of several of these communications. Knautz depicted a grim but realistic picture of the debt situation. He implied that Hoeger did not know how to handle finances. Beginning in 1930, Knautz said that in 18 months, he had succeeded in installing an adequate bookkeeping system for the Good Samaritan Society. He stated that the system had worked for three years before Hoeger took charge, after which the records became chaotic.[11] Regarding the bondholders for the Society's hospital at Aberdeen, South Dakota, Fred Knautz told the Board of Directors that "They [the bondholders] absolutely refuse to deal with the Good Samaritan Society and stated very frankly that the many unfulfilled promises, their slipshod and haphazard business methods had resulted in such a lack of confidence and trust that they would, under no condition, have any further dealings with said Society."[12] In the same letter, he said, "We have gotten along with cheap help, because on the whole our Society has become to some extent, cheap itself, which has made it extremely difficult to obtain the services of men and women of any great experience and ability in this type of work."[13] It was his conviction that shifting funds from one institution to another must cease. Knautz wanted a Home to be adjacent to a hospital in a community. He felt it was the only way a community could afford a Home. Hoeger tended to favor a Home without a hospital affiliation. The Society's business manager believed as well that the times called for consolidation and retrenchment rather than expansion.

While Knautz was warning the Board of Directors of imminent bankruptcy, the gulf between him and Hoeger was widening. The rift between the two men ultimately led to a division between Superintendent Hoeger and the Board. Knowing that his management abilities were being questioned, August Hoeger prepared a memorandum in which he expressed his concern for a hierarchy of authority. He stated that if there was too much work for the General Superintendent, an assistant superintendent should be hired to check reports of institutions and to maintain a complete record of legal documents, *etc.* He went on to say that all work must be done under the supervision of the General Superintendent. Hoeger continued, "The Board, not the Society, elects the Superintendent and he is responsible to the Board. All other employees are responsible to the Supt." He concluded the memorandum by saying, "Thus, each man knows exactly to whom he is responsible, and nowhere are there two bosses. As Christ said, `No man can serve two masters.'"[14]

Seeds of doubt had been planted in the minds of the Board of Directors, and they began to question Reverend Hoeger's leadership. They wondered how long the Society could sustain its increasing debt? How long would it be before the Society was faced with foreclosures, bankruptcy, and possible law suits which might close down the entire operation? Knautz had successfully conveyed to the Board his fear of the impending bankruptcy of the Good Samaritan Society if unplanned expansion continued. Fearing the worst, the Board, on November 8, 1937, instructed Reverend Walter Keller to draw up a plan for the reorganization of the Society. A month later, he presented his plan, recommending that the Society change its name to the Lutheran Hospital and Homes Society of America (LHHS). The Board instructed Keller and Knautz to work out the details of the plan and refer it back to the Board for final adoption on January 3, 1938. At that time, the Good Samaritan Society would turn over to the reorganized Society its assets and liabilities. F. R. Knautz was to be the general manager of LHHS and General Manager of the Society until the reorganization was effected.[15] Hoeger opposed the ideas of reorganization and after first going along with it reluctantly resigned from the board of the Lutheran Hospital and Homes Society.[16]

On January 3, 1938, the Lutheran Hospital and Homes Society was established, but the Board decided it was not advisable to reorganize the Good Samaritan Society. The rationale for this latter decision cannot be documented. The minutes simply state that the Board of Directors moved to drop the reorganization issue and that it instructed Knautz to continue as General Business Manager of the Society. At this same January meeting, the LHHS purchased with all assets and liabilities the Good Samaritan facilities at Hot Springs, South Dakota, the Old People's Homes at Valley City and Jamestown, and a hospital at Baker, Oregon. The newly constituted organization agreed to manage hospitals at Bowbells, North Dakota, and Terry and Jordan, Montana.[17] Thus, at the beginning of 1938, a second corporation (LHHS) existed which had all of the same board members and administrative staff as the Good Samaritan Society. Reverend Keller was named president of the LHHS board with Rev. J. F. Graepp serving as secretary. In reality, Knautz was in charge of the LHHS; he began as Business Manager, then as General Manager, and ultimately as its Executive Director.

Eleven days after the formal creation of the LHHS, Knautz wrote another lengthy letter to the Board of Directors. Toward the end of the letter, he wrote:

> We are now to believe that a new organization has been formed. I cannot see it as a new organization, at least not plainly enough or clearly enough to sell the idea to the people concerned about the above named institutions, because we still have the identical group and surely we cannot fool ourselves into believing that men who have been are in large part in business enterprises and of the caliber of men that we have to deal with in these various communities, will believe for a minute that we have a new organization or that our business methods and dealings will be any different than they were in the old organization, because we do still have the same Board of Directors and the same officers.[18]

He went on to recommend a mix of Good Samaritan Board members and several new people plus a new group of officers to head up the LHHS. He concluded his letter by offering to resign from "the Board of Directors of the old Good Samaritan Society and the new Lutheran Hospital and Homes Society, to take effect immediately."[19] The Board rejected his offer to resign.

Hoeger was very unhappy with what was taking place. He was the founder of the Good Samaritan Society, but he was being removed from the decision-making process. The Board told him that there would be no further expansion without its permission. There would be no switching of funds from one institution to another, and the General Superintendent was told that his borrowing of money would be monitored.[20] His daughter, Dr. Agnes Hoeger, in mid-June 1938, wrote him a wonderful letter of encouragement from London, England, where she was enrolled in the London School of Tropical Medicine. In it, she said:

> ...It is a fearfully hard struggle that God is test-
> ing you with; but that only goes to show that God
> is examining you for the next higher degree and
> He must be sure that you will not fail otherwise
> He would not have given you the test.

> Personally, Dad, I feel that God has a much
> greater work for you in store and that this terri-
> ble crisis will prove to be a great blessing. It
> seems to me that He is showing you that His
> Kingdom is not built of outward things but of
> inward things. And, although your best friends
> can stop you from building the Kingdom of God
> outwardly, they can not stop you from building
> His Kingdom in the hearts of human beings.[21]

Agnes Hoeger recommended that he outlive, outlove, and out-laugh his enemies. She urged him to love them and outlove them — the most Christ-like virtues.[22]

The financial state of the Good Samaritan Society was at an all-time low in 1938. There were insufficient funds to pay Home office expenses, including the salaries of the Superintendent, General Manager, and one District Manager. Gilman Wang, the District Manager, was released on September 1, 1938, and Knautz took over his responsibilities. Counties were unable to pay their $30 a month for welfare residents. Because of unpaid bills, there was a threat to turn off the electricity at the Arthur Home. In an effort to raise operating funds, the Society proposed to sell the Harvey, North Dakota, Hospital to the Roman Catholic Church for $37,000 with $35,000 being the lowest bid that the Society would accept.[23]

On January 13, 1939, the Board of Directors made the decision to divide the properties of the Good Samaritan Society, stating that in the event of bankruptcy or foreclosures, all of the facili-ties would not be lost. The Lutheran Hospital and Homes Society purchased, for one dollar each, including all assets and liabilities, the Good Samaritan facilities in Fargo, North Dakota; Sheldon, Iowa; Eureka, South Dakota; Columbus, Nebraska; and Sterling, Colorado.[24] Within the next two years, the LHHS took over all but four of the Good Samaritan Society's facilities, the latter facilities being located at Ambrose and Arthur, North Dakota; Greeley, Colorado; and Sioux Falls, South Dakota. Reverend Hoeger was the primary victim of these transfers as the Good Samaritan Society was left with most of the debt of the two organizations.

In the midst of the foregoing transfers, Knautz continued to pass judgment on the dire financial straits of the Society. In a 16-page report to the Board in October 1939, he reviewed the high incidence of failures of Good Samaritan facilities. Knautz felt the Good Samaritan Society had drifted along with no direction and poor business practices. He stated that in more than one case, no written contracts existed on lease agreements. In his conversations with the Board, he said the plan drawn up in late 1937 by the LHHS and adopted by the Good Samaritan Society would to a great extent have been successful had it been followed. He implied that Superintendent Hoeger was at fault. In his view, Hoeger had not been cooperative, the Board had not received a report and the Society had not conducted an audit.[25]

After several pages of pinning responsibility for the Society's financial plight on Reverend Hoeger, Knautz attempted to absolve himself from being associated with efforts to undermine Hoeger and the Good Samaritan Society. He wrote:

> I have been accused of disrupting and upsetting the ideals and ideas of the Good Samaritan Society. I have been accused of holding secret meetings. I have been accused of wanting to get Reverend Hoeger out of the organization and many other things. I care little about these accusations; they are untrue.[26]

In the spring of 1939, the beleaguered Good Samaritan Society had come under the scrutiny of the Commission on Charities of the American Lutheran Church. Meeting in Chicago on April 11-12, 1939, the Commission considered a letter from Reverend A. H. Fritschel, Jackson, Minnesota, to Dr. Em. Poppens, President of the ALC, concerning Hoeger's failure to pay the interest on a long overdue note of one of his parishioners. Fritschel complained that very little interest had been paid on the note, that the woman's letters of inquiry had been ignored, and that no explanation had been given of why the payments were not being made. Fritschel wanted pressure from above to make Reverend Hoeger meet his obligations. The Commission on Charities agenda included a statement from the pastors of the Wisconsin District of the ALC, stating that they had lost confidence in the management of both the Good Samaritan Society and the LHHS. They complained that the congregations at Fond du Lac and Oconomowoc, Wisconsin, had suffered because of the loss of credit and the poor management of the homes for the aged in those cities. Beginning with a motion to make a casual and exploratory survey of the institutions and agencies affiliated with the Society and LHHS, the Commission undertook an investigation that lasted until the summer of 1940.[27]

The ALC's Commission on Charities reconvened in Chicago on October 31, 1939, to listen to a highly subjective report from Dr. C.E.Krumbholz, the Executive Secretary of the Welfare Department of the National Lutheran Council. He had conferred with Reverend Hoeger and had visited the Society's institutions at Arthur and Fargo. Krumbholz began his remarks by saying that the Society's facilities had poor administration, heavy indebtedness and standards that were no credit to Reverend Hoeger or the Lutheran Church. He then stated that the rank and file of the Lutheran constituency in North Dakota had confidence in Hoeger. They had money invested in his institutions and the state's "laymen see nothing objectionable in the standards of Hoeger's institutions because they themselves are satisfied with rather meager and primitive accommodations and facilities in their own homes, and know little about standards prevailing in eastern states."[28] Krumbholz appeared oblivious to what had transpired in rural North Dakota during the 1930s. His observations were solely confined to the physical factors he had noted in his brief visit to the Good Samaritan facilities. He made no attempt to contrast the care for both body and soul that the people received in the Arthur and Fargo Homes with that in county poor farms and state institutions. He could not visualize how it was to simply survive approximately 20 years of a depressed farm economy and nine years of climactic adversity. Basically, he existed in a different world. Closing with a bureaucratic pronouncement, he said there was no way to bring about the compliance of Reverend Hoeger because "The confidence which the laity seems to have in Hoeger's enterprises, plus the general approval of a considerable number of clergymen to the projects, creates a practical problem."[29] Eugene Hackler, who later served on the Board of the Good Samaritan Society and as its legal counsel, attributed some of the action against Hoeger to the professional jealousy of a faction within the ALC hierarchy.[30]

The Commission then instructed one of its members, Reverend William von Fischer, to obtain more definite information on investors' complaints against the Good Samaritan Society. When he reported that it was difficult to obtain documentary evidence because interested people did not respond, the Commission invited Frederick R. Knautz and Reverend Walter Keller to appear before the Commission to discuss the financial conditions of the Society.[31]

Keller and Knautz appeared before the Commission at the Atlantic Hotel in Chicago on February 27, 1940. Keller said the Lutheran Hospital and Homes Society had been organized to handle and to administer new institutions. This statement contradicted what had occurred in 1938-1939 when the LHHS had obtained control of most of the existing institutions operated by the Good Samaritan Society. Keller told the Commission that the LHHS had no legal responsibility to pay off the debts of the Good Samaritan Society, but that it felt morally obliged to do so. No serious effort was ever made to fulfill this obligation.

Regarding Superintendent Hoeger, Reverend Keller said he "was a man of prayer, devout, sincere, honest, but not a business man `although he thinks he is.'"[32] Keller further stated that the Board of Directors had checked Hoeger's penchant for expansion and his policy of indiscriminately borrowing of money. Superintendent Hoeger had been told that his job was to manage the Arthur Home and to pay off its debts and obligations. In his remarks, Knautz said the LHHS had been organized to check Hoeger's activities. Under the new structure, Reverend Hoeger could not write checks or transfer any money from one institution to another. When Knautz said the Society had not drained money from the ALC, Dr. Em. Poppens had replied that that was not the issue. The ALC, he said, had not clarified the problem of charities since the merger in 1930. The old Ohio Synod had only synod-owned institutions; the old Iowa Synod had synod-owned, society-owned, and synod-recognized institutions. "The whole issue," according to the ALC President, "is whether this scheme of taking on more institutions, borrowing money, and transferring from one institution to another shall continue."[33]

Before they left the meeting, Knautz and Keller were instructed to prepare statements for the following points:

1. Why two societies?
2. A list of the institutions for which you assume responsibility.
3. A paragraph relative to the position and to the scope of the duties of Reverend Hoeger.
4. A statement listing the total amount of notes and other obligations, and a plan for liquidating them.

Reverend Hoeger, who had not been invited to the meeting, was asked to respond to the foregoing four points by mid-May 1940.[34]

Superintendent Hoeger responded to criticism of his work in the *Sunshine*. He stressed that the money borrowed to build his humanitarian work occurred during the so-called "good days." He did not know at that time that ten years of depression were coming, that there would be crop failures and a dust bowl. Hoeger continued, "And still when we are criticized, you would think that we were to blame for it all."[35]

He had received a further rebuke from the Board of Directors in mid-December 1939. It announced that the Business Manager would have charge of all the business of the corporation and that he should be acceptable and responsible to the Executive Board and the Board of Directors only. The Superintendent would be responsible for his duties to the Board of Directors and the Executive Board.[36] The worst blow fell during the Board meeting on April 9, 1940. On that day, the entire Board of the Good Samaritan Society and the administrative staff, with the exception of Reverend Walter Keller, resigned, along with Louis Heiden, manager of the farm at Arthur, and Reverend Wilko Schoenbohm, the principal of the Good Samaritan Institute. Superintendent Hoeger was told to move the Society's records from the Fargo office to Arthur. After shifting their allegiance exclusively to the LHHS, these former friends and colleagues of Hoeger elected Knautz as General Superintendent and General Manager.[37]

Approximately two months later, on June 2, 1940, the Commission on Charities made its report to the Board of Trustees of the American Lutheran Church. The Commission's report viewed the LHHS in a favorable light, commenting that the officers and Board of LHHS had shown every willingness to cooperate with the Commission on Charities by way of supplying information and readiness to counsel. Expressing confidence in the management of the Lutheran Hospital and Homes Society, the Commission recommended no official action on the part of the ALC at that time.[38]

It was a different story when the Commission considered the Good Samaritan Society. Its members said they respected Hoeger for his piety and sincerity, but they did not have confidence in his financial administration or in his judgment to refrain from unwisely establishing new institutions. "The considerations," the report stated, "cause us to fear that the administration of the Good Samaritan Society brings the American Lutheran Church into disrepute." Relative to the Society, the Commission recommended to the Board of Trustees that they adopt the following Resolution No. 5:

> Be it RESOLVED, that the American Lutheran Church officially disclaim any responsibility for the financial administration of the Good Samaritan Society, and be it
>
> FURTHER RESOLVED, That the American Lutheran Church officially disclaim any responsibility for any new institution opened without the approval of the Church's Commission or Board of Charities.[39]

Learning of the Commission on Charities' Report, Reverend Walter Keller wrote to August Hoeger, Sr., on June 15, 1940, stating that it was necessary that the Society and the LHHS come to a better understanding and, if possible, pull in the same direction. He continued, "We will have to face the Board of Charities and Synod next Fall whether we want to or not and therefore our house must be in order. I have received some more threatening letters pertaining to those notes and steps must be taken very soon to satisfy those people or they will make bad for the Society and us at the synodical meeting." Keller asked Hoeger to convene the old Board of the Good Samaritan Society, even though they had resigned earlier, to discuss the issue that he had raised.[40]

In response to Keller's request, Hoeger probably wrote one of the longest letters of his professional career. It expressed his anger and frustration over the way he had been treated since the creation of the Lutheran Hospital and Homes Society. His feelings are best expressed in the first paragraph, which reads:

> Dear brother,
>
> When I received your letter Saturday evening, I did not know if I should laugh or cry, but I did know that that was not my friend Walter of many years standing. In every line I read the doing of Knautz. Don't you think, Walter, that it's getting to be high time that you and I were doing some thinking of our own instead of letting Knautz try to run this whole affair? Not Knautz and not you, but I am the guilty one who started this whole work of the Good Samaritan Society. I have put the best years of my life in it and also my reputation, and with God's help I intend to live up to principles on which this work was founded. It was Knautz, with your assistance, who cooked up the whole idea of separating the Good Samaritan Society and Hospitals and Homes. Not one word was breathed to me, everything was done in secret and like a gang of high-way robbers. Then you expect God's blessing to rest upon it. At that meeting, April ninth, I was told that I was to have the debts and a few institutions left to the Good Samaritans — that I was the leader. I accepted this work and I have taken ahold of this affair and I absolutely refuse to have Knautz butt into this work. He has more than his hands full with his Hospitals and Homes. You also will have to realize that I am the president of the Good Samaritan Society and also the superintendent, and you'll have to work out the problems of the Good Samaritans with me and not with Knautz. We are saving and paying every cent we can and if this had been done the last three years, many thousands of dollars would have been paid off.[41]

Reverend Hoeger went on to say that he would take care of the letters referred to by Keller. Concerning the Synod, he had answered the four questions the Commission on Charities had posed long ago. Midway through the letter, he made his position clear that he would continue as the head of the Good Samaritan Society. He wrote:

> My dear Walter, my heart is heavy and of course the easiest would be to take up a congregation and let you people run things your way. Seventy-five percent of those noteholders are my personal friends. They still have confidence that I will see that they get their money back. My whole life belongs to God and until he shows me that he wants me someplace else, I intend to stand up and fight like a man for this cause. I have been patient nearly three years, I have been praying and hoping that you people would come to your senses. I have built this work from the very beginning, not on dollars but upon Christian workers.... They look up to me as their leader and I am not going to let a little business manager upset this whole blessed work and put a different spirit into it. If you cannot agree with our principles you have the right, the same as the others, to resign, but you do not have the right to upset the apple cart.
>
> .... Finally, neither you nor I will always be here, but Christ's work goes on. Again I say, I am the one who founded this work; I have spent these eighteen years in it and have certain principles that we're working on. I believe it is my privilege to see if a work so consecrated and born can exist.[42]

He concluded his *"Hier Ich Stehe"* remarks with the following words: "I hope you will accept it [the letter] in the spirit it was written. I love peace and go to the very limit to keep it, but I'm up against the wall now and cannot back up any farther. I therefore demand that you respect the office I hold. If you're not satisfied you can tell the society which is over and above both of us."[43]

The problems of the Good Samaritan Society were the primary subject of discussion at the annual meeting held at the Arthur Home on July 14, 1940. Superintendent Hoeger referred to the Arthur Home as not only the mother institution but also as the experimentation of the Society. Mistakes were made, he said, but other homes may benefit from them. "Our greatest mistake, if you want to call it such," he remarked, "was that in the years of depression we did more charity than our friends gave us the means to do." Acknowledging that the Society's members lived in troublesome times where nothing was secure, Hoeger concluded his report by saying, "But over and above it all is the Almighty God who always has the last word and in His Hands we commit the work of the Good Samaritan Society."[44]

In the early fall of 1940, the Executive Boards of the Society and LHHS met to clarify a few matters regarding the split between the two organizations. It was decided that there should be separate maintenance between the two bodies. The LHHS published in papers that the Good Samaritan Society was in no way connected with the Lutheran Hospital and Homes Society. Twenty-one days later, on October 16, the Executive Boards, meeting at the main office of the LHHS in Fargo, brought an official "peaceful separation" between the two organizations. The Good Samaritan Society was represented by Superintendent Hoeger, the vice president, Reverend T. S. Severtson of Ambrose, and the Society's secretary, Sister Margaret Moehring of Arthur. The documents and papers of the Society and some office equipment which had been purchased jointly, were conveyed to Arthur. The question of how the LHHS would help pay joint debts was set aside and nothing was done about it.[45]

In the final edition of the *Sunshine* for 1940, there was a special notice, indicating that the Good Samaritan Society specialized in work for epileptic, feeble minded, mildly insane, adult cripples, aged and sick. The work with and for crippled children had been taken over by a separate society. Donations for the work of the Good Samaritan Society should be sent to the Good Samaritan Home, Arthur, North Dakota.[46]

In the fall of 1940, a distraught August Hoeger was left alone with four Homes and with most of the debt of both the Good Samaritan Society and LHHS. All of the debt that could be transferred was assigned to the Good Samaritan Society. Much of 18 years of hard work had been taken from him. The Board members who had switched allegiance, at one time, had been his best friends. For a while he withdrew from those about him. His sons reported that the household was like a tomb for several days. Hoeger seriously considered returning to the parish ministry. Bertha Bosch Christian said she did not see him for three days, that he secluded himself and engaged in prayer.[47] He poured out his heart and hurt to District President George Landgrebe of the ALC. President Landgrebe urged Reverend Hoeger to stay the course and not to abandon his work with the Good Samaritan Society. Landgrebe told Hoeger that he should not make a hasty decision and that he should keep praying, asking for God's guidance.

In his 1940 Christmas letter to the Society staff, Superintendent Hoeger told the Society's members that "we were not criticized for our work but about our finances." He emphasized that the Good Samaritan Society was not on any church budget, that it did not receive state aid and that it was not the recipient of funds from a community chest drive. The Society worked on a different principle; it solicited its own support.[48]

Although he sometimes lacked business acumen and could not be described as a team player, there was no excuse for the maltreatment he received between late 1937 and the fall of 1940. Much of what occurred took place without his knowledge. The man who had built the Society was ignored when crucial decisions were made. The Board secured control of the Homes which had the strongest financial base and told Hoeger that he would have to solve the significant debts of the remaining Good Samaritan Homes at Arthur and Ambrose, North Dakota; Sioux Falls, South Dakota; and Greeley, Colorado. When Reverend J. F. Graepp, president of the LHHS board in 1943, questioned the propriety of some of the actions taken against Hoeger between 1938-1940, Knautz wrote that in assigning the responsibility for the Arthur Home debt to Hoeger, they were doing him a favor! His argument was that the Arthur community was willing to support the Home with contributions, that the community contained a certain amount of wealth, thus, it was not the worst situation. He felt that LHHS had taken a great load from the Good Samaritan Society and left it with only the task to clean up the Arthur debt. In the same letter, Knautz said that he was careful not to advertise or publicize the LHHS. This was being done so as not "to draw or distract from Good Samaritan Society or in any way hinder or jeopardize that organization from soliciting donations or contributions for their institutions."[49]

The split left painful emotional scars. Hoeger cut off relations with all of the Society Board that transferred their allegiance to the LHHS. He did not speak to Fred Knautz until a meeting was arranged between the two men in 1968. It was Reverend Hoeger's style to be non-confrontational. Thus, he did not talk about the men who had betrayed him. He would not say a bad word about them. He simply would not have anything to do with them.[50]

Throughout the entire crisis, the workers at the several Good Samaritan Homes remained loyal to Superintendent Hoeger. They, too, encouraged him to continue with the work he had begun in 1922. With the support of those people who surrounded him in this hour of trial coupled with his own determination and firm belief in the rightness of his cause, Reverend Hoeger decided to carry on. The survival chances for the Good Samaritan Society appeared minimal, but he determined to rebuild the Society. As the United States stood on the verge of entering World War II, August Hoeger set about reducing the organization's debt, creating a new Board of Directors, and adding to the Society's roster of Homes. He told his wife Amelia that the split "will not stop us. I'm not going to quit. I'm going right on."[51] In creating a new board, he thought of the loyal Home administrators (or managers) that had stood by him during the darkest hour of the Good Samaritan Society. He decided that the new Board of Directors must include administrators. Bertha Christian and Viola Baugatz were among the first administrators to serve on the Board. In the years that followed, Hoeger moved with more caution in acquiring new facilities. He was reluctant to make commitments which involved large sums of money.[52]

The controversy had involved strong but different personalities. Neither Hoeger nor Knautz would be subordinated to the other. Both men were convinced of the rightness of their position. Both men worked long hours in striving to reach their objectives.[53] Some participants in the controversy have said that it was too bad that Hoeger and Knautz could not have worked together, that there was strength in the diverse approaches of both men. Nevertheless, both organizations achieved success with little conflict between them. The Lutheran Hospital and Homes Society stressed ownership or management of hospitals while the Good Samaritan Society stressed the ownership or management of nursing homes. In 1988, Lutheran Health Systems (the former Lutheran Hospital and Homes Society) owned and operated 60 facilities in 11 states, including clinics, chemical dependency units and the Anne Carlsen School for Disabled Children at Jamestown, North Dakota. Through diversification, LHS established or acquired three subsidiaries. The subsidiaries, which collectively covered 14 states, included:

1. Concord Health Services, Incorporated, specializing in durable medical equipment and home health care agencies.
2. LHS Management Company, offering management services to hospitals and nursing homes, and
3. Diagnostic Medical Systems, distributing medical technology.

A new chapter in the Good Samaritan Society had begun. In the two decades following 1940, it would acquire or build a multitude of homes throughout the central part of the nation. Three and a half decades after the split, Clarence Austad commented that Reverend Hoeger "got the dirty end of it, and boy, that dirty end looked like a rose before he got done with it."[54] The schism had been a trying time for Reverend Hoeger, but it had also been a significant learning experience. In rebuilding the Good Samaritan Society, he would carefully monitor the Society's financial accounts, recording income and expenditures with a pencil in notebooks or on the back of envelopes.

Chapter Six
REBUILDING THE VISION, THE GENERAL SUPERINTENDENT

"Have no anxiety about anything but in everything by prayer and supplication with thanksgiving let your requests be made known to God." —
Philippians 4:6.

John T. Flanagan wrote that "A man's life virtually defies capture." One can narrate the events, record the activities, define the attitudes, describe the personality, evaluate the impact on others and quote the written word but never capture the whole person.[1] This is certainly true in attempting to describe the professional career of August Hoeger, Sr., after 1940. Nevertheless, there are certain things that can be said about him with certitude. He was a leader, a man of great faith, a visionary, a compassionate individual, and a person of conviction and perseverance. Possessing these qualities, he quickly overcame the setbacks brought about by the Great Depression and the tearing asunder of the Good Samaritan Society in the spring of 1940. The beginning of his remarkable recovery, however, was overshadowed by another global tragedy.

As the pall of the Great Depression began to lift from the land, the shadow of the next traumatic event, another general war, gave people little cause for rejoicing. While the forces of aggression worked their will in East Asia and Europe, the American economy slowly recovered. In 1940, the worst days of the Depression were over but almost ten million Americans, 17 percent of the work force, were without jobs; about 2.5 million found their only source of income in government programs.

On the same day that a mass resignation of Good Samaritan Society board members had occurred, April 9, 1940, German military forces invaded Denmark and Norway. Five weeks later, following the Nazi attack upon the Low Countries and France,

President Franklin D. Roosevelt, on May 16, 1940, asked Congress for appropriations to rearm the nation. The demand for armaments stimulated the American economy. The Great Depression ended, but its termination would see thousands of young American men dead or wounded on foreign battlefields and social disruption at home.

In early December 1941, the United States became directly involved in World War II. The increased demand for food put farmers in a favorable bargaining position. Farm production reached a new high on the Prairie Plains during the war years. Agricultural prosperity continued after World War II. There was a mild recession in 1946-1947, but the American economy quickly recovered and began to expand. The millions of starving people in Europe and Asia created a high demand for American farm products. Coupled with favorable growing conditions on the Prairie Plains, production and marketing increased dramatically. Farmers, as well as the Good Samaritan Society, now could move to eliminate the indebtedness they had incurred during the Great Depression.

The rebuilding of the Good Samaritan Society occurred in a very different social environment. Better living conditions accompanied an improved economy because a veritable technological revolution followed World War II. The switch from animal power to gasoline engines was completed. Isolated rural life ended with improved roads and motorized transport. By 1951, the corn crop was harvested with mechanical pickers and small grains with combines.

Electric power came to rural areas in the American heartland in the late 1940s. Electricity, more than anything else, reduced the differences in country and city living. It brought many farm homes and small towns into the modern age. Life became easier with electric-powered machines and home appliances. By 1953, the television set was becoming a fixture in rural areas providing another link with the wider world. The Arthur Home, through donations from members of the community, installed a 21-inch RCA set in the dining room. The matron commented, "You should have seen the faces of our people when they not only [could] hear, but [actually could] see the people talking to them. It becomes a little difficult to get them to go to bed at night."[2] During World War II, the Society's homes experienced a shortage of necessary furniture, beds, bedding, washing machines, and refrigerators. Home managers coped with rationing along with the remainder of American society. Some of the elderly could not understand why certain items were not available. Staff workers showed them newspaper headlines which indicated that only so much sugar, for example, could be obtained. The Arthur Home was fortunate enough to churn its own butter and to have its own milk, eggs, hogs, steers, and garden produce.[3] There was a shortage of help everywhere. Many people were attracted to jobs in defense industries, and, of course, millions of men and women were in the armed forces. Personnel at the Arthur Home interceded with the Cass County draft board to reclassify people needed to run machines and supervise workers on the 480 acre farm.[4]

Despite the wartime shortages, Reverend Hoeger determined to forge ahead. The Society could not fold its hands and do nothing because the need for homes for the aged was too great. The Society could not sit idle and wait for better days. Overcoming wartime obstacles, the Society had opened five additional facilities by 1945. Although his first love had been serving youth, Hoeger became convinced during the 1940s that care of the elderly was the most acutely needed of all works of mercy. The elderly were living longer and there were more of them.

With no visible means of support, the debt-ridden Good Samaritan Society had appeared headed for bankruptcy or worse in 1940. Excluding a growing economy, the credit for the Society's recovery belongs solely to Superintendent Hoeger. Except for occasional secretarial help from his wife, Amelia, he alone was responsible for keeping the Society operational and for building it anew. It was a remarkable accomplishment for a person who had not completed college, who did not spell very well, and who constantly mispronounced people's names.

In the spring of 1945, on the eve of his greatest achievements, August Hoeger, Sr., was nearing his 60th birthday. Physically, this Christian entrepreneur did not stand out in a crowd. Small in stature, approximately 5 feet 7 inches tall, he weighed about 155 pounds. As a young man, he had dark, wavy hair. It grayed prematurely, and he became bald as the years progressed. The blue-eyed Superintendent Hoeger had a rather long, full face, and he wore glasses. Behind his right ear, he had a large, fatty tumor which he refused to have removed. The Reverend Hoeger had little sense of dress. He favored conservative, dark suits of a comfortable cut. Amelia usually purchased his shirts. A very frugal man, Hoeger often wore the same clothes until they wore out.

He lived simply, with no pretense of any kind. When his $200 per month salary was raised to $400 a month, Reverend Hoeger continued to live on $200.[5] When traveling by train, he never used sleeper accommodations, or if by car, he always sought the motels with the lowest rates. The General Superintendent, however, was not a stingy person. He was very generous. Hoeger determined that he would not waste a cent that could be used to help the needy. Self-denial was the first lesson in Christ's school, and one of the vital requirements in Hoeger's staff was performance. If traveling on Society business, the question was — "How would I live if on my own?"[6]

The energy which emanated from August Hoeger was demonstrated from the lectern and the pulpit. He had large, expressive hands, and he used them extensively when he spoke. He seldom used notes when speaking, and he was at ease with large audiences. Being enthusiastic and vibrant, Hoeger was able to excite an audience. Bertha Bosch Christian said that when Reverend Hoeger was in the pulpit "He had the thunder of Simon when he preached, and what he preached, he meant."[7] He was not an evangelist. Preaching from the heart, his message was plain and direct. His natural simplicity of outlook enabled him to express in common terms his faith in God, "and with a special eloquence the thoughts and feelings of humble expression to the common man."[8] He feared church people were not carrying out the God-given task of going out and making disciples. Hoeger spoke to the essential point of the human's lost condition and the need of salvation by the grace of God through the crucified Christ. The crucifix, to Hoeger, was the inspiring symbol of God's great love for humankind.[9] He wanted evidence of Christ on the cross. He did not believe that the empty cross enhanced remembrance of the suffering that Christ endured for the purpose of redemption.[10] Hoeger also had a great love for stained glass windows. They were found in the chapels of several of the Society's facilities. Stained glass windows provided a visual means of expressing the Gospel to the non-literate. The medium contained the message.[11]

Superintendent Hoeger engaged in vertical thinking. He looked upward. Genuine life came through devotion, religion and tradition — from the vertical plane. He lived life in two worlds — a dual existence in the heavenly and the earthly worlds. His leader in each was a present-future God who was in control of all circumstances. Life to Dad Hoeger was a seasonal journey in these two worlds where all life was holy.[12]

Reverend Hoeger was broadminded about all religious denominations. He was not particularly concerned about doctrinal differences provided one had a personal relationship with Christ. He approved of administrator William Goldbeck's giving communion to all denominations at state institutions in Nebraska although the "old" American Lutheran Church frowned on it.[13] Reverend Hugo Schwartz said that Hoeger was "pretty much ecumenical though his heart was in the Lutheran Church."[14]

The General Superintendent maintained a good balance between action and devotion. He spent hours by himself, but they were productive hours. His peace of mind and will were strengthened through prayer and meditation, and these qualities played a major role as he continued to build the Good Samaritan Society. Prayer was a constant in the Hoeger household. Family devotions occurred on a daily basis. All members of the immediate family were to become full-time church workers. Daily devotions also became an integral part of the Good Samaritan Society. As of 1997, the staff at the Society's national headquarters continued to participate in morning devotions each day of the work week. Pastor Hoeger was not a critical theologian or a critical Biblical scholar. He accepted the Word of God without subjecting it to a critical analysis.[15] Even so, he loved to read theological books, including the works of Helmut Thielicke. At night, Hoeger would quickly fall asleep, no matter what problems he had encountered during the day, but he would often wake up at 2 or 3 a.m. and read until daybreak.[16] "God willing" was often his response to questions and requests, since he believed that God directs all life.

The General Superintendent was quite outspoken concerning the proper behavior of Society personnel. There were rules for female employees and their "boyfriends." The women should associate only with "honorable Christian men," otherwise everyone's reputation was in jeopardy. The women should entertain their male friends only in sitting rooms or parlors or else the residents would lose respect for workers. The female staff should be in by 10 p.m. when the doors were locked except one night a week when they could stay out until midnight. Good Samaritan workers were to have high ideals, maintaining the reputation of the Society as a Christian institution.[17] Although he did not consider dancing a carnal sin, Reverend Hoeger believed that "As children of God we do not find our joy in dancing." As long as he was alive and General Superintendent, he declared, there would be no dancing permitted in any of the Good Samaritan homes. One of the administrators, he stated, had square dancing for the elderly. The administrator lost, and he was not there anymore. In 1969, Hoeger stated, "The downfall of the churches today can be put in one word, `permissiveness.'"[18]

Reverend Hoeger seldom looked people in the eye except when speaking to large audiences.[19] Yet, August Hoeger, Sr., was charismatic in conversation and personal contact. When he gathered with a community group, which usually included businessmen, city councillors, and pastors, Hoeger was very comfortable with them. He used a low-key effective approach. The General Superintendent impressed his listeners with his integrity and absolute trust in God. His sincerity hurt at times. To a hypochondriac woman, he said, "I don't think you have been sick a day." The woman felt she was sick all of the time, and she was quite upset over his blunt statement.[20] His spirit of honesty, meekness, and humility inspired confidence. There was no deceit when he responded to questions.[21] Eugene Hackler, the Society's legal counsel for many years, said that when Reverend Hoeger testified in court, usually on a tax matter involving the Society, he did not have to speak to win favor with the jury. "His [Hoeger's] mannerisms and his attitude and his sincerity," said Hackler, "was sometimes electric."[22]

Reverend Hoeger loved wit and humor but he did not indulge in it. He did not mind being teased about his fire engine red pajamas and that he feared onions and sin equally. In good humor, he accepted criticism of his failure to maintain his automobile and his driving thousands of miles without a spare tire.[23]

Rural people were impressed with his great interest in and extensive knowledge of livestock, flowers, and gardening. Hoeger was comfortable with farmers and small-town merchants. When he resided in Fargo, he would drive to Arthur on Saturdays. Shortly after his arrival, he could be found conversing with the farm manager, asking how the crops were doing and what were the current grain prices. One of his primary concerns was checking on the cattle, particularly the purebred Holsteins. The General Superintendent was very proud of maintaining their registration.[24] His hands were work worn. Residents at Arthur, and later at Hastings, Nebraska, were accustomed to seeing Hoeger in coveralls, digging in the dirt, painting, or hammering nails.[25] Lucille Greer Wedge, an employee of the Arthur Home, said that Dad Hoeger would bring boxes of tomato plants from Fargo, don a pair of bib overalls, and he would soon be found crawling along a row, placing plants in damp holes, and packing soil around them.[26] Several of his contemporaries indicated that he planted over 7,000 trees in his lifetime. When asked about his great interest in this endeavor, he replied, "I don't plant trees for myself — I plant them for those who will follow after me — the young people."[27] At the Arthur farm, he would spend a whole day preparing a brooder house, regulating water fountains, and securing ground feed. The next morning, Hoeger would bring 500 baby chicks from a Fargo hatchery, remaining to make sure everything was working properly.[28]

The loss of all but four Society facilities in 1940 had left Reverend Hoeger deeply shaken, but he was the type of individual who preferred to discuss the possibilities of the future than to talk about the past. He always looked forward to a new project with great anticipation. Twelve years after the crisis of 1940, the Good Samaritan Society had 32 homes in seven states. He continued to transform large homes and former schools and hospitals into residences for the elderly. Many of these were structures that no one wanted, and he purchased them with no down payment. Dr. Samuel Miller, the founder of the Lutheran Bible Institute, said Superintendent Hoeger would "quiver like an aspen tree whenever he saw an old mansion he could make into a home for old people."[29]

In the post-World War II period, Miller's description of Hoeger's desire for large, old homes must be questioned. At the time of the split, he had been attacked for his lack of organizational and managerial skills. Pastor Hoeger never forgot those difficult years, and after the Great Depression, he proceeded with caution. Erv and Betty Chell, longtime administrative employees of the Good Samaritan Society, said that Hoeger "could be a hard-headed business man" and that promoters of a new project had to work hard to justify it. He would closely scrutinize the financial costs. Erv Chell commented that he [Chell] would work on a financial presentation for days. The senior Hoeger, through his longtime familiarity with balance sheets and operating statements, would briefly skim Chell's work and quickly provide an analysis of it. Chell argued that Hoeger was sharper than the critics who thought he was not businesslike.[30] Reverend William Goldbeck commented that Hoeger always insisted that the Society maintain a safe balance between assets and liabilities. After the 1940 experience, he had to know that the Society's investments were safe.[31] His philosophy became — "Add three or four rooms or a half-dozen rooms. Just don't bite off more than you can chew."[32]

Through experience, he developed a great ability to judge whether or not a Society Home could support itself in a particular community. August (Augie) Hoeger, Jr., recalled:

> Dad always had an uncanny way of making pay a place that others couldn't. I remember when I was a kid, going with him to inspect a hospital in Iowa that he was being asked to take over. He took a quick look around and told them the place had too many rooms not equipped for patients; the place had not allotted enough room for paying occupants in proportion to its size and overhead costs.[33]

Into the early 50s, Superintendent Hoeger continued to ignore the Board of Directors' wishes in purchasing some homes. When Reverend William Goldbeck began working for the Society, he observed Hoeger buying property and signing contracts without asking anybody about the wisdom of the purchase. Goldbeck assumed that this was standard procedure.[34] When federal and state regulations forced the Society to sell the old mansions at a minimal price, almost compelled to give them away, Hoeger never considered it a loss because these homes had been used for several years to care for people.[35]

The 1950s proved an opportune time for expansion. The Hill-Burton Act, which primarily provided money for the construction of hospitals, allotted funds for nursing homes. Although Hoeger did not want to get involved with the federal government, these government monies made available other resources to him. It was time for the Good Samaritan Society to grow.[36]

Throughout the decade, Reverend Hoeger preferred founding homes with a limited number of residents, favoring no more than 20 residents per facility, in smaller communities, wanting to keep people near their homes, families, and memories. He never went into a community to establish a home unless invited. John Bosch, another longtime employee of the Society, drove Hoeger to organizational meetings in several communities. A local committee would always be waiting for the General Superintendent. When Hoeger arrived alone, the local group would ask where his committee was. Bosch remembered that Hoeger would just smile and point up to heaven and say — "It's just us."[37] During the meeting, he expressed his philosophy concerning age and loneliness. He told his audience that the elderly might be able to care for themselves "but they do not do well living alone." Hoeger believed that "The disease of loneliness is common to all elderly people."[38]

Reverend Hoeger called his meetings with local committees the "sowing of the seed sessions." A strong motivator, he aroused enthusiasm for carrying out the project. He used a "we approach," that together we can do this. In the 40s and 50s, the local committee performed many of the functions later done by the regional directors of the Good Samaritan Society. When the Society began to construct homes, the Superintendent urged the local committee to visit a community where a Society home had already been constructed. In this way, he believed, a local group would know how to do the project from start to finish.[39] Hoeger always left the details in starting up an operation to others. His forte was not in the details, but the overall picture.

From the 1920s through the 1940s, homes could be opened with no concern for regulations. For many years, a license was not needed to operate, and when the first licenses were issued, few standards were required. With the imposition of state requirements in the 1950s, the Society along with other organizations caring for the aged, were forced to give up the old mansions and hospitals and to begin constructing new homes. Usually the state would allow a two-year grace period for the construction to be completed. To keep a newly constructed facility licensed, state Departments of Health in the northern Prairie Plains began to insist on a high level of operation. This meant improved training of administrators and workers to care for the residents in the homes.[40]

The new rules and regulations irritated the founder of the Society. He wanted to take care of old people, and he felt the new laws and restrictions handicapped his efforts.π Paper work and bureaucracy never appealed to him, and he was not fond of institutional structures, public or private. Hoeger can best be described as an apolitical person. He seldom discussed politics except for inflation and government funds for nursing homes. One of his pastoral colleagues, Reverend George Unruh, said that Hoeger was not interested in world affairs. He was a good citizen, Unruh stated, but he doubted that Hoeger ever voted.[41] Although he had to yield to the new welfare regulations, Hoeger continued to insist that the primary requirement in all Society facilities was to provide a Christian family atmosphere in which the workers had a generous supply of the healing balm of Gilead.

Reverend Hoeger saw the Lord's plan in small steps. "A man's mind plans his way," he said, "But the Lord directs his steps." With little money for starting a home, small steps were a necessity. He informed Bertha Halvorson Holstein when she started a home at Lakota, North Dakota, that she must watch every penny. He told her to buy a place setting for each resident as she filled the facility, plus one extra setting for any person who might knock on the door and need a meal to keep body and soul together. According to Halvorson, Hoeger instructed her that "If someone should drop and break a glass, just go to the dime store and replace that one glass (one or two cents). We couldn't afford to buy an extra one. Every penny was treasured."[42] Viola Baugatz and Bertha ("Bertie") Bosch first lived in an unfinished attic at the Society home on North Minnesota Avenue in Sioux Falls. When a dish was broken, they had to replace it before dinner as there were no extra dishes available at the facility. The prevailing philosophy was to be good stewards and avoid waste.[43]

The Good Samaritan Society Superintendent constantly reminded home managers that to control overhead they should limit their hiring of additional staff in order to stay within budget. The administrators were told to hire workers for no more than 40 cents per hour. Hoeger believed that no more than one-third of the Society's income should go into salaries because of the organization's other contractual obligations.[44]

He opposed hiring too many people with specialized training, such as registered nurses or accountants, because of his budgetary concerns. By being the sole person in the Central Office, he became the role model for managers. No funds were directed to excessive administration. By the mid 1950s, he seldom made a risky investment. In deciding whether the Society should purchase a facility, he could pretty well at a glance see what he thought was a safe margin. The General Superintendent carefully watched the ratio between the value of the purchase, the total assets of the Society, and its obligations.[45]

Despite his mathematical talents, accountants disapproved of Reverend Hoeger's record keeping. Clarence Austad, an accountant and an administrator of Society homes for many years, said that some of the statements that came out of the Society's headquarters made no sense. He called for a regular budget and annual audits of the Society's finances.[46] Yet, Austad admired Hoeger's efforts. Each home would send in the federal tax for its employees; Hoeger would compile it and remit the total to the Internal Revenue Service. He made few errors in remitting the money.[47]

Hoeger's bookkeeping tactics became legendary within the Good Samaritan Society. He built a multi-million dollar operation by recording data on the backs of envelopes or in small spiral notebooks that he carried in the inside pocket of his suit coat. His unofficial office was usually his vest pocket or his car. His recording instrument of choice was the "common, lowly lead pencil" that he always carried in his coat pocket.[48] His official office was in one of the bedrooms of his home. A three-drawer steel filing cabinet, containing the Society's records, was located in Amelia's clothes closet. When a reporter visited the Hoeger home, the Society's Superintendent pulled open the empty bottom drawer, commenting, "And I use only two drawers, too. I don't believe in a lot of organization. I'm just interested in caring for people."[49] Some of the home administrators were given Big Chief writing tablets on which to prepare their reports for submission to Hoeger. They were told to write the names of patients and income, including donations, on one page. On another page, the administrators listed all expenditures, including salaries.[50] Upon receiving the reports, Reverend Hoeger would take over the kitchen or dining room table in his home, and using his adding machine, determine the financial state of each facility and the Society as a whole.

One of Hoeger's greatest strengths was his phenomenal memory. He remembered the names of the administrators, whether or not they were married, how many children they had, and where they were in school. When he heard of a certain building or person that might be available or useful for Society work, he would quietly file that information in his mind where it would be available should it be needed at some future time. He attained this knowledge by being a good listener when he wanted to listen. Although he seldom engaged in small talk, Pastor Hoeger demonstrated his interest in the Society's workers by these well received references to their families. With his remarkable memory, he could quickly analyze a financial statement. He knew what he needed to look at and foremost among these items was how much money was being spent for labor.[51]

Most administrators observed that one of his significant weaknesses was his lack of correspondence. This failing may be attributed to his self-acknowledged shortcomings in grammar and spelling, to his lack of secretarial assistance, and to his occasional attitude that if you ignore something long enough, it will go away.[52] Ray Conlon, a former member of the Society's Central Office staff, said that Superintendent Hoeger would put a letter from an administrator in a desk drawer and leave it there for 30 days. When he opened the drawer, the problem would be gone. By this time, the administrator would have solved the problem.[53] During the 1950s, Reverend Hoeger did use the telephone extensively in responding to administrators who reported problems in the operation of their respective homes.[54] His comments were usually brief and terse with the recipient expected to interpret his remarks.

His best influence came through direct contact with Society personnel. He loved to travel, and he became restless if he were at home too many days. Although Reverend Hoeger did not like traveling during the winter, John Hoeger estimated that his father was away from home about half the time.[55] At age 73, he was still driving about 30,000 miles every year. Until his death, Superintendent Hoeger probably gave the dedication speech at 95 percent of new Good Samaritan facilities or additions to existing homes.[56]

August Hoeger, Sr., formed a corporate endeavor similar in several ways to the J. C. Penney Company. In the January-February, 1951, issue of the *Sunshine*, he related how the Society used two practices identified with the successful department store chain. James Cash Penney had begun with one store, through which sufficient surplus capital was accumulated to begin a second store, then a third one until there were 1,600 J. C. Penney stores in 1951. Hoeger used the same principle in the growth of the Good Samaritan Society. After a home was up and running well, any surplus monies generated by that facility would be used to start another one. Donated money, however, would not be used for that purpose. The second similarity emphasized local control. Each store or home was operated by a local manager, not by a corporate headquarters.[57] Local administrators would hire the staff, admit the residents, and run the home as if it were their own. Hoeger trusted his administrators by giving them "elbow room" to run their respective homes. He had a talent for finding dedicated people, working with them, and understanding their weaknesses. He did not judge character, he simply assumed the best.

His critics, particularly in the 1930s and 1940s, did not like his informal management of the Society's facilities or his great trust in the administrators. His management style, however, was not as casual as it appeared on the surface. Hoeger may have been ahead of his time. The Society's work was being carried out through people of conviction, people who were dedicated, loving and enthusiastically carrying out the mission of the Good Samaritan Society.

What was important in hiring managers was that they cared for people. At one meeting of home administrators, Superintendent Hoeger told them, "My dear people, don't mistreat any of God's children." The Good Samaritan Society would help the local administrators develop their administrative skills. One hiree felt he could not do the job. Hoeger's response was that "if he had said he knew everything about it, he wouldn't want to hire him."[58] He believed that if you put a good manager in a small home he would do just as well as if he managed a large one. If you put a poor manager in a large home, he would continue to perform poorly.[59] In the main, he attracted dedicated workers because he was a good role model. People were hired if they were Christian in belief and practice; he saw in them love and a willingness to serve.[60]

Reverend Hoeger told administrators that they should conduct devotions in their own thoughts and words after they, themselves, had taken a portion of the day for meditation and prayer. Staff members should also be present for devotions and not "rattling pans in the kitchen" when devotions took place.[61] Time after time, he told facility managers that "The patients must therefore be and remain the main object in all our reports. In other words, they take first place." When registered nurses became home administrators, Hoeger reminded them that they should not run their facilities like a hospital. It was the residents' home and they (the administration) should make it so. "It is not supposed to be an institution," he said, "It is a home."

Pastor Hoeger recommended special treatment for special people in a special place. Tablecloths, even if they were only paper ones, should adorn the tables for Sunday dinner. Residents would be putting on their better clothes and tablecloths would help make the weekly event something special. Food was served family style in the old homes with eight to ten people sitting around the table. Family style service ended with the introduction of government regulations.

Hoeger encouraged the lodging of residents in double rooms. He believed it was not good that people be alone because loneliness was a terrible sickness. He wanted as many contacts within the home as possible between residents, with the administrator, and with the staff.[62] The General Superintendent emphasized the self-help of residents, whom he wanted to be independent. Residents could get some exercise, he told administrators, by carrying urinals from their rooms to the bathroom and securing another one.[63] What made Good Samaritan homes particularly special, something altogether different from other homes for the elderly, was that in a Society residence they were looking after the spiritual lives of the people as well as their physical well being.[64] Emphasis must be placed on hope, Hoeger said, because it held faith and love together. Society members, like its founder, were to preach a message of hope in Christ.

The General Superintendent believed that all workers were equal. He did not view workers as hired help; they should have a call from God to serve Him by taking care of those His least. He firmly believed in Martin Luther's concept of *vocatio* (to call), that all vocations are equal in the sight of God. Luther wanted people to seek God's will for the great and small decisions of life in our vocations. August Hoeger, Sr., was a practitioner of Luther's thesis that through our callings God holds the world together, preserves humanity and gives people great and holy joy. God calls us to serve Him and His world.

Unfortunately, not all administrators had Hoeger's sense of calling. There were some who took advantage of his "elbow room" concept and his faith in them. During the latter half of the 1950s, some of the facility administrators misused Society funds for personal gain or managed a home's affairs in a way that totally went against Hoeger's and the Society's operating philosophy. He was asked once if he ever ran into pitfalls because he put too much faith in his managers. He replied, "Yah, out of 86, I missed on three. Jesus had 12 and he missed one out of 12, so I have a pretty good average."[65]

He missed on more than three, but he was always willing to give a person the benefit of the doubt. He trusted people too much. Reverend Hoeger disliked firing anyone because he had great sympathy for people, and he couldn't bear to be disagreeable to someone he liked. In addition, he had difficulty meeting problems head on. As noted earlier, the General Superintendent never dealt with many complaints that came in, and some of the problems did go away. On other occasions, they did not, and people questioned whether he was in charge of affairs as he should be.[66] He avoided confrontation as much as possible. Hoeger seldom openly confronted a Home manager who was obviously corrupt, incompetent, or derelict in his or her duties. Usually someone else was sent to fire the errant manager. Dr. Erwin Fritschel, who was instrumental in founding the Bonell Home at Greeley, Colorado, observed that there were occasions when he had to go to the fight.[67]

In building the Good Samaritan Society, Hoeger proceeded by faith, but it was not a blind faith. Certainly, he had complete trust that God's will would be done and things would be all right. Yet, as his son, August Jr., observed, he did not move blindly ahead on a project unless he had it all figured out on paper, examining potential income, expenses, and indebtedness. He estimated the potential pay-out for each Home brought into the Society. Superintendent Hoeger believed that each action would turn out according to God's will. It did not mean, however, that each action would be a success.[68]

What role did his wife, Amelia, and the Good Samaritan Society's Board of Directors play in rebuilding the Society? During the first half of the 1940s, Eleanor Roosevelt, wife of the Nation's president, was told that her imprint on the nation would be as great as her husband's. "Nonsense," she had replied, "The function of women is to ease things along; to smooth them over." Amelia Hoeger fit the once traditional role described by Mrs. Roosevelt. Her practical and pragmatic view of life, gained from her father, actually complemented her husband's visionary outlook, a man who walked by faith, who considered all things possible, and whose feet, sometimes, were not on the ground. Amelia's feet were always on the ground. She helped make her husband's vision work by, for example, pouring generic catsup into a Heinz bottle during the "hard times" of the Great Depression.[69]

If August Hoeger, Sr., came home keyed up, she was the calming force in the household.[70] She sometimes questioned some of his ideas and the continual acquisition of homes. She often told Mrs. Henry Foege, the wife of Reverend Henry Foege, one of Superintendent Hoeger's closest associates, "Oh, what do they think about, they are starting another Home, when will this ever end? Why don't they quit?[71] When August Hoeger, Sr., opened a facility in the small community of Osnabrock, North Dakota, (population of approximately 300) in 1968 with 24 beds, despite the Board of Director's earlier decision that no home should be started in a community of less than 1,500, Amelia cried out in exasperation, "*bist du verruckt?*" (are you crazy?)[72] She questioned some of her husband's affairs, but she was always supportive, inspiring August, Sr., onward because "he was more interested in how the Lord could do the impossible rather than the probable."

Throughout the 1940s, Superintendent Hoeger continued to make arbitrary decisions. He often consulted the Board of Directors after the fact. He did not always listen well. If his knowledge in a given area was as good as that of Board members, he followed his own dictates.[73] Hoeger was not an organizational man with a sense of corporate structure. He always viewed the organization as a Society — a community working together. He did not permit Board opinion to stand in the way of his vision.

The bringing of new people on the Board from various backgrounds and professions during the 1950s caused the Board to become more assertive in handling the business of the Society. Men such as Carl Becker and Eugene Hackler wanted the Society's business conducted on a better business and financial basis. The Board found Hoeger's reliance on individual managers hindered the creation of standardized records and the opportunities for the joint purchase of food, furniture, and other supplies.

Reverend Hoeger opposed sudden changes in the constitution of the Good Samaritan Society. In a 1957 letter to the Society's membership, he commented on the Society's unique structure. Most organizations, he declared, had boards that met once a month. Hoeger continued, "Putting emphasis on the Manager of the local home is the cornerstone of our organization." The General Superintendent went on to cite his prerogatives and responsibilities. He was the watchdog; he appointed and dismissed all managers. No debt could be made without his consent. Field men were his helpers and responsible to him. He must approve all loans and blueprints. The Board of Directors would act when a new home was planned or purchased. Hoeger advised the membership that any efforts to change the constitution must proceed slowly.[74]

August Hoeger, Sr., belonged to a generation of strong leaders found throughout the Lutheran Church, its related agencies, and its higher education programs. He believed in having the right person in the right place, Institutions were successful when there were able people in key places. Policies might need clarification but it was people who made the difference. He was convinced that fewer policies and better people would provide the resources needed for positive institutional health and growth. Hoeger would have strongly agreed with the statement that no monuments have ever been erected to committees.

By the close of the decade, Hoeger was willing to listen, to accept input and to make changes, yet he always spoke out against centralization, a growing tendency in American corporate society.[75] He feared that the Society would become top heavy with administrators. Reverend Hoeger did not foresee that as the Society became larger, more departmentalization, more regulation, and more administrative personnel would be required. By September 1957, the Society had an Assistant Superintendent, Reverend E. M. Mueller, hired in September 1949, and a secretary-bookkeeper, who handled Social Security and income tax data for employees. In addition, furniture was being purchased for Homes on a volume basis.

In fulfilling this mission, August Hoeger, Sr., gained a reputation as a pioneer in the field of geriatrics, one of the most innovative men of his time. He had a vision of what ought to be done for people in need, and he was ahead of his time in terms of care for senior citizens. American society was changing: the extended family was disappearing, and many of the elderly did not have any form of economic or social security. Aside from the family, the only other solution to care for the elderly in the 1920s and 1930s was the county poor farm. There were no entitlement programs. Hoeger proposed to take care of people in a new and different way. Dr. Erwin Fritschel argued that the founder of the Good Samaritan Society could be called the father of the nursing home movement.[76]

With the help of other dedicated people, inspired by Hoeger to develop and administer nursing homes on shoestring budgets, the Good Samaritan Society weathered all kinds of problems to become a leader in long-term care in the post-World War II era. Every knock was truly a boost to Hoeger, and he had many knocks. The ALC took formal action to censor him. The Society was torn apart in 1940, government gave him many knocks as did the Board, colleagues, and friends, but he persisted.

On May 30, 1956, August Hoeger, Sr., received an honorary degree from Wartburg Theological Seminary, Dubuque, Iowa. Hoeger, a 1908 graduate of the Seminary, was awarded a Doctor of Divinity degree for the many years he had served the elderly of the Prairie Plains. In accepting the degree, he told Dr. Bernard J. Holm, the president of the Seminary, "I hope it will help me to become more humble and fill me with more zeal to build the Lord's kingdom."[77] He was inducted posthumously into the North Dakota Entrepreneurs' Hall of Fame at Grand Forks, North Dakota, in December 1992. The Hall of Fame, begun in 1986, was sponsored by the Center for Innovation and Development at the University of North Dakota. It recognized North Dakota entrepreneurs and inventors for their longstanding contributions to the state and the nation. Hoeger was recognized as a pioneer in the field of geriatrics and long-term care. He had caused local people to respond to the needs of the elderly.[78]

Crucial to Reverend Hoeger's success was his strong Christian faith. He knew that he had a Helper, who was far greater and wiser than he was. His success can also be attributed to his decentralized administration. He permitted the administrator of each home to develop the project as he or she best saw fit in the light of the local situation, using his or her own special talents without restricting that person with many rules and regulations. Hoeger, who had approved each community venture, kept a close eye on the progress of each facility, and he provided guidance and encouragement to the administrator.

The General Superintendent went beyond inspiring people to meet the needs of the elderly in their community. Hoeger wanted homes to be "hubs" to communities. Nursing homes should be more than a place to stay until death; they should be a vital part of the community.[79] He introduced new concepts of care, created Helpers' Clubs, and made the Good Samaritan Home a "Center" for all of the aged in a particular community. These centers would provide all types of meaningful, leisure time activities. Under his guidance, home administrators gained representation in management, and improved resident facilities became a reality.[80] The December 1961 issue of the Senior Citizen stated that the Good Samaritan Society had made "...A vast and almost unbelievable contribution in the fields of housing and hospitalization for growing legions of aging." The Society entered only those communities where they were invited and remained only to help those, who according to Superintendent Hoeger, meant business. In other words, the Society would assist those communities willing to buckle down and give a hand in doing whatever was needed to make the Home a going concern. At the annual meeting on September 17-18, 1957, Hoeger could report that the Society operated 50 homes in 12 different states.[81] The Society had come a long way in 17 years. The vision which seemed on the verge of failure in 1940 was now being fulfilled on a national level.

Above: Working at the rug loom, where thousands of rugs were woven of rags made from old clothing.
Right: Sewers at their machines.

Chapter Seven
REBUILDING THE VISION: ARTHUR AND OTHER RURAL VENTURES, 1940 - 1957

*"But if you stay in Me and obey My
commands, you may ask any request
you like, and it will be granted.
    My true disciples produce bountiful
harvests. This brings great glory to my
Father." — John 15:7-8.*

Despite the opposition of August Hoeger, Sr., to increased
governance, the continued growth of the Society necessitated significant changes in the administrative structure.
In rebuilding the Society, the structure and functions of the Board
of Directors were modified, and changes were made in the procedures for securing funds for new Homes. Administrative districts
were created, field men assigned, and a greater emphasis placed
on technical training for staff and Home administrators.

At the annual meeting in 1947, Society members voted to
increase the Board of Directors to 15 people. Board representation, at first confined to residents of North Dakota, now included
people from several states as the Good Samaritan Society expanded across the Prairie Plains. In the same year, the Board determined that in the expansion process, the General Superintendent
must take two or three Board members to visit a proposed acquisition. This special committee would then submit its recommendation in writing to the entire Board, and its members would
express their approval or disapproval by mail. The Board of Directors also requested that all local institutions establish advisory
boards.[1]

Having funds available for the establishment of new homes
dominated discussions at the annual meeting two years later. As
of 1949, new homes received financial assistance from funds
either donated to the Good Samaritan Society or provided by

some of the established facilities that were financially able to provide aid, with no set amount being designated. The Board of Directors recommended that each home remit 1 or 2 percent of its income, or a certain percentage of its income over ongoing expenses, to the Central Office to be used for facility expansion.[2] Despite opposition from certain Board members, Hoeger continued, as late as 1955, to insist that all homes financially able to do so should assist in the establishment and maintenance of sister institutions. He told administrators that one of their duties was to set aside a regular part of their home's income for the reduction of the debts of the Society's institutions.[3]

The rapid acquisition of Homes led Superintendent Hoeger to recommend that the Good Samaritan Society be divided into administrative districts.[4] Four districts were established with the district administrators managing local homes, allotting their time between visiting other facilities in their assigned areas, and administering their particular homes. By October 1957, there were six field men, including:

Dr. Erwin Fritschel — Colorado
Reverend E. M. Mueller — Iowa
E. H. (Hugh) Adams — Kansas and Missouri[5]
Clarence Austad — Minnesota
Oscar Deines — Nebraska
Dr. August Hoeger, Sr. — North and South Dakota.[6]

At the annual meeting during the preceding month, the discussion centered on making the field men full-time directors without the responsibility of operating a local institution. The possibility of paying their salaries from the general treasury was explored.[7] Following up on the recommendation of Eugene Hackler, the field men became full-time regional directors in 1959.[8] To better fund Central Office operations, each facility was required to contribute 50 cents per bed on a monthly basis beginning January 1, 1958. A portion of these dues, which were estimated to raise $10,000 to $12,000 per annum, would pay the General Superintendent's salary which had been raised from $3,000 to $5,000 per year.[9]

As indicated in Chapter Six, state Departments of Health began to create regulations and standards for homes for the aged in the 1950s. A large number of old family residences, hospitals and hotels that had been converted into homes did not measure up to state requirements. On December 10, 1953, Dr. Albert J. Chesley, head of the Minnesota Department of Health, demanded that the Society remodel five of its institutions in Minnesota.[10] Verne Pangborne, of the Nebraska Department of Health, made a similar request, ordering the Society to replace some of its older homes in that state with new construction.

The new requirements called as well for better trained staff and administrators. The Board of Directors first considered rein- stituting a Bible School, similar to the earlier programs at the Good Samaritan Institute in Fargo and at Allen Memorial Hospi- tal in Waterloo, Iowa. This idea was set aside in favor of one- week institutes that would involve intensive study of nursing adminis- tration and practical work.[11] Before that decision was made, a code of ethics was prepared for Society workers and distributed at the 1952 annual meeting. Hoeger and the Board of Directors believed it necessary to acquaint new workers with the spirit needed to do their work in the right way.[12]

With increased state requirements, changes took place in the content of annual meetings. Parts of ensuing meetings were given over to technically oriented sessions. Topics included the Proper Diet for the Aged, the Care of Bed Patients, Public Relations, the Training of Workers, Occupational Therapy, and Family Housing for the Elderly.[13] The annual meetings, traditionally held either at Arthur or Fargo, North Dakota, were held at other sites beginning in the mid-1950s. The 1955 and 1956 meetings were held at the Ingham Bible Camp, Wallingford, Iowa.

Beginning in 1956, Superintendent Hoeger and the Board of Directors entered into lengthy discussions with the Board of Christian Social Action of the American Lutheran Church regard- ing recognition of the work of the Good Samaritan Society by the ALC.[14] Reverend Hoeger's good friend Dr. Erwin Fritschel wanted the Society to get together with the ALC. Hoeger argued that it could not be done and should not be tried. Although the Good Samaritan Society would benefit in terms of publicity, counsel and support, it eventually rejected the ALC's proposal. The Board for Christian Social Action proposed that if the Society became an agency of the ALC, the Church Board would have two official rep- resentatives on the Society's Board of Directors.[15] Hoeger, howev- er, opposed the ALC's request for reorganization of the Good Samaritan Society, which meant surrendering control of the Society's facilities to local Lutheran direction.[16] The General Superintendent also recognized that in the old American Luther- an Church, national boards made key decisions for each institu- tion, decisions related to budget, building plans, fund raising, and certain personnel matters. The Society and Hoeger would have been unable to tolerate such tight control.

The financial status of the Good Samaritan Society improved significantly after World War II. Delinquent payments became a thing of the past and the Society had greater maneuverability in arranging contracts and making purchases. Some financial assistance came via the federal government. Following the passage of the Social Security Act in 1935, the federal government was obligated to match state funds for the care of the destitute aging. States retained the right to set eligibility rules and benefit levels. A grievance procedure was set up in order that anyone could appeal to the federal government if it was felt that the state or county had been unfair. Assistance became a right; it was no longer a charity. Social Security payments, which began in 1940, paid for part of the care for qualified people who chose to enter nursing homes. The amount of old age assistance was small and those people who could not afford hospital care but who needed an institution that stood between a boarding home and a hospital often chose a nursing home. Thus, these payments contributed to an increased number of nursing homes nationwide.

One of Hoeger's wise financial decisions was to maintain the Good Samaritan Society as a one-corporation organization. With one balance sheet or financial statement, the Society had the capability to throw its financial weight behind one specific area or new enterprise.[17]

Three of the four homes remaining with the Society after the split in 1940 flourished after World War II. The homes at Arthur, Sioux Falls, and Greeley became the "Mother Homes" for North Dakota, South Dakota, and Colorado respectively. In the late 1950s, they were joined by other pioneering facilities in Kansas, Nebraska, Minnesota, and Iowa. The Arthur facility, which was the "Mother Home" of the entire Good Samaritan Society, had an indebtedness of $130,000 prior to America's entry into World War II. This debt had been eliminated by 1954.[18] The Arthur Home's financial recovery was indicative of the Society's growing strength in a resurgent economy.

The Mother Home:
Arthur, North Dakota

On December 13, 1939, Gilman Wang, assistant administrator, provided the Society's Board of Directors with a detailed report on the financial condition of the Arthur Home. Twelve North Dakota counties were 2-7 months behind in paying their obligations for residents at Arthur. One county paid in registered warrants, and they were used to pay off the home's account at the Arthur Mercantile. In December, the Society paid out $1,100 toward its current account. The Arthur Farmers' Elevator denied further credit. The Home owed the Elevator $2,500, and the manager demanded a payment of $900 plus suitable real estate for the remainder. The Society had been fortunate to receive a donation of 44 tons of coal in November from lignite producers in western North Dakota.[19]

Despite the debt, August Hoeger, Sr., never thought about closing the Arthur Home. He hoped that it would be debt free by 1948. He was overly optimistic. It was not until September 1954 that he could inform the Board of Directors that the Arthur Home no longer had any liabilities.[20] He vigorously supported the program carried on at Arthur. In a general letter, the Superintendent informed its readers that there was no need to send a family member who might be feeble-minded, epileptic, or senile to a state institution because Arthur provided the needed services. He wrote, "This is the only home in the northwest that specializes in caring for the aged who are senile, the feeble minded and the epileptic, many of whom are also crippled, blind, deaf and dumb." Reverend Hoeger further stated, "These people are in the world not to be punished or to live out their misfortune their endowment gave them to begin with. But they are in the world to provoke and arouse our love."[21]

There were good reasons for the delay in debt retirement. One of Hoeger's primary goals was to honor a pledge that he made during the 1930s, that workers would receive back wages once the economy improved. Thus, in the early 1940s, loyal workers such as Bertha Christian and Viola Baugatz, who had not been paid for three years, received the money due them. Superintendent Hoeger continued to develop the Arthur complex's physical facilities, as well. Rightly convinced that the best therapy for many of the residents was physical and meaningful work, Hoeger began a fund drive in 1940 for the construction of an industrial building. He proposed a frame structure with six rooms that could house print, shoe, small repair, and cabinet shops plus a Gather-Up Department.[22] Funds and construction help came from the Arthur community and by the fall of 1941, the 50-foot long and 30-foot wide building was almost completed.[23]

Handicapped workers were in charge of almost every department in the new Industrial Building. Lucille Greer, of Beresford, South Dakota, who had contracted infantile paralysis at age five, supervised the Gather-Up Department. She had taken high school courses and business training at the Good Samaritan Institute in Fargo. She processed the donated clothing and shoes that came to the Home, channeling some of the donated items into other activities in the Industrial Building.[24] Shoes that needed minor repair work were directed to the shoe shop, where the shoemaker, who had received his training at the Good Samaritan Institute, also repaired shoes for people in the Arthur area.

Rug-making became a new industry affiliated with the Gather-Up Department. Ruth Erickson, of Moorhead, Minnesota, supervised two workers and five residents in making rugs from rags derived from worn-out clothes. The workers manned an automatic, hand-driven loom and two sewing machines.[25] Rug weaving was done for 50 cents a yard when the rags were furnished. By the late 1960s, over 5,000 rugs had been made at the Arthur Home.[26] The print shop produced a variety of printed materials, including bulletins, the *Sunshine*, the Luther League paper for the Dakota District, duplicating work, and stationery.[27] A sheet of stationery and an envelope sold for a penny in the 1940s. The activities in the Industrial Building provided residents with first-rate occupational therapy. Over the years, many of them learned a trade and supported themselves when they left the Home.

Throughout the 40s and 50s, the farm also played a significant role in providing therapy for the residents as well as sustaining them at the dinner table. Goodwin "Goodie" Nelson, the farm manager, adhered to Reverend Hoeger's philosophy that "People do not feel caged in when they are doing some sort of farm work."[28] Residents who had a rural background helped with the small grain and corn harvest from the 480-acre farm. They also worked in the garden and the orchard. In the early 1960s, staff and residents continued to can or freeze substantial amounts of fruits and vegetables. Residents and employees cared for 40 head of pure-bred Holstein milking cows, 150-300 hogs yearly, and 200 laying hens.[29] Eggs, poultry, and pork remained as staples in the diets of residents and staff alike. One of the reasons resident rates at the home averaged only $65 per month during the late 50s was the residents' active role in the labor force and the reliance on home-grown foodstuffs. The milk from the dairy herd was sold, since the law now stipulated that only pasteurized milk could be used for baking and drinking.[30]

In the immediate post-World War II period, staff and residents continued to live in a world of their own on the outskirts of Arthur. The home's activities were, in many respects, dictated by the rhythm of the seasons. Most workers derived comfort and sat-isfaction from their work and relationships. In commenting on her experiences at the Society's Mother Home, Bertha Christian said, "I got rich, not in money, but in a feeling of doing something worthwhile. I loved it. It was hard, but I would gladly do it again."[31]

Adjusted to the rhythm of rural life, the male residents and staff, shortly after daybreak, proceeded to the barn to milk and feed the Holstein cows. Residents scattered wheat on the ground for the Leghorn hens before feeding the hogs and horses. By this time, the bell, located near the dining hall, rang out the first call for breakfast. As the men finished washing up, the last bell for breakfast sounded. Before leaving the table after eating, a famil-iar hymn was sung, and the matron read a short devotion.

Residents, under the supervision of the staff, then took up their assigned tasks, depending upon the season. If it were fall, some of the men harvested produce from the garden or picked corn. Oth-ers went to their daily work in the Industrial Building. Some of the women labored in the laundry, carrying baskets of wet clothes to the outside lines to snap them out and pin them in place. Main-tenance tasks in and outside of the buildings provided work for other people — including building shelves, glazing storm win-dows, and repairing harnesses for the horses. The evening supper bell was always a welcome sound after a day of shared labor. Before the staff prepared the residents for bed, they all gathered in the dining room to hear Bible lessons, to sing, and to relate any problems they might have.[32]

Like most people, residents and staff anticipated special days or occasions that provided a change from their daily routines. Two such occasions were Christmas and Home Day. Home Day, or Good Samaritan Day, which was patterned after the church festi-vals of the year, took place on the second Sunday in July for sev-

eral years before being shifted to the fall harvest season.[33] During
this open house, a large tent was erected to shelter those in attendance. When Home Day was held on Sunday, pastors of area ALC
churches cancelled their own church services and urged their congregations to attend a combined morning worship service at
Arthur. People from Casselton, Leonard, Amenia, and as far away
as Enderlin gathered in the huge tent.[34] Visitors brought their
picnic lunch and the Society provided free coffee. In the afternoon,
there was a program with music provided by area choirs.[35] In the
early years, the annual meeting of the Good Samaritan Society
was held in conjunction with Home Day.

In later years, Home Day became a harvest festival. Goodie
Nelson, who capably managed the Home's farm from 1940 to
1987, provided much of the direction for this event. A long-time
collector of antique farm machinery, he used a Case steam engine
to power the threshing machine. Two hundred acres of oats or
wheat would be cut with a binder and shocked by the residents.
Known for his tenderness and patience in working with the residents, Nelson had them haul bundles and pitch them into the
threshing machine on Home Day.[36] For several years, it was one of
the premier fall attractions on the western slope of the Red River
Valley. People came to visit family members or to view the work.
Nelson commented, "We like to have all these people come and
watch and have lunch with us. After all, threshing is one of our
social events of the year."[37]

Another of the major social events was the annual Christmas
program. Practice for this endeavor began the day after Thanksgiving. The residents loved the rehearsals. Excitement reigned.
No matter how many rehearsals, however, the staff did not know
what the performers might do on the night of the program. The
staff simply sat back, relaxed, and enjoyed it, as did the community. Standing-room-only crowds gathered to witness and play a
part in the celebration of the birth of Christ.[38] The program was
presented in the dining room on Christmas Eve, where a large
tree had been erected. The Christmas story from the Gospel of
Luke was read in three languages, English, German, and Norwegian. There was a sudden burst of youthful rejuvenation when
several of the older people recited Bible verses and pieces of
Christmas poetry they had memorized 50 or 60 years in the past
at their church, home, or school. The Christmas story was presented in pageant form, as well. Two of the residents played Mary
and Joseph and several of the older men, dressed as shepherds,

most often wearing bathrobes, knelt by the manger. "Silent Night, Holy Night" was sung by the Home's choir in the three languages named above.[39] Reverend Hoeger presented a sermonette and following the closing prayer, the program ended with the celebrants singing "Joy to the World, the Lord is Come."[40]

From the opening of the Arthur Home until his departure to Hastings, Nebraska, in 1968, Pastor Hoeger regularly conducted Sunday worship services at the Home. Sunday was a special day for food for the body and soul. The practice of using white tablecloths for dinner continued when residents sat down to the traditional rural fare of roasted meat, mashed potatoes, a vegetable, and rhubarb or apple pie. Reverend Hoeger conducted a worship service at 2 p.m. and spent the remainder of the afternoon visiting with the residents, looking at livestock, and during the growing season, checking on the garden and the crops. Sunday supper usually consisted of sandwiches, cake, sauce, and coffee, followed by a Luther League meeting at 7:30 p.m.

Superintendent Hoeger insisted there be complete interaction between residents and staff. They were to be friends, eating together, singing in the choir together, and sharing problems together.[41] How well he related to the residents was indicated in his relationship with Henry, a physically able but somewhat retarded individual. Henry had heard staff members talking about their vacations, and he asked when he was going to get a vacation. Having overheard him, Hoeger patted him on the shoulder, saying, "I can't take a vacation, either, Henry. I guess you and I will have to take our vacation in Heaven." A satisfied Henry was later heard bragging to residents that he and Reverend Hoeger were going to take their vacations together in Heaven.[42]

Despite evidence of rural tranquility, a self-supporting economy and daily routines, life at the Arthur Home was far from idyllic. Developing good relations with the community and the State of North Dakota were concerns of both the Home's administrator and Superintendent Hoeger. Beginning in the 1950s, the State Department of Health began a regulatory program that became almost overwhelming in the decades to follow. After an inspection of the Arthur facility in December 1952, the Department of Health informed Hoeger that the Home would not be licensed for 1953 unless 1) additional staff was hired to meet residents' needs and to ensure safety procedures, including the use of a night nurse or an attendant, and 2) improvements were made in the furnace area for better fire protection.[43] This was only the beginning of required changes in physical facilities and procedures for resident care.

The Home's relationship with the Arthur community improved dramatically when Mrs. Dorothy Fowler, a registered nurse, became the administrator in November 1959. She was a strong enough person to do the things she wanted done, regardless of criticism.[44] The citizens of Arthur became partners in the Home's activities as Fowler enlisted volunteers in an auxiliary and solicited support from church groups. She began an adoption program whereby a community person did many things for or with a resident. The facility's advisory board, which in the past usually met only to engage in fund raising activities, became more active. The Home contributed to the local economy as more women from the Arthur area were employed to work with the residents.[45] The people of Arthur were welcomed to the facility to share a cup of coffee and conversation.[46]

August Hoeger, Sr., had said that the employees must be with the residents in order to get them to grow mentally and socially. Fowler had the ability to unite the staff and residents into one large and happy family. She introduced many improvements in the care of the residents. She and her fellow workers attempted to determine the aptitude of the mentally or physically disadvantaged people in their care and made them feel needed by assigning them meaningful tasks. One resident raised and lowered the flag, another went to the post office for the daily mail, others answered the telephone, made change for the vending machines, set the tables, or, under proper supervision, cut rhubarb and peeled apples for pies.[47] Residents likewise took care of the garden and maintained community flower beds in Arthur as well as in the nearby town of Hunter. They participated in the erection of a series of latticework and trellis that screened the view of the old buildings at the Home and the planting of flowers in the Prayer Garden adjacent to the Center. This project was given special recognition by the Fargo Green Thumb Garden Club.[48] Inspired by Hoeger, the Prayer Garden emphasized the theme of Calvary, and it included a large crucifix, a stained glass depiction of Christ's ascension into Heaven, and several pieces of statuary, all positioned along several walkways.

The Center's employees began a program of one-to-one relationships with the residents in an effort to make them more voluble, to enhance their sociability, and to improve their memory. Through these personal conversations, a certain amount of background information concerning each person emerged. If the person died, this data was used in the obituary. Remotivation sessions were used with residents who spoke very little. They were asked to bring something to a daily session and to state what it meant to them. Magazine pictures of old schools, stores, and pumps often stimulated their memories to the degree that they would comment on the item, but they never engaged in conversation.[49]

During Dorothy Fowler's tenure, a systematic keeping of medical records was introduced and drugs were made available for those patients subject to epileptic seizures. With money more readily available, special equipment for physical rehabilitation was added. Major and minimal changes in the appearance of the Arthur facility took place. Rusco windows were installed and new mattresses and beds were placed in each room. Five building projects were undertaken over a 15-year period. Projects included a new residential wing (1965), an activity room and an enlarged dining room. Three cottages were erected in 1968; they were rented to retired people who could care for themselves. Two years later, a four-plex for the elderly was constructed.[50]

For over 40 years, the Arthur Home had been a basic or custodial care facility. In the newest residential wing, 16 beds were given over to Intermediate Care. An Intermediate Care Facility (ICF) was defined as a level of care between Basic Care (room and board) and Skilled Nursing Care. IC facilities received their license from the State Department of Health while Basic Care facilities obtained their license from State Social Services. The introduction of Intermediate Care meant meeting higher standards, leading to higher costs that were met by private pay residents and tax revenues. Implementing Intermediate Care at Arthur obligated Fowler to add a full-time registered nurse, two licensed practical nurses, a social worker, and a cook, who took food courses from a licensed dietitian.[51]

When Dorothy Fowler retired in 1974, state authorities, using new building code standards, refused to issue a license for the Arthur Center.[52] Henry J. Reith, who replaced Fowler as administrator of the Arthur Center, was immediately involved in a fundraising campaign to replace two of the deteriorating original buildings. The campaign received a significant boost from Bertin C. Gamble, chairman of the board and chief executive officer of the Gamble-Skogmo Corporation. Gamble was born and reared in the Arthur area, and his father was associated with the local bank, Gamble made a $100,000 gift from the Gamble Foundation toward the building replacement fund.[53]

A new 98-bed Intermediate Care Facility was dedicated on September 12, 1976, with the state's governor, Arthur A Link, as the featured speaker.[54] In meeting federal and state requirements, the Center employed a physical therapist, more professional nursing care, and arranged for regular visits by a physician from Fargo.[55] With the addition of another four-plex in 1980, the Center served over 120 people, providing four levels of care — Retirement Apartments, Basic Care, Intermediate Care, and Skilled Nursing Care.

Gifts of farm land to the Good Samaritan Society in the postwar period enabled Reverend Hoeger to begin other facilities in a pastoral setting. He used the opportunity to create a spiritual refuge for troubled youth near Fargo. In the James River Valley, near Parkston, South Dakota, he dreamed of creating a second Arthur. In addition, the Society created a retreat in the Rocky Mountains where administrators and their families could go for physical and spiritual renewal.

Mapleton Boys' Ranch
1949-1952

Throughout much of his life, August Hoeger, Sr., debated whether to work with youth, who had their whole lives ahead of them, or to work with the elderly. Although he came to favor working with the elderly, from time to time the Good Samaritan Society involved itself in youth work. One such effort was the Society's Boys' Ranch located 1.5 miles northeast of Mapleton, North Dakota. As early as 1940, Reverend Hoeger discussed a possible farm for problem boys. Protestants did not have a home on the Prairie Plains for so-called problem children. He felt that state institutions (reformatories) did not solve the youngsters' problems, primarily because they lacked the Word of God.[56] He admired the work being done at Starr Commonwealth, Albion, Michigan, and at Boy's Town in Omaha, Nebraska, but he believed the latter was too large and too urban.

Hoeger envisioned a site consisting of ten cottages for 100 boys, ages 10-17, for his ranch complex. His prayers for a site were answered in the early stages of World War II. A woman from Illinois, who owned a farm near Mapleton, looked for an organization working with children to make use of the farm. When the Good Samaritan Society was recommended to her, Hoeger told her of his idea for a boys' ranch. She agreed to give 320 acres, located about 12 miles west of Fargo, near Mapleton, to the Society when it was ready to use it. Superintendent Hoeger told her that the debt on the Arthur Home had to be reduced before any action could be taken on the proposed ranch.[57]

America's entry into World War II had created significant social disruption on the home front. Children were neglected because of the war; fathers were in the military service and mothers were employed in defense industries. Pastor Hoeger, however, was unable to fulfill his new vision until 1949. By that time, the Society's financial picture was brighter and building materials, directed to national defense between 1941 and 1945, were available.

After being uninhabited for ten years, the farm home near Mapleton was in considerable disrepair. During the summer of 1949, August Hoeger, Jr., who had just graduated from Concordia College, Moorhead, Minnesota, enlisted several of his classmates to repair and repaint the farm home and to clear the brush from the surrounding land. Albert Bartz, a high school teacher from Valley City, North Dakota, was named ranch superintendent. Calvin Berg was recruited to be farm manager,[58] and soon there were six boys living in the farm home.[59]

Superintendent Hoeger announced that the purpose of the Boys' Ranch was "to take neglected boys and boys who have gotten into difficulties and lead them to a higher standard in the fields of physical, social, mental, and spiritual development."[60] Once the ranch was established and operating funds were available, trades and crafts would be taught. Hoeger proposed to construct a general workshop where blacksmithing, welding, wood craft, printing, and other trades might be learned. The boys were encouraged to participate in the FFA, 4-H, and the Boy Scouts. During the school year, the youngsters attended public school in Casselton. Hoeger was primarily concerned that the boys heard the Word of God, and they were required to attend the church of their choice every Sunday.[61]

Once the ranch was underway, the need for additional housing became immediately apparent. In November 1950, Hoeger located a 12-room house only two miles from the Ranch. Purchased at a reasonable price, the dwelling was moved to the Ranch. The newly acquired home accommodated another eight boys, bringing the total to 14. When the youngsters were not in school at Casselton, they helped with plowing, summer fallowing, swathing, and combining at the farm-ranch, and they repaired an old granary which was to be used as a barn.

Despite abundant donations, which included a team of horses, a riding horse, other farm animals, farm equipment, and thousands of dollars, the Society decided to end activities at the Boys' Ranch in 1952. Another boys' ranch, also with Christian sponsorship, had been started at Cavalier, North Dakota. Believing there were insufficient troubled boys in North Dakota for two such refuges, the Good Samaritan Boys' Ranch was merged with the excellent facility at Cavalier. Fifteen years were to pass before the Society again entered into the care of troubled youth with the opening of a Boys' Home at Corona, California.[62]

The Colony of Mercy
Parkston, South Dakota

During the 1950s, Reverend Hoeger continued to believe that the Society should have a farm in each state for certain classes of mentally disabled who did not fit into town homes for the aged. By this time, the Good Samaritan Society had thriving farms at Arthur, New Rockford, Iowa, and Parkston, South Dakota. These farms proved invaluable for the raising of produce and livestock that could be used for the residents and staff as well as saleable cash crops.

The Parkston ministry had begun in 1946 when the Society acquired 107 acres of land from Jacob Lindemann on August 26, 1946, for $10,500. Lindemann, who was very enthusiastic about beginning an old people's home, remarked: "I don't expect this will be paid as long as you and I are alive." He was mistaken; the debt was paid within two months. Mr. and Mrs. Friedrich Doering of Parkston, good friends of the Good Samaritan Society, having retired and wanting to sell their farm and move to town, gave the Society a $10,000 gift to be used in founding the Colony of Mercy. In return, the Good Samaritan Society gave the Doerings "... an annuity bond which pays them interest as long as they live." The Doerings also had 160 acres for which they had paid $125 an acre. They traded that land for 160 acres at the Colony and willed it to the Society. Wanting a farm of at least 400 acres, Reverend Hoeger hoped and prayed that someone else would follow in the footsteps of the Doerings and help the Society secure at least another 160 acres.[63] His prayers were answered the following summer when Fred Kapperman of Arthur, North Dakota, purchased a quarter of land from the Doering farm and deeded it to the Good Samaritan Society. The Society gave him an annuity for the remainder of his life.[64] Hoeger envisioned a dairy operation, hay and pasture land, an orchard and tillable soil at the Parkston site. He wanted the Colony of Mercy to be the garden spot of South Dakota.

The land, including several well-constructed buildings, had originally been the site of the New Elm Springs Hutterite Colony, established in 1879. It was the site of the first Lehrerleut Hutterite colony in North America. When the Hutterites moved to Canada in 1930, Jacob Lindermann had acquired their land. The Hoeger family spent an entire summer at the new acquisition, located 12 miles south of Alexandria in the James River Valley, readying the property for its first residents. Hoeger's two sons, John and August Jr., (Augie) did much of the outdoor work. The abandoned Hutterite Colony was known to locals as the "Snake Farm." One of Augie's onerous tasks was to be lowered to the bottom of a shallow well, catch the hundreds of snakes that were slithering around, hit their heads on the side of the wall, put them in a bucket, and John hauled them out. John, later quipped, "Anyway, you can see that Augie started at the bottom" in the Good Samaritan Society.[65] John, just out of the seminary, and administrator of the new facility, was the designated tree planter. One day while he was watering the young trees with a sprinkling can, his father came up to him and said, "Son, you don't water trees with a sprinkling can. Get a five gallon bucket and soak them down. When you just sprinkle, the roots only stay on the surface and the first hot sun will dry them out and kill the tree. Soak them down so the roots will go deep into the soil."[66] John served as administrator at the new facility from 1948 to 1950.

The Parkston Colony of Mercy, which became known as the Country Center in the 1960s, had 40 handicapped elderly residents. They were former patients of Yankton State Hospital and the Redfield School for the Mentally Handicapped. At one time, 25 of the residents were mentally disadvantaged while alcoholism, blindness, and emotional disturbances afflicted the others.[67]

John Hoeger, in his first experience as an administrator, received invaluable assistance from Rita and Nikolais (Kola) Reinfelds, beginning in October 1949. They were among the 50-plus displaced persons sponsored by the Good Samaritan Society after World War II. The Reinfelds fled to Germany in 1944 as the Soviet Red Army advanced into Latvia, their native republic.

From 1944 to 1949, they lived in a displaced persons' (DP) camp at Kleinkoetz, Germany. Rita's brother, who had come to North Dakota at an earlier date, and who was working on a farm near Fargo, met with August Hoeger, Sr., and discussed the plight of his sister and brother-in-law. Reverend Hoeger filed an affidavit with the federal government that the Reinfelds would have a place to work and to live in the United States if they were employed by the Good Samaritan Society.

John Hoeger said it was a happy day when he met the Reinfelds at the train depot in Sioux Falls on October 6, 1949. For the next 31 years, they blazed a trail for many to follow in patient care, sound fiscal management, and efficiency. In patient care, they developed a long list of innovations from self-help devices to the latest in plant therapy programs.[68] Rita, a surgical dentist, and Nikolais, a Lutheran pastor, became the matron and orderly respectively at the Colony of Mercy.

After giving the Reinfelds a basic understanding of how to run the Parkston facility, Reverend John Hoeger left for Kansas in 1950 to begin a home mission congregation. As the new administrator of the Colony, Rita Reinfelds began to care for 26 residents with a staff of four people: herself, her husband, Kola, a Latvian girl who did the housekeeping, and a cook. In addition to being the administrator, Rita was in charge of nursing. Her position was a 24-hour-a-day job. A medical doctor came to the Colony of Mercy only once during the Reinfelds' tenure, when a resident had cut an artery and was in danger of bleeding to death. The Colony, at that time, kept no medical records.

The Reinfelds were handicapped by a lack of knowledge of American culture and rural life. The Colony raised 300 chickens, a key part of the food chain at the facility. With her medical background, Rita was expected to kill the chickens. She chopped off their heads, but she did not know how to remove the feathers or eviscerate them. Eventually, however, she learned how to do it. The Home had linoleum floors, and being a very meticulous person, Mrs. Reinfelds cleaned them quite frequently. Unfamiliar with liquid waxes and cleaners in Europe, she applied a new coat of wax each time the floor was cleaned, so that residents, staff, and visitors soon trod on a thick coat of wax with a yellowish hue. She was finally informed that you had to remove some of the wax before applying a new coat.[69] In February 1951, Superintendent Hoeger transferred the Reinfelds and their young son, Uldis, to the newly opened home at Olathe, Kansas.

Opal Maggert became administrator of the Country Center in 1969. With her nurse's training and a correspondence course in administration, she took the licensure exam, a recently installed requirement for nursing home administrators in South Dakota. Mrs. Maggert said that the Parkston Country Center was the most challenging work of her life. She discovered that the residents loved to sing, so she organized a choir and secured robes for the singers. The residents were also given work assignments, including the maintenance of a large garden. The Center had a van which was used to transport several of the residents to nearby stock car races. Her husband, Glen, an experienced carpenter, did considerable construction and remodeling at the center and at the nearby Boy's Ranch, which had been established in 1970.[70]

It was announced at the Good Samaritan Society Board meeting on November 17, 1972, that the Society had disposed of the farm equipment, stock, and feed and was thereby abandoning its farming operations near Parkston. The Society sold 607 acres of the farm, for $150 per acre, to the New Elm Springs Hutterite Brethren, Incorporated, with the stipulation that the Hutterites could buy the remaining acres if the Good Samaritan Society discontinued operating the Country Center.[71] The Society retained forty acres of tax exempt property on which it planned to continue to operate the Center and the Boys' Ranch for as long as possible. The facility was left with only horses and gardening.

One Society wit stated that "The Parkston Center went along as long as the state was not aware of it." That lack of awareness ended in 1974 when the South Dakota Department of Health informed the Society that it would no longer license the Country Center for supervised living. The Health Department indicated three problems facing the center:
1. Inadequate fire protection
2. A shortage of help
3. Lack of approval of the water and sewage systems
   by the Environmental Health Agency.[72]

After studying the possibility of building a new site, the Society's Board of Directors decided to close the Country Center on June 30, 1975, and move the residents to other centers. Colonel Charles Peterson, Regional Director for South Dakota, said the Society still owned 36 acres and would hold the James River Ranch Camp in the summer.[73]

When Superintendent Hoeger visited the Country Center in the fall of 1969, he had decided that a site along the James River was "an ideal setting for a camp." He envisioned a place that would serve neglected and unloved boys who had been deprived of any Christian influence. The camp would provide an opportunity for a small group of urban boys to live, work, and play for a period of two months under the direction of a devoted Christian leader. A wholesome country and farm experience would be provided with a strong emphasis on Bible study. Hoeger immediately met with area people and talked up his idea. Beginning in February 1970, Colonel Charles Peterson and John Rude from the Central Office, assisted by Hoeger, firmed up plans for what became the Jim River Ranch.[74] The Ranch was first opened to young boys, 10-17 years old, with good potential and no record of delinquency. They were referred to the Society by teachers, pastors, welfare workers, organizations, and individuals.[75] It was expected that the boys, who came from low income families, would develop a joy of life, an acceptance of others and an attitude that we are one in Christ while at the Ranch. Through discussion groups, prayer, and friendship, they would learn to serve and share and to develop respect for others.[76] Volunteers from five counties contributed their labor as well as materials, furnishings, cleaning services and financing. The camp served Aurora, Davison, Douglas, Hanson, and Hutchinson counties. Money given by individuals, churches, clubs, and groups funded Ranch operations. The 36-acre Ranch, which fronted on the James River, included three cabins, with the main one being winterized. A college couple was hired each summer to serve as camp hosts, to give guidance to the campers, to strengthen the youngsters' Christian beliefs, to listen and to lead discussion groups. In each of the three 2.5 week sessions, the boys participated in a variety of activities, including archery, baseball, body building, canoeing, gardening, horseback riding, housekeeping tasks, lawn care, daily Bible study, and attendance at the church of their choice on Sundays.

The Jim River Ranch later expanded to serve both boys and girls and to provide retreat facilities for numerous Christian groups. At the end of the summer camping program, it became the Jim River Retreat Center. In the so-called off-season, church groups, couples clubs, group homes, 4-H members, the Boy Scouts, and the staffs of Society homes gathered for retreats at this picturesque site on the banks of the James River.

Following the closing of the Country Center, there were fewer donations to the Jim River Ranch. The Society's Board of Directors closed the Ranch as of December 15, 1982, because of increasing costs and a dwindling number of campers. The Ranch, including all surrounding property and all improvements, had been sold the preceding day to the New Elm Springs Hutterian Brethren for $37,000.[77] In the same year, the former Country Center was placed on the National Register of Historic Places.

A few Parkston residents expressed their displeasure over the sale of the land to the Hutterites, without area people having a chance to bid on the parcels. It was their belief that the accrual of land in the hands of the Hutterian colonies would work to the disadvantage of small farmers. The protestors pointed out that much of the land being sold to the Hutterites had been given to the Society by a Parkston resident, Friedrich Doering.[78] The disgruntled residents asked that the Society use the money and interest acquired from the sale of the property to the Hutterites and the sale of a farm at Delmont, South Dakota, to help Parkston build on to its hospital which needed funds to remain operative.

Following the final sale of Country Center property in 1982, the Good Samaritan Society responded to requests from members of the Parkston community to discuss long-range plans for the two remaining facilities within the city. In response to the community's needs, the Society had constructed a home in Parkston in 1955, and, in 1966, the Society had acquired the former St. Benedict Hospital and converted it into an Intermediate Care Facility. The Society said it would maintain the licensure requirements for these facilities as long as possible. High costs, however, and an uncertain resident census, made future building uncertain.

When a proposal to build a new 70-bed facility in the Hutchinson County community was denied by the State Health Department, which stated that there was no need for another care facility in the area, the Society's board discussed building on to the hospital and renovating the present facilities. After considering the costs to upgrade both Centers, the large number of nursing home beds within a 30-mile radius, 669 in May 1987, and an unhealthy farm economy, the Board of Directors formally transferred ownership of the two facilities to the Benedictine Health Care System on August 7, 1988, for $50,000 cash.[79]

The Society, beginning with the Colony of Mercy (Country Center), had served Parkston residents for more than 40 years. In that time, an estimated 3,200 area residents and their families received invaluable spiritual and physical assistance from Society workers. The objective that humanity must be served in body and soul, no matter for what period of time, set by August Hoeger, Sr., had been fulfilled once again.

Luther Lodge
Estes Park, Colorado

Dr. Erwin Fritschel, one of the founders of the Bonell Good Samaritan Center at Greeley, Colorado, purchased a beautiful 40-acre site in the Rocky Mountains for $2,000 shortly after World War II. He donated the property to the Good Samaritan Society for use by its administrative and executive personnel. In September 1952, Superintendent Hoeger recommended that each Good Samaritan home contribute $100 toward building a cottage on the land. The cottage would be used for vacations, Bible Study Camps, and other purposes.[80] Within a year, Fritschel moved to acquire another site, approximately a quarter mile away from the original purchase. The new location, costing $6,000, consisted of 2.5 acres of land with three small cabins and one large cottage.[81] Writing to Hoeger, on July 4, 1953, Fritschel told Hoeger that he could secure $2,000 from the Bonell Home but that the remainder of the money would have to be borrowed in Greeley or from one of the Good Samaritan facilities.[82]

At the Society's 1953 annual meeting, it was decided that various facilities would assist in paying for the cottage and one of the cabins.[83] The structures, located in Estes Park with a view of Mount Meeker, became a vacation site for hundreds of Society personnel and their families in the decades that followed. In the spring of 1967, two of the cabins were destroyed by fire.[84] The two remaining buildings, Pine Cabin and Luther Lodge, were modernized, providing comfortable accommodations with kitchen and bath facilities.[85]

In 1970, the costs for operating Luther Lodge totaled $900 for the year. Vacationing administrators paid $35 per week for use of the Lodge and $20 per week for the smaller cabin.[86] Two years later, the Society's Board of Directors authorized $7,000 for the construction of another cabin at the site. The Board took this action with some misgiving because there had been ongoing discussions, dating back to 1965, on the limited use of the vacation facility. In the summer of 1974, the Board seriously considered disposing of the Luther Lodge property. Few administrators took advantage of the facility; costs not covered by rental fees were being absorbed by the Bonell Center at Greeley, and some of the guests had been irresponsible concerning fire safety.[87] When the Board members met again in November 1974, they decided to keep Luther Lodge, authorized improvements and made it more attractive to Society personnel.

Of all of the facilities begun under the leadership of August Hoeger, Sr., the Arthur Center remained his ideal. He was at Arthur for Home Day shortly before he died on October 8, 1970. The Arthur facility met his initial criteria for a home: it was in a rural setting; it had been built from scratch — step-by-step; its census was small, contributing to a family atmosphere; it maintained and practiced his basic philosophical and religious beliefs, and for him, Arthur was always home.

For many years, administrators did not remain long at the Arthur Home. Hoeger sent them out to open or develop new facilities. Among those dispatched from the Mother Home for this task were Augusta Priewe, Etta Janssen, Bertha Bosch Christian, Viola Baugatz, Bertha Halverson Holstein, Marie Walz, Mr. and Mrs. Clarence Blake, Marie (Schugaan) Bosch, and John Bosch. Dad Hoeger gave the bride away when the Boschs were married in 1946. From the Mother Home at Arthur, the Society from 1936-on, in an extension of Christ's hand, opened a Mother Home in each of the several states of the Prairie Plains.

Above: *Buildings and grounds at Arthur, North Dakota.*
Below: *The Good Samaritan Home at Olathe, Kansas. Once intended as a hospital, the Victorian building was purchased by the Good Samaritan Society in 1952.*

Chapter Eight
REBUILDING THE VISION: MOTHER HOMES IN THE HEARTLAND 1940-1957

*"If you don't make good use of the
old, you don't deserve the new."*
— Old German Saying.

As Americans celebrated their hard fought victory over the forces of fascism in the summer of 1945, August Hoeger, Sr., could once again fully engage the Society in meeting the needs of the elderly. The *Sunshine*, in its first post-war issue, proclaimed in a front page story — "Still Going Ahead." With a renewed sense of urgency, Hoeger, one step at a time, began to establish Good Samaritan nursing homes in the several states that composed the Northern Prairie Plains. He was dedicated to ending the ultimate humiliation for many elderly who were completing their lives on county Poor Farms where commissioners doled out money and food as they saw need. Many of these poor farms had acquired dismal reputations because of abuses within the system.

In his prayer life, he continued to ask, "What is the Lord's plan?" The Society had come this far because of an unshakable faith in God. What did He have in store for the Society in the future? Reverend Hoeger said that "A man's mind plans his way. But the Lord directs his steps!"[1] During the early 1950s, a ripple effect occurred as Good Samaritan facilities were established in rapid succession in the Dakotas, Colorado, Iowa, Kansas, Minnesota, and Nebraska. The Society home at Arthur was, of course, the "Mother Home" for North Dakota and the Mother Home of the Society. This chapter considers the first homes in the other states that composed the original "Heartland" of the Good Samaritan Society.

Sioux Falls Home
Sioux Falls, South Dakota

In the midst of the Great Depression, the Good Samaritan Society established a home in Sioux Falls, South Dakota. On March 15, 1936, the Board of Directors affirmed the purchase of the former J. W. Parker residence, and one-half block of land, for $10,000.[2] Built in 1886 of Sioux Falls jasper, the stately home, located at 400 West Third Street, overlooked the city. Following Parker's death, the residence became a home for alcoholics and later for unwed mothers, the building having room for 18 residents. One of Parker's daughters, Carrie, wanted the Ark of Refuge, as the home was then named, to be used for the care of the aged.[3]

Following the acquisition of the Parker home in 1936, the Society renamed it the Lutheran Home for the Aged. Reverend Hoeger sent Sister Etta Janssen from Arthur and Rose Glennen from Fargo to administer the new facility. On December 1, 1936, the Home had 17 patients, two of whom were charity cases. Following the return of Sister Etta to Arthur in 1938, the Lutheran Home for the Aged had a succession of supervisors for the next two years. During this time, it briefly operated under the auspices of the Lutheran Hospital and Homes Society.[4] The LHHS board named Mr. and Mrs. M. M. Logelin, of Aberdeen, South Dakota, as the new supervisors. By 1940, the Lutheran Home for the Aged faced serious financial problems for two reasons. First, the resident occupancy rate was far below census capacity, and there were few new applications.[5] Secondly, the Logelins had made the home a credit risk in the business community by "running up bills" all over town.[6]

Following the dismissal of the Logelins, the dire situation was turned around in 1940 when Hoeger sent Bertha Bosch and Viola Baugatz from Arthur to administer South Dakota's "Mother Home." They were joined shortly thereafter by Marie Schugaan and John Bosch. Bertha Bosch reported that when she arrived the Old People's Home, as it was popularly known in Sioux Falls, was filthy. The facility had no money, no financial credit, and only twelve residents, two of whom were total charity cases.[7]

The shortage of residents was attributed to a lack of awareness of the Society's Home in southeastern South Dakota. The Good Samaritan Society had found it difficult to publicize the home because there was no congregation of the old American

Lutheran Church in Sioux Falls. Reverend Hoeger was not well known in the area, and synodical differences loomed large in the 1940s. Striving to create an awareness of the Lutheran Home for the Aged, and hoping, thereby, to increase the number of residents, a group of Society workers under Pastor Hoeger's direction made a goodwill tour of ALC congregations in southeastern South Dakota in the fall of 1941. The tour group consisted of Alma Sather, Lucille Greer, Ruth Erickson, and Viola Baugatz. They presented a program of musical readings and songs after which Reverend Hoeger provided information about the Sioux Falls Home.[8] In the following year, 1942, St. John Lutheran Church was organized in northwestern Sioux Falls. This congregation, in the years that followed, provided assistance to the home. The publicity tour proved productive. The Sioux Falls facility soon had 31 residents, using all of the available space. Rollaway beds were brought out at night and set up in the hallways. Staff members were on call 24 hours a day. Without the assistance of professional nursing care, basic home remedies were prescribed for residents who were not seriously ill. Bed rest was the solution for flu victims, soda was prescribed for an upset stomach, and aspirin was given for headaches. The rooms in the former Parker House were very large, like a dormitory, each room accommodated 5-6 beds. There were few modern conveniences. During the winter months, staff members spent considerable time shoveling coal into the furnace that heated the facility. The laundry room consisted of two wringer-type Maytag washing machines.The washing was hung on outside lines to dry during the entire year, and in the winter, after being exposed to the elements, the clothes had to be thawed out and further dried in the home.[9] The administrators and staff were forced to move into rooms in the attic and basement of the old three-story mansion. The attic had little ventilation and became unbearably hot during the summer months. There were evenings when the workers took their bedding down to the lawn and slept there.

As of 1942, because of the war, help was often difficult to find, and even though more room was desperately needed, wartime shortages of building materials prohibited the construction of additional housing. A considerable amount of the food consumed by residents during the 1940s came from a large garden on the home's property. Bertha Bosch's mother supervised the garden, from the planting of seed in the spring to the harvesting of vegetables in late summer. Some of the area churches had ingather-

ings for the facility. As at Arthur, garden vegetables were canned
for consumption during the winter months. During the 1950s,
this practice came to an end when the State Health Department
ruled that home-canned food could no longer be served in nursing homes and retirement centers.

The Home's administrators had to contend with a mounting
number of regulations. After a rigorous inspection in the spring
of 1944, the State Fire Marshal gave the Lutheran Home for the
Aged a positive report. Bertha Bosch wrote to Superintendent
Hoeger on April 26, 1944, stating "The health inspectors have yet
to come, and the fire chief said they were tough. But we're not
worried, there's always a chance of joining the WACs."[10] The last
remark was made undoubtedly with tongue in cheek.

In the same letter, Bosch asked Hoeger's permission to give
the workers a raise as they were getting restless. Board and
room had been a part of their pay in the early 1940s. The home
became a financial success, and the Sioux Falls facility, after having taken care of its own debt, was able to pay the back salaries
due several of the people who had worked at the Arthur Home for
many years. In the late 1950s, the Sioux Falls Good Samaritan
Center was able to provide financial assistance for starting new
Society centers at Parkston and Tyndall, South Dakota; Poca-
hontas, Iowa; and Luverne, Minnesota.

Immediately following the end of World War II, in 1945, the
federal government gave the Good Samaritan Society permission
to construct a 22-bed addition. On June 2, 1946, the East Wing
was dedicated. The new construction, which cost $65,000, con-
tained six rooms for workers, private baths for some of the residents, and a large solarium with glass on three sides. This new
addition was soon filled, and the workers returned to their former quarters in the attic and the basement of the Parker home
as residents were given their rooms in the East Wing. The staff's
charitable spirit was truly tested in 1950. A five-room house to
lodge the workers had been constructed on the grounds, but after
a brief residence in their new quarters, they once again moved
back to their old haunts in the mansion in order that the center
could house additional applicants.[11]

As the 40s drew to a close, Bertha Bosch left Sioux Falls to
begin a home in an abandoned Coast Guard station near Groton,
South Dakota. Viola Baugatz became the administrator of the
Sioux Falls Good Samaritan facility. In 1958, a West Wing was
added to the growing complex. With this addition, 25 more resi-

dents were added to the census. The new construction, which cost $113,000, included a new kitchen, dining room, and lounge. A registered nurse became a part of the staff. A craft department was begun, and a part-time supervisor was employed.[12]

The Society's Board of Directors decided to raze the original building in the early 1960s. The old mansion and the solarium were reduced to rubble on August 1, 1965. A new two-story unit, containing space for 58 beds, plus a solarium and a distinctive sun deck overlooking the city, was dedicated on August 14, 1966. Senator George McGovern (D-South Dakota) spoke at the dedication of the $400,000 unit. The south end of the structure housed the national offices of the Good Samaritan Society until 1970.

When Viola Baugatz transferred from the Sioux Falls Center to the Good Samaritan Village at Hastings, Nebraska, in 1968, the "Mother Home" of South Dakota had 108 residents in a completely new and modern facility. By 1980, the Sioux Falls Center had a professional nursing staff, a licensed dietitian, a registered physical therapist, a Director of Activities, and a full-time Director of Social Services, plus assistants, and a food service staff. Available programs included craftwork, music, and game activities. Spirituality remained part and parcel of the total care of each resident. Morning devotions were held each day of the week with special services every Sunday in the Center chapel led by a community pastor.

Beginning in the 1970s, during Norman Stordahl's administration, the Good Samaritan Society began placing interns at the Center to learn administrative procedures. After the Central Office moved to new quarters in 1970, the vacant area at the center was remodeled and first used by the Development of Adult Services (DOAS). Later, the Aging Services Center and Senior Companion programs were located at the Sioux Falls Center. The recovered space also included a chapel, an expanded area for crafts, and a larger dining room.

A continued increase in the census led to a further expansion of the Sioux Falls Center in 1973.[13] In early 1996, the facility had room for 139 residents. Plans were made at that time for additional construction that would permit the Center to offer rehabilitation and other care to elderly residents who planned to go home after a stay in the hospital. The new type of care, called subacute, would provide a level of care the elderly normally received in a hospital setting. The Center would be able to provide less expensive care in a non-hospital setting, preparing the short-term residents to return to their homes. The decreasing availability of Medicare funds led to shorter hospital stays.[14] Because of a decline in the Center's census and uncertainty over subsidy payments, implementation of the expansion was delayed.

The Bonell Home
Greeley, Colorado

In December 1937, Superintendent Hoeger, via a newsletter, informed his co-workers in the Good Samaritan Society of a new venture. He wrote:

> We are still going ahead. So we have gone ahead and opened an Old People's Home at Greeley, Colorado. These buildings used to be an Episcopalian Seminary. We now have 8 people there. It took a lot of scrubbing and painting to put the dormitory in livable shape. The beginning was also hard there, but now the future looks brighter.[15]

The beginning of this facility occurred during the summer of 1936. Returning from a trip to California, August Hoeger stopped in Greeley, Colorado, to attend a Sunday worship service. Following the service, the pastor of the church, Reverend Erwin Fritschel, invited Hoeger to his home for dinner. Knowing of Hoeger's penchant for seeking out abandoned buildings that could be transformed into Society Homes, Fritschel kidded him that there was an old Episcopal Seminary closing because of financial difficulties. Reverend B. W. Bonell, Dean of St. John's College (the Seminary) owned the building and everything in it. Reverend Hoeger was interested, and a meeting was arranged with Bonell for the next morning. When Bonell heard that the Seminary would become a home for the elderly, he was interested in selling the buildings, located on ten acres of land, approximately two city blocks, on the outskirts of Greeley.[16]

The Society agreed to pay $20,000, paying off the obligation over 20 years at $1,000 per year with no interest.[17] The Good Samaritan Society agreed to name the facility for Bonell and to pay him 50 dollars per month for the remainder of his life.

Bonell, who was 70 years old at the time and who had had a recent bout with tuberculosis, was not expected to live long. He defied the odds and died at the age of 92.[18]

In his newsletter, Hoeger had mentioned that the beginning was hard — that was an understatement. In June 1937, the Society sent Edna Borchardt, of Oconomowoc, Wisconsin, to get the Home under way, but it was beyond her ability to bring about the undertaking. The buildings were run down, and the weeds around the buildings were waist-high. People in Greeley had not grasped what the whole venture was about. Most of its citizens still thought of any type of home for the aged as a Poor Farm.[19]

Fortunately, the first resident, Uncle John Detweiler, became legendary for his work in improving the grounds and in repairing furniture and beds in preparation for additional residents. The weeds fell victim to his scythe, and the trees and flowers began to flourish because he dutifully watered and cared for them. The Hoeger family spent summers working at the Bonell Home, and Detweiler was joined by a Mr. Phenix, a capable "fix it" person with hammer, saw, and paint brush.[20]

Reverend Fritschel, the first administrator of Bonell, played a pivotal role in the success of the Greeley facility. The Bonell Home could not borrow money — but he could, a thousand dollars at a time from a local bank. He lived only a block from the home, and he often spent his summer vacations repairing rooms, painting, and purchasing equipment with his own funds.[21] Pastor Fritschel directed the overall program at Bonell until 1958. When he became president of the Central District of the American Lutheran Church, he rallied various church groups toward the support of the Bonell Home.

By the summer of 1940, the Greeley facility housed 30 residents. Hoeger anticipated creating rooms for an additional 30 people. In the *Sunshine*, he sang the praises of the region, stating that the area had lots of sunshine and that the climate was wonderfully dry.[22] It was during the same year that Mrs. William (Marie) Walz became the matron of the Bonell Home. Marie had gained her experience at the Mother Home in Arthur. She had been in charge of the corridors from 3 to 11 p.m.. Coming from Fargo, North Dakota, Marie arrived in Greeley on August 4, 1940. When she arrived in the city, she knew of the Bonell Home only as T.O.P.H., and no one knew where that was. A taxi driver finally guessed that it might be old St. John's College on the hill.[23] She was not overly impressed with the three-story building that first housed the home. No one could be placed on the third floor, for example, because it was in such a bad state of disrepair. In performing her duties at the Bonell Home, Marie took nurses' training at the local hospital, and she was certified as a licensed practical nurse.[24]

Described by Fritschel as a "terrific matron," Marie Walz, in her 18-year tenure, established a new spirit at Bonell through her unselfish service to the residents. One resident recalled that there were evenings when Mrs. Walz would visit the room of a sick person, reading until that individual forgot his ills and smiled with appreciation. On one of the city blocks that came with the purchase of the seminary from Dean Bonell, a series of single family cottages were constructed for older married couples. Bonell was at the forefront of the Good Samaritan Society's experiment with independent-living apartments and various levels of care. The cottage residents had fellowship with people of their own age, and they could maintain small flower gardens outside of their dwellings. If there was a need for medical assistance, a nurse from the Home was available.[25] The cottages sold for about $5,000, a large amount of money for the time, on a Life Contract dependent upon the age of the occupants.[26] Eventually, the Bonell complex, along with the Good Samaritan Village at Hastings, Nebraska, would provide seven levels of care, ranging from complete independent-living apartments to intensive nursing care.[27]

The departure of Marie Walz to California and Fritschel's decision to give up his supervisory duties necessitated a search for new leadership for the Bonell Home in 1958. Prior to his leaving, Reverend Fritschel recommended Erv Chell as his replacement.[28] Erv and Betty Chell arrived in April 1958 to administer the Greeley complex. They had been missionaries to India. Chell assumed direction of expansion of Bonell while Betty worked in the Center's office.[29]

A massive construction program ensued over the next nine years. The buildings constructed between 1959 and 1967 included:

1959	Walz Unit (Walz Personal Care Building and the Walz Multi-Purpose Lounge).	$145,000
1961	Row Apartments.	$170,000

1962   Manor Units. $367,000

1963   Circle and 1/2 Circle
       Apartments $350,000

1967   Seven-story Tower Central
       facilities and Hoeger Nursing
       Unit . . . . $2,000,000.

Over 25 percent of the funds for the construction of the seven-story Tower Central came from a $600,000 grant received through the Hill-Burton program.[30] While further refining the multi-level program introduced by Fritschel and Walz, the Chells beautified the grounds with gardens, fountains, and streams. One of the annual highlights of the Bonell complex was a banquet and fall bazaar. The banquet attracted hundreds of people from the Greeley community, and the bazaar fulfilled a year's work in the Activities Department.[31] After ten years in Greeley, the Chells moved to Sioux Falls, South Dakota, in 1968, to join the staff of the national office of the Good Samaritan Society.

The Olathe Home
Olathe, Kansas

Reverend John Hoeger left his position as administrator of the Colony of Mercy, Parkston, South Dakota, in July 1950. He journeyed to a suburb of Kansas City, Missouri, to begin mission congregations at Overland Park and Olathe, Kansas. When his father visited him in early 1951, they decided to check the yellow pages of the Kansas City telephone directory to determine the number of nursing homes in the area. Finding a few homes listed, they thought it would be nice if the Society could take over a home that was already established rather than buy a large building and begin from scratch. Father and son visited the Johnson County, Kansas, Welfare Department to check on the laws and regulations for providing care for the elderly in Kansas. As they were leaving the Welfare office, a woman said, "By the way, there is a home for sale here at Olathe. A young couple is running it, but they are not 21 years old and so we cannot give them a license."[32] Superintendent Hoeger remarked, "We considered that [the woman's comments] an answer to our prayer."

After a visit to the Cedar Crest Nursing Home, at 414 East Cedar, Olathe, Superintendent Hoeger leased the facility, purchased the equipment, and the Society took over in seven days. It was the 16th home opened by the Good Samaritan Society and the first Society Home in Kansas.[33] The new acquisition was a three-story stone structure, constructed in 1868 and used as a flour mill for 33 years by the Christian Martin Ott family. Augie Hoeger, who was pursuing a Master of Arts degree in clinical psychology at the University of Missouri, Kansas City, briefly served as administrator at the old, grey stucco building. He was replaced by Rita and Nikolais (Kola) Reinfelds in February 1951. Rita had been the administrator at the Parkston, South Dakota Colony of Mercy. The Reinfelds had gained administrative experience under John Hoeger's tutelage when he had charge of the Parkston facility between 1948 and 1950.[34]

Rita experienced several difficulties when she first took over the 22-bed Olathe Home. There were 13 residents at the time, five of them in restraints. No tranquilizers were used at the time, and she had limited help. As recent immigrants from Europe, they had left a displaced persons' camp in Germany in the fall of 1949; the Reinfelds had some problems with the English language. She could manage if talking directly to people, but conversing over the telephone was another matter. However, Rita was a quick learner, and in a short period of time, she became fluent in English. Augie Hoeger, who resided at brother John's home while a student at the University of Missouri, helped maintain the Home's account for two months. The old building needed considerable modernizing, and capital was secured to install a new furnace and sink.[35]

The Good Samaritan Society purchased a large Victorian home, located at 572 East Park, Olathe, from the City of Olathe in July 1952. The Society offered $20,000 for the building, once intended to be the first Olathe Hospital, payable over a three year period.[36] The new acquisition, first licensed for 17 residents, became the Olathe Home as operations ended at the East Cedar site in January 1955, and its residents were shifted to the new location.[37]

At its new location, the Olathe Home prospered, and in the next 27 years, 1955-1982, six additions were made to the facility. One of the most significant of these additions was the construction of a $350,000 licensed skilled nursing care unit for 93 residents, dedicated on May 2, 1965.[38]

The Reinfelds were caring, efficient, and innovative administrators. The Olathe Center gained a reputation in the Society for its well kept grounds. Rita remembered what Reverend Hoeger had said when she and Kola were at Parkston. He had stated that the first view of a home is from the outside. If you kept that in order, then everyone would know that you are going to be a good keeper of those things that were inside.[39] In 1976, the *Kansas City Star*, after extensive investigation by its reporters, rated the Good Samaritan Center at Olathe as one of the top three nursing homes in the Kansas City area.[40]

When the Reinfelds moved to the East Park address in 1952, they began with 17 residents plus one other paid employee. At the time of their retirement on February 1, 1981, they administered a modern brick complex worth $2 million that cared for 162 residents and employed 120 people plus consultants.[41] They exemplified Superintendent Hoeger's conception of the ideal administrator. In 1965, he had stated that the Society needed an administrator who would work — "Not one who sits at a desk and tries to do something, but someone who can and will even get his hands dirty." He wanted an administrator who had his heart and soul in his work, one who knew how to save, using efficient business management practices.[42]

At the time of their retirement, the Reinfelds felt they were being smothered with paper work. The residents' needs and the regulation of nursing facilities were changing dramatically. With growing government intervention, the amount of documentation required by federal and state authorities cast administrators in a new role. Costs increased with the government's insistence that each center employ a dietitian plus occupational, physical, and speech therapists. Requirements and personnel changed, but the old structure at 572 East Park in Olathe had not changed. With growing maintenance required on the old facility, the Society constructed a new building, on a new site, that was dedicated on May 6, 1995.[43]

St. Luke's Home
Kearney, Nebraska

A sharp contrast in function and inhabitants marked the history of the Good Samaritan Society's "Mother Home" in Nebraska. St. Luke's Home was originally located in a building that housed the Kearney Military Academy. The three-story structure that was once filled with noisy boys disciplined for a potential career in the military, as of 1953, was filled with the elderly, enjoying the twilight years of their lives.

Towards the end of the 19th century, the economy of Kearney, Nebraska, was on the upswing and the community was growing. Representatives of the United Brethren Church approached a group of businessmen about establishing a low cost academy in Kearney. Although they were offered 25 acres in east Kearney and money to construct one building, the United Brethren decided to build at York, Nebraska, where they received a better offer. Main street merchants made the same offer to Episcopal Bishop Anson R. Graves, who had arrived in 1890, and he set forth to begin the project.

In 1891, he attended a meeting at Yonkers, New York, to solicit funds at a missionary meeting. At the meeting, he told the story of a 12-year-old boy who had come to him when he was at Broken Bow, Nebraska, and asked "When can the church take me and educate me for the ministry?"[44] Mrs. Eva J. Cochran responded to the Bishop's story by offering $3,000 for the establishment of a school. On September 6, 1892, the Platte Collegiate Institute, a coeducational school for training students for the ministry, opened. The campus included a brick building and two wooden dormitories. For a time, the school thrived but enrollment gradually dropped and financial pressures took their toll.

Following the outbreak of the Spanish-American War in 1898, the Institute was transformed into the Kearney Military Academy for Boys. The change in the Academy's mission increased attendance but the condition of the school's buildings deteriorated. Deciding that a new building was needed, Kearney's civic leaders turned once again to Bishop Graves. They promised him that if he would raise $25,000 for a new and modern building for the school, they would contribute another $25,000.[45] Bishop Graves turned again to his Eastern benefactor, Mrs. Cochran. The "true mother of the school" responded with the necessary matching funds. On December 18, 1906, the people of Kearney gathered to dedicate the modern, fireproof building that still looms above the Platte Valley in east Kearney. With Bishop Graves presiding and William Jennings Bryan delivering an oration, Cochran Hall, built of reinforced concrete and finished in pressed brick, became the Academy's new home. During the following year, the Episcopalian vestry, needing a larger church for the Kearney Diocese, voted to build St. Luke's, from which the Society home derived its name.[46]

George A. Beecher, who became the bishop of the Kearney Diocese in 1910, assumed control of the Academy and Cochran Hall on June 1, 1913. Under his guidance, the school became not only an efficient military academy but a more diversified educational institution. Courses were offered in agriculture, manual training, and sociology.[47] The remaining years of the decade were described as the "golden years" of the school by one of its students, Vine V. Deloria, D.D., who attended the Academy between 1917-1921.[48] The Academy's fortunes, however, were subject to sudden change. The school closed on September 5, 1923, following declining enrollment and a fire which destroyed an annex, the boiler house, and the gymnasium.[49]

The property in east Kearney remained abandoned for almost two decades with Cochran Hall the only building remaining. In 1940, an agreement was reached between officials of the Episcopal Church and the City of Kearney that Cochran Hall and the surrounding 31 acres be deeded to the City with the provision that the property be for public use only.[50] The building was refurbished and reopened as a National Youth Administration (NYA) Work Center, one of the many programs instituted by the New Deal during the Great Depression. During World War II, Cochran Hall housed German prisoners of war as well as American military and civilian personnel.

Cochran Hall underwent another change in 1948. Under the auspices of the First Lutheran Church of Kearney, the building was renovated and opened as St. Luke's Hospital. This latest chapter in the history of the venerable structure proved a financial nightmare. In an effort to save the venture, First Lutheran Church sought the help of the Lutheran Hospital and Homes Society. The Nebraska Department of Health issued a provisional license to the LHHS to operate a general hospital, with 51 beds and ten bassinets, on November 7, 1951.[51] The hospital could not be saved, and it was closed in 1952.

Reverend Hoeger often drove past Kearney on his way to Gothenburg, Amelia's home town. He could see Cochran Hall in the distance, and he commented that he would like to make it a Society home some day. When the building became available, he acted quickly. On June 3, 1952, Hoeger indicated that the Good Samaritan Society would take over the hospital property and convert it into a home for the elderly. Cochran Hall was purchased for $250,000. During the next months, the Society sold the hospital's equipment to competitive bidders.[52] In June 1953,

St. Luke's Home opened in Cochran Hall under the management of the Good Samaritan Society. Eighty beds were available for prospective residents. Ten years later, Oscar Deines, the Home's administrator, indicated that more space was needed for social and physical therapy. St. Luke's employed 26 full-time workers and five part-time people. The average age of the residents was 81 years with 66 percent of them being ambulatory.[53]

Three years later, on August 28, 1966, a new, one-story, 60-bed facility was constructed southwest of Cochran Hall. In future years, the new structure would be referred to as the "main building." It featured 40 units, 20 double-bed rooms, and 20 single-care units.[54] The new construction proved timely because the State Fire Marshal condemned the use of Cochran Hall as a nursing home in 1975. Dan Apple, then the administrator of St. Luke's Home, said, "My first intentions were to have the building torn down. However, after talking to several people, I learned of the building's historical value. I also learned that it was structurally sound."[55] Cochran Hall, where between 1,200 and 1,500 aged and infirm people had been cared for over 20 years, stood empty again.[56]

In the same year that Cochran Hall was phased out, the Society moved eight buildings to its 38-acre site. Each of the buildings was divided into four apartments, each with an emergency hook up to the nurses' station in the "main building." The apartments were available to married couples or single people who were 65 or older and able to live independently. The residents of this small village shared a recreation room, and they staged monthly pot-luck dinners.

The current St. Luke's Center was refurbished in 1978 when all of the rooms were repainted and decorated with new draperies. An addition to the Center provided space for a laundry and a larger kitchen and dining area. Cochran Hall did not remain vacant. The Good Samaritan Society, working with the board of directors of the Rhyme and Reason Community Child Care organization, renovated the first floor of the historical building. Following scrubbing, painting, and ensuring that the structure met the required codes for plumbing, heating, and electrical work, Cochran Hall became a community day-care center. The sounds of youth which reverberated through its halls at the turn of the century were repeated as the 20th century drew to a close.[57]

West Union Home
West Union, Iowa

The first Society home in Iowa was another former hospital. Dr. Frank Whitmore promoted its construction in West Union in 1898, and he named it the Maple Leaf. The hospital failed financially and Whitmore departed for China to become the secretary of the Nanking YMCA. By 1910, the interior of the building was remodeled; it contained a grocery store and a general merchandise and shoe store on the ground floor. The second floor was given over to professional offices.

In 1919, the City purchased the building, and it was reopened as a hospital in 1920. When West Union opened a new health care facility, Palmer Memorial Hospital, 29 years later, in 1949, the Good Samaritan Society took over operation of the new building. The hospital was leased to the Society for one dollar per year on May 1. The lease stipulated that the Society would take all of the revenues and meet all of the expenses including maintenance and upkeep of the facility.[58] In 1951, The Society purchased the old hospital from the City of West Union for $10,000 and opened it as a 40-bed nursing home. Local citizens contributed $3,329 to help restore the building. Pat Camp served as the first matron until she moved to California.[59]

The Good Samaritan Society began planning for a new facility in January 1965. Community contributions to the endeavor included $30,000 cash and the proceeds from a farm given to the Society by Adam Musselman. The money was used to purchase 9.6 acres north of Palmer Memorial Hospital. The $350,000, 50-bed home was dedicated on October 9, 1966.[60] The old facility continued to operate as a custodial care home for 25 people until the Iowa Public Health Department ordered its closure in 1974. These residents were moved to the new facility. The Society donated the old building to the Fayette County Historical Society for one dollar in 1975.[61] Four single bedroom apartments were constructed adjacent to the Nursing Center in 1973. The apartments were financed through donations from the community and Nursing Center funds. In the spring of 1975, the West Union Center added an additional wing which included ten double rooms, bathing facilities, a chapel, office space, and a multi-purpose room.[62] The Good Samaritan Society decided to withdraw from the hospital setting on June 30, 1975, and to focus on long-term care in West Union. The hospital and its equipment was sold to Palmer Memorial Hospital, Incorporated, for $51,263.92.[63]

Iowa's oldest Good Samaritan Society Center housed 71 residents in 1991, employed 72 full-time and part-time people, and operated with an annual budget of nearly $1,254,000.[64] In the 90s, the Center adopted a legislator program. State legislators were invited to the Center "to learn long term care issues, to hear about facility concerns and to discuss possible solutions." They were taken on tours of the facility, and they listened to explanations of the Center's operations and how it served the community's needs. The program was an eye-opener for a number of legislators who did not realize the vital role nursing homes played in the health care continuum. One of the unique classes conducted at the center was a German language class.[65]

Clearbrook Home
Clearbrook, Minnesota

Minnesota's oldest existing Society home opened at Clearbrook in 1952. The Home was an outgrowth of a hospital that did not materialize. The community gave the incomplete building to the Society, which undertook to complete the project. The Good Samaritan Society ended up razing the ill-fated structure and in its stead constructed a two-story building for long-term care residents. The 56-bed facility, on the south edge of Clearbrook, added an East Wing in 1963 which included 32 additional beds, two solariums, and an elevator. Nine more beds, a chapel, another solarium, beauty shop, new kitchen, and a storage room were added to the center three years later. The first administrator of the present 93-nursing-bed facility was the Reverend Carl G. Berg.[66]

Mother Homes were to be established in other states during the 1950s and 1960s as the Good Samaritan Society extended its influence across the Southern Plains into Oklahoma and Texas. In the midst of this expansion, Dad Hoeger remarked in 1958 that a man should slow down a little as he aged. Statistics belie this statement as the Society more than doubled its facilities in the next decade. At age 75, he continued to traverse the Prairie Plains in his Dodge automobile visiting each of the growing number of Society facilities. His mind continued to generate new ways in which the Society could continue to carry out Christ's mandate to serve the needy. Growth carried with it new problems but as in the past every knock became a boost.

Above: *Remnants of Spencer Park, in Hastings, Nebraska, known as "Chimney Town," which was replaced by the Good Samaritan Village.* **Below:** *A bird's eye view.*

Chapter Nine
MORE GROWTH, MORE PROB-
LEMS, MORE IDEAS
1958-1967

*"We are an organization that is not
only in debt to God, but also in debt to
human beings." — August Hoeger, Sr.,
Good Samaritan Society Annual Meeting, August 1967.*

August Hoeger, Sr., celebrated his 50 years in the ministry
at a special dinner at Fargo, North Dakota, in 1958. After
a series of tributes to his achievements and steadfast
faith, he responded that a person should take it easier as he gets
older, "but he shouldn't exactly retire, just slow down a little."[1]
Hoeger did not slow down. In November 1963, the General
Superintendent did miss his first Board meeting in 41 years.
Amelia had broken her hip, and he stayed home to take care of
her.[2] At 73, he was always on the go. Like Robert Frost, he had
"miles to go" and "promises to keep."

The Good Samaritan Society continued to grow. The number of
facilities more than doubled, from 47 in 1955 to 101 in 1965. The
annual operating budget was seven times larger in 1965 than it
had been ten years earlier, increasing from $1.3 million to $9.6
million.[3] Driving a late model Dodge, Hoeger visited one home
after the other during the summer months, driving at least
30,000 miles per year. He seldom stayed longer than an hour at
a home, but as his son Augie said, "Dad can't stand to go past one
of his Homes!" In some respects, Reverend Hoeger was a modern
version of the circuit-riding preacher of pioneer days.[4] His brief
visits bolstered the morale of home administrators. "Dad"
Hoeger, as he became affectionately known throughout the
Society at this time, was the "best tonic a person can have,"
observed one facility administrator.

In championing the Society's continued growth, Hoeger often
found himself challenged by the Board of Directors. His relation-

ship with the Board began to change during the 1950s. During the early years, most of the Directors had been clergy. After the split in 1940, many of the Board members were home administrators. By the late 1950s, the number of administrators who could serve on the Board had been reduced, and other professional people were being elected Directors as the Board's membership became national. Board membership was always voted on at annual meetings with at least two nominations required for each opening.[5]

Dad Hoeger was never enamored of the Board of Directors as a working mechanism. He had a board because he believed that banks, governments, and certain individuals viewed boards as a necessary part of any institutional endeavor. Boards, in his view, became too tied up in technicalities; he wanted to use them only as a consentual body. Otherwise, he believed a Board of Directors would become an obstacle to growth.[6]

A member of Reverend John Hoeger's congregation at Olathe, Kansas, Eugene Hackler, an attorney, served on the Society's Board for 15 years, and as treasurer of the Society for 12 of those years. The Good Samaritan Society relied on his legal counsel on tax matters for 20 years. Hackler was a stickler for meeting financial obligations, and he was one of the Board members who often challenged Hoeger's expansion plans. Hackler worried about acquiring new facilities because Superintendent Hoeger had no staff and did things pretty much from memory, jotting down minimal data on the backs of envelopes or in small spiral notebooks.[7]

There was a growing feeling on the Board of Directors that administrators had too much leeway in carrying out their duties. Some of them did encounter financial difficulties and Board members feared that the administrators would overcommit the limited funds of the Society.[8] After a meeting of the Board on November 2, 1962, home administrators were reminded that the Board had complete authority between annual meetings and that the Superintendent was responsible to the Board. The Superintendent, in turn, or his assistant, had complete authority to carry out all policies and directives of the Board.[9] Later on, the Board conducted a study to develop a standard reporting system for financial and statistical reports to the Central Office.[10]

At a tension-filled Board meeting in Omaha, Nebraska, Eugene Hackler moved that the Directors declare a moratorium on building. The motion, which carried by one vote, stipulated that no property should be mortgaged or purchased until the Society's records were better organized.[11] Superintendent Hoeger tended to ignore the moratorium. He was a shrewd politician in the manner in which he presented his position. He quickly perceived people's interests and brought out from them their interest in helping him in his work. He chose specific occasions to ask Board approval for new facilities. As a result, homes continued to be built during the moratorium period. As late as 1962, the Board continued to discourage expansion unless an unusually good proposal was forthcoming whereby a local community would have a large part of the funds necessary for construction.[12]

Hastings Village

One such occasion when Hoeger ignored the moratorium on further expansion was in the development of the Good Samaritan Village at Hastings, Nebraska. This remarkable project was first brought to Dad Hoeger's attention in 1956 by Reverend William Goldbeck, who had been the chaplain at the Hastings' Regional Center, a state facility for the mentally impaired and handicapped. Goldbeck suggested that the Good Samaritan Society acquire Spencer Park, a large housing complex owned by the City of Hastings.

The complex dated back to World War II when a large naval ammunition depot was located east of Hastings. The federal government acquired Spencer Park, on the southeast edge of Hastings, and began the construction of concrete block apartments to house the people working at the ammunition depot. The first residents moved into the 840-unit complex on October 16, 1943. The employees were conveyed to and from their employment on "cattle wagons" or "barges," actually flatbed trucks fitted with benches. At the end of the war in 1945, the housing complex contained nearly 6,000 people.

The Navy maintained control over Spencer Park until 1954 when all of the units were sold to the Hastings Housing Authority for $44,918. The Housing Authority rented the units to the residents of what became known as "Chimney Town" to local citizens. The number of residents in Spencer Park declined rapidly, and the housing deteriorated without the maintenance that the Navy had provided. Spencer Park became an eyesore with tall weeds and an accumulation of trash. In addition, the park became identified with crime and violence.[13]

Hoeger was intrigued with the possibilities offered by the park. Visionary that he was, he believed that the Good Samaritan Society should continue what had begun at the Bonell Center in Greeley, Colorado: the development of independent living units located in close proximity to available skilled health care.[14] He believed such units would attract the mobile elderly because of their convenience, security, health and wellness programs, meal services, and the sense of belonging to a small community where individual freedom could still be expressed.[15] Hoeger and Goldbeck met with the Hastings City Council to discuss the purchase of the southern half of Spencer Park for a retirement community. In their conversations with the Hastings' officials, Hoeger and Mayor Barth discovered that they had attended grade school together. Barth had confidence in Reverend Hoeger, knowing of the Society's work at its Home in Kearney, Nebraska. The sale of the property would eliminate two problems for the City Council. Under its contract with the Navy, the city was obligated to pay for demolishing the complex if the housing program proved unsuccessful. In addition, the city would no longer have the responsibility of evacuating tenants from some of the apartments in the northwest corner of the park. Because of the violence in that area, people did not drive through it at night.[16]

When Superintendent Hoeger recommended to the Board of Directors that the Society purchase the southern part of Spencer Park, the Board was unanimously opposed, having considered the state of disrepair of the apartments and the social problems involved. Seeing the future possibilities for the apartments and believing it was God's will, Hoeger went against the Board's wishes and purchased 50 acres of land and 420 apartments, which could provide room for 500 people, from the City of Hastings for $112,500 in the fall of 1957. The General Superintendent announced his *fait accompli* at the Society's annual meeting.[17] He considered the purchase a wonderful gift. The property was valued at $1.5 million, and the Society paid less than one cent on the dollar for it.[18]

Reverend Goldbeck, the Village's first administrator, and his wife, Dagmar, took over renovating the first apartments on January 1, 1958. Diligently painting, papering and cleaning 15 apartments, they began to solicit applications in April. All of the first applications were from out-of-town as Hastings' residents had difficulty eradicating from their minds the traditional image of "Chimney Town." The first residents arrived, and Villa Rest opened on July 14, 1958.[19] By 1961, three other villas, Villa Peace, Villa Hope and Villa Faith, had been developed. Little by little, the word was spread about the Village's advantages. The American Medical Association published an article about the seven levels of care offered at Hastings Village. Residents were admitted to the villas according to the amount of care they required. Villa Rest, for example, was a care home for ambulatory people who needed a minimal amount of nursing care.[20] The sixth and seventh levels included nursing care in a care home and infirmary care.

The Good Samaritan Society gradually acquired the remainder of Spencer Park. In 1966, the Hastings Housing Authority sold the Society an additional 48 apartments for $18,000. Two years later, for $82,500, the remaining apartments became Society property. All of Spencer Park was now a part of the Village except for 11 apartments and one other building, all occupied by the Hope Training School. Once again, a vision of Reverend Hoeger became a successful reality. According to Reverend Goldbeck, "With Hoeger, if a thing worked, let's go ahead and use it."[21]

Two major events occurred at the Hastings complex in 1966. William Goldbeck retired as the Village administrator to become the chaplain. Reverend John Hoeger resigned his ministerial position at Ontario, California, to be the new Village administrator. At the get-acquainted tea held to welcome him to Hastings, John attempted to juggle a plate holding tea and crumpets while shaking hands. He tipped his plate and some of the tea ran down his pant leg. One of the Regional Directors phoned John shortly thereafter and greeted him, "Hi, John. Have you got your feet wet yet?"[22] The other major event was the dedication of a $775,000, 156-bed Intermediate Care Facility on October 2, 1966. John Hoeger named the new building Villa Grace. He and his family resided in the Goldbeck's former apartment. Finding several items with the name Grace on them, he assumed he was naming the building in honor of Goldbeck's wife. He soon discovered that Grace was their daughter. The situation was rectified with the dedication of a new four-story brick apartment building, the Goldbeck Towers, on June 25, 1972.

Goldbeck had built up a $100,000 reserve at the Hastings' complex. When John Hoeger began to spend some of the money for personnel and needed equipment, Dad Hoeger, who never forgot his experiences of 1938-1940, cautioned him to watch his expenditures. John asked Viola Baugatz to come to Hastings as an assistant administrator. He asked her to cut down on overstaffing, which was accomplished gradually. She later took over purchasing plus managing the housekeepers.[23] John's sister, Dr. Agnes Hoeger, became the first medical director of the Village. She had served as a medical missionary in New Guinea for several years. When John Hoeger was asked to join the Central Office staff in 1972, the Society's Hastings Village covered 90 acres and housed 1,257 residents in more than 700 apartments. It was a city onto itself with paved streets and sidewalks, all utilities and a small lake.[24]

The building program continued under John Hoeger's successor, the Reverend Jacob B. Jerstad, who was married to Laura Hoeger, one of the six daughters of August Hoeger, Sr., and his wife, Amelia. By 1970, the four small Villas were becoming obsolete and it was only a matter of time before they would not meet the regulations of the State Health Department. With a large grant from the Edwin Perkins' Foundation, the $1.4 million Perkins Pavilion, a 263-bed home, was dedicated on April 8, 1973. Once the Pavilion was completed, residents were moved out of the old historic villas. Over the next five years, 59 of the beds were licensed for Medicare-approved skilled care while the remaining 204 beds were licensed for intermediate care. George Paulson became the administrator of the Hastings Village in 1977 when Reverend Jerstad joined the Central Office in Sioux Falls, South Dakota, as Spiritual Ministries Director for the Society.[25] Before he left Hastings, Jerstad had begun the tradition of holding fall Bible conferences.

Aside from Arthur, the Hastings Village became Dad Hoeger's favorite Good Samaritan facility. After spending the winter months at Hastings for two years, he completed his move to the Village in 1968 to be with family members and to be near his dear friends, the Goldbecks and Reverend and Mrs. Henry Foege. He made the Village his base of operations for the remainder of his life with periodic commutes northward to his beloved Arthur and to the Central Office in Sioux Falls. During the last week of his life, Hoeger, with hammer and hand, worked on the construction of another of his dreams, a Prayer Chapel at Hastings Village.

Nursing Home Builders

The contractor for the construction of Villa Grace at Hastings had been Nursing Home Builders of Broken Bow, Nebraska. During a single decade, from 1959 to 1969, Nursing Home Builders would construct more than 100 new facilities for the Good Samaritan Society.[26] State requirements forced Superintendent Hoeger to abandon remodeling and adding to old structures and to construct new buildings. As long as possible, he had adhered to his particular concept of a home. He had been adverse to single rooms, believing that they promoted loneliness. State requirements forced him to include so many single rooms in new construction.[27] He had favored facilities with no more than 20 residents. The cost factor in new construction dictated that there be a minimum of 40 beds in a new home. Dad Hoeger found the new requirements hard to take. He had a quirk when it came to secular authority. His son, Augie, reported that when Hoeger, Sr., was told by officials of the Minnesota Department of Health that Good Samaritan facilities would be licensed only if certain requirements were met, he asked them, "How many of you have cleaned up poop after a resident?" When they had done that, they could start telling him what to do. When they left the meeting, Augie asked his father how many times he had cleaned up after a resident. One source indicated that the Society's Superintendent had spent only one night in a nursing home.[28]

The president of Nursing Home Builders, Ray Brown, first made contact with the Good Samaritan Society through Reverend Goldbeck. Later, Brown, and his partner, Don Denesia, journeyed to Fargo to visit with Dad Hoeger. Although Brown was concerned about Hoeger's style of bookkeeping — his use of a pencil and school tablet to record data for an organization with a $6 million balance sheet — a bargain was struck between the two men. Brown was deeply affected by Reverend Hoeger. He remarked that "...He [Hoeger] changed everybody that knew him. You can't know him like he was and not change."[29] The Society built facilities according to what a rural community could handle. As a rule, a home contained 40 beds along with a kitchen and dining room that could accommodate 60 people. In the early 60s, a home was constructed for between $130,000 and

$150,000.[30] Brown could build a facility according to the Society's specifications for about half the price of other contractors. With an efficient and specific design and his own construction crew, Brown's Nursing Home Builders could construct a home in nine months. Exceptions were made to the basic design when a local group wanted a certain feature.[31] Using funds available through the Hill-Burton Act was another matter. The federal government had its own set of specifications in constructing housing for the elderly. Nursing Home Builders continued to build homes for the Society after August Hoeger, Jr. became its Executive Director.[32] At one time, all of Brown's business came from the Society. In the 70s, the construction firm began to build for non-profit corporations nationwide, and the name of the firm was changed to Medical Facilities.[33]

The Society's Tax-Exempt Status

As the number of new facilities increased, state and local governments looked for ways to tax the Society's revenues. A letter from the U. S. Treasury Department, dated May 24, 1955, reaffirmed the Good Samaritan Society's exemption from federal income tax because it had been organized for charitable purposes. The government also assumed that the Society's farming operations were for the benefit of its members and/or patients and "not commercial farming ventures for profit."[34] In 1961, the concern of four states — Idaho, Minnesota, North Dakota, and Oklahoma — that any tax exempt property in their particular jurisdictions should remain in their area if the Good Samaritan Society ever dissolved, caused Superintendent Hoeger to recommend the following amendment to the Society's constitution:

> In the event this corporation is dissolved for any cause whatsoever, the property and assets of every character including all funds, real estate and personal property, shall become the property of non-profit organizations in the area where the Society is operating an institution, after all just debts and obligations have been paid.[35]

County assessors frequently challenged the tax-exempt status of facilities in their jurisdiction. Eugene Hackler, the Society's general tax counsel in the 50s and 60s, gained a national reputation in his successful defense of the tax-exempt status of Society homes. His defense of the homes at Beatrice and Wymore in Gage County, Nebraska, was to be cited repeatedly in other tax cases as a standard foundation case. It became one of the most cited cases in tax exemption law.[36] The case reversed the trend of tax exemption being denied by many states. The Nebraska Supreme Court held charity to be something more than mere alms giving or the relief of poverty and distress. The Court said charity is broad enough "to include practical enterprises for the good of humanity operated at a moderate cost to those who receive the benefits."[37] The justices further ruled that no one in the Society was receiving "private" profit. The Supreme Court's opinion stated, "Nursing homes for the aged and infirm are analogous to hospitals in that they perform largely the same services available in hospitals...." The Society's services were limited to a large extent to the aged, the infirm and individuals who were mentally subnormal.[38] According to August Hoeger, Jr., Hackler became the expert in the field of tax exemption for non-profit organizations. Over time, he had 40-60 cases in the court system.[39]

As late as 1978, the Society had to carry a case to the Iowa Court of Appeals to overturn a Fayette County decision which rescinded the tax-exempt status of the West Union Good Samaritan Center in 1973. The Appeals Court rightly ruled that the center "was not operated with a view to pecuniary profit."[40] The Court, considering income over expenses, said that a reasonable return would be 10 percent at a home. The Good Samaritan Society worked at ".1 of 1 percent in 1972, 5 percent in 1973, and 3.12 percent in 1974." The reason that the Society had some excess income over expenses was due to low management salaries and an abundance of volunteers. The justices further stated that the Society's "objectives are charitable. To require that the Society sustain operating deficits in order to perpetuate its real estate tax exemption is unsound and would discourage responsible management practices."[41] Maintaining the tax-exempt status of all of the Society's homes helped save costs for residents.

Reverend Hoeger had to move against litigation of another sort, as well. For years, the Society did not have liability insurance on some of its property. Hoeger believed that if people knew the Society had insurance, it was more likely to be sued. The doctrine of charitable immunity — which meant that any not-for-profit charitable institution would not have to pay if someone was hurt on its premises or if there was malpractice — no longer existed. After considerable persuasion by legal counsel, Dad Hoeger agreed that the proper insurance had to be purchased.[42]

Community Centers

The physical growth of the Good Samaritan Society and the problems that accompanied growth did not deter Hoeger from coming up with new ideas by which the Society could better serve the elderly and the distressed. In 1963, he recommended that all of the Good Samaritan homes for the elderly should change their names to centers. He pointed out that two-thirds of the old people in a community would never live in a nursing home. The Society could assist them by making the home a center where they could meet, have Christian fellowship and become one with the center's residents. Together, they could form an association or club. Modifying a statement from Abraham Lincoln's Gettysburg Address, Superintendent Hoeger said, "It should be an organization of the old people, for the old people and by the old people."[43]

In addition, he envisioned a Helper's Club which would involve center staff members and community volunteers in a program that would enable the community's elderly to put off entering a care center. Composed of all Christian denominations, his Christian Senior Citizens Association would assist in providing recreation for the elderly and taking them to places of interest, including a day at a lake, ball games and lectures.[44] Local administrators and their staffs would play a key role in coordinating such outreach programs as Meals on Wheels, telephone reassurance, homemaker services and home health care. Meetings of the Helper's Club would be in the center.[45]

By the mid-1960s, several of the homes had Helper's Clubs. At the Good Samaritan Center at DeSmet, South Dakota, volunteers made daily phone calls to the elderly in the community. The Center also staged a hobby and craft show for residents and community people. Another center made 150 pairs of mittens for Indian children; another Good Samaritan facility held a Christmas party for 350 elderly people.[46] Hoeger's concept was 10-15 years ahead of its time. In the early 1970s, federal and state governments finally realized the importance of the services that could be offered to senior citizens and began to underwrite such efforts. The federal government would call its "Johnny-come-late-ly" program an alternative to long term care.

Corona Boys' Home

August Hoeger, Sr., had one more chance to sanction an opportunity for the Society to work with troubled youth. In 1967, William G. Steiner of California appeared before the Society's Board of Directors to plead for the Society's support of a new approach to helping troubled and homeless boys, ages 11-18. For several years, Steiner had worked with California's juvenile courts, and he had been depressed by the lack of adequate treatment for these youths. He asked the Board if it would be interested in a new type of center, where boys could live together in a wholesome environment and secure the type of help needed to return them to normal community life. With the blessing of the General Superintendent and Executive Director, the Board responded to Steiner's request with a vote to develop a center along the lines that he had recommended. The main center for the youth program at Corona, California, was a former millionaire's mansion that had been used as a retirement home.

The Corona Boys' Home opened in 1967 with Steiner as administrator. Its primary purpose was to provide "a comprehensive rehabilitation program for boys who have emotional and adjustment problems."[47] The program provided positive group living experiences, including remedial academic education on the grounds, arts and crafts instruction, psychotherapy, group counseling, casework services, religious training, and moral guidance.[48]

An Interest in East Asia

Dad Hoeger had been a staunch supporter of overseas missions ever since his call to be a pastor on the North Dakota plains in the early 20th century. In the last years of his life, he involved the Good Samaritan Society in another overseas effort. He recommended that residents of homes be given the opportunity to contribute to a special project, a home in Hong Kong, through collections at worship services.[49] At the Society's annual meeting in August 1965, the Hong Kong project was approved, subject to study and action by the Board of Directors.[50] At a Board meeting the following February, Dr. Carl Becker suggested Vietnam as the location for a home. After investigation, it was decided that a home for the elderly would not be appropriate because East Asians were firm believers in the extended family. Becker's suggestion, however, had sparked Superintendent Hoeger's interest. At the time, full-scale war raged in Vietnam and the plight of orphaned children stirred his feeling of compassion and a belief that the Good Samaritan Society was called to do something about it.[51] In February 1967, Hoeger recommended that Reverend William Goldbeck, a former Air Force officer, go to Vietnam on a fact-finding mission for the Good Samaritan Society. Funds contributed by the Hastings Center and offerings from other centers subsidized Goldbeck's trip.

Goldbeck easily made contacts in Vietnam. Traveling extensively by helicopter and Air Force planes, he even visited sites near the demilitarized zone. He contacted representatives of the Christian Missionary Alliance, a primary purpose of his mission, explaining the Society and its interest in some type of service to the victims of the conflict.[52] Goldbeck made it clear to the Alliance that if the Society should eventually pull out of the venture, it wanted a Christian community in place to provide ongoing support. He reported to the Society's Board of Directors in June 1967, supplementing his comments with anecdotes and pictures. With the understanding that the Society would work through existing agencies and that only free-will offerings from the homes and individual contributions would fund the mission effort, Dad Hoeger drafted a letter to all of the Society's facilities on April 29, 1968, getting the Vietnam Project underway.[53]

On November 17, 1966, August Hoeger, Sr. spoke to the annual convention of the American Association for the Aging at Milwaukee, Wisconsin. Prior to his remarks, he had been given the Association's highest award — the Award of Honor — for his "creative and distinguished service to nonprofit homes." At the time, the Society had 105 Homes in 14 states. In his comments, Dad Hoeger responded to growing demands for racial integration in homes for the elderly. Noting that the federal government said that such homes must treat all races equally, he said that the Good Samaritan Society had been doing it for 20 years. Hoeger asked, "What is this Johnny-come-lately business?" The census of Society homes listed Indians, blacks, and Hispanics along with the predominant white population residing in the northern Prairie Plains states.[54] It was another evidence of his prescience and compassion for all human beings in need.

The concern for racial equality was only one of several issues being debated bitterly in the United States in the 1960s. American society was being pressured to change on several fronts; often this pressure took the form of mass demonstrations and violence in the streets. The Good Samaritan Society also underwent change in the 60s: a change in leadership and a change in management style. The Society's change, however, was peaceful and rational, accompanied by a continued growth in facilities and services.

Above: *August "Augie" Hoeger with "Dad" Hoeger.*

Left: *John Hoeger.*

"Dad Hoeger remained more than a figurehead in the Society throughout the 1960s. He continued to mold the direction of the Society. He still studied centers' balance sheets thoroughly, and he gave careful consideration to new building plans and remodeling projects. He constantly warned against making physical growth more important than spiritual growth."

Chapter Ten
TRANSITIONS
1960-1970

"Given the right employees, you can do anything." — *A Good Samaritan Society Administrator*

Americans entered the 1960s riding a wave of optimism. They enjoyed an economic boom, with steady growth, full employment, no inflation, balanced federal budgets, a rising standard of living, a low crime rate, and stable families. Yet, many of the country's citizens felt a deep sense of discontent and unease. Growing dissatisfaction, particularly among the young and racial minorities, bubbled beneath the surface of the country's social structure. Mounting discontent erupted into mass demonstrations and street violence as alienated groups attempted to disassemble public and corporate authority.

Elie Wiesel, in *The Fifth Son*, summed up the decade with the following words:

> Ideas and ideals, slogans and principles, rigid old systems and theories, anything linked to yesterday and yesterday's supposedly earthly paradise was rejected with rage and scorn. Suddenly children struck fear in their parents, students in their teachers.[1]

The 60s became a decade of movements: a free speech movement, a civil rights movement, and movements against traditional education and sexual mores. "Don't trust anyone over 30" and "Power to the People" became standard verbiage for those wanting to alter American society radically. Their adoption of a "hippie culture" and communal life was directed against what they perceived as the evils inherent in corporate capitalism. Discontent culminated in an overwhelming protest against the participation of the United States in the Vietnam War. American forces were fully committed to this struggle in 1964 by President

Lyndon B. Johnson. Johnson, who succeeded to the presidency in November 1963, after the assassination of John F. Kennedy, chose not to run for re-election in 1968 because of the bitter opposition to his Vietnam policy. It was this same President Johnson who had pushed his Great Society legislation through Congress in 1965. This landmark reform legislation had included the Medicare and Medicaid programs that would have a significant impact on the future of the Good Samaritan Society.

The Society, too, underwent considerable change during the 1960s. The changes were not as dramatic and traumatic as those taking place in the greater society, but they were very significant for the future of the organization. Dad Hoeger surrendered much of his executive authority after four decades of inspired and visionary leadership. Team leadership, fostered by August Hoeger, Jr., replaced individual leadership. In the ensuing years, the administrative structure of the Good Samaritan Society would undergo major change as it took on some of the characteristics of a modern corporation.

The growth of the Society resulted in an undeniable need for more management. August Hoeger, Sr., recognized that he could no longer oversee 68 facilities by himself. At a meeting of the Board of Directors at Omaha, Nebraska, in 1959, he first suggested procedures for choosing an Assistant Superintendent to eventually replace him as General Superintendent. A few weeks later, Hoeger recommended that a nominating committee be appointed to choose candidates, one of whom to be selected by ballot by the Society's membership at the next annual meeting. Following training sessions for a year or two with Doctor Hoeger, the Assistant Superintendent would succeed him. It was important, he stated, that "the Society should elect this man from among their membership as they would have to work for and with him in the future."[2] In the same year, two of the field men were relieved of their home administrator duties to become full-time regional directors; they were E. M. Mueller and E. H. Adams.[3] According to Eugene Hackler, he and his wife worked out the plan for regional directors in the basement of their home, and he presented it at the next Board meeting.[4] Bertha Bosch Christian supported Hackler's claim to being the proposer of the reorganization scheme and building moratorium.[5] Dad Hoeger reluctantly approved the use of regional directors because he believed their use implied a definitive hierarchical structure. The inclusion of another level of management was contrary to his standing principle that administrators should manage their own Society homes. His contacts with the field men and regional directors remained primarily by phone. When asking these men to check on the various facilities, new ideas often emerged from the conversations.

Throughout 1960, Superintendent Hoeger continued to handle the affairs of the Central Office by himself. One of the most laborious tasks each month continued to be the preparation of the Social Security statement. By the tenth of each month, each home remitted 3 percent of each worker's monthly wage along with a matching 3 percent. Hoeger totaled all of the tax and remitted it to the government within the next five days.[6] He maintained a positive attitude despite the growing burden of his office. In an addendum to his 1960 Christmas letter to his co-workers in the Society homes, he wrote, "Now 85 homes. Some fun. With cloth I weigh 145 pounds. Feel fine, thanks to Dr. Agnes. Keep looking up and enjoy yourself. Dad."[7]

The Society's membership never did elect an Assistant Superintendent. On December 27, 1960, in a letter to all home administrators, Dad Hoeger announced that he had appointed E. Hugh Adams as his assistant. In the same newsletter, he informed the administrators that the Board of Directors had increased the monthly dues of each facility from 50 cents to one dollar per bed per month. The increase in dues would be used to develop "new places and new ways to serve our old people."[8] Adams, who had first met Hoeger in Lenexa, Kansas, in 1952, would have his office at Salina, Kansas. He took over much of the Society's public relations work, publishing a monthly newsletter on a ditto machine. In addition, he functioned as regional director for Kansas, establishing several new Society homes in that state.[9] Home administrators had mixed feelings toward Adams. One person described the Assistant Superintendent, a former Marine, as a real Christian in the line of duty.[10] Another home manager was not impressed with the purchases Adams made for his facility. Adams, he said, preferred to buy high-priced furniture rather than the more practical pots, pans, plates, and kitchen sinks.[11]

By 1962, the Society had become too large for Reverend Hoeger and his Assistant Superintendent to manage effectively. Hoeger had taken the Society as far as possible with its prevailing administrative structure. Additional supervision was needed as some of the home administrators were not living up to the Society's requirements for competency and honesty. Board mem-

bers expressed concern over the poor handling of certain financial notes and the need for more equitable and business-like procedures. However, Hoeger's age and whether he could properly
handle the Society's affairs were never discussed at Board meetings. One Board member wrote to Dad's son, August Hoeger, Jr.,
asking Augie to tell his father to retire, suggesting that Dad
involve himself in the affairs of some local home.[12]

Augie Hoeger had been named president of the Good
Samaritan Society Board of Directors in 1959, after having
served on the Board for two years. At the time, he was chairman
of the Religion Department at Dana College at Blair, Nebraska.
During the summer months, he often traveled to various homes
with his father. Augie left Dana College in June 1960 to become
campus pastor at Mankato State University, Mankato, Minnesota.

At this time, the majority of the Society's growth was taking
place in the central and southern Plains' states. After careful
study by an Improvement Digest Committee, the Board of Directors decided to accept the committee's recommendation that the
Central Office be moved from Arthur to Sioux Falls. The Board
brought the recommendation to the floor of the annual meeting
at Sioux Falls between August 22-24, 1962. Three other sites,
Denver, Kansas City, and Omaha were recommended from the
floor. Viola Baugatz made such a persuasive presentation favoring Sioux Falls that the vote was almost unanimous for the
southeastern South Dakota city.[13] The Improvement Digest Committee advanced the following reasons for favoring Sioux Falls:
(1) The city was centrally located; (2) It was large enough to provide useful facilities and good transportation to the Society's
facilities; (3) There was the good possibility of the future construction of an office building on the Society's present property in
the city; and (4) It was located near several operations that
would be helpful in establishing a training school for administrators and other staff members.[14]

At the same annual meeting, Society members made other
important decisions concerning the administration of the Good
Samaritan Society. Because the Central Office staff consisted
only of Doctor Hoeger, Assistant Superintendent Adams, still
residing in Salina, Kansas, and a full-time office worker, the delegates voted to add staff according to need and available
finances. This was done with the caveat, undoubtedly expressed
by Dad Hoeger, that there be no "top heavy" administrative

structure. The assembly also agreed to establish uniform operations throughout the Society. Henceforth, there would be standardized forms for reports and records. The Central Office would
be the depository for all records of the Good Samaritan Society,
and the General Superintendent would be relieved of handling
the time consuming task of compiling Social Security and with-
holding tax data.[15]

Wanting to secure assistance for August Hoeger, Sr., as quick-
ly as possible, the Executive Committee of the Board met in
Sioux Falls on December 19, 1962. A motion was made by the
Board's vice president, Wallace J. Estenson, that August Hoeger,
Jr., be called to a full-time position in the Central Office at a
salary of $525 a month plus housing and car allowances totaling
$175 per month.[16] Approximately one month later, on January
16, 1963, the full Board met at the Sheraton-Cataract Hotel in
Sioux Falls with Estenson presiding. After Bertha Christian formally nominated August Hoeger, Jr., Board members voted to
call Augie to the Central Office as Administrative Assistant to
the General Superintendent, offering the financial conditions
outlined in the meeting of December 19.[17]

Four members of the Board of Directors came to August
Hoeger, Jr.s' home at Mankato one night just as he was getting
ready for bed. When they asked him if he would become his
father's assistant, he said no, stating that he enjoyed working
with young people at the university. After the members left,
Betty questioned his decision. She asked him how he could be so
callous toward his father's lifetime work. After much prayer and
lengthy discussion, Augie was persuaded to call Estenson. He
agreed to accept the position as Administrative Assistant for five
years.[18] Following his move to Sioux Falls, August Hoeger, Jr.,
would become the Executive Director of the Good Samaritan
Society in February 1963. At that time, the Society had 68 homes,
containing 3,000 beds. He and Dad Hoeger divided up the territory with Augie supervising the southern half while his father
administered the northern part, which included North Dakota,
where Dad Hoeger had been in the same synod and same conference for 55 years.[19]

Born on August 7, 1927, Augie Hoeger grew up at Fargo, North
Dakota. When he was 14, he began to drive for his father during
the summer months. He was also designated negotiator for Dad
Hoeger, who did not like to bargain but always wanted the lowest price for a hotel or motel room. When stopping for the night,

it was Augie's task to go to the prospective lodging's front desk and state that "We won't pay more than two dollars." If they could not get a room for that price, Dad ordered him to drive on to the next place.[20] Driving across the northern Prairie Plains with Superintendent Hoeger continued to be an act of faith as he never took care of his cars, neglecting oil changes and tune-ups and never checking the air pressure in the spare tire.

Augie had demonstrated his leadership abilities while attending Fargo Senior High School. He was president of the National Athletic Society, the band and the boy's glee club. He served as vice president of the orchestra and of the *a capella* choral group. In 1945, he was named representative student of the year. He lettered in basketball, football, and track. Weighing 185 pounds, Augie not only captained the football team but as an all-state quarterback led the team to the state high school championship.[21] Dad Hoeger thought it was okay for Augie to play football, but he and Amelia had misgivings about the brain concussion and broken bones their son incurred.[22]

August Hoeger, Jr., continued his football career at Concordia College, Moorhead, Minnesota, where he received a Bachelor of Arts degree in Psychology and Philosophy in 1949. He assumed administrative functions at the Good Samaritan homes at Parkston, South Dakota, and Olathe, Kansas, between 1949 and 1952. While at Olathe, he had completed work on a Master of Science degree in Clinical Psychology (1951) at the nearby University of Missouri in Kansas City. Continuing further graduate study at the University of Southern California, Los Angeles, he met Elizabeth (Betty) Helen Dahl, a young woman from Minnesota, who was a roommate of Augie's younger sister, Gertrude (Trude) Hoeger. Augie married Betty Dahl on February 23, 1952. Five children would be born to their marriage, three sons and two daughters.

Following his receipt of a Bachelor of Divinity degree from Wartburg Seminary in 1955, August Hoeger, Jr., served pastorates at Ankeny, Iowa, and Englewood, California. The latter call enabled him to do further graduate work at the University of Southern California. From Englewood, he had moved to Blair, Nebraska, in 1957, to be the head of the Religion Department at Dana College. Three years later, he had accepted the position of campus pastor at Mankato State University.

The Prairie Plains offered him a greater opportunity to pursue bird-watching, an avocation he shared with his father. He later served as president of the South Dakota Audubon Society.[23] In 1987, Augie ranked second among bird watchers in South Dakota for the number of different species he had seen. Tennis was another of his leisure-time pursuits. It was an activity that he and Betty enjoyed in Sioux Falls and during the winter months in Florida, following his retirement as president of the Society in 1987.

In the latter part of February 1963, the new Executive Director first located the Society's Central Office in the finished basement of his home on West 35th Street in Sioux Falls. Betty served as secretary and looked after the Society's affairs while Augie was on the road.[24] Along with Dad Hoeger, who resided in North Dakota, they were the Central Office staff as Hugh Adams resigned suddenly as Assistant Superintendent. He apparently believed he was in line to be the Executive Director and that the Board of Directors had aligned Augie against him.[25] Adams talked about starting his own nursing home business, but he was financially unable to do so.[26]

During his first three years as Executive Director, Augie spent seven out of eight days on the road. He had to take immediate action to correct conditions at several Homes. His management brought more order and structure for the firm development of the Society. Several administrators had created their own little kingdoms. They had taken unfair advantage of Dad Hoeger's elbow-room concept and his faith in them. In his first round of visiting homes, Augie immediately dismissed 17 administrators after hearing reports from staff people and local advisory boards of dishonesty or incompetence.[27] Dad Hoeger said that the behavior of these administrators was a source of disappointment and heartache. A repetition of this experience had to be prevented, and he counseled all Society workers to "watch and pray that you do not fall into temptation."[28] Fortunately, the inadequate administrators made up only a small number of the Society's employees; the majority of the administrators were giving their all for Good Samaritan Society.[29]

Dad Hoeger remained more than a figurehead in the Society throughout the 1960s. He continued to mold the direction of the Society. He still studied centers' balance sheets thoroughly, and he gave careful consideration to new building plans and remodeling projects. He constantly warned against making physical growth more important than spiritual growth. "If he was out to pasture," said Richard Gorsuch of Sioux Falls, "Dad still exercised a lot of muscle."[30] General Superintendent Hoeger always reminded the Board and the staff when they were considering monetary matters — "Now remember fellows, it is the people here that are important."[31] Dad Hoeger never shied away from offering opinions at annual meetings. He would present his view and Augie would often follow with an opposing view, providing a balanced presentation. Despite the differences of opinion, the Society continued to grow.[32]

A basic difference between the two men was in leadership style. Augie was more of a team player whereas his father was very often the sole decision maker. The new Executive Director set about forming a solid management team that stressed participatory management. Eventually, the team was composed of Central Office personnel, administrators, and Board members. In advancing the cause of the Society, he used "whatever energy, expertise, experience, and insights that were available."[33] He compensated for a lack of experience in business management by surrounding himself with good advisers.

One of the first people hired by Augie Hoeger was Colonel Charles E. Peterson, described by John Hoeger as the "ultimate organizational man."[34] Peterson, known to Society members as "Pete," had retired from the U. S. Air Force on August 31, 1963. He began his service in the Air Force in 1941, participating in World War II and the Korean War. At the close of his military career, Colonel Peterson was attached to Headquarters Strategic Command, working in the health care field, supervising 13 Air Force hospitals. Returning to Sioux Falls, where his parents resided, the 45-year-old Peterson applied for employment with the Society. Augie was immediately impressed with Pete and asked him to join the Good Samaritan staff on September 1, 1963. The Executive Director took Peterson to the Society's 1963 annual meeting at Fargo. Still wearing his Air Force uniform, Pete visited the Home at Arthur, where he pitched bundles and played horseshoes with the residents. He was very impressed with the work begun by Dad Hoeger four decades earlier. One vivid memory he had of the Arthur Home was a large wall poster which read, "Our Good Samaritan Home at Arthur, North Dakota, `A COLONY OF MERCY.'" The central figure on the poster was Christ at Gethsemane, with the question — "He did this for us; what are we doing for Him?"[35] Dad Hoeger became Peterson's tutor as they drove many miles together. Hoeger explained the modus operandi of the Society. He instructed Pete on how to sow the seed in a community and his basic criteria for choosing an administrator — "You should choose a person who has a love of God and His people."[36] At the dedication of a home, Hoeger always told the audience that the easiest part of the job was over, raising funds and finishing the building.

Charles Peterson began his work with the Society as regional director for the Southern Area in September 1963. His territory included Nebraska, Kansas, Oklahoma, Texas, and Colorado. He found the Society Homes to be a conglomerate of buildings, including old hospitals, mental institutions, a hotel, an Indian school, former military housing, and converted large houses. The Colonel discovered disturbing conditions in many homes. There was a need for paint, furniture, and draperies, and he encountered a host of plumbing problems. He discovered corruption and, on one occasion, neglect of duty. The administrator at one home had purchased a clothes dryer and a record player with the home's funds, and he had taken them with him when he left the facility. In another case, Pete discovered a 15-year-old girl was running a home while her mother was in the hospital.[37]

A great believer in efficiency and structure, Colonel Peterson, on September 25, 1963, sent a letter to administrators in his area requesting from each of them the following information:

1. A copy of a monthly report on the operations and financial conditions of the Home.
2. Periodic progress reports on a potential building program and/or expansion plans.
3. Expansion possibilities for the Society in adjoining communities.
4. Clippings on local publicity and promotion brochures.
5. Notification of actions taken or proposed by local or state officials which would affect the operation of the administrator's facility.
6. The administrator's suggestions for improving his operation.
7. The availability of qualified personnel who would be assets to the Society.[38]

At Augie's request, Peterson relocated from Hastings, Nebraska, to Sioux Falls ten months after joining the Good Samaritan Society. He served as regional director for Iowa and Minnesota for a short time before being named administrative assistant to the Executive Director. He was used to organization and functional charts with definite channels to follow. Pete was concerned that there was no budget procedure in place for facilities. In 1964, he developed the first budget system for the Society, and he managed it for approximately ten years.[39]

Colonel Peterson became the regional director for South Dakota in 1966. With Peterson's move to Sioux Falls, the Southern Area was divided between Harold Tompkin, an associate in an architectural firm at Lincoln, Nebraska, and the Reverend Henry Foege, who had been the administrator of a 70-bed nursing home at Waverly, Iowa.[40] Tompkin had charge of Homes in Colorado and Nebraska while Foege supervised facilities in Kansas, Oklahoma, and Texas.

After operating for about a year out of his basement, Augie moved the Central Office to an addition recently made to the Sioux Falls Center on North Minnesota Avenue. In June 1964, the office staff, aside from Augie, included Betty Hoeger, Colonel Peterson, Harold Tompkin, and June Baker, the Society's first full-time secretary.[41] Because they were often called on for advice, Eugene Hackler and Henry Foege were a part of the core group. For ten years or more, the entire Central Office executive staff met in the Executive Director's office, at least weekly, to talk about the issues and to come up with some sort of consensus. Augie Hoeger's emphasis on decisions arrived at through a democratic process by his administrative team proved successful. In the 1960s and 1970s, the Good Samaritan Society underwent its most dramatic growth; for a 15-year period, the Society added about 1,000 beds per year. This growth came primarily through the construction of homes that were in the 40-60-bed range.[42]

The new management style brought greater order and structure to the Society's development, and increased growth meant that the Society would have to be managed like a modern corporation. The increasing centralization of the Good Samaritan Society's operations was not accepted readily by some of the home administrators. Superintendent Hoeger's elbow-room concept was an individual affair. He carried the banner for the Society, and he trusted each administrator to follow the guidelines he had established. Under August Hoeger, Jr., elbow room came to mean each administrator carried out his duties but within defined boundaries, always taking into consideration his fellow team members and always willing to accept advice and recommendations from others.[43]

Augie stressed the importance of nurses' aides in the operation of any facility. Of all the employees in a facility, residents relied most on the aides because the residents were best acquainted with them. The irony of the situation was that the aides, so vital in resident care, under current law needed little training. The greater the distance from the bed, the more training that was required. Licensed practical nurses needed one or more years of specialized education; a registered nurse had advanced training for three to five years, while an administrator often needed more education. Given these circumstances, Hoeger said that administrators must provide a thorough orientation program for their aides, explaining all of the technicalities of their new obligation. During the training session, the administrator should emphasize the Society's philosophy of Christian care and concern for the worth and dignity of each resident.[44]

The Society might change but not its basic philosophy. A Philosophy Committee, composed of members of the Central Office staff, prepared a statement of principles in the early spring of 1966. The committee agreed that the cornerstone of the Good Samaritan Society remained the love of God through Jesus Christ. In response to the question, what makes the Society unique?, the Committee advanced eight basic reasons for its uniqueness. The Society's distinctiveness meant:

1. Sharing oneself, not being condescending.
2. Ministering to the total person, not a fraction.
3. Talking with people, not at them.
4. Not only a sermon, but a discussion.
5. Freedom spiritually, not habitual bondage.
6. Sharing one's hope, in Christ, not coercion.
7. Encountering life, not escaping from it.
8. An open honesty with our fellow man.[45]

While creating a new administrative structure, Augie Hoeger served actively on several national associations and boards. He was a part of President Lyndon Johnson's commission for the formulation of the entire Medicare program. Appointed to the Medical Assistance Advisory Council by Wilbur J. Cohen, the Secretary of Health, Education, and Welfare, Augie joined 20 other council members in providing advice to the federal government in its administration of the medical assistance programs authorized by Title XIX of the Social Security Act.

In January 1965, President Johnson had proposed a compulsory hospital insurance system for all persons over the age of 65.

Johnson's signature on amendments to the Social Security Act of 1935, which established the Medicare and Medicaid programs, culminated thirty years of Congressional debate on health care. The impetus for favorable legislative action came from a 1963 government survey which revealed that about half of the elderly in the United States had no health insurance. Title XVIII of the Social Security Act provided health insurance protection for persons aged 65 and over who were entitled to receive Social Security or Railroad retirement benefits. Part A, of Title XVIII, had some significance for the Good Samaritan Society since it provided hospital insurance for short-stay hospital care and limited post-hospital care in skilled nursing facilities and home health services. The hospital insurance was funded through the Social Security payroll tax.

Medicaid, established by Title XIX of the Social Security Act, contributed significantly to the Society's growth. Title XIX was a means-tested entitlement program, providing medical assistance to low income persons, including the aged. Medicaid was structured as a federal-state matching program, within which each state was to design and to administer its own requirements, set eligibility and coverage standards, and establish specific reimbursement policies. Under broad federal guidelines, states were required to cover care in a skilled nursing facility. Through the use of general revenues, Title XIX provided for grants to help states pay the medical expenses of the low-income elderly population.

The Society had to decide if it wanted to put any of its homes under the new entitlement programs; doing so would involve considerable modifications in facilities and the employment of more nurses to meet federal requirements for skilled nursing care. Following a decision to participate, Colonel Peterson issued Medicare Memo No. 1 on September 9, 1966.[46] Medicaid became the program of choice for the Society and other nursing home organizations. Some of the income from Medicaid's reimbursement program enabled the Society to construct and operate new facilities. The Good Samaritan Society could more readily assist communities who came to the Society to develop nursing homes in their localities.[47] In 1983, 60 percent of all nursing home charges in the United States were paid by Medicaid. Medicare paid an additional 7 percent. Three years later, in 1986, 55 percent of the census in the Society's nursing facilities was funded primarily through the Medicaid program. The remainder of the residents, including 5,000 apartments, were private pay.[48]

Funds for the construction of new facilities continued to be available through the Hill-Burton Act (1946). Changed to the Hill-Harris program, the competition for funds was vigorous by 1967. Standards were high, and not all of the Society's centers qualified for the program.[49] Funds for projects at centers, such as recreation, crafts and social services, became available through Title III, P.L. 8973, the Older Americans Act.[50] By turning to the government for funds, the centers faced mounting requirements for nursing homes. Dad Hoeger, of course, found this difficult to accept. August Hoeger, Jr., who had to deal with these requirements, commented that government regulations increased from almost nothing to utterly ridiculous proportions. In addition, construction costs had skyrocketed and expenses had exploded. Rates rose accordingly, from $2.00 per bed per month in 1963 to $4.00 per bed per month in April 1967.[51]

Government assistance was not the only reason for the growth of nursing home care in the 60s and 70s. The shift of population from farms to urban areas, creating limited living space, tended to discourage three generations living under the same roof. After studying the changing demographics, the Society decided to place more emphasis on constructing homes in larger urban areas. The increased mobility of families sometimes left the aged stranded in their home community. Finally, Americans were living longer because of better health care, diets, and working conditions.

Augie continued to assemble an efficient Central Office staff in the latter half of the 1960s. People were brought to the Sioux Falls office who would play key roles in the Society's development over the next two decades. Mrs. Nordiss Winge joined the staff on April 13, 1965. Over the next 18 years, she would serve as Executive Secretary, Assistant for Operations and Services, Director of Administrative Services, and Assistant to the President.[52] Harold Tompkin moved from Lincoln, Nebraska, to Sioux Falls to become an architectural consultant for the Society in the spring of 1965. Henry Foege assumed Tompkin's responsibilities as regional director for Nebraska.[53]

Several other key administrative decisions were made early in 1966. When Colonel Peterson was named Administrative Assistant to the Executive Director, Ray Conlon became the regional director for Iowa. Betty Hoeger, who had edited the Society's periodical, *Smoke Signals*, for three years, relinquished her position to P. A. Hendrickson, of Lennox, South Dakota, a former newspaperman.

Dad Hoeger was finally persuaded that centralized purchasing would be best for the Good Samaritan Society. From the Society's beginning in Arthur, he had always favored buying locally as much as possible. Augie sent a memo to the Board's Executive Committee, stating that the Society needed a full-time purchasing agent, who would also coordinate the shipment of supplies to the institution's facilities and supervise the setting up of equipment. Purchasing in bulk would mean considerable savings for the Society.[54] In August 1967, the Executive Director announced that Ken Harmon would be the purchasing agent.

A few administrators threatened to resign as the Central Office continued to move inexorably toward centralized accounting. These same administrators objected as well to the Society's move to insure its centers collectively. In the past, they had purchased their center's insurance from a local insurance agent.[55] The increasing amount of government regulation and the unprecedented move into the nursing home field by a number of national corporations necessitated closer direction of the Society's affairs. Fred Friedrichsen, the president of the Board of Directors, in his report for 1968, said the Directors would have to study each new project, as well as the entire operation, more carefully than in past years. Augie tempered the growing move toward centralized accounting by saying, "So let the cold statistics of this Report be warmed by the deeds of the love they represent."[56]

In recruiting key management people, the Executive Director tended to draw from the ranks of the Society. One exception was Robert J. Molgard, who served briefly as controller, beginning on March 1, 1968. Within the next four months, Erwin Chell, a former missionary to India and more recently the administrator of the Bonell Center, was named purchasing agent. Ray Conlon joined the Central Office staff as the new center (project) developer.[57] Chell became the Society's "adaptable man." As of November 1, 1968, he took charge of the insurance program and the other responsibilities of the controller. When plans were made for a new headquarters building that would house a complete computer department, Chell began training to direct that department. Conlon, in turn, became Director of Development and Purchasing.[58] Two other appointments, one representing the

Society's progression toward a modern corporate structure, and the other representing the Society's heritage, completed August Hoeger, Jr.'s management team as of 1970. John Rude was placed in charge of recruiting personnel, the training of new employees, and the preparation of appropriate manuals and forms. However, Augie made the final decision in the selection of an administrator after a lengthy interview. The Society established a training procedure for new administrators which included an internship in a center for two months.[59] Rude also became the Public Relations director for the Good Samaritan Society. The Reverend Calvin Berg had fulfilled this function along with being a regional director. With the growing emphasis on multi-culturalism in American society, Rude made visits to the ghetto areas in Chicago and Kansas City to explore the possibility of new projects for the care of the elderly.

Dad Hoeger wanted a reaffirmation of the Society's spiritual dimension, and to that end, he proposed a Spiritual Uplift Program. He wanted evidence of what a center was doing in a community. To carry out this objective, on November 15, 1968, the Board named the Reverend John Kilde as the Spiritual Adviser for Good Samaritan centers in South Dakota.[60] In addition, he would serve as chaplain at the Sioux Falls Center. Kilde would review, evaluate, and develop the spiritual ministry in each facility.[61] Dad Hoeger encouraged other states to emulate South Dakota.[62] He emphasized that the greatest needs of the residents continued to be emotional, social, and spiritual needs. Nursing care was not enough. Quality care could not be given by people who did not care.[63] Responding to vehement opposition to the way the program was being conducted, the Board of Directors voted, in late June 1970, to discontinue the Spiritual Uplift Program; the idea, nevertheless, was not dead.[64] Seven years later, the concept was revived in a different form when the Reverend Jacob Jerstad became Director of Spiritual Ministries.[65]

Augie and Betty Hoeger experienced a welcome change of pace during the summer of 1969 when they traveled to Western Europe and visited several sites that cared for the aged and for the physically and mentally impaired. Two German locations that were a part of the heritage of the Good Samaritan Society were on the itinerary. They visited Neuendettelsau, from which the founders of the Iowa Synod had come, and which was the departure site for 200 missionaries to New Guinea. The Hoegers spent time as well at the Bethel Institute at Bielefeld, a center providing activities and therapy for epileptics and the mentally impaired. Several of the world's leading authorities on epilepsy resided in Bielefeld. Their visits to care centers took the Hoegers as far north as Oslo, Norway.[66]

Before the Hoegers departed for Europe, the Board of Directors had engaged in preliminary planning for a new Central Office building. The Board wanted the regional directors to have their offices in the national headquarters. New quarters would be needed to house them and the growing management team. The Directors wondered whether some other urban center would be better located for the regional people to carry out their work.[67] After considering Denver, Kansas City, Minneapolis, and Omaha, the Executive Committee of the Board agreed that the Central Office should remain in Sioux Falls. In mid-April 1969, a building committee, composed of Wallace J. Estenson, Albert Hanson, and Walter Person from the Board and Calvin Berg, Erwin Chell, Ray C. Conlon, and Charles E. Peterson from the Central Office staff, began to examine possible sites for the new structure.[68] A month later, the Board's Executive Committee approved the building committee's proposal to purchase five lots on the east side of West Avenue North in Sioux Falls for $86,100.[69] During the 1969 annual meeting, the committee displayed sketches of the proposed new headquarters plus a detailed floor plan. Delegates learned that a computer, to be obtained through a leasing arrangement, would be incorporated into the new building. The Central Office staff was authorized to borrow up to $350,000 for the building project.[70]

The dedication ceremony for the new headquarters at 1000 West Avenue North took place during the 1970 annual meeting. The delegates had an opportunity to view the new data processing center. Dad Hoeger gave the opening devotion. During the three-day meeting, he presented what turned out to be his last report as General Superintendent. He told the assembly to "Look up to the Cross and find the value of your work."[71]

By this time, the Good Samaritan Society had a new logo or official emblem for use in or outside its facilities. Augie had asked one of his former colleagues at Dana College, Reverend F. W. "Bill" Thomsen, a native of Denmark and the chairman of the Art Department, to design the emblem.[72] The symbol contains a cross at the foot of which Christ is kneeling to pick "up a victim along life's road." Christ's purpose was to make the person "whole and set him on the way." The logo called on Society members to kneel and serve others and Christ. Christ helped each person and each person should help another. According to John Hoeger, the emblem represented a Society "staff member helping a resident, a volunteer helping a resident, a resident helping a resident; a resident helping a staff member .... each serving the other with joy."[73]

Dad Hoeger, at age 83, continued to carry out his duties as General Superintendent. In 1968, he was the principal speaker at every one of the Society's center dedications. He drove thousands of miles to visit centers, even flying additional miles, something he said he would not have done at age 81. Hoeger did give up the regional directorship in North Dakota as he moved to the Village at Hastings, Nebraska. From his new residence, he continued to be interested in the Helpers' Club, the Vietnam Project, and the overall religious and spiritual conditions of the Society.[74] During the 1968 annual meeting, on August 13, a "This Is Your Life" program was staged on the occasion of the 60th anniversary of Dad Hoeger's ordination. Among the people present was Fred Knautz, and the two former adversaries conversed on a social basis for the first time since the split in 1940.[75]

The founder of the Good Samaritan Society died suddenly on Thursday morning, October 8, 1970, at Hastings, Nebraska. As usual, he was active up to the moment of his death. On Monday, hammer in hand, he had worked with others in the construction of a prayer chapel at Hastings Village.[76] A resident held the nails while Hoeger, with one arm disabled, pounded in the nails with a one-clawed hammer.[77] The next day he participated in a funeral service, delivering a discourse on the Twenty-Third Psalm. He rode to the cemetery with the mortician and asked him what the cost would be for conveying a body to Arthur North Dakota. Hoeger felt the mortician's charge, ten cents per mile, was reasonable.[78] Dad had indicated his desire to be buried at Arthur on his last trip to Arthur Day the preceding month. Speaking to a group in the dining room, he turned around and said, "Well, Hoeger is going to die some day. He'll be buried over there behind the trees. I don't want you to be sorrowful about this. I want you to be happy, because I am going to be with my Maker."[79]

Hoeger had attended mid-week worship services on Wednesday; Reverend Goldbeck had delivered the sermon. The General Superintendent was in the midst of preparation for a trip to Brainerd, Minnesota, where he planned to dedicate a center on October 11. On Thursday morning, after purchasing groceries and taking clothes to the dry cleaners, he returned home and collapsed in the bathroom at approximately 11:30 p.m.[80] In an announcement to Society members, Augie Hoeger said, "This was the day he [Dad] had prayed for and even eagerly anticipated his whole life."[81]

A plain man with a deep faith had passed from the scene. "His emphasis had always been on the individual with no thought of personal glory; he always sought to give care in a manner that would preserve the dignity and pride of the receiver.[82] "Funeral services were held in All Saints Chapel at the Hastings Good Samaritan Village on October 12. Two of his closest friends, the Reverend William Goldbeck and the Reverend Henry Foege, assisted with the service. Interment took place at the Good Samaritan Center Cemetery at Arthur, North Dakota.

Dad Hoeger believed nothing was impossible when the Lord guided and directed one's life. His philosophy was that all one needed to do was to tell the Lord, "I'll go where you want me to go. I'll be what you want me to be." Russell Cox, a Sioux Falls columnist, wrote:

> I've never met a more sincere, more dedicated
> man in my life than Dad Hoeger. Nor have I met
> anyone who had such a profound understanding
> of the meaning of the word we call love. Nor have
> I ever been acquainted with any individual who
> had a more unshakable faith in God.[83]

August Hoeger, Sr., had a remarkable ability to transmit his faith and vision to the thousands of men and women who associated with him in the work of the Good Samaritan Society. A poet once wrote — "They are not dead who live in lives they leave behind. In those whom they have blessed they live a life again." The people entrusted with carrying on his legacy, the Good Samaritan Society, did not falter.

In the years following his death, the Society continued to grow and to increase its services to the elderly, remembering and practicing Hoeger's firm conviction that "the one thing every old person really needs and wants is love. We all want to be loved. And that's the most important difference between a Good Samaritan Home and many others."[84]

Transitions can be difficult, be they individual, institutional, or societal. In contrast to what was occurring politically and

socially on the national scene during the 1960s, the Good
Samaritan Society moved ahead in a positive and peaceful manner. Augie Hoeger, with little training in business administration, had put together a management team, which because of the
Society's growth, found it necessary to introduce certain aspects
of a modern corporate structure. At the same time, he maintained the spiritual and philosophic integrity emphasized by his
father.

Chapter Eleven
MINISTRIES BEYOND THE CENTERS' WALLS
1970-1995

*"Whatever your task, work hearti-
ly,... as you are serving the Lord."* —
Colossians 3: 23-24.

*We give thee but thine own,
Whate'er the gift may be;
All that we have is thine alone,
A trust, O Lord, from thee.*[1]

The first verse of John Montgomery Bell's familiar 19th century hymn speaks to the Good Samaritan Society's mission
efforts during the 1970s and 80s. By 1970, the Society was
in a position to bring Christ's healing balm to troubled people
outside of its centers for the aged in the nation's heartland. Outreach programs were initiated to provide physical and spiritual
succor for people in war-ravaged South Vietnam, overpopulated
and poverty stricken Bangladesh, the inner city of Chicago,
urban California, and the rural population of the Prairie Plains.
Not since the 1920s, when Dad Hoeger worked tirelessly for the
Iowa Synod's (ALC) involvement in overseas and inner mission
work, had the Good Samaritan Society entered into a mission
effort of the magnitude that it did in the late 1960s and early
1970s.

Project Vietnam

It took almost three years of careful planning and investigation for the Good Samaritan Society to establish an overseas mission project in Southeast Asia. This was the third mission effort
undertaken by Dad Hoeger. During his first years in the ministry, he had helped begin the Iowa Synod's participation in a
Lutheran mission at Papua, New Guinea. At a later date, he
played a decisive role in founding the Lutheran Orient Mission,
an outreach to the Muslim Kurds of Iraq. Dad Hoeger now envi-

sioned a home for the elderly in Hong Kong which would be a place of refuge for those fleeing Communist China with no worldly goods. The funds for such a venture would be obtained through the Sunday worship service offerings at the Society's growing number of facilities (See Chapter Nine).[2] His attention shifted to Vietnam when military hostilities in that country escalated after 1964.

In March 1966, August Hoeger, Jr., the Society's Executive Director, communicated with different agencies in Washington, D.C., via Senator George McGovern (SD), soliciting informed views regarding the wisdom of such an undertaking. The East Asian experts all agreed that the care of the elderly was, historically, a family responsibility. An official of the Agency for International Development stated that the "family group prohibits the placement of elders in nursing homes." He went on to say that orphanages in Vietnam did need help.[3] Augie Hoeger quickly solicited the views of several center administrators and residents and found that they were interested in the Vietnam orphanage project.[4]

Reverend William Goldbeck, who developed a consuming interest in such a project, established a Vietnam Committee at Good Samaritan Hastings Village, Hastings, Nebraska. Gaining approval from the Society, Goldbeck flew to Vietnam on March 14, 1967. It was his task to do the research and ground work for a proposed child care center among the war-ravaged people of that nation. When Goldbeck reported to the Board of Directors in the latter part of June, he recommended that the Society support a parochial school in the Mekong Delta area of South Vietnam and a refugee project in the capital city of Saigon. In his report, Goldbeck said:

> It should not be taken lightly that for many years Dr. Hoeger was led to believe that the Good Samaritan Society should have a mission arm reaching out to a far distant land.
>
> Such a conviction, we believe, was God given and we doubt that there can be found a justifiable Christian reason for failing to join in this effort....[5]

The Board decided to create its own Vietnam Committee which would meet with the Hastings Village Vietnam Committee before the Directors' next meeting in August.[6] The Vietnam Committee from Hastings included Reverend and Mrs. Goldbeck, Reverend Henry Foege, and Reverend John Hoeger. Chosen from the Board for the Vietnam project were David Brewer, Erv Chell, and Eugene Hackler. Five people from the two committees were to be chosen to serve on a permanent Project Vietnam Committee with Dad Hoeger to be a permanent member of the committee.

The formal constitution and by-laws that were drafted as the Society entered into this venture indicated its significance. The constitution began with the following words:

> NAME: Project Vietnam and Other Overseas Missions shall be the name of the overseas arm of The Evangelical Lutheran Good Samaritan Society.

> OBJECT: It shall begin with child care projects in Vietnam but may from time to time be altered and expanded by the membership of the Society.

Project Vietnam would be directed by a five member committee with the General Superintendent or Executive Director being an *ex-officio* member. The committee would be responsible to the Board of Directors through the Executive Director. Center administrators were asked to organize a local committee of not less than three members who would organize themselves to develop the most effective ways for creating a desirable atmosphere for the promotion of Project Vietnam.[7]

Project Vietnam created some controversy and opposition. The American public was divided regarding the participation of U. S. military forces in the Southeast Asian conflict. In an effort to make the Society's venture non-political, the Board of Directors, on November 20, 1967, passed a resolution which stated that "If further politics are discussed, all fund raising will be stopped and no further money will be allocated for Vietnam."[8] Some administrators objected to the undertaking because they thought resident contributions should be used only in the community. The success of Project Vietnam also depended on how supportive a regional director was of the program.[9] Dad Hoeger responded to

those administrators who opposed the project because they
believed it was wrong to ask the elderly for a donation. Hoeger
compared worship services at a center to worship services in a
church — people expected the offering plate. He further noted
that Project Vietnam had been approved at the annual meeting
of the Society.[10] In a longer than usual letter to the administrators, he wrote about his aim in life. Regarding the Society's role
in Vietnam, he said:

> Just to pray the Lord's Prayer "Thy Kingdom
> Come" and then do nothing - that is not God's
> way.... I can not do all these things myself and
> that was never my aim in life: just to see how
> much I could do. But my aim is to see how many
> people I can get interested in building God's
> Kingdom, this is also why you are an adminis-
> trator. You also should try to see how many peo-
> ple you can get interested in building God's King-
> dom.[11]

For five years, Reverend William Goldbeck dedicated his
boundless talents and energy to directing the Society's efforts to
help Vietnamese children. As project director, he worked with
each Society center upon approval of the regional director and
the local administrators. He spoke fervently for the project, and
he and his wife distributed posters and coin banks as they commuted from one center to another. By January 1970, the funds
derived from Sunday chapel offerings by member centers and
supportive private gifts enabled the Society to send between
$2000 and $2,500 a month to assist Vietnamese children. The
funds supported three schools, including the Freedom Village
School, located in a Saigon suburb; the Cholon Gospel Chapel at
Cantho, the largest city on the Mekong Delta; and a school in the
Phu Tho Hao area. In mid-1970, 581 children attended the three
schools. When they came each day to their respective sites of
learning, they received academic instruction, some food, occasional clothing and most important — Gospel teaching. Goldbeck
told the 1970 annual convention of the Good Samaritan Society:
"We are convinced that this has been, and is, a most effective
ministry, and an expeditious use of gifts dedicated to the Lord's
work."[12]

Nineteen months earlier, the Project Vietnam Committee had decided that a person from the Good Samaritan Society should be sent as a site supervisor and worker to Saigon. Dad Hoeger and Henry Foege brought the Committee's proposal to the Board of Directors on November 15, 1968.[13] Rather than send a member of the Society to Saigon, Good Samaritan officials, in the summer of 1969, contacted the World Relief Commission, Inc. (WRC) to administer and direct Project Vietnam. Delegates to the 1970 annual convention approved associating with WRC, "believing that time and distance made it difficult to make the necessary judgment for growth and expansion of work in Vietnam." The World Relief Commission was the overseas relief arm of the National Association of Evangelicals, non-denominational in service and interdenominational in fellowship. It had become a nationally recognized conduit for churches and organizations wanting to provide aid to people who experienced the ravages of war, disease, poverty, and illiteracy.[14] The WRC had begun its work in 1944, during World War II. Using the slogan "Food for the body and food for the soul," WRC provided a channel from the "haves" to the "have nots." Through educational and technical assistance, the World Relief Commission prepared refugees to become self-supporting and to assume leadership roles with the expectation that these victims of political and social tragedy would eventually be able to return to their home areas.[15] Beginning in 1971, and for the next four years, the Society's Central Office maintained an official relationship with Dr. Everett S. Graffam, the Executive Vice President of WRC.

One of the new facilities supported by Project Vietnam through its working relationship with WRC was the Hao Khanh Children's Hospital, located north of Danang. Using their own money, U. S. Marines from the Third Division, in cooperation with Navy Seabees, had built the hospital and turned it over to the World Relief Commission on June 7, 1969. The modern 120-bed hospital was one of the largest medical facilities of its kind in Southeast Asia. Over 100 children a day received medical and surgical care at Hao Khanh.[16] Funds from the Society's centers were used to purchase medical bandages, drugs, food, clothing and blankets for the hospital.[17] Desiring a first-hand report of work at the hospital, Reverend and Mrs. Frank Wilcox, on leave in the United States from their missionary post in Nepal, agreed to the Society's request to visit the hospital on their return trip to Nepal. After visiting the Hao Khanh facility between August

15-20, 1972, they reported back to the Central Office via pictures and tape recordings.

Funds from Project Vietnam likewise went to support the Bao Ank Orphanage at Dalat, a facility dedicated by the World Relief Commission in May 1971. At Dalat, 60 Montagnard boys were "taught the Gospel of love and saving grace" plus a trade they could use later in life. This emphasis upon serving "the needs of the whole person — body, soul and spirit" fit the vision brought to reality by Dad Hoeger five decades earlier at Arthur and at the Good Samaritan Institute in Fargo.[18]

In the early fall of 1972, Reverend Goldbeck and his wife withdrew as leaders of Project Vietnam, going on to assume other responsibilities in the Society's work. From its inception, they had directed the Project, putting in thousands of hours of work at no cost to the Project and almost singlehandedly keeping the Project at the forefront of the Society's attention.[19] The Goldbecks requested that the Central Office take over the entire operation and that John Hoeger become the director of Project Vietnam.

John Hoeger had been a member of the original Vietnam Committee at Hastings Village, and he continued to be a vigorous supporter of the Project and of the Society's relationship with WRC until military and political conditions forced the termination of the program in 1975. Delegates to the 1972 annual meeting of the Society were told that the "...Project Vietnam ... mission resulted from the obedience of Dad Hoeger to the Spirit's prompting, that the Good Samaritan Society would be true to its image in reaching even to the children who had fallen victims of war."[20] In his response to the financial assistance given by a member of the Society to the projects of the WRC in Vietnam, Everett Graffam, on January 7, 1975, wrote to thank her for her interest and help "through the wonderful administrative help of the Good Samaritan Society, and particularly Dr.[sic] John Hoeger, who for many years has been a dear friend and keenly interested in the work at the hospital and the various projects WRC has in that needy country [Vietnam]."[21]

A series of military reverses, the corruptness of the South Vietnamese government, and a growing lack of support for the war in the United States led to the withdrawal of American forces from Vietnam and the triumph of the Marxist government of North Vietnam. On March 26, 1975, John Hoeger asked Graffam if he had any news concerning the Hao Khanh Hospital.[22] Graffam had ordered the evacuation of the American staff in

Vietnam, commenting that there were 60 qualified Vietnamese Christians, members of the Christian Youth Social Service, on the hospital staff.[23] The capture of the hospital and Danang by the Viet Cong and the North Vietnamese Army on March 30, 1975, occurred shortly after it had been turned over to the Christian Youth Social Service.[24]

Project Vietnam came to an abrupt end when Communist forces captured Saigon on April 30, 1975. The end came to this worthy project after seven years of striving to better the conditions of innocent victims of war, particularly children. Like a center forced to close because of a declining census or limited finances, Project Vietnam had ministered to the bodily and spiritual needs of God's people during its period of service. At the Hao Khanh Children's Hospital, over one-quarter million child care days (in and out-patient) had been provided since the hospital was built. In the spring of 1975, up to 40 children a month were becoming Christians. From 1970 to 1975, WRC assistance to Vietnam totaled over $6 million.[25] Although only one-third of the Good Samaritan centers supported Project Vietnam, it was still possible to send at least $2,000 each month to Vietnam to relieve the suffering.[26] Ninety-two cents out of every dollar went directly to the places of need described earlier, a statistic which indicated the integrity of the program.[27]

As the American military and political situation declined in South Vietnam, the Good Samaritan Society began looking for another overseas mission program. The General Director of the World Mission Prayer League (WMPL), an independent Lutheran Missionary Society, directed the Society's attention to the great needs of the people in Bangladesh, a small state on the Asian subcontinent. Bangladesh, an over-populated country, suffered from recurring wars, violence, and monsoon floods. WMPL planned to build a 50-bed hospital and a chain of dispensaries to serve 1.2 million people having no medical resources. In addition, WMPL intended to bring the Gospel to Islamic Bangla-desh.[28] When the Good Samaritan Society decided to support the Bangladesh program, Project Outreach was born.

Project Outreach

Delegates to the 1974 annual meeting of the Good Samaritan Society voted to support the World Mission Prayer League's project in Bangladesh, in addition to Project Vietnam.[29] With the conquest of South Vietnam by the Communist North Vietnamese in the spring of 1975, Society members grew more interested in the Bangladesh mission effort. When they gathered for their annual meeting in the following year, the offering was designated for medical assistance to the newly founded state.[30] Bangladesh was only three years old when the Society began its support of mission work in the northwestern section of that country. Prior to 1946, the new republic had been a part of India before the Indians gained their freedom from Great Britain. From 1946 to 1971, what is now called Bangladesh was known as East Pakistan. Located in what was once eastern India, Bangladesh faced on the Bay of Bengal. Excessive population had become its nemesis as approximately 66 million people resided within a 55,134 square mile area.

On September 11, 1975, Reverend John Hoeger informed Everett S. Graffam, Executive Director of the World Relief Commission, that, henceforth, offerings from the participating Society centers would be designated for the Bangladesh Project.[31] The WMPL had broken ground for a hospital six months earlier. The medical facility was to be located approximately two miles from the city of Parbatipur. The World Mission Prayer League planned to establish a series of dispensaries within a five mile radius of the hospital. There were over a million people living in that area who were not served by any medical facility. The Society's first intent was to direct its donations to the hospital. The title given to the over-all project was LAMB (Lutheran Aid to Medicine in Bangladesh).[32]

Following the groundbreaking ceremony for the hospital, WMPL officials emphasized the repair and building of a seven-mile road that would connect the LAMB Project with the one major highway that wound through Bangladesh.[33] There were no bulldozers, cranes, or cement mixers, and without machines, the road project took time. Red bricks were smashed to make gravel. The construction project provided "work for food" for 55 heads of families who built the road by hand; it was estimated that 400 people were able to eat because of the wages earned by these men, who had no other means of livelihood.[34] A huge well was sunk at the proposed hospital site which would supply adequate water for the medical facility.

In 1976, the Good Samaritan Society contributed $20,000 to the Bangladesh project. While the hospital was being constructed, the Board of Directors decided to support a related project, the purchase of a van that would function as a mobile clinic in providing medical help for the thousands of people who lived in small villages outside of Parbatipur. Starvation and malnutrition were prevalent in many of the villages, compounding immediate health care needs.[35] In addition to providing medical care, the personnel in the mobile clinic were to accumulate data on the needs of the people, to teach public health and preventive medicine, and to preach the Gospel. The van needed for this work did not arrive in Bangladesh until late September 1979, after which the mobile clinic went into operation. In the late 1970s, the number of centers contributing to Project Outreach in Bangladesh fluctuated between 51 and 84.[36] Frank Wilcox, Director for Spiritual Ministries, reported to the Society's Board of Directors, in August 1984 that the LAMB Hospital had finally opened for a full medical ministry. The hospital's goal was to establish a holistic health program, promoting health understanding, care and cure. In 1992, the hospital served 350 patients a day.

During its August 12-15, 1984, meeting, the Board of Directors approved a second Outreach program — a non-denominational World Hunger Program that would divide money equally between World Vision and Bread for the World.[37] Bread for the World, based in Washington, D.C., had as its goal to educate the Congress on hunger issues — when considering legislation, Congressmen should take seriously the needs of hungry people around the world. World Vision was a child care sponsorship program. For $24 a month, a person or group could provide the basic necessities of life for one particularly needy child. World Vision similarly directed other programs that tried to provide food, clothing, and medical care for poor people around the world.

The Society had its largest outpouring of gifts for Project Outreach in 1987. The centers participating in the Project, approximately 25 percent, gave a total of $33,250. LAMB Hospital in Bangladesh received $19,692.00 of that amount.[38] In 1995, monies given to Project Outreach totaled over $31,000 with over three-fifths of that amount going to LAMB Hospital.[39] The need in poverty-stricken Bangladesh had not diminished. A staff member at the Hospital, Diane Krueger, reported:

> Life is just harder to get through each day. The poverty is more extreme, illness and disease often more deadly. Yet, the differences are not always so vast. The hopelessness and futility peo-

ple live with may seem to me more evident here
— but it is the same in the States. No, I don't
think knowing Jesus as Lord and Savior will
make the floods stop, or bring mechanized equipment here or even make the homes bigger. I do
know that knowing Jesus as Lord and Savior will
remove hopelessness and futility.

Krueger went on to thank the Society for its regular gifts for
LAMB Hospital, stating that "Your generosity allows us to serve
so many more poor patients without financial means. It is also
such an encouragement to all of us here, knowing your gift is
given with many prayers."[40] Dad Hoeger's strong personal vision
of an overseas mission for the Society had been fulfilled as the
organization prepared to enter the 21st century. Project Outreach was a success. Under the supervision of the Director for
Spiritual Ministries, it had become an integral part of the
Society's dedication to providing physical and spiritual care for
the needy.

Christian Action Ministry

A growing awareness of the plight of racial minorities, in the
aftermath of the civil rights movement of the 1960s, induced the
Society's Board of Directors, in June 1970, to mandate the establishment of a nursing home in an inner-city area.[41] Adhering to
the Board's request, the following inquiry was addressed to pastors of churches in cities containing a sizeable minority population — Chicago, Denver, Kansas City, and Omaha — by the Central Office staff:

... Our Executive Board is very interested in having more information on the "inner city" and its
needs, especially in the area of health care with
the thought that we might in some way serve a
part of these needs.[42]

A response came from Christian Action Ministry (CAM), a
church-sponsored organization in Chicago's westside black community. Located in a densely populated section of the "Windy
City," 150,000 people in a two mile area, CAM was attempting to
serve the needs of a district in which one-third of the families

were unemployed and/or on welfare. Christian Action Ministry had begun its work in 1965 when fourteen churches, representing six denominations, banded together in an attempt to build a workable community. In five years, CAM had made significant progress in education, housing, black business, employment, day care, and youth programs.[43]

Four members of CAM came to Sioux Falls in November 1970 to meet with the Society's Board of Directors. The CAM representatives explained their plans for constructing a new medical facility, and they wondered if Christian Action Ministry and the Good Samaritan Society could work together in developing the project. Their proposed Center for Human Development would include a 225-bed nursing home, a medical clinic, and a day care center. At its next meeting in March 1971, the Board recommended that CAM contact appropriate government and private funding agencies to seek grants for the proposed center. If the monies were secured, it would permit the Chicago based group to own the facility and the Society to serve as management consultants for the proposed project.[44]

Christian Action Ministry, having no experience in operating a nursing home, wanted the Good Samaritan Society to assume this task because the Society best exemplified what was wanted in terms of quality, loving, and financially viable care for elderly, long-term patients. On July 27, 1971, the Society entered into an agreement with Christian Action Ministry whereby the Society would assist in the development of a design for the center, furnish consultative services for all phases of the operation and otherwise assist CAM in preparing a feasible scheme of operations. The two parties agreed that if the project was not completed, the Society would expect no reimbursement from CAM for the assistance provided by the Central Office.[45]

Executive Director Augie Hoeger sent David Walters, Wayne Muth, John Rude, and Les Kleeb to Chicago to visit the proposed site of the Center for Human Development in late September 1971. The Society task force first met with Pastor David Nelson of Bethel Lutheran Church, one of the 14 congregations supporting CAM. The four men also met with David's sister, Mary Nelson, who was Program Coordinator for CAM. At the time, she was a strong supporter of the building project and five years later she had become the Director of Development and Planning for CAM. The task force recommended that the Society continue its involvement in the development of the center.[46]

The Central Office staff and the Board watched with great interest as CAM launched a $5.4 million fund drive for the new facility in the mid-1970s. As the monies came in, including a $1.2 million Hill-Burton grant, the Good Samaritan Board of Directors reaffirmed its pledge to use the Society's expertise in helping select and train an administrator and other key staff for the inner city nursing home.[47] The Board also loaned CAM $250,000 toward the building project with the assurance that the loan would be repaid in conjunction with a minimal management fee over a seven-year period.[48] When the Society sent the money to CAM in the spring of 1977, the Society had already commenced training an administrator for the projected Chicago home.[49]

A formal management and consulting agreement had been signed the previous month, on March 3, 1977. Christian Action Ministry appointed the Good Samaritan Society as its full and exclusive managing agent for the nursing home, starting January 1, 1978. For its services, the Society agreed to charge only $2,000 per annum. CAM reserved the right to hire all of the personnel for the nursing home, including the administrator and department heads. The Good Samaritan Society, however, was responsible for the direct supervision of the forenamed employees according to the five-year agreement. The Society would provide up to one year's training for the administrator and up to six months for an assistant administrator, sharing the costs with Christian Action Ministry. During the management term, CAM retained the right to hire and discharge employees but with the concurrence of the Society if the administrator was involved.[50]

Midway through the construction of the Center for Human Development, Mary Nelson, the Director of Development and Planning, informed John Hoeger, on April 20, 1978, that she was resigning after 13 years of service to Christian Action Ministry.[51] She had become critical of the actions of several of her CAM administrative colleagues, and there is evidence that she was "eased out" of her position. A project which had gone along well when Mary Nelson was playing a leadership role began to go bad.[52]

Approximately two months later, the congregation where her brother had served as pastor, Bethel Lutheran Church, by unanimous vote, gave notice that it was withdrawing from CAM on June 30, 1978. The deteriorating situation within CAM's administration was revealed in the reasons that Bethel cited for withdrawing from the denominational support group. Bethel accused CAM of:

1. A lack of moral integrity necessary in a Christian organization
2. Unfair personnel practices which rewarded friendship instead of performance
3. Questionable financial arrangements resulting in personal profits
4. A management structure which avoided dealing with problems and issues instead of solving them.[53]

The Good Samaritan Society continued to provide complete managerial assistance for the 225-bed skilled care nursing home then under construction. The Society remained committed to helping the inner city elderly and to providing the best conditions possible for these deprived individuals. John Hoeger, Executive Vice President of the Society, spoke at the ribbon cutting ceremony and dedication of CAM's Center for Human Development on November 4, 1979.[54] He recalled that it was a unique speaking experience for him. The frequent interruptions of amen and hallelujah from the audience gave him more than adequate time to collect his thoughts.[55]

Less than two years after the dedication ceremony, Christian Action Ministry took action to remove the Good Samaritan Society from its managerial role. In a letter to Al Brown, Regional Director, and August Hoeger, Jr., the Executive Director, CAM administrators requested the termination of the management contract as of June 30, 1981. The CAM officials said that closer "hands on" professional supervision of CAM by local experts in the nursing home field was necessary if the center was to become self-sustaining in the shortest possible time.[56]

Following a year and a half of negotiations, CAM, which had filed for bankruptcy in 1982, agreed to pay the Society $42,000 in full and final settlement of the $250,000 advance that the Society made to the Chicago based group at the time the Center for Human Development was constructed.[57] Meeting on February 18-19, 1983, the Society's Board of Directors, attempting to salvage what they could from an almost impossible situation, agreed to write off $200,000 of the $242,000 CAM still owed the Society.[58]

What began as a valiant and humane effort ended in tragedy. In late July 1983, four elderly patients at the Chicago nursing home died during a heat wave because of a lack of proper air conditioning. CAM officials had known for several months that the cooling system needed repair but took no action. Immediately following the tragedy, local and state health authorities charged the nursing home with 113 code violations. The home was shuttered and the 190-plus residents were transferred to other nursing home facilities in the Chicago area. Seven officials of CAM and the Center for Human Development, including the Executive Director and the administrator of the nursing home, were indicted by local authorities.[59]

The tragic situation could have been avoided if the Society had been permitted to manage the home and to evaluate the competency of the administrator and the staff. Unfortunately, the Good Samaritan Society was barred from ensuring that the home met licensure standards as of the summer of 1981. CAM officials lacked the necessary fiscal and management skills to carry out the plan they conceived in the early 1970s.[60]

The failure of the inner city project was not the fault of the Society. The restrictions built into the agreements with CAM made it impossible for Society personnel to provide the expertise, integrity, care, and compassion needed to make the project work. In all other situations, the Good Samaritan Society successfully cared for elderly, minority people in its nursing care and independent living Centers — be they the Chippewas of northern Minnesota or the Navajo of the American Southwest, Chicanos in Texas, blacks in a variety of urban settings, or East Asians in Hawaii. Dad Hoeger's conviction and practice that the Society must show compassion for ALL human beings in need continues to be a basic part of its credo as the Society looks forward to the 21st century.

Corona Boys' Home

The Corona Boys' Home, which opened in October 1967, had a very successful beginning. On March 1, 1968, less than six months after its founding, the home was filled to capacity. Described by a state supervisor as the finest child-care home in California, the Corona facility, initially housed 42 boys.[61] Within another three years, the program served 110 boys at six different locations throughout the state. The boys were referred to the Society by the State of California's Welfare and Probation departments. Eighty percent of the youngsters came from homes broken by death, divorce, or desertion. Many of the boys had been abused, neglected, and/or unloved.

No boy was accepted who was considered a serious delinquent. Many of the young residents at Corona had histories of truancy, academic failure, incorrigibility and emotional problems. They came from all economic backgrounds, and they represented all races and religions. Under the supervision of a competent staff of counselors, teachers, and social workers, efforts were made to help the boys learn to trust adults, gain confidence in themselves, and learn more acceptable ways of dealing with their problems.[62] Boys who fell behind in their education were prepared for public school through small enrollment, remedial classes, tutoring, and other means of individualized instruction.

The Society and William Steiner, the Executive Director of the Corona Boys' Home, soon introduced group homes to avoid two problems often associated with growing up in larger institutions — becoming excessively dependent and institutionalized. The group or residential home helped to bridge the gap between institutional care and the return to community life. While the main campus at Corona remained the center of operations and the residence of the younger boys, group homes were established in Corona, El Cajon, Danville, Fair Oaks, Riverside, and Upland, California.[63] The boys were placed in residential homes according to their age. Several homes served boys between 12 and 15 years of age while other residential sites met the needs of youths 16-18. The group homes for the older youngsters were designed to prepare them for freedom and independent living. They attended public schools, held part-time jobs, and were an integral part of the community.

Adjacent to each of the residential homes was a small cottage where the older boys could reside if their counselors believed they could handle increased privileges and responsibilities. The cottage dwellers purchased their own food, prepared their own meals, cleaned their quarters, shopped for their own clothes, and arranged for their own medical appointments. Although the program was designed to create self-sufficiency, boys needing help could turn to the counselor who lived next door. For many of the young men referred to the Society's California Boys' Home complex, the transition back into the general community was made easier through the "half-way home" experience.[64]

Ironically, when the California Boys' Home reached a new enrollment height in 1973, 160 youths in eleven facilities, it began to experience financial difficulties. Executive Director Augie Hoeger told the Board of Directors that the California enterprise was no longer self-supporting because of cutbacks in welfare and increased expenses. The ten group homes remained financially sound but expenses at the headquarters in Corona exceeded income.[65]

Concluding that the spiritual dimension of the California facilities needed strengthening, the Good Samaritan Society, in the summer of 1977, decided to use a portion of the Project Outreach funds to support a chaplaincy program for the California youth centers. By this time, the 11 youth homes had spread over a 650 mile radius and were serving 220 young people between the ages of six and 18.[66]

A conservative mood in the United States during the 1970s contributed to Corona's financial problems. One of the conservatives' goals was to reduce radically the welfare system. An elderly Californian, Howard Jarvis, became nationally recognized when he successfully led a petition drive to place a radical tax reduction measure, Proposition 13, on the California ballot. California voters approved Proposition 13 in June 1978. The tax cutting referendum reduced the state's property tax 57 percent, and it resulted in stringent limits on state spending for social programs, including financial assistance to homes caring for boys with emotional and social problems.

Enactment of Proposition 13 increased the financial problems of the Corona facility. Reimbursement was frozen for two years at the same time that standards of care were increased. Reverend August Hoeger, Jr., recommended that the Society's continued involvement in California be decided within the next two years.[67] The situation at Corona worsened in the fall of 1979 when Steiner resigned and a replacement was not readily available. In addition, the State of California refused to renew the Society's license unless the dormitory at the main facility was renovated.[68] The Menninger Foundation, of Topeka, Kansas, agreed to evaluate the work at Corona and to recommend if the Society's work should continue in the Golden State. In their report, the Menninger people said the work being done at the Corona Center was of historic proportions and urged its continuance.[69]

The Society's Board of Directors decided in February 1980 to operate the headquarters at Corona for one year under the close scrutiny of personnel from the Central Office.[70] A year later, Augie Hoeger recommended that only the main campus at Corona be retained by the Society. Three of the group homes in the Sacramento area were put up for sale.[71]

Vinton Bruflat, a regional director for the Society, prepared a detailed report in early December 1982 on the deteriorating situation in California. His report emphasized the financial and spiritual conditions in the California Boys' Home Ministry. The State of California refused to pay totally for the delinquent and emotionally troubled youth under its jurisdiction. It paid approximately 90 percent of the expenses incurred by a facility. Worse yet, the State's rates as of July 1981 were frozen, and social workers throughout California predicted that there would be no rate increase through July 1984.

Bruflat did not find a strong spiritual presence in the homes. The Christian ministry came primarily through the administrator and the 20 hours per month of the chaplaincy. Christian leadership was strongest in the northern California homes where the home supervisors were more inclined to apply Christian principles to everyday life. Bruflat concluded: "The Christian thread throughout the total program at Corona was not that strong."[72]

Two days after Board members received Bruflat's report, they decided to continue the Boys' Home endeavor only until another acceptable organization or organizations could assume operations, including the debt load, or other uses were found for the facility.[73] Fifteen agencies expressed an interest in taking over the California homes, the real estate having been appraised at $2 million. The Society's accountants determined that if the properties were sold for $1,200,000, the Society would not have expended any money on the Corona homes.[74] In early June 1983, the Board accepted an offer of $1,115,000 from the Guadalupe Home for Boys, Inc., for the facilities at Corona and Sacramento.[75]

The sale ended the Good Samaritan Society's 60 years of work with youth. The work had taken many forms — working with mentally impaired youth at Arthur, physically handicapped youth at the Good Samaritan Institute in Fargo, young men with social and emotional problems at the Mapleton Boys' Ranch and the California Boys' Home Ministry as well as economically and socially deprived youngsters at the Jim River Ranch. Many of the young people who were cared for, counseled, and taught in these various facilities became constructive and contributing members of society in their adult years. Through the actions of the Good Samaritan Society, they had been nourished intellectually, physically, and spiritually.

DOAS and Senior Companions

The Good Samaritan Society, as part of its Fiftieth Anniversary observance, developed a bold new outreach ministry on the Prairie Plains. Beginning in 1971, Executive Director Augie Hoeger said that the major emphasis for the year would be the outreach of the Society's centers into the community. Eight years earlier, Dad Hoeger had advanced this concept. The time was ripe for its implementation.[76]

This new ministry began to take shape when Hoeger announced that the Good Samaritan Society and Lutheran Social Services of South Dakota (LSS) planned to sponsor jointly a special outreach program to assist communities in providing services to the retired and the elderly in their homes. The program would initially focus on southeastern South Dakota and adjacent communities in Iowa and Minnesota. Eduard (Ed) Kilen, a social worker with Lutheran Social Services, directed the program. Kilen had graduated from Augustana College with a composite major in the Social Sciences and a minor in Education. He went on to receive a Master's degree in Social Work from the University of Minnesota, after which he worked for two years with Family Service of St. Paul, Minnesota. Returning to South Dakota, he joined Lutheran Social Services and also taught Social Work courses for four years at Augustana College.[77]

Augie Hoeger and Colonel Charles Peterson, a member of the board of LSS, brought the idea of home health services and "Meals on Wheels" for the elderly to Lutheran Social Services. The proposed ministry was enthusiastically embraced by Oliver Bergland and Milton Erickson from LSS. It was agreed that Kilen would be located at the headquarters of the Good Samaritan Society. He was asked to establish a program that would assist communities in the development of services to people in their own homes that would enable them to enjoy a happy, healthy, and more productive retirement.

Ed Kilen assigned himself six objectives as he undertook the pilot project for the Development of Adult Services (DOAS). He proposed:

1. To develop services for the elderly in the community.
2. To bring the community's elderly to the Society's centers.
3. To deal with the being [the Spirit] in the body.
4. To train people to work with the elderly in the community.
5. To prepare training and resource materials.
6. To seek grants to expand service to the elderly.[78]

Two programs, with similar objectives, emerged from the planning that took place in 1971-1972. DOAS, fulfilling Dad Hoeger's proposals of the early 1960s, became a Society-wide program in 1973. The guidelines for DOAS called for retirement and care centers to "help persons deal with the problems of age, illness, disability, family relationships, and spiritual life — the needs of the entire person." The Aging Services Center, under the aegis of the Good Samaritan Society, became a pilot program in southeastern South Dakota. Kilen secured a three-year planning grant from the South Dakota Office of Adult Services and Aging. The federal government finally recognized the value of proposals advanced by Dad Hoeger almost a decade earlier. With Title III funds in hand, the Society established the forenamed Aging Services Center at the Central Office in Sioux Falls. The center served Region II, six counties in the southeastern corner of the state, coordinating services for the elderly.

A crucial part of the latter program was recruiting and training volunteers. Kilen developed a specific methodology in recruiting people for the project in the first pilot communities, Parkston, Tripp, and Centerville, South Dakota. He asked Good Samaritan Society Center administrators to call an organizational meeting. In advance of the meeting, administrators were requested to tell Kilen what organizations there were in the community — such as churches, service clubs, and senior centers. Two representatives from every organization were invited to the meeting. If the community had a National Guard unit, delegates from that organization were deemed essential because the Guard could provide invaluable service during severe winter weather.

Using a pyramidal approach, assembled representatives formed sub-committees and selected a six-person steering committee, which included two members at large, a secretary, treasurer, and co-chairs. Kilen found through experience that a person more readily accepted a leadership position if there was someone else to share the responsibility. It became the responsibility of the committee members to tap the volunteer pool, members of the various community groups, to conduct the program. In organizing a community, Kilen carried certain essential items to each meeting: newsprint, marking pens and a polaroid camera. He always asked the steering committee to remain after the meeting, took their picture, and placed it along with a story on the program in the local paper. He discovered that this kind of public exposure made it difficult for people to renege on their prior commitment.

Federal officials were so impressed with this organizing procedure that they asked if it could be used as a model in other regions of the country. The Society's center administrators were invaluable to the project's success. They not only developed community contacts and encouraged local participation, but they also served as liaison people between the particular community and the Aging Services Center in Sioux Falls.[79]

The Good Samaritan Society took the lead in two other outreach programs — Life Enrichment for the Elderly (LEE) and Senior Companions. In 1974-75, the Aging Services Center, in partnership with Lutheran Social Services of South Dakota, participated in LEE, funded by the Lutheran Brotherhood Insurance Company. The primary objective of the LEE program was to identify and meet the needs of southeastern South Dakota's elderly. The success of the program depended upon the involvement of community people, including pastors, nursing home staffs, business people and senior citizens.[80]

The other major outreach program of the Aging Services Center was the Senior Companion Program. The program began in September 1978 following the receipt of a grant from ACTION, the federal agency for volunteer service. Senior Companions agreed to work with the elderly in hospitals, rest homes or private residences, the primary emphasis being on helping older people to remain in their own homes. To be a senior companion, a person had to be over 60 years of age and interested in working with the elderly. Volunteers underwent 40 hours of orientation, monthly inservice sessions, and refresher courses. They received tax-free compensation, reimbursement for transportation, on-the-job accident insurance, and a free physical examination.[81]

The Senior Companions became a part of a client's care team, providing social support, assistance with personal home management, and a link to community services. Kilen decided that the Aging Services Center should emphasize nutrition and transportation programs in Region II. He asked Fern Chamberlain, a coordinator for Region II, to do research and collect statistical data on the need for a nutrition program for the elderly in the southeastern sector of South Dakota. She found that prior census data had missed many elderly people in rural areas, particularly in the area northwest of Sioux Falls. The result was the creation of an entirely rural Meals on Wheels program. At noon during the week, the parking area at West Nidaros Lutheran Church, located in the countryside a few miles north of Sioux Falls, was filled with cars as the Senior Center at the church carried out the rural nutrition program. The Good Samaritan Society decided to opt out of the nutrition program because of its many other obligations to research, outreach and service, and the responsibility for the Meals on Wheels program was assumed by senior centers in the region.[82]

After its inception in 1978, the Senior Companion Program continued to grow because of changing social conditions and health care policies. The number of people ages 85 or older increased yearly. Their family members with job obligations were unable to provide these seniors with the necessary daily living assistance they required, and economic factors and changes in the national health care system similarly increased the need for home care.

The Society's sponsorship of the Aging Services Center provided firm footing for the type of community outreach program envisioned by Dad Hoeger. The Senior Companion Program became an integral part of the Good Samaritan Society. Nathan R. Koehler, a graduate of Augustana College (Sioux Falls), became executive director of the program in the 1980s. As a result of the DOAS and Senior Companion programs, the needs of the entire person were met through the following services — Meals on Wheels, special dietary services, in-home services (handyman assistance, health service, and homemaker service), telephone reassurance, visitation and volunteer programs, transportation, the senior center as a home away from home, spiritual guidance and solace, and employment opportunities for seniors involved in the Senior Companion Program.

Saigon, Parbatipur, Chicago, Corona, and West Nidaros were geographical locations often discussed in Society circles as the Good Samaritan Society, with commitment and ingenuity, widened the scope of its mission activities in the 1970s. The staffs of the Central Office and the Society's growing number of centers, along with the residents of many of these centers, became "Good Samaritans" on a national and world-wide scale as they brought material aid and the Gospel message to thousands of people victimized by war, poverty, dysfunctional social units, or loneliness. Ideological and political forces prevented the Society from continuing its mission in some of the locations noted above. Project Outreach, however, continued to flourish on the international level, and the Society's Adult Services and Senior Companion programs continued to carry out the plan conceived by Dad Hoeger in the early 1960s. The Society in the post-World War II years had been blessed with considerable success, and, in turn, it had responded with a mission program that had enhanced Kingdom work in several parts of the globe.

May we thy bounties thus
As stewards true receive,
And gladly as thou blessest us,
To thee our first fruits give.[83]

Chapter Twelve
EQUIPPING THE SAINTS
1970-1989

"God does all the healing,; healing
is an essential part of His plan for
salvation, not just a byproduct. God is
the healer, we are the enablers."
— Rev. August J. Hoeger, Jr.

On December 12, 1986, August Hoeger, Jr., asked to be relieved of the Good Samaritan presidency at the annual meeting in 1987.[1] During his 25 years at the helm, the Society had experienced remarkable growth. At the close of 1962, the Society had 68 facilities with a residential capacity of 3,000 people. Under Augie Hoeger's leadership, the Society had become the largest nonprofit, long-term care organization in the United States. It included over 200 facilities, caring for 24,000 residents in 26 states. The growth of the Society necessitated the creation of a modern corporate structure to better serve the residents and staff of the various centers. In 1987, the Central Office of the Society housed comprehensive accounting and data processing services and the necessary consulting and support personnel to carry out the Good Samaritan ministry.[2] In the last months of Augie's administration, the Society formally affiliated with the American Lutheran Church and the Lutheran Church in America, becoming an arm of the Church in long-term care.

In leading the Good Samaritan Society to new heights, Augie always kept the mission and guidelines, established by his father, in the forefront. The soft-spoken Executive Director went about his task quietly. He used teamwork in "Equipping the Saints." Emphasis was placed on the selection of quality personnel, structure, technology, the development of expertise, and the preparation of forms and manuals to assist the administrators and thousands of staff people in the centers to better care for the residents in their trust. What had been accomplished took its toll in energy and time away from the family. At the end of 1969, Augie stated that his work for the year had necessitated 64,000 miles of air travel and 40,000 car miles in the 163 days he was out of the office visiting one center after another.[3] During the 80s, he listened to taped books while traveling to each of the 200 facilities that he visited at least once every three years.

For the most part, the work was enjoyable. There were, however, a number of administrative "headaches." One of the most vexing and longstanding problems, concerning the facility at Mason City, Iowa, was not resolved until the summer of 1970. The Society's interest in Mason City had begun 24 years earlier, in February 1946, when Dad Hoeger met with five area pastors to discuss the purchase of an unfinished building originally intended to be a hospital. Construction of St. Luke's Hospital had begun in 1923. Because of the depressed economy, the 100-bed structure had never been completed. With only three floors finished, the building stood vacant for 20 years.

In the summer of 1946, Hoeger returned to Mason City and began negotiations with the current owner of the proposed hospital. Dad asked one question before he began to bargain with the owner. "Do you pray?" he asked the man. The latter replied, "Sure, I'm a praying man!" The Society purchased the building for $20,000 with no down payment. Hoeger agreed to make improvements each year and to pay $1,000 annually toward the debt.[4]

John Hoeger had accompanied his father on the summer trip to Mason City. John felt the former owner had been thrilled to get rid of a giant-sized lemon. That night, John could not sleep, wondering where the money would come from to complete the building and who would operate it. His father, however, no more than two minutes after he had gone to bed, began to snore; he was sound asleep. John later surmised that the two minutes were for prayer, perhaps a simple little prayer — "Lord, you take care of the details. Amen."[5] Upon his return to Fargo, the General Superintendent opened his mail and found a $5,000 check. A woman from Illinois had surrendered her farm to help the elderly. In her accompanying letter, she wrote that "she did not need all this money and that it should be put to a good cause." A few days later, Hoeger received $3,000 from a person in California.[6]

Through the efforts of the Society, the building, which had been a vacant eyesore, opened as a nursing home on December 8, 1946. From the beginning, there were problems. Rev. E. M. Mueller, the administrator of the Mason City facility and, for a time, an Assistant Superintendent of the Society, often took the initiative in establishing new facilities without consulting Dad Hoeger or the Board of Directors.[7] In addition, the Mason City Home had been incorporated separately. The Society owned the Home but never managed or operated it. The facility had always been managed by a local corporation, composed of area Lutheran churches.

In the spring of 1958, the Mason City corporation ran afoul of the Society's Board of Directors when the Mason City group attempted to secure a loan of $250,000, using the property as collateral to obtain the money. It was quickly indicated to them that the legal owner of the property was the Good Samaritan Society.[8] The separate corporation was also an embarrassment to the Society in a more public way. The Central Office received many complaints regarding the Mason City Home from staff, residents, relatives, and State of Iowa health officials. The Society was powerless to correct deficiencies because the local board would always overrule them.[9]

In 1962, the Society decided to take steps to disassociate itself from the Mason City operation. As of April 7, 1962, the board of the Mason City Home accepted Rev. Mueller's resignation.[10] By December 1962, the Society's Board of Directors had made a gift of approximately $1 million in assets (the home and surrounding land) to the local Mason City board. In February 1963, the facility was incorporated locally under the ownership of the Lutheran churches in that area of Iowa. To ensure that the local board did not make a personal profit from the gift and turn it into a proprietary home, the Good Samaritan Society insisted on holding continuous membership on the board with veto power to see that this did not happen. For awhile, Dr. Carl Becker was the Society's representative on the Mason City board.[11]

Augie Hoeger used the services of Eugene Hackler, the Society's legal counsel, to move things along. On April 19, 1965, Hackler sent a Quit Claim Deed and two Special Warranty Deeds to an attorney at Mason City.[12] Less than two months later, on June 9, 1965, Articles of Incorporation were filed with the Secretary of State of Iowa, which changed the name of the Mason City Home to the Good Shepherd Geriatric Center, Inc. By the summer of 1970, the American Lutheran Church asked the Society to relinquish its membership on the Mason City board. The Executive Director breathed a sigh of relief when the Society's Board of Directors, in late June 1970, approved a motion to relinquish all claim, votes, and authority over the Mason City facility. The Good Samaritan Society surrendered all claims when word was received from the American Lutheran Church that the Good Shepherd Geriatric Center had been accepted by the ALC.[13]

Adding to the Executive Director's concerns, the Good Samaritan Society navigated some stormy financial waters during the 1970s and 1980s. The Golden Age of American capitalism came to an end in the early 70s. Real per capita income in the United States had grown at 2.25 percent per year between 1950 and 1970. Real (in terms of purchasing power) average weekly wages peaked in 1973 at $308.03 (1982 dollars). By 1991, these wages had fallen to $260.37, a decline of 15.5 percent. The post-World War II economic boom came to an end with the Arab oil embargo beginning October 6, 1973. The Organization of Petroleum Exporting Countries (OPEC) enacted the embargo to pressure Americans into taking a pro-Arab stance as Egypt and Syria engaged in a war against Israel. The American population, which had grown up on cheap, abundant energy, had made no effort to conserve its energy resources. By the fall of 1973, the country imported one-third of its oil supplies.

Although most of OPEC's members lifted the embargo in March 1974, oil prices remained high, rising 350 percent between January 1973 and January 1974. The boost in the price of imported oil reverberated throughout the entire economy. It drove up both inflation and unemployment, inflation increasing to a frightening 13.4 percent in 1979. Inflation eventually came under control as the federal government reduced spending and the Federal Reserve Board raised interest rates. Unemployment, however, reached 10.2 percent in the early 80s, with many workers being laid-off in the ailing "smokestack industries" — auto, steel and rubber. In 1981-1982, the nation experienced the most severe of nine recessions since World War II.

The recession was particularly hard on the original heartland of the Good Samaritan Society. Easy credit in the latter half of the 1970s caused many farmers to borrow more money than they could afford for farm land, expensive machinery and irrigation equipment. The nation's farm debt in 1971, $54.4 billion, soared to $165.8 billion at the end of the decade. Drought conditions in the late 70s, low commodity prices, and burdensome debt incurred at high interest rates compelled many farmers of the Prairie Plains to file for bankruptcy or to lose their property through mortgage foreclosures and farm auctions during the 80s.

Financing the Saints

Throughout this era of economic turbulence, the Good Samaritan Society quietly continued to grow. Augie Hoeger, as Executive Director, set no limits as to size; the Society, he said, would grow in accordance with needs.[14] The Society, nevertheless, responded to the economic realities of the time. It continued to adhere to a set ratio of 60-40 of assets to maximum indebtedness, the ratio having been suggested by a home administrator at an annual meeting. In the summer of 1973, the Society changed from bed dues ($4 per bed per month) to a percentage based on the operating income of a Society center. The Board of Directors decided a percentage basis would be more equitable. On July 20, 1973, the Board said that dues and accounting would be computed at 2 percent with the proportionate share charged to accounting to be increased to perhaps one-half that amount.[15] Within four years, the percentage required from each local center's operating income increased to 2.25 percent. The Central Office pointed out that similar organizations charged from 6 to 12 percent. One percent of the operating income paid for accounting, data processing, a computerized payroll system, and other services that contributed to the financial health of the centers. The remaining 1.25 percent provided each center with guidance from a regional director and consulting services that included spiritual ministries, social services, in-service education, printing, purchasing, community relations, construction, fund development and management.[16]

The Society decided that a fund raiser must be employed to ensure that adequate funds would be available for a long-range program. Claiming that he was too old, a reluctant Reverend Henry Foege, the regional director for Nebraska, accepted the position in February 1973. By the end of the year, Foege, one of the Society's most committed workers and a close friend of Dad Hoeger, had died from a heart attack.[17] In the fall of 1975, Clinton Gehring was appointed Director of Fund Development, working in areas where the Good Samaritan Society had existing facilities and assisting in the development of continuing contribution programs.[18] Gehring's appointment followed a lower profit margin in 1974 because of price controls, rapid inflation, and an increase in minimum wages.

The Society felt the full brunt of the nation's economic problems beginning in the late 1970s. Because of inadequate reimbursement from state Medicaid programs and census problems, money was tight at several facilities. Reverend John Hoeger, the Society's Associate Director since 1972, urged centers to put some monies away for leaner years.[19] On June 30, 1978, 52 facilities showed deficits in their accounts. Ten of these facilities had failed to meet their budgets by $30,000 or more.[20]

With the speed of its expansion limited by financial considerations, the Society sought a formula to guide its growth. The Society's borrowing potential was limited; each added facility had to stand on its own financial feet. The Society's Development Committee, attempting to ensure that new facilities operated in the black, increased the requirements for new construction. Dad Hoeger had believed that if a community was committed and involved in the planning in bringing a new center into being, it could not fail. In the mid-70s, the Society required a community to raise funds equalling 30 percent of the anticipated project cost and to provide an approved site of at least five acres (preferably ten to 15 acres) with utilities located within five feet of the proposed building.[21] The Development Committee, desiring adequate funds in the face of the inflationary times, stipulated that start-up money for new construction be increased from $1,000 to $2,000 per bed.[22]

Cooperating with the federal government's attempt to cool an overheated economy, the Society, in 1979, announced that it would do less in construction and concentrate more on managing centers. State legislators, particularly in states where agriculture was a dominant industry, sought new sources of revenue, and they began to question The Evangelical Lutheran Good Samaritan Society's status as a nonprofit corporation.[23] It became John Hoeger's task to explain to these covetous legislators what was involved in being a nonprofit organization. He repeated, time and again, that the Society was not organized for making a profit as an end in itself. No financial gain went to any individual and no individual could receive an excessive salary. The excess income over expenses was used for the benefit of residents, as a margin of safety in the event of a loss of income or unusual expenses, and as a growth factor. It was easier for the Society to secure loans if it could prove that it had the ability to operate with a comfortable financial margin.[24]

The Hoeger brothers expressed their concerns to these same legislators about the reductions in Medicaid payments at the same time that operating costs at centers continued to rise. Costs for both skilled care and intermediate care exceeded welfare payments in the early 1980s. Facing possible Medicaid cuts in the future, the Society in June 1981 reactivated its Resource Development Department. Reverend Raymond Mehl, the Director of Development and Public Relations at Waldorf College, Forest City, Iowa, became the Good Samaritan Society Director for Resource Development.[25] When employing Mehl, Augie Hoeger said that the Society must maintain a strong financial base; it was as much the organization's Christian responsibility as the care it gave.[26]

Practicing good stewardship, the Good Samaritan Society managed to maintain a positive financial balance in the early stages of the recession of 1981-1982. The total equity of the Society increased in excess of $14 million in 1982.[27] Nevertheless, the chairman of the Board of Directors, A. Robert Langemo, continued to express caution. With the slowdown in the economy, the Board put all major expansion plans on hold until the bond market improved and the economy showed signs of recovery. Because of skyrocketing costs and drastic reductions in operational income, all components of the Society had to trim their budgets to meet the challenge.[28]

During the remainder of the decade, the Good Samaritan Society expanded at a cautious and conservative rate. Operational costs continued to rise because of new services to residents and persistent inflation. A shortage of labor in certain areas of the country, particularly trained nurses, caused Society officials to re-evaluate the wage scale. Most significant, strained state budgets resulted in below-cost medical reimbursements for over half of the Society's residents.[29]

In 1988, the Society's new president, Reverend John Hoeger, recommended that the organization hold back on expansion and concentrate on upgrading services to the 200-plus facilities. Emphasis would be placed on providing highly skilled care, securing more sophisticated rehabilitative equipment, and upgrading data processing equipment and software.[30] The Board of Directors increased the dues to 3 percent of the operating income of each facility.[31] Although the debt load was reduced, John Hoeger reported that the Society incurred a deficit in its net operating income during 1988. With the Society "skating on thin ice," he recommended that operating costs be lowered by 2 percent, and he provided guidelines for a cost containment program. For a short while, it appeared that the extension of the Society's ministry was grinding to a halt as the banking world said "no" to financing new projects.[32]

In 1989, the labor costs for the Society approximated 60 percent but over a decade and a half, the cost of Central Office operations had increased only minimally. In 1972, the cost of the Central Office as a percentage of the total costs of the Society was 1.8 percent. In 1988, the cost was 2.26 percent. Much of the increase had related to updating the Society's computer technology. Other increases were attributed to a rise in architectural fees, maintenance, printing costs, and the employment of additional specialists.[33]

The nursing home industry had become highly competitive, particularly in the "Sun Belt" and on the West Coast. Given this competition, the Society marketed its concept of retirement living — the Good Samaritan Society provided a quality of life not found in the competition's homes. Dr. Mark Jerstad, at the time the Society's Vice President for Operations, said that the Society's mission to give quality care would never be compromised despite the pressures of finance, meagre reimbursement for care given, staff shortages, and the increasing burden of workers' compensation costs.[34]

In meeting the ongoing financial challenge, the Central Office requested that all facilities participate in Medicare Part B and be certified for Part A. Such certification would provide a significant new source of income by reimbursing overhead costs not captured in the Medicaid program. It also allowed facilities to attract private paying residents who would benefit by having a portion of their care paid for under the Medicare program.[35]

By the beginning of the 90s, the Good Samaritan Society had successfully weathered the financial storm that first struck the nation in 1973 and which intensified during the 1980s. The challenges had been met through good stewardship, efficiency, prudence, and prayer. The very size of the Society, its purchasing power, specialists, and its many friends, contributed to its stability. Despite the financial "belt tightening," quality had not been sacrificed.[36] Collectively, "The knock was a boost" for the Society as its services to the needy increased and additional facilities joined in the mission begun at Arthur in 1922.

Serving the Saints

An increase in services to residents via center administrators and staffs meant an increase in Central Office personnel. Described by one longtime staff person as "a tremendous personnel man," Augie Hoeger had begun putting together a team in 1963 to guide the destinies of the Good Samaritan Society.[37] With a dedicated, caring style of leadership and an open display of his faith, he became a role model for the Society's employees. Ray Conlon, a member of the Central Office staff in the 1960s, said that the Executive Director had a knack for being liked. The staff did not always agree with him, and sometimes they complained, but they were always ready to defend him.[38]

Michael O. Bice, the president of Lutheran Health Systems (the former LHHS), Fargo, North Dakota, described August Hoeger, Jr., as a quiet visionary who led by example. His faith was unshakable and a wonder to behold. Bice went on to say, "I've learned more about people and the nature of our organizations than I can ever repay. Indeed, he [Augie] is my mentor."[39] Hoeger selected people for his team who could work independently within and for the Society's philosophy and mission. He was described as sometimes being cautious with talented people in giving them management opportunities that they wanted, but over all he had more acceptance of independent and aggressive talent than most chief executives.[40] A few staff people felt that he was too gentle, but no one denied his courage. One observer noted that Augie's most courageous move had been to assume the helm of the Good Samaritan Society.[41]

Two people made up the administrative team when Augie assumed the helm in 1963, he and his wife, Betty. They were soon joined by Colonel Charles "Pete" Peterson. The Society's new Executive Director became aware of Peterson's availability through a visitation pastor who had called at the Bennie Peterson home in Sioux Falls. Their son, Charles, recently retired from the U.S. Air Force, was home for a visit. Pete was looking for continued work in health care, and he wondered if Augie would be interested in him. Needless to say, the Good Samaritan Society's Executive Director was, and thus began Peterson's long and dedicated service to the Society.[42] During his early years as executive, Augie relied extensively on three Board members for counsel: Dr. Carl Becker, Eugene Hackler, and Wallace Estenson.[43]

Dad Hoeger often said, "Try to remember not to become top heavy." August Hoeger, Jr., attempted to adhere to this policy but he realized that better patient care could be achieved only if able and dedicated personnel were added to the Central Office when needed. Augie adhered as best he could to the elder Hoeger's cautionary advice. The selection of Erwin Chell, on July 1, 1968, as purchasing agent for the Society was one of Hoeger's key appointments. Chell, who had been administrator of the Bonell Retirement Community, Greeley, Colorado, for ten years, went on to become Director of Accounting, the first director of the Society's computer program and the Director of Finance by the mid-1970s. He closed out his career as a regional director, retiring in April 1983 after 25 years of service. His wife, Betty "Betts" Chell, retired a year and a half later after being co-administrator at the Greeley facility, a bookkeeper in the Central Office, and regional director for the Northwest Area beginning in 1977. In the latter position, she became the first female executive in the Central Office. During their collective 51 years of service, the Chells did much to shape the policies and procedures of the Good Samaritan Society.

The Board of Directors made a pivotal move in February 1972 when it appointed Reverend John Hoeger as Associate Director of the Society.[44] John gave up his position as administrator of the Hastings, Nebraska, Good Samaritan Village to assume the newly created position. The Board, at first, viewed John Hoeger's new assignment as a succession to the position held by Dad Hoeger after 1963. Initially given the assignment of deepening the spiritual life of the Society's membership, John rapidly assumed other administrative functions. He felt strongly about education, and he sought to employ administrators who had a college or university degree.[45] If his brother had not come to the Central Office, Augie indicated that he would have vacated the Executive Director's position at a much earlier date.[46] The brothers became an excellent administrative team. Michael Bice described them as pioneers and innovators. According to Bice, "Their continuous self-renewal enabled the Good Samaritan Society to transform itself into the premier aging services company in the country."[47]

When the Society celebrated its 50th anniversary in 1972, the Central Office administrative staff included the Hoeger brothers, four Directors — Accounting (Erv Chell), Purchasing (Ray Conlon), Personnel and Training (John Rude), Development of Adult

Services (Eduard Kilen) — and seven regional directors, including Craig De La Barre, who along with Colonel Peterson and Ed Kilen continued to serve the Society in 1996 from the national headquarters.[48] Mrs. Nordiss Winge, who came to the Central Office in 1965, served as Executive Secretary.[49]

At the time of its 50th anniversary, the Society had 160 facilities operating in 20 states. A contest was held to select a theme for the anniversary year. The winners, Mrs. Don (Ethel) Wischer, an aide at the Arthur Center and Leonard (Bud) Witt, a center administrator since 1968, came up with the theme — "In Christ's Love, Everyone Is Someone." Believing that the theme truly reflected the philosophy and objectives of the Society, it was formally adopted as the Good Samaritan Society's motto in convention at Moorhead, Minnesota, on August 6, 1972.[50]

As the need arose, new specialists continued to join the Central Office team. When the decision was made to employ an auditor, the Society's leadership wondered how the administrators would react. Would they feel that the Central Office was exerting too much control? The auditor would spot-check the accounts of Society facilities to ensure that the Society's accounting policies were being followed. He would also play a vital role in formulating the annual budget for the Central Office. To lessen the fears of those administrators who might feel threatened, the Executive Director emphasized that the auditor would report financial findings only and that he would not evaluate personnel.[51] The Central Office received its first audited financial statement in 1977. It became a key element in financial planning, particularly in understanding state reimbursement formulas.[52]

Another essential position was filled in 1977 when the Reverend Jacob Jerstad came to the Central Office as the Director of Spiritual Ministries. Jerstad had been the administrator of the Good Samaritan Village at Hastings, succeeding John Hoeger in 1972. Beginning in May 1978, he began holding workshops for the centers' chaplains; topics included "Bedside Visitation," "Handling Grief and Depression," and "Pastoral Styles." Jerstad staged spiritual leadership retreats for administrators and interns, as well, underscoring the Christian atmosphere of a Good Samaritan Center.[53]

At his retirement in 1987, Augie Hoeger commented that 23 members of the Hoeger family, at one time or another, were on the Society's payroll.[54] Dr. Agnes Hoeger, the eldest daughter of Dad and Amelia Hoeger, was one of the people referred to by the president of the Society. She had a long and distinguished career in medicine and in serving her Lord and Savior, Jesus Christ. A 1934 graduate of the University of Minnesota Medical School, Agnes served as a missionary to New Guinea until World War II. She then enlisted in the U. S. Army and as a military physician was assigned to Peru. Dr. Hoeger returned to New Guinea after the war, remaining there until 1965. She served as Medical Director at the Good Samaritan Village, Hastings, Nebraska, from 1966 - 1977. After taking a one year medical records course at the College of St. Mary in Omaha, Nebraska, Agnes began working at the Central Office in 1978 as the first medical consultant. In this capacity, she visited every Society facility. Possessed of great stamina, courage, and a desire to serve humankind, she joined the Peace Corps for 18 months at age 72. Agnes returned to the Central Office as the medical records consultant in 1983, before she retired in 1985.[55]

Shortly after his completion of a study leave at the University of California, Los Angeles (UCLA) Graduate School of Management, Augie Hoeger took steps to reorganize the administrative structure of the Central Office.[56] Central Office personnel held a retreat at the Parkston Country Center on October 12-13, 1976, to discuss reorganization. Decision-making in the past had involved the entire Central Office staff bringing their chairs to Augie's office and collectively advising the Executive Director. The entire staff attended the same meeting, reviewed the same material and made known their thoughts on the issue under discussion. One observer described Central Office meetings in Sioux Falls as "a country kitchen." Each day started with daily devotions around a large coffee table. As Dad Hoeger, in the past, had met with staff over a cup of coffee at one of the old homes, management decisions were still being made informally amidst friendly surroundings. By 1976, however, 20 people made up the staff, necessitating some change in procedure. The discussion at the retreat centered on procedures for allowing everyone some kind of input while reducing the number in attendance.[57]

The reorganization discussion went on for two years. Several staff members did not want to abandon the decision-making process that had been used since the 60s. There was some mistrust as not everyone could be on the new Management Council. Those favoring the Management Council asked how democratic a growing organization could be.[58] Other staff people believed Augie and John Hoeger should be the final decision makers. During the discussions, the Hoeger brothers warned against creating a corporate or big business image of the Society. They reiterated that it was the task of the Central Office to be the servant of the centers, to equip the saints, and to be less of a corporate head-quarters.

The expanded staff meeting, another decision-making forum, was not changed until late 1983. Local administrators had been asked to sit in on meetings at the Central Office when decisions were made that would affect the Society's facilities. The growing complexity and variation of regulations from state-to-state necessitated a change in this method of securing advice. Society officials decided that each region should elect a representative to sit in on an expanded staff meeting to be held each year in May.[59]

At the annual meeting in 1978, the membership approved new titles for the Hoeger brothers by revising the Articles of Incorpo-ration and By-Laws. With the revisions, August Hoeger, Jr., became President of the Society, rather than Executive Director, and John Hoeger became Executive Vice President. Ronald Pat-terson and Nordiss Winge were named Vice President and Trea-surer and Secretary respectively. The changes in office titles relieved the Board of Directors of perfunctory signatory duties which were inefficient and uneconomical.[60] Between 1976 and 1986, the staff of the Central Office doubled. In 1986, there were 12 regional directors, each supervising 10-20 centers, and eight department directors with their staffs. They were represented on committees whose proposals went to the Management Council, made up of representatives from the regional directors and departments, for final Central Office action.[61]

Unifying the Saints

More than a modern managerial structure was needed to keep the growing organization unified. Communication and a common philosophy played vital roles in keeping the Society's personnel informed and attentive to their mission. From 1923 to 1955, the *Sunshine* had provided information on what was taking place in the Society's homes. First published at Arthur, the four-page periodical tended to give more attention to the "Mother Home" than the other facilities of the Society. Hugh Adams, from his operating base in Kansas, published dittoed *Good Samaritan* newsletters between 1955 and 1963, following the termination of a Society-wide distribution of the *Sunshine*. In late 1967, the first edition of *The Good Samaritan*, a quarterly newsletter, was distributed to the entire Society, to families of residents and to other interested people. Its contents included information on the Society's personnel and facilities, new programs for caring for the elderly, future planning, and the organization's mission.

Three periodicals have been used for in-house communication. For several years, *Sioux Smoke Signals*, later changed to *Smoke Signals*, was distributed to administrators, department heads, and other staff to promote an exchange of ideas.[62] When Patrice Meier became the publications editor for the Society on January 18, 1977, new ideas and new formats were introduced. A new monthly publication, *Vital Signs*, made its appearance on July 1, 1977. In medicine, the vital signs had always been "temperature, pulse, and respiration" (T.P.R.) whereas in the Society T.P.R. stood for "Together People Respond." *Vital Signs* provided better communication between the Central Office staff, administrators, and interns. Each month, the periodical contained information on purchasing, personnel changes, reports on conventions and other meetings, a calendar of events, and feature articles on long-term care issues. Distribution of the most recent in-house publication, *The Administrator*, began in 1989. Its content was similar to its predecessor, *Vital Signs*.

Dad Hoeger had lived his personal life and managed the Good Samaritan Society in accordance with the tenets of the Christian faith. No person better exemplified the Society's ideals and mission than its founder. It was important that future members of the Good Samaritan Society know of his dedication and faith in bringing the Good Samaritan Society into being and his commitment and struggle to make it a viable institution. Thus, shortly after his death, discussions ensued regarding a book as a memorial to him.[63] In the fall of 1971, a Memorial Committee began to search for a professional writer to write a biography of Dad Hoeger that included the early history of the Good Samaritan Society, the book being financed through memorial gifts.[64]

The preparation of a history of Dad Hoeger's life took on a life of its own. Ten years elapsed before the publication of the biography. At the annual meeting in 1974, it was announced that Ken Halvorsrude would be researching the senior Hoeger's life and that he would be soliciting information from Society members.[65] Halvorsrude conducted interviews with over 125 Society members, past and present. His research proved invaluable in understanding Dad Hoeger's long and illustrious career. The following

February, Dr. Herbert Krause, Professor of Literature at Augustana College (Sioux Falls), began a fictionalized history of Dad Hoeger's life. After completing 50 pages of manuscript, Krause became ill, and he was unable to complete the project. After first considering Carl Becker to author the biography, the Board of Directors, in August 1976, asked Dr. Agnes Hoeger to undertake the assignment. She immediately began collecting data and with the assistance of Mrs. Walter (Irma) Person completed *Ever Forward*, 148 pages, for distribution at the 1981 annual meeting.[66]

Other memorial monies were used to create a prayer garden to celebrate Dad Hoeger's love of flower gardens, bushes, and trees.[67] One of his favorite hymns had been "In The Garden." He believed that a thing of beauty, such as a flower, was a letter from God telling of His love for His people.[68] The memorial garden, completed in 1976, was located in the Central Office complex at Sioux Falls with the conference room overlooking the garden.[69] The garden, which included flowers, shrubs, and a statue of Christ in Gethsemane, became a place of meditation.

A memorial for Amelia Hoeger also became a part of the new Central Office, located at 1000 West Avenue North in Sioux Falls. Six years after the construction of the Society's new headquarters, officials were forced to remove a window on the southwest side of the computer room because it caused variations in temperature and humidity in the room. Unable to match the brick for the wall, which was adjacent to the main entrance to the Central Office, the Board of Directors commissioned Dr. F. W. (Bill) Thomsen, who had designed the Society's logo, to design a mosaic — "Jesus Christ, the Bright Morning Star" — as a memorial to Mrs. Hoeger.[70] The mosaic remained in place until 1995, when the Society moved into its current national headquarters in southwest Sioux Falls. This beautiful piece of art work was placed in the lobby of the new headquarters where it immediately catches the eye of visitors and employees when they enter the building.[71]

Out of necessity, the Central Office became a major presence during the 1970s and 1980s. More than tender loving care was required of nursing home administrators and their staffs. They had to maintain medical records, create care plans and provide various kinds of therapy for their charges. Financial management was much more sophisticated than it had been in the first half century of the Society's operation. The Central Office was present to further equip the saints. The growing number of services needed could only be met through increased personnel at the national headquarters. As the Society grew and became more complex, as government regulations increased, careful financial supervision and additional consulting services were necessary. To help centers meet the standards for quality care, formally established in 1983, the Central Office prepared guide books and manuals and conducted an extensive in-service education program for all staff personnel at the center level.[72] Further assistance came through accounting services, data processing, and consulting assistance in activities, community and staff relations, construction, insurance, printing, social service, and spiritual ministries.[73]

The growing sophistication of the Society's operations did not lessen the contacts between Central Office personnel and administrators. Nor did it lessen the need for administrators to engage in person-to-person contact at their respective centers. Augie Hoeger, always concerned that direct and personal communication be maintained at all levels of the Society, gave the following instructions to administrators at area meetings in 1986:

He instructed them:

1. to secure feedback from residents, to listen to them, to talk to them,
2. to actively supervise their staff by getting out from behind their desks,
3. to find out what goes on at night and on the weekend in their centers,
4. to know if food needs are being met,
5. to hire and keep good staff,
6. to talk to the families of residents and
7. to treat residents as independent adults, not like wrinkled babies.[74]

Housing the Saints

Seven years after Augie Hoeger assumed the leadership of the Good Samaritan Society, the number of facilities totaled 145, an average increment of 11 centers per year. The Society did not sustain this phenomenal growth during the 70s and 80s because of the adverse economic conditions. Proceeding with caution, much of the Society's efforts went toward improving services in the existing centers. The Good Samaritan Society, nevertheless, doubled its number of facilities between 1965 and 1987.

Several factors contributed to the growth of the Society during the tenures of Augie and John Hoeger. Early on, many rural communities became concerned with the plight of their elderly. Smaller towns saw the economic advantages of having a nursing home in their midst; a nursing home often became the life breath of many communities. To meet their concerns, they turned to the Good Samaritan Society, offering the necessary land and money to establish and maintain facilities.

St. Ansgar, the oldest town in Iowa, population 1100, was such a community. Having heard that a nursing home had been built 20 miles away, the residents of St. Ansgar invited Augie Hoeger to meet with them. The Executive Director sat down at a table with five farmers and main street businessmen. Immediately, Hoeger told them that he believed the town was too small to provide adequate staff for a nursing home. Augie went on to indicate what the Society required of the citizens if they wanted a facility — $1,500 per bed (in 1965, the Society was building 40-bed homes) and a minimum of 15 acres in the best part of St. Ansgar. The townspeople would also have to establish an advisory board, the heart and soul of the project. The town's representatives "hardly said boo" after they heard the requirements. Augie said goodbye, asking the group to let him know if they wanted to proceed any further. He drove immediately back to Sioux Falls and told Betty, his wife, that he did not expect to hear from the group. He was wrong. At that moment, the telephone rang; a representative of the St. Ansgar community was on the line. He said that they had met all of the requirements, and he wanted to know what they should do next.[75]

After 1966, Medicaid and Medicare, coupled with increased life expectancy and higher hospital costs, contributed significantly to an increased nursing home census and, in turn, the need for new facilities. In many areas, there was a lack of affordable housing for the elderly as well as a dearth of supportive home services and transportation. The increased mobility of families left many aged stranded in their home communities. Intrafamily relations also played a role. Some of the elderly chose not to live with relatives and there were many families that were unwilling or unable to care for aging members.

Following the opening of a new center, the Society, by way of the administrator, continued to develop a close working relationship with the community. Various local organizations were encouraged to adopt a resident, and visitors to the facility received the same expression of love and concern that the center sought to provide for its residents. The administrator sought and accepted as many speaking engagements as possible.[76] At several facilities, civic organizations were invited to hold their biweekly or monthly meetings in the new center's dining room.

The early years for a new facility were often deficit years because it took time to fill every bed. A limited number of residents still required a full range of services, and as a result start-up expenses could not be paid out of current income. This situation resulted in a number of locally owned nursing homes being turned over to the Society for management. The Good Samaritan Center in Metropolis, Illinois, opened in 1965, was the first location for which the Society provided management services.[77] On the occasion of the Society's 50th anniversary, 22 such homes were managed by the Good Samaritan Society.[78]

Changing demographics determined where the Society would construct new facilities. The shift of population from farms to urban areas accelerated following World War II and reached its peak during the farm crisis of the 1980s. Adhering to a policy of selective expansion, the Society began to emphasize construction in the southern and southwestern areas of the nation. New Society facilities sprang up in Arizona, Florida, New Mexico, and Texas. It was tempting to invest in these rapidly growing areas where the facilities would always be filled and where loans would eventually be paid. The Society, however, did not shirk its obligation to the small towns of the Prairie Plains, the original "heartland" of the Society. Central Office personnel faced the dilemma of being faithful to service in a dying community where it was often difficult to find staff for the local center. Administrators and Central Office personnel sought alternative ways to use empty beds and to serve the community by identifying positive circumstances.[79] In late February 1988, a Rural Task Force was created to decide when to close a rural facility.[80]

During the 1970s, the Good Samaritan Society took over nursing homes in humid subtropical areas of the United States. In 1974, the Society purchased the Laniolu Retirement Center in downtown Honolulu, Hawaii, from the American Lutheran Church.[81] Six years later, the Society acquired the Pohai Nani retirement complex, Konehoe, Hawaii for $9 million. The Pohia Nani complex, containing 200 apartments and 40 nursing beds, had been owned by a bankrupt corporation.[82] The acquisition of Kissimmee Village, near Orlando, Florida, followed protracted negotiations. In the early 70s, a large number of elderly people purchased bonds to finance a retirement village in central Florida, a few miles from Disneyworld. Known as the Aldersgate Project, the Village contained 861 garden-type apartments, 277 mobile home pads, 26 personal care beds, and 266 nursing beds. It was situated on 238 acres, complete with lakes. Due to overexpansion, the organization filed for bankruptcy in 1974.

A delegation of residents and bondholders from Kissimmee came to Sioux Falls and asked the Good Samaritan Society to purchase and operate the Village. Following prayerful deliberation, the Society decided to purchase the facility. Eleven delays followed as another corporation became interested in the property, promising a higher purchase price. The constant legal maneuvers and the delays tested the patience of the Society's leaders. The Society had borrowed a large sum of money to pay for the property, and the interest mounted each day of the delay. On the morning of May 4, 1979, officials at the Central Office prayed to the Lord "to show us how?" After hearing that the presiding judge had ordered another delay to consider another bid, the Society ordered its attorney to withdraw the Society's bid. When the attorney for the trustees of the bondholders heard of the Society's action, he immediately called the Central Office, stating that he would take quick action to accept the Society's bid. He was able to contact, via telephone, the federal circuit court judge handling the case while the judge was between flights at a Canadian airport. The judge awarded the contract to the Good Samaritan Society for $9,750,000. The bank remained open late, the papers were signed, and the transfer was made on the same day that had started with prayer. In the years that followed, Kissimmee Village, like Hastings Village and the Bonell Center, became a flagship facility of the Society. Immediately after the completion of the transaction, one of the Society's leaders observed that the greatest reward from all these proceedings was knowing "that our Lord is with us and that He listens to our prayers and in His own time and way, He answers."[83]

For many years, when the Society needed to construct a new facility, the contract had gone to Nursing Home Builders Incorporated (NHBI), Broken Bow, Nebraska.[84] In constructing centers for the Society, Ray Brown, an owner of NBHI, argued that his firm built homes for the Society below national average costs. Desiring an assurance of quality, the Board of Directors of the Society asked a Sioux Falls architectural firm, Spitznagel, Incor-

The Growth of the Society, 1942-1993			
	Facilities	**Employees**	**CO Employees**	**Residents**
1942	5	48	1	317
1947	9	116	1	611
1952	34	232	1	1,268
1957	59	623		1,870
1962	79	1,879	2	3,847
1967	112		15	9,246
1972	160		35	13,414
1977	181	11,116	54	17,641
1982	191	13,900	75	20,725
1986	200	15,700	98	23,943
1987	201	15,936	102	24,061
1993	236	21,000		28,000

- Annual Reports of the Good Samaritan Society, 1987,1993

porated, to study one of the centers under construction by NHBI to see if standards were being met, whether the standards were minimum or higher.[85] Following the study, the Society decided to continue with NHBI, which had constructed or been involved in the building of more than 100 nursing homes for the Society.[86]

The relationship with Nursing Home Builders continued until January 1984 when, at a regional directors' retreat, the recommendation was made that there be no new projects by the Broken Bow firm. Instead, the Society's expertise, using recently formulated plans of a model facility, would provide the blueprints for a structure meeting Good Samaritan standards for quality control.[87] With centers being constructed far from the Society's original heartland, it was deemed advisable to deal with contractors familiar with construction in a particular area, be it Arizona, Florida, or Texas.

The availability of funds from the Housing and Urban Development (HUD) Department for construction of rent subsidized housing caused The Evangelical Lutheran Good Samaritan Society to form a new corporation. On January 24, 1979, Good Samaritan, Incorporated, a South Dakota nonprofit corporation, began operation. The new corporation provided a means for an expanding array of services beyond those allowed under the Society's Articles of Incorporation. Although it was a separate legal entity, Good Samaritan, Incorporated, shared officers and Board members with The Evangelical Lutheran Good

Samaritan Society. Corporate headquarters were at the Central Office in Sioux Falls.

Facilities were financed under Sections 8 and 202 of HUD's funding guidelines. The first of the new facilities, a 100-unit apartment complex, opened at El Paso, Texas, in December 1980.[88] Within the next decade, Good Samaritan, Inc., operated seven facilities with others under construction. Later, changes in HUD regulations necessitated the formation of a separate corporation for each new housing project. Boise, Idaho, Good Samaritan Housing was the first to be incorporated, in April 1985.[89] The federal government required that people be 62 years of age or older or that they be handicapped or disabled to reside in the facilities built with HUD revenue. Their income limits were set by the county in which the building was located. HUD also stipulated that the residents must live independently with no staffing of "nursing care rehabilitative services."[90] The low rent subsidies covered all expenses of the Society with the exception of depreciation. Within the various facilities, the Society and tenant councils organized a variety of activities, including potlucks, drawing classes, creative writing, Bible studies, book discussion groups, gardening, dance, and other activities.[91]

The continued increase in Central Office services and the corresponding increase in personnel necessitated larger quarters. The new national headquarters for the Society at 1000 West Avenue North in Sioux Falls was dedicated on August 16, 1970. The new building housed the Society's own computer service.[92] Additions to this structure followed in 1977 and 1980.[93] Within a year, when the need for additional space in the future became apparent, the Board of Directors began discussions regarding the purchase of the Western Surety Building, across the street from the Society's headquarters.[94] The discussions culminated in the purchase of the "908 Building," so-called because of its address, for $900,000 in the summer of 1989.[95]

By the late 80s, adapting to changes in attitude and life-style, the Good Samaritan Society placed increasing emphasis on the construction of apartments and assisted living facilities. Apartment dwellers had more independence and responsibility for their own care; they were actively involved in managing their own lives. In assisted living units, the residents did not need 24-hour skilled nursing service. Medical assistance and supportive services were available if needed. These units provided for an emergency call system, complete meal service, activities, scheduled transportation and supervision of medications.[96]

The same decade saw a corresponding decline in the census of nursing homes in the Prairie Plains. The changing demographics and the emergence of assisted living services contributed to the availability of beds in nursing facilities. In 1988, the State of South Dakota ordered a moratorium on nursing home construction and expansion, currently in effect until June of 2000. A multi-level living environment, nevertheless, remained the dominant type of Good Samaritan facility as the 1980s drew to a close. The management of these facilities had become much more sophisticated with the introduction of new rehabilitative services, social activities, increased government regulations, numerous forms, and more complex computer systems. Administrators had to be planners and local fund raisers. Most important among their responsibilities was to serve as the spiritual leader of the facility, demonstrating a commitment to serving God.[97] As the Society rapidly expanded, Dad Hoeger's concept of "elbow room" for administrators came under considerable stress as they carried out their duties within a growing corporate structure and an increasing number of state and federal mandates.

Chapter Thirteen
"ELBOW ROOM"
1970 - 1995

"Freedom is participation in power"
— *Marcus Tillius Cicero*

Longtime center administrators looked back to the years before 1965 as the "good old days" in the Society's nursing homes. Life, to them, seemed less complicated and less intense. Nurses spent most of their time providing direct care to patients in the so-called good old days, whereas since 1965 they have spent most of their time documenting information about the residents. In the good old days, people who worked the night shift baked bread and cookies for the residents and staff. Sometimes they would put a load of clothes in the washing machine. Most of the staff was made up of farmers' wives who could be counted on to give a good day's or night's work. Their training was on the job, and they loved the residents. Prior to the advent of the Great Society legislation, life, to these administrators, seemed simple; there were few rules and regulations. No more of that. With the advent of Medicare and Medicaid, government involvement intensified, and operating nursing homes became one of the most regulated industries in the United States. With new governmental oversight, the physical care of residents improved dramatically. The administrators, in turn, lost some of their independence as they had to assume responsibilities never considered before that time.[1]

Shortly before his death in 1996, Colonel Charles E. Peterson, as he concluded his 33rd year with the Society, wrote that the Society had changed from a close family type operation with considerable facility involvement to a corporate structure with more long-range planning, accountability, task forces, and many committees. The changes in structure were necessary to successfully run an organization of the Society's size.[2]

The great majority of administrators of the 1950s and 60s were dedicated Christians from all walks of life. Many had no formal training in administration or management. They were often

second career people, having been former farmers, missionaries
or teachers. In some instances, there were three or four members
of the same family serving as administrators in the same state.[3]
Quite often there were spousal teams managing a home. For
many of these people employed by Dad Hoeger, it was on-the-job
training. Licensing became a headache for them in the early 70s.
One of the dreaded aspects of the job was supervising nursing
care. Because of their lack of medical knowledge, administrators
delegated authority when confronted with problems of nursing
care.[4]

Thus, they came to their administrative positions with little
background experience except they had love and compassion for
the people in their charge. With these qualities, they met Dad
Hoeger's criteria for an administrative position. He told Colonel
Peterson, "Give me a people person who loves and trusts his God,
and we can train him to be an administrator."[5] Administrators
should be "confessing, practicing Christians, active in the worship and life of a Christian congregation."[6] It was essential, Dad
Hoeger stated, that they believe in the holistic care of people. In
a letter written two years before his death, he told administrators:

> You should look upon this work of our Good
> Samaritan Homes as first of all being a home
> where we take care of the whole man, not only of
> his body but also of his spirit. That we want to
> bring food not only for their body but also for
> their soul. Seek ye first the Kingdom of God, is
> what Christ ordered us to do; all these other
> things would be added on to it; they will come
> more or less from themselves. And so we hope
> that when you become an administrator, you will
> realize that your first and biggest duty is to look
> and see that the souls of your older people are
> just as well taken care of as the body.[7]

August Hoeger, Sr., who was never enamored of the government's role in the nursing home industry, had given the Society's
administrators considerable freedom in carrying out their duties
in their respective facilities. "Elbow room" was the term he
applied to this freedom given to administrators. Dad Hoeger
equated elbow room with trust. Betty Chell commented that dur-

ing her first five years at the Bonell Center in Greeley, Colorado, she had hardly any dealings with the Central Office. The Central Office was too far away so "she did her own thing" and relished the independence.[8] Later evidence indicated that some of these administrators were given too much freedom.

According to John Hoeger, there were certain extremes under the old system that contributed to centralized control. Under the system that emerged during the 1940s, conscientious administrators, wanting to promote the welfare of the Society, and desiring to please Dad Hoeger, would affect economies that were not necessarily good for the Home they managed. They tended to buy used furniture and to underpay themselves. They were the sacrificial group, giving funds to those administrators at the other extreme who "lived high off the hog" and bought the finest furniture. These administrators were not diligent in their work; they were guilty of undercharging and overstaffing.[9] Others spent too little time in their respective centers. Augie Hoeger said that they should spend more time in the halls and rooms and that they should give greater effort and thought to the preparation of daily devotions.[10]

The tremendous growth of the Society during the 60s and 70s necessitated the imposition of several formal guidelines on facility managers. They were free to manage their facilities in the way they saw appropriate but this management had to be carried out in full agreement with the Society's mission statement, its philosophy and objectives, and in accordance with a detailed job description. A case in point, on November 24, 1976, Augie Hoeger sent a memo to all administrators that under no circumstances should they or other employees benefit personally from transactions involving the Society. Modest Christmas gifts from suppliers, in no way a bribe, were permitted. The violation of the policy could result in dismissal. The memorandum likewise discouraged center administrators from handling residents' funds. There was always the danger of mingling resident funds with those of the center.[11] In all matters, guidance and encouragement would be provided by the regional directors and the support staff at the Central Office.

By the 1980s, because of the centralization of authority that accompanied growth, and growing government intervention, administrators found they had much less room to extend their elbows. Metaphorically, the administrator could be depicted as standing in the center of a room with the four walls gradually moving in and restricting the movement of his or her elbows. The four walls were federal regulations, state standards, community codes, and the Society's policies. Administrators had the freedom to manage, lead, operate, and function in their facilities to the extent they did not bump their elbows up against the growing number of regulations, standards, codes or policies.

Regulations, Standards, and Codes

The staff at the Central Office assumed responsibility for informing administrators of new local, state, or federal requirements. Additional staff, including many specialists, had to be employed to keep up with the increasing amount of nursing home legislation. In the early 1960s, Kansas set the tone for what was to come. As of January 1, 1963, a skilled nursing home license in that state was granted only if the facility had a registered nurse, trained in physical therapy, on each shift, and a local advisory board that included a physician, nurse, religious adviser, and other community members.[12] South Dakota began to license and classify skilled care facilities in 1967. Standards were the essential part of classification — standards for the staff, physical plant, care given, and record keeping. Classification determined the fees that would be allowed for residents receiving Medicaid. Licensing meant meeting the standards, the preparation of numerous reports and the regular inspections of nursing homes by state health officials.

Administrators soon found that they, too, would have to be licensed. The federal government mandated that as of July 1, 1970, each state must have a licensure law in effect for administrators or the state would not receive matching federal funds for nursing homes. Administrators had until July 1, 1972, to be licensed.[13] Center managers, in place, could take courses approved, and sometimes planned, by the Department of Health, Education and Welfare (HEW). Following a lengthy discussion among members of the Society's Board of Directors and Central Office staff, the Society decided to train its own people on a long-term basis rather than attempting to attract experienced administrators from other nursing home corporations.

Education and Training

An intern program was begun in May 1971. People with college degrees who wanted to pursue a career in nursing home administration were hired for the program. Local Centers agreed to share in the expenses of an intern.[14] Each intern would gain a minimum of one year's experience under the supervision of a licensed administrator. The interns — there were eight in the first group — first received a month's orientation at the Central Office. In this initial session, they became familiar with the Society's history, philosophy, and policies. The Executive Director, August Hoeger, Jr., emphasized that Society nursing home administrators and their staffs must have a basic love and concern for those they served. True high quality care could not be given by those who did not care. The Christian commitment of the administrator should be transmitted throughout the facility through regular devotions and Bible studies.[15]

There followed a very structured introduction to all of the departments in the facility where the intern would serve. The training sites were not all alike. Some were large with multi-levels of care, others were average-sized skilled or intermediate care facilities. Some were in communities where the Society operated a hospital and a nursing home. Others were located where an intern could relate to two or three nursing homes within a 20-30 mile radius.[16]

By August 1973, John Rude reported that 25 interns had been in the program and that 15 of them had already been placed as administrators. Twenty-two center administrators had served as preceptors. The program proved to be a learning process for administrators as well as interns. Administrators gained from the ideas, feedback, and new perspectives that the intern brought to the facility. Interns quickly developed rapport with the residents and the staff, confidence, and a knowledge of procedures. One of the interns to come out of the program caught its essence when he said that his training to be an administrator would help people realize they are somebody.[17]

Although the intern program was a success, the Society needed additional good licensed administrators. John Rude asked the Board of Directors to consider changing the Society's policy of hiring three Lutheran administrators for every non-Lutheran. He believed that a person's capability rather than religious denomination should be the first priority in the hiring process. The Board agreed, and on November 15, 1974, removed the 75 - 25 percent denominational requirement.[18]

As government requirements continued to multiply, the Central Office, seeking to ease the work load of administrators, developed a variety of in-service programs for staff at the centers. Using the resources of the American Health Care Association, a series of training films were prepared especially for the long-term care facilities. The films emphasized patient care instruction for nurses aides, food service, housekeeping, maintenance, fire containment, infection control, and the proper handling of drugs. Some of the programs were designed specifically for the Society's spiritual program. The first film, "Go and Do Thou Likewise," described the history, philosophy and operations of the Society. Another film, "Death and Dying," taught a center's staff how to be of assistance to the dying and to those loved ones left behind.[19]

The Central Office similarly made available modular, self-paced training programs which provided an overview of the aging process and the role of the nursing assistant in providing care to the residents of a long-term care facility.[20] By the 1980s, administrators were deluged with a variety of manuals and report forms. The new materials which flowed from the Central Office were designed to enhance quality care and to increase management efficiency. One of the significant manuals was the two volume Staff Development Manual. Meeting federal and Society regulations and standards, it became the foundation for a center's staff development program. The manual not only included data on resident care and center operating procedures but it also contained teaching concepts and the characteristics of an adult learner.[21] Other manuals prepared by Good Samaritan headquarters that became part of an administrator's resource library included volumes related to finance, nursing services, construction standards, deferred giving, and a three-volume resource catalog.[22] Administrators now had less time to walk the halls and visit with residents and staff as much of their time was committed to keeping abreast of policies and regulations and to completing a multitude of reports.

The Central Office considered the relationship between administrators and their staffs to be of vital importance. During the 1980s, some facilities, particularly those in rural areas, faced real or potential problems in securing adequate staff. The exodus

of rural inhabitants to larger urban locales accelerated during
the farm crisis of the 1980s. It was reasoned that a satisfied staff
would more likely remain at its present work site. The move by
labor unions to unionize service industries related as well to good
employer-employee relations. Although few center staff members
ever made the attempt, the Central Office worried about possible
efforts to unionize the Society's employees. The Board minutes
for November 16, 1972, indicated that one Society facility had
voted for unionization. In this case, the Society believed that an
ounce of prevention was worth a pound of cure. The Society
adopted uniform personnel policies, conveyed to center administrators via an Employee Personnel Policy Handbook, and the
Central Office urged administrators to keep the lines of communication open with employees, listening to their concerns about
benefits, wages, and working conditions.[23]

The walls continued to close in on administrators' elbow room
in other ways during the 1980s. The Board of Directors created a
Model Facility Committee in June 1980. The committee was told
"to develop guidelines for the 1985 model facility that would be
multi-leveled and as self-contained as possible with the flexibility for various sized communities and local demands of climate,
government, and persons to be served."[24] The Committee found it
impossible to develop a specific model facility and switched its
efforts to identifying characteristics and services which should
be a part of any Good Samaritan facility. The Model Facility
Committee, however, did identify 28 basic standards for each
Good Samaritan owned or managed facility. The measurements
for each of the standards were prepared and sent to the various
center administrators to evaluate the compliance of their respective facilities. Society headquarters reasoned that the project
would determine needs and enhance the quality of care.[25]

New federal regulations, mandated under the Omnibus Budget Reconciliation Act (OBRA) of 1987, would increase the
Society's costs and further add to the work load of administrators
and the Central Office staff. The OBRA legislation called for
more specialized employees, additional nursing personnel, more
staff training, new screening and assessment of present and
prospective residents, additional rehabilitative services for residents and changes in the structure and design of several of the
Society's buildings.[26] One portion of the new regulations called
for additional training of nursing assistants. Complying with the
new regulations would prove costly to the Society. The federal

decision makers said that the staff changes and added training were necessary to bring the nation's nursing homes up to a standard called "nursing facility."[27]

It became obvious that administrators needed additional education to deal knowingly and responsibly with the ever-increasing demands placed upon them. On March 17, 1986, Al Erickson and Elliot Thoreson advanced a resolution requesting that the Good Samaritan Society and Augustana College (Sioux Falls) explore the feasibility and desirability of developing a joint venture in offering degree programs in gerontology, geriatrics, and health care at the B.A. and M.A. levels. The Augustana College Board of Regents, preoccupied with the recent resignation of President William C. Nelsen, did not approve the resolution at its May 1986 meeting.[28]

Shortly thereafter, Dr. Mark Jerstad, who was then the Society's Vice President for Facility Services, entered into negotiations with North Texas State University, Denton, Texas, and Luther Northwestern Seminary, St. Paul, Minnesota, to create a second-level program at the M.A. level that would train administrators who moved into multi-level facilities. In 1988, the Good Samaritan Society received the Preceptor of the Year Award from the Center for Studies in Aging at the Texas school. The Society was recognized for its contribution to the field of aging through the training of its student interns.[29] An agreement was formalized in the summer of 1988, and 12 Good Samaritan administrators enrolled in the three-year Masters Degree program at North Texas State in September 1989. The Good Samaritan Society agreed to pay the tuition, fees, and $1,000 per year in related expenses to each participant.[30] Recipients of the financial aid agreed to commit three years of service to the Society following the acquisition of their degrees. The Masters program combined management theory with Biblical and theological concepts. At the North Texas Center for Studies in Aging, the Society personnel took courses in management, finance, and gerontology. On the Luther Northwestern campus, the students received a rich foundation in the Christian gospel.[31] The first graduates of the program in long-term care administration completed their coursework in 1992.

Within the Society, the orientation and training of new interns and the education of administrators for licensure credit continued. A new Administrator-in-Training (AIT) program was introduced in 1988. Medicare workshops were conducted at the regional level. A scholarship program was begun in 1990 to encourage center staff members to study subject areas related to their work in the field of aging. Staff members who participated in the program became eligible for promotions and salary increases.[32]

While meeting the demands for better educated administrators and staff, the Society did not neglect its spiritual mission. The Central Office, in 1990, established a scholarship program to help clergy in Good Samaritan centers, either chaplains or volunteers, to take a basic unit of Clinical Pastoral Education (CPE). Chaplains spent one day per week in a classroom, in a discussion and group process. The clinical part of their course work was carried out in nursing homes.[33]

The Director for Spiritual Ministries, Greg Wilcox, devised a retreat program for administrators in 1992. Every third year, an administrator would have the opportunity to participate in the Triple R program — Reflections, Relationships, and Risks. The periodic retreats gave center administrators an opportunity to evaluate themselves as spiritual leaders within their facilities, to realize their strengths, and to correct their weaknesses.[34]

Elbow Room Versus Requirements

As the walls continued to limit an administrator's freedom to manage his or her facility, the Central Office strove to lessen their load and to assist them, wherever possible, in their administrative tasks. Through consultants, education programs, data on the constant updating of requirements by governmental agencies, the preparation of forms and manuals, financial and computerized accounting systems, and assistance from regional directors, the Central Office worked diligently to meet the needs of each facility.

The infringement upon local management was a nationwide phenomenon. Bureaucratic and corporate growth, products of the post-World War II era, affected almost every service and manufacturing industry. As elbow room declined, Society leaders emphasized participation. Always the team player, Augie Hoeger reaffirmed the Society's traditional practice of participatory or open management. He made note of the presence of administrators on the Board of Directors since the 1940s.[35] Administrators continued to have an excellent perspective on the Society's operations, and they continued to attend annual meetings in large numbers. At the annual sessions, they spoke with a strong voice regarding Society policies and practices. In addition, they were represented on the expanded staff, which met at least once a year. Administrators, from their vantage point, equated the concept of elbow room not only with trust but also with fairness. They appreciated consistency in the carrying out of the Society's policies. Fairness, to administrators, resulted when regional directors acted in accordance with the guidelines set down at the administrative level within the Central Office.[36]

President Lyndon Johnson's "Great Society" legislation had a great impact on the Good Samaritan Society. Medicare and Medicaid played a major role in the Society's growth and the changes in care and management at each of the facilities. Labor rates went up and resident rates increased accordingly. The government demanded more but the demands were tempered by the cost reimbursement factor. A considerable amount of a center's operating funds came through payments from the various state governments for Medicaid.[37] In 1986, 55 percent of the census in nursing care facilities was Medicaid funded.[38]

The Good Samaritan Society faced significant challenges to its mission upon entering the decade of the 90s. The figurative avalanche of state and federal requirements, the increased longevity of residents, and growing competition for workers from other nursing home corporations, resulting in shortages of nurses and trained aides, were challenges to be met and overcome. Over three decades, the skilled care hours required for each resident had doubled as serving the aged became more labor-intensive. Labor costs increased as well as costs for new equipment and the modification of facilities. Adhering to Dad Hoeger's motto of "Ever Forward!" (*Immer Vorwaerts!*), the Society continued to meet these challenges and to improve resident care in the process. Several of the new programs for residents introduced in the Society's facilities during the past quarter century merit description.

Resident Participation and Rehabilitation

Americans do not give the aged the respect, honor and dignity that they deserve, thus spoke Augie Hoeger, the Society's Executive Director, at the 15th anniversary of the Lincoln Lutheran Home, Racine, Wisconsin, on February 24, 1970. Care of the elderly, outside of the family setting, had gone through two stages in the 20th century. Earlier in the century, the county poor farm had provided food and shelter. The elderly had a roof over their heads, and they received a hot meal. In the second stage, nursing homes added tender loving care — love, concern, and compassion. This was not enough, Hoeger told his Racine audience. He said, "Even the best food, shelter, love and compassion are not enough without honor. Do we give them [the aged] the respect, honor and dignity they deserve?" Honor implied a sense of worth. If able in mind and body, the elderly should be engaged in meaningful activities. Their talents, the Executive Director said, should be used in leadership, politics, writing, research, volunteer work, and the church. The elderly were a font of wisdom.[39]

In 1963, August Hoeger, Sr., had written:

> Our aged are our treasure. They are the depository of our wisdom, storehouse of our know-how, guardians of our honored traditions, stabilizers of our economy, who through young and middle years helped make America great.[40]

Dad Hoeger emphasized work therapy; people had a basic need to be productive. His son, Augie, now determined to move the interests of the Centers' residents beyond "B-B-C" — Bingo, Bible Study, and Crafts. Able residents should become involved in political and civic affairs. They should give something to the whole community, not the other way around. In doing so, residents would feel worthwhile.

In the 1970s, the Good Samaritan Society introduced a variety of social activities to stimulate the mind and to achieve greater interaction between residents, staff, family, and community.[41] Federal mandates, in the mid-1970s, accelerated the Society's emphasis on social services. The growth of social service programs and the employment of qualified social service personnel could be largely attributed to the Nursing Home Standards (1974) which mandated that facilities "provide or arrange for social services as needed by the resident, designed to promote the preservation of the resident's physical and mental health."[42] The Standards stated that residents had a right to receive certain stipulated services. The presence of social workers in the Society's centers was soon required. For a while, the Society resorted to using qualified social work consultants and part-time social workers. Eduard Kilen, the Society's Director of Resident and Community Services spent considerable time seeking to employ qualified full-time social workers. On one "good" day, he was able to hire two of them, one of them following an interview at the Ortonville, Minnesota, airport.

Society officials, following through on Dad Hoeger's admonition that centers were "to take care of the whole person, body and soul," developed the Care Team concept. It called for Care Team planning for the total person. Each care plan included meeting the following six needs: 1) health care, 2) dietary, 3) spiritual, 4) restorative-rehabilitative, 5) activity, and 6) social service.[43]

In meeting activity and social needs, the Society introduced The History of Our Lives (THOOL) Performance Project in 1981. Emphasizing drama, history and heritage, residents of the centers were given the opportunity to share events from their lives. Jim Meyer, a representative of the South Dakota Arts Council, tested the concept's workability in several nursing homes. Residents who participated in THOOL developed a feeling of confidence and accomplishment. The project had a particular appeal to residents who were unwilling or unable to participate in other activities; THOOL was a means whereby they could maintain contact with the outside world.[44]

In preparing skits that depicted incidents from bygone days, residents developed their own scripts and reenacted events without props, giving realistic and enthusiastic performances. At an annual meeting, residents from the centers in George, Iowa, and DeSmet, South Dakota, provided presentations. The George group performed a general store skit while the DeSmet contingent humorously depicted the family's first ride in the first family car. Dad, of course, got mixed up with the foot pedals and was unable to stop the car. Car and family ended up in a nearby haystack. Many of the skits dealt with one-room country schools, a site of learning fondly remembered by many residents. Viewers were amazed at these performances. One woman, who was usually disoriented, played her role perfectly.[45]

Some individuals wrote histories of their experiences while others recorded their reminiscences on tape. Unfortunately, the THOOL project had a short life. Many staff people felt they did not have the ability to carry out the program. Other staff members did not have time for it as they were tied down with gathering data on the residents. A local thespian, who had community support, was needed for a center to participate successfully in a THOOL performance.[46] While it lasted, THOOL provided residents with an opportunity to give something back to the community and to enhance their sense of worth.

The leadership skills of the residents were cultivated through the creation of Resident Councils in the mid-70s. "A voice, a choice" became the theme of the Resident Council. Council members helped plan the particular facility's activities and programs. They shared their ideas, made decisions, contributed to the implementation of their proposals and recruited other residents to serve on the council's committees. Resident Councils played a major role in setting up field trips for their fellow residents. Such field trips might involve a once a month dining out experience at a restaurant selected by the council. Other trips involved sightseeing tours, a fishing expedition, shopping at a mall, or attending Sunday service in a nearby church.[47]

Honor, dignity and a sense of worth were cultivated through the One To One (Person To Person) program. The program, inaugurated by the Central Office on January 1, 1973, asked every staff person in a center to "adopt" one or two residents. Every day, the staff member took 10 - 15 minutes to visit with a particular resident, visiting or sharing in whatever way they desired. The basic idea was to develop friendships in the belief that having a real friend was excellent therapy for the resident.[48]

Another important activities program developed in the Society's centers stressed reality orientation and remotivation. Present comprehension was used to reawaken interests and to enlarge awareness for those residents who were lonely, confused or who had lost contact with the world around them. The Pleasant View Center at St. James, Minnesota, established four objectives in carrying out its remotivation program. The facility's goals included 1) developing methods which would motivate residents to take an interest in life, 2) furnishing mental stimulation, 3) providing opportunities for socializing and fellowship, and 4) breaking the monotony of the nursing home routine. The St. James Center designed a special activities program for those residents who had speech problems, physical handicaps, or a loss of memory. Activities were geared to finger dexterity and body coordination. The residents folded and packed dressings and made May baskets and Christmas decorations. Good readers were encouraged to read aloud poetry and short stories.[49]

The establishment of the Family Discussion Group in 1976 further promoted communication between the families of residents and a center's staff. Ed Kilen pioneered the family discussion group program at the Society's facilities. Center staff members were to serve as catalysts, providing a place to meet, bringing families together, and enabling them to share their feelings and to become supportive of one another. The discussion groups helped families of residents to feel they were a part of the Good Samaritan family.[50] However, Kilen encountered some difficulties in getting the program underway. In the first small group meetings, families tended to direct their comments and questions to a staff member rather than interacting with one another, so Kilen changed the format of the first meetings. He formulated questions that family members could talk about, and he supplemented the preliminary discussion with appropriate audio-visual materials. The Society's Director of Resident and Community Services discovered that the family members really began to open up during the coffee and cookie breaks. When the groups reassembled, they selected their leaders and engaged in good discussion. The groups' ideas and queries were carried to the general session where the participants freely expressed themselves on cost and care in nursing homes.[51] Following Kilen's presentation of a paper on "Family Discussion Group Meetings" at the convention of the American Health Care Association (AHCA), a more detailed description of his work was published in the January 1978 AHCA Journal.[52] The Good Samaritan Society, through a variety of social programs, many of them generated by the Society's social workers and activity directors, created new ways for senior citizens to grow and to find new areas of self-expression. Residents responded when stimulated to develop their talents and interests.

The Care Team concept called for restorative-rehabilitative services for residents, as well. These services helped residents to relearn lost physical skills, to develop new skills, and to stay active and independent as long as possible. Different types of therapy programs helped each resident to reach his or her full potential. An imaginative walking program for able residents was devised by Don and Florence Toft, administrators of the Northern Pines Good Samaritan Center at Blackduck, Minnesota. Formerly with the YMCA at Sioux Falls, South Dakota, Toft had a lifelong interest in the value of exercise for people of all ages. He provided both the opportunity and motivation for those residents physically able to begin a walking program. A paved path was constructed around the facility. Seventeen times

around the center equalled one mile. The progress of every walker was recorded. Over six years, two of the residents walked, in
recorded miles, the distance from Blackduck to New Orleans,
Louisiana, and back. One of these two residents had struggled to
walk one block when he began the program. Homemade plaques
were awarded to any resident completing 25 miles. Over 20 residents received plaques to hang on the walls in their rooms. In
addition to improving blood pressure and flexibility, the participants enjoyed a new zest for life because of the walking program.[53] Music was similarly used as a therapeutic tool with exercise being added to the music, exercises such as clapping, foot
stomping, and swaying.[54]

Using modern technology, residents confined to wheelchairs
could engage in horticulture therapy. Memories of farming and
gardening were revived as they applied their horticultural skills
to agri-tub portable gardens, round containers that rotated at
eye level. This type of therapy brought to its participants not only
the sounds and smells of summer, but also a sense of accomplishment as they sampled the produce from their mini-gar-
dens.[55]

Physical therapists helped residents to maintain and enhance
their strength. They worked, as well, to prevent complications
and deformities. The work of occupational, speech, and physical
therapists or rehabilitative specialists included bowel and blad-
der retraining, positioning and transferring, range-of-motion
exercises, recovery of speech following a stroke, and ambulation
therapy to enable certain residents to walk with or without assistance once again.[56] Centers' nurses and staffs worked closely
with the therapists, assisting in this specialized care. All of the
rehabilitative services provided by the Society's facilities were
consistent with physicians' orders.[57]

A special emphasis on improving health during long-term care
occurred in the 1980s. Health care was viewed as a balance of
mind, body, and spirit; the whole person must be considered. Centers stressed physical fitness, nutrition, stress management,
safety, and medical care.[58] Daily or weekly visits by primary care
physicians to Society centers became a common practice in the
late 1980s.

In the spring of 1986, a geriatric clinic was established at the
Good Samaritan Village in Sioux Falls, South Dakota. A room
was set aside for an examination table and blood pressure cuff.
The clinic was open for three hours every Wednesday afternoon.

Up to 12 patients were seen each week by licensed physicians who were finishing their family practice residency. They saw residents with minor or routine health concerns.[59] Three years earlier, the Good Samaritan Nursing Center at Idaho Falls, Idaho, employed a geriatric nurse practitioner to provide outpatient service for older adults.[60] The Whispering Pines Good Samaritan Center, Pine River, Minnesota, opened a satellite clinic on May 1, 1988. During its first year of operation, the primary care physicians saw 135 patients per month. In the Northwest, the Boise, Idaho, Samaritan Village entered into an agreement with the University of Washington Geriatric Fellowship for Physician Training in February 1989. This training site for geriatric care physicians proved beneficial to residents and physicians alike.[61] The Boise facility also included a mobile dental operating unit as of August 1988. A local dentist set aside nine to 15 hours per week to examine residents. In addition, the Boise Samaritan Village had funds available to employ a part-time hygienist and to purchase dental supplies. Problems such as the transportation of residents and treating people in wheelchairs in the dentist's office were eliminated. What occurred in Boise helped meet the OBRA requirements that long-term care facilities must assist residents in securing routine and 24-hour emergency dental care.[62] Wherever clinics were established, the residents appreciated the hands-on care and not having to leave their respective centers for this basic health care.

In the final decade of the 20th century, the Good Samaritan Society continued to be in the vanguard in developing new means to care for the afflicted. The Society's Idaho facilities proved to be fertile ground for initiating different forms of care. Beginning in January 1972, the Valley Sunset Home, later to become Boise Samaritan Village, began to care for up to 28 severely physically handicapped adults who possessed normal intelligence. Ranging in age from 22-44, the new residents required considerable assistance in dressing, eating, and performing their bathroom functions.[63]

In the late 70s, Dwight Wuenschel, then the administrator of the Good Samaritan Village in Moscow, Idaho, became one of the leaders in applying hospice concepts in a nursing home setting. The Moscow facility emphasized quality of life, not the quality of death, meeting the holistic needs of the family and the dying resident. Wuenschel indicated that facilities engaged in hospice care needed a medical staff that could provide pain control, volunteers to sit with the family and their loved one who was close to death, and a staff skilled in interdisciplinary care.[64]

Proper care for victims of Alzheimer's Disease and related disorders became another Good Samaritan Society priority during the 1980s.[65] The Society created special units at several Society centers for persons with Alzheimer's and related disorders (for example, age related dementia or a severe decline in intellectual functions). The interior design and furnishings of these special units were modified to meet the behavioral problems associated with Alzheimer's Disease. The walls and ceilings were painted in soothing colors, patterned floor tiles were removed, along with potentially dangerous items, and a quiet public address system was introduced. Trying to make the residents' stay as safe and comfortable as possible, the Society increased nursing care and modified meal service and activities.[66]

With the acquisition of the Good Neighbor Homes in Minnesota during the fall of 1992, the Good Samaritan Society entered care programs in two very different areas. A Huntington's Disease Unit and a Chemical Dependency Unit were located at the University Good Samaritan Center in Minneapolis, Minnesota. The 25-bed Huntington's Disease Unit opened in August 1993. One of six such centers in the United States, it was the only one in the Upper Prairie Plains specializing in the physical and behavioral aspects of this genetic disease.[67] The 30-bed Chemical Dependency Unit, housed at the University Center, operated two programs. The Bridgeway Elders Program, begun in 1976, met the physical, emotional, social and spiritual needs of chemically dependent senior citizens. The goals for its patients were sobriety, freedom, and restoration of self-esteem. The Bridgeway's Brain Injury, Disability, and Illness (BIDI) Program worked with chemically dependent people between 18 and 50 years of age. The program strove to make its clients sober and healthy people ready to meet any challenge that life might offer.[68]

Introducing new and better methods of care has been a constant at the Society's centers over the past quarter century as the Good Samaritan Society met increasing governmental requirements and studied and adopted new techniques for the physical care, remotivation, and rehabilitation of the residents at its many facilities. The Society, through its own personnel, developed innovative ways to provide better care and to honor and to promote the self-worth of the people given to its trust.[69] Society officials continued to emphasize participatory management. The

Central Office, however, had full authority and responsibility to see that each center operated as a true Good Samaritan facility. The administrator was responsible for directing affairs within the facility, but he lived in two communities — the local community which he dealt with on a daily basis and the community of the Good Samaritan Society. Society officials believed that the Good Samaritan Society was structured in such a way that an administrator could live effectively in both communities. Elbow room for administrators declined, but the physical care of the people placed in their charge improved dramatically. Modern medicine now dictated the type of care practiced in the Society's facilities. The frail and elderly were living longer, necessitating more care. In the midst of all of this significant change, the Society never forgot its central mission, to care for the soul as well as the body.

Chapter Fourteen
RELATIONSHIPS
1970-1996

"Make it your aim to be at one in
the Spirit and you will inevitably be
at peace with one another."
— Ephesians 4:2-3.

Throughout its major growth period in a national culture becoming increasingly secular, the Good Samaritan Society remained true to its Christian mission. Augie and John Hoeger constantly reaffirmed Dad Hoeger's operating philosophy that the Society existed to serve the Lord and His people that were in need. Augie said that the Society was begun in poverty and born out of Christian piety with a deep faith in God together with a hope in Jesus Christ.[1] The Executive Director warned Society members present at the annual meeting in 1978 not to become self-satisfied. He said, "The more I have, the more likely I am to resist God's will in my life. Because the more I have, the more I stand to lose."[2] At a regional meeting in the same year, John Hoeger said that the Good Samaritan Society could easily go the way of many other organizations. They were organized by dedicated Christians, prospered, then forgot their heritage and Lord and permitted materialism to dominate their lives.[3] In explaining the Society's long-range goal, he said:

> Heaven is our goal, the cross the energizer. The
> plan was to stay in His grace, follow His will, and
> serve Him day by day as He would direct His will
> to be done on earth as it is in heaven.[4]

Often called "Bottom Line John," John Hoeger wore the title with gratitude because, he said, the true bottom line was Christ's mission. "If our finances ever become the end purpose instead of just a means of accomplishing our mission," he declared, "then we would utterly fail as a harvesting tool because then we are no longer in Christ's hands or even working in his field."[5] The Good

Samaritan Society was a service organization, not a money organization.

Spiritual Relations

Two years before his death, Dad Hoeger expressed his concern
about the Society maintaining its proper relationship with Kingdom work. He believed administrators were becoming too caught
up in finances and in contending with fire marshals, doctors, and
welfare forms.[6] The paramount concern of the Society, he wrote,
is a sound evangelical spiritual ministry for its residents and
workers. Wanting to assist administrators with their spiritual
programs, in late 1968, August Hoeger, Sr., distributed guidelines
for a spiritual program and appointed Pastor John C. Kilde, the
former administrator of the Sioux Falls Center, as area Spiritual
Coordinator.[7]

Kilde's tenure had been brief and a formal spiritual ministries
program was not restored until the Reverend Jacob B. Jerstad
was named the first full-time Director of Spiritual Ministries on
June 1, 1977. Jerstad, a graduate of Concordia College, Moorhead, Minnesota, and Luther Theological Seminary, had served
several parishes before becoming administrator of the Good
Samaritan Village, Hastings, Nebraska, in 1972. He married
Laura Hoeger and to their union six children were born, including Dr. Mark Jerstad, who became the president of the Good
Samaritan Society in 1989.[8]

An enthusiastic and firm believer in the importance of witnessing for Christ, Jacob Jerstad carried out a series of witness
programs at the centers between 1977 and 1980. Through area
workshops, he challenged center staffs to become involved in the
spiritual well-being of their residents. Workers were trained 1) to
be alert to any of the spiritual needs of residents, 2) to witness in
a kindly way for Christ, and 3) to pray with and for the residents.
Jerstad then conducted a resident witnessing program at the
Society's facilities. Reminding residents of the Savior's call — "Ye
shall be my witnesses" — they were enlisted and trained to personally win and nurture their center neighbors and friends for
Christ. Spiritual needs would be met on a one-to-one basis. He
reminded uncertain participants in the program of Christ's
words in Luke 12:12 — "The Holy Spirit will teach you at that
time what you will say."[9]

The Reverend Frank Wilcox became the Director of Spiritual Ministries in September 1982, following the retirement of Jacob Jerstad from active ministry in December 1981. Wilcox, a graduate of Augsburg College and Luther Theological Seminary, and his wife Amelia ("Billie") Hoeger, served as missionaries to India and Pakistan under the World Mission Prayer League from 1945 to 1956. They were in Nepal from 1970 to 1976, where Reverend Wilcox served as Executive Secretary for the United Mission to Nepal. Prior to joining the Central Office staff, Wilcox directed a Lutheran Bible School in Los Angeles, California. While on the mission field, Frank and Billie had three sons, one of whom, Gregory, succeeded his father as Director of Spiritual Ministries.[10] Frank Wilcox continued Jerstad's initiative of traveling to centers to conduct workshops for staff and residents, he conducted spiritual retreats for new administrators and chaplains who served the facilities, and he led in ministry at the Central Office. In addition, Wilcox prepared simple Bible studies to be used to further enhance spiritual life in the Society's facilities.[11]

On September 16, 1988, Pastor Wilcox retired from the Central Office to be a part-time chaplain at the Good Samaritan complex at Kissimmee, Florida. His successor, his son, Pastor Gregory Wilcox, was born in Taxila, Pakistan, when his parents were stationed there as missionaries. The younger Wilcox graduated from Augustana College (Sioux Falls) and from Luther Northwestern Seminary, St. Paul, Minnesota. While attending college and the seminary, he worked as a nursing home orderly, gaining valuable insights into the care of the elderly and the Society's work. Before joining the Society in mid-September, Greg Wilcox had served as a pastor at Hendrum, Minnesota, since 1983.[12]

One of the major challenges faced by the new Director of Spiritual Ministries was the ongoing struggle by administrators to keep the Christian faith central to their work. At times, they were almost overwhelmed by other matters, including federal and state regulations, finances, politics and health care, supervision of staff and residents and community relations. Wilcox reminded them:

> Nothing can claim more importance than our faith. It is what makes us unique and it is the very reason for our existence! There is no more important part of the Good Samaritan Society than its faith. A relationship with God in Christ

lies at the heart of who we are. It explains our
past, gives meaning to our present, and direction
to our future. There are no questions about that,
only different voices affirming the same reality.[13]

He urged the continuance of Society-wide devotions. Although
their preparation might be difficult and time consuming, administrators, as the spiritual leaders of their facilities, were obligated to prepare them. As spiritual leaders, administrators needed
to have their own faith continually challenged and strengthened.[14]

Three new spiritual programs were introduced by Greg Wilcox
in 1992. The programs included:
1. STAR — Staff Affirming Residents
2. SEASONS — (Ecclesiastes 3:1) "For everything
   there is a season, and a time for every matter
   under heaven." Administrators would be called to
   a yearly retreat.
3. TRIPLE R — Reflections, Relationships and
   Risks - A yearly evaluation of each administrator's spiritual leadership.[15]

Between 1992-1995, the STAR program was expanded with
the expectation that it would become an integral part of the orientation for all Good Samaritan employees. When inaugurated
in 1992, the program consisted of two-day inspirational and educational workshops for all Society administrators plus one staff
member from each facility. In 1995, 18 mini-retreats were held
under the auspices of the STAR Program. In addition, there were
34 STAR inservice sessions involving approximately 2,200 staff
members. Sessions emphasized listening, compassion, empathy,
servant leadership, lamenting with the lonely, and sharing the
Gospel as a gift. Workshop participants left the sessions with an
understanding of the basic premise of STAR — If one felt loved
and affirmed by others, he or she could capture a new sense of
what it was like to be loved and affirmed by God. The feeling of
being accepted by God was at the heart of the STAR Program.[16]

Church Relations

The Good Samaritan Society's formal relationship with the
Church was resolved in 1986. Relations with national Lutheran

Church bodies, particularly after 1935, were not always harmonious. Dad Hoeger's individualism did not always sit well with the Church hierarchy. He had been influenced by the German practice that the Church's functions were to teach and preach; mission and charity work were separate entities.[17]

Cooperation and togetherness were a part of the small-town culture of the Prairie Plains in the 20s and 30s, and many local Lutheran Churches were staunch supporters of the work of the Society. From 1922 to 1930, the Good Samaritan Society was an official part of the Iowa Synod. When the Iowa Synod merged with the Ohio and Buffalo Synods in 1930 to form the "old" American Lutheran Church (ALC), the Society became a recognized arm of the ALC with one ALC person attending all Society Board meetings. This Church representative, however, had no vote but he could make recommendations on how the Society should proceed. Tensions rose during the schism years, 1938-1940 (See Chapter V), when Church officials became critical of Dad Hoeger's business methods and the physical state of several of the Society's facilities, arguing that they were below the standards of most national nursing homes.[18] Hoeger was not particularly interested in national standards. Rather, his concern was an immediate reality: he wanted to care for old people, and finances and good records were not important if the needs of the elderly were being met. He did not want impositions placed on him by state welfare departments, lawyers, or Church bureaucrats.

In 1957, the Good Samaritan Society sought and received recognition by the Board for Christian Social Action of the American Lutheran Church. The recognition was provisional and only of the "operating Society as a service organization." None of the Society's homes were included in the recognition. Within a year, the ALC threatened to withdraw its recognition because of Dad Hoeger's "go-it-alone" actions. The ALC charged the Society with moving into California without benefit of close geographic ties and a lack of supervision. Hoeger was similarly criticized for entering new communities without the prior knowledge and approval of the Society's Board of Directors. The Christian Social Action Board of the ALC also accused the Society of using the general recognition as a means for soliciting funds for local institutions. Another Lutheran body, the Evangelical Lutheran Church (ELC), had informed ALC officials that they did not want the Society to enter certain geographic areas without their approval.[19]

When the "new" American Lutheran Church (a merger of the "old" ALC and the ELC) was formed in 1960, the Good Samaritan Society was no longer recognized by any Lutheran synod. As the merger of the two Lutheran Church bodies took place, the ALC made an offer to establish a relationship with the Society but on the Church's terms. The ALC insisted on a reorganization of the Society to give control of its various facilities to local Lutheran control. The proposal was rejected by the Society and the offer withdrawn.

Conversations with the ALC resumed in 1961 after the Society's Board of Directors passed a resolution directed at seeking a closer relationship with the Church. While negotiations continued over the next quarter century, the Good Samaritan Society remained a fellowship of Lutherans, providing "physical, spiritual, mental and emotional care in the spirit of Christ."[20] During the 70s, Augie Hoeger had voluminous correspondence with John M. Mason, Director of Services for Aging of the ALC, regarding the recognition issue. Mason was sharply critical of the Society's past policies and the status of its facilities. He wrote that the recognition of the Society in 1957 by the old ALC was only a conditional recognition and that the Church was planning to withdraw this recognition if the 1960 merger had not occurred.[21] He intimated that the Society was in trouble with the Internal Revenue Service. Augie replied that "In almost 51 years, we have never had the slightest suggestion of difficulty with the IRS."[22] Regarding Mason's stance toward the Society, John Hoeger believed that John Mason felt that the Good Samaritan Society was behind the times. Hoeger thought that Mason would have been very much for what the Good Samaritan Society had become, an organization with up-to-date facilities and skilled administrators and staff.[23]

The American Lutheran Church, adhering to the philosophy of the former ELC, refused to compromise, insisting that either the Church (or a recognized constituent body of the Church) must own and operate the Good Samaritan Society or there would be no relationship. As correspondence and negotiations continued through the 70s, Pastor Jacob Jerstad served as chairman of the Society's Liaison Committee. The ALC's Board of Social Action finally issued an ultimatum that either every member of the Society's Board of Directors would have to be elected by some

body of the Lutheran Church or the ALC would have no relationship with the Good Samaritan Society. Augie Hoeger wrote to
Dr. David W. Preus, the Acting President of the ALC, that the
offer was unacceptable to the Society. It would mean the complete demise of the Society as a corporation. The Board of Directors firmly rejected the proposal.[24] Despite the deadlock, the
Society continued to express its desire to work more closely with
the ALC, to be recognized by the Church, but to retain the
Society's autonomy.[25]

In the mid-1980s, the dialogue between the two entities finally moved toward a positive conclusion. In 1985, the ALC indicated that it wanted to recognize the Good Samaritan Society and
asked the Society to draft a proposal which Church officials could
review and approve. Key issues that were resolved to the
Society's satisfaction included: 1) the continued operation of the
Society as an independent organization, as it had for 64 years,
and 2) a stipulation that no Society funds would be diverted for
Church use.[26] At the Society's annual meeting, August 10-13,
1986, the members approved an affiliation agreement with the
American Lutheran Church and the Lutheran Church in America (LCA). The affiliation, as defined by the Division for Social
Ministry Organizations of the ALC and representatives of the
Society, meant recognition by the Churches that the mission of
the Society and the mission of the Churches were fully integral
to the achievement of God's mission.[27]

The agreement stated that the parties could exchange knowledge, expertise, share resources and services:

> ...while preserving the Society's freedom to oper-
> ate independent of Church ownership or control
> and safeguarding both Society and Church funds
> in such a way that the Society is not required to
> support Church facilities and activities, nor are
> the Churches, either corporately or through local
> congregations, required to support the Society or
> its Centers.[28]

Starting with the 1987 Annual Meeting, the Society would
designate four of its Board members for approval by the ALC and
the LCA or their successors. These Board members were free to
vote on Society business without instruction or direction from
the Churches. The four individuals were not required to report to

or be responsible to the Churches for their participation in Society affairs.[29]

Formal affiliation continued with the creation of the Evangelical Lutheran Church in America (ELCA) on January 1, 1988. Three church bodies, the LCA (2.9 million members), the ALC (2.3 million members), and the Association of Evangelical Lutheran Churches (110,000 members), merged to form the fourth largest Protestant denomination in North America. Through the merger, the ELCA related to more than 300 social service agencies through its Division for Social Ministry Organizations, in addition to the Good Samaritan Society, with its more than 200 nursing homes.

Through the efforts of President Mark Jerstad, The Evangelical Lutheran Good Samaritan Society was also recognized by the Lutheran Church-Missouri Synod (LCMS) on September 25, 1990. The LCMS granted the Society "Recognized Service Organization" status through its Board for Social Ministry Services. This new affiliation helped the Society to reaffirm its Christian heritage and to broaden its denominational character. In listing the Society in The Lutheran Annual, officials of the LCMS said, "We recognize your ministry is one through which the mission of the Church becomes the people of God responding in the name of Christ to those 'who thirst, are naked, were sick, lonely and in need of comfort' and we pray God's blessing upon it."[30]

As the century drew to a close, the Good Samaritan Society continued to strengthen its relationship with the organized church. At the Annual Assembly of the South Dakota Synod (ELCA) in 1994, a resolution (#71) was approved, recognizing the Society's desire to be "more closely related to the life and mission of the South Dakota Synod." The resolution put the Society on the synod budget for 1995 and for following years for a $1.00 partnership in synod ministry. The Society would serve as a resource to synod congregations and its personnel were invited to participate in the synod's ministry.[31]

The Good Samaritan Society, under Mark Jerstad's leadership, likewise became a major participant in the Association of Lutheran Social Ministries Organizations (ALSMO). ALSMO came into being in April 1995 with the merger of the National Association of Lutheran Ministries with the Aging (NALMA) and the Coalition of Executives (COE). ALSMO's national office was established at the Minnesota Regional Service Center of the Good Samaritan Society. In late May 1996, the Society co-sponsored with ALSMO, the Minnesota Lutheran Long-Term Care Council, Luther Northwestern Seminary, and the Center for Studies in Aging, at the University of North Texas, a Midwest Regional Conference in St. Paul that considered "Leadership in Long-Term Care: Leaders in the 21st Century."[32]

In summation, Dad Hoeger had formed the Society in 1922 as an "arm" for congregations to use in ministering to those in need. In the 20s and 30s, local congregations provided an important means of support for the Society's early work. Beginning in the 1940s, national Lutheran Church leaders began to take an interest in the Good Samaritan Society. These officials were often critical of the Society's management and its facilities. Sometimes they were condescending toward and demanding of August Hoeger, Sr,. and his son, August Hoeger, Jr. Father and son continued to maintain the independence of the Society as they built it into the largest nonprofit nursing home corporation in the United States, known for its quality long-term care. They wanted to work with Church officials, not under them, and after decades of negotiation, a successful relationship was established in 1986. In gaining recognition from the several national Lutheran Church bodies, the Society remained true to its origins. The Board of Directors was an intersynodical group when the Society began in 1922. While diversity became a part of the Society's heritage, the dominant objective continued to be the Christian mission of sharing God's love in word and deed.

Board Relations

Religious diversity as it related to administrators, voting privileges and representation on the Board of Directors also underwent scrutiny during the 70s and 80s. During the first 48 years of the Society's history, only Lutherans were employed as administrators. The new licensure laws for administrators, required by Medicaid, necessitated the hiring of non-Lutherans as administrators to manage the Society's growing number of facilities. To alleviate the shortage of qualified people, the Board of Directors, on March 5, 1970, ruled that Christians of any religious denomination could serve as administrators.[33] At the Society's annual meeting, August 8-11, 1971, voting rights were extended to non-Lutheran administrators. The Lutheran identity of the Society was maintained by requiring that Board members, regional directors, and all Central Office specialists must be Lutheran.[34]

Board members continued to be elected at annual meetings. They could serve two consecutive three-year terms and at a later date could be reelected. Six of the 15 members were Society administrators. With their first-hand knowledge, they helped the Board make the correct decisions on planning, policy and personnel. The remaining nine members could not be employed by the Good Samaritan Society, including the corporation's officers, and served without remuneration. The Board met quarterly. The Executive and Associate Directors served at the Board's pleasure.[35]

The issues of the composition of the Board of Directors and the qualifications of Board personnel continued to be modified through periodic changes in the Society's By-Laws. In August 1987, a change in membership was formalized. Board members, henceforth, were to be active Christians with at least nine (the non-employees) being Lutheran. The requirement that all of the corporation's officers be Lutheran remained unaltered.[36] The governance structure and functions of Board meetings were refined in the early 1990s due to the efforts of the Board's chair, Dr. Marilyn Stember. Board members were assigned to one of three standing committees — Board Development, Finance, or Planning, and to the ongoing Audit and Nominating Committees. In July 1995, there were further revisions in the Articles of Incorporation. Of significance, Article VI - Board of Directors, now stated that the Good Samaritan Society would be administered by a Board of no less than 15 people nor more than 25. All non-employee members, all active affiliates of a Lutheran Church, would be selected, designated, and submitted to the Evangelical Lutheran Church in America or its successor for approval. Article V was revised to stipulate that the Society's affairs in the future would be administered by a Board of 16 people — nine non-employees, six administrators, and the President of the Good Samaritan Society, who became a voting member of the Board.[37] The changes in the Articles of Incorporation and By-Laws were approved by the Society's membership at the 1995 annual meeting. Because of the Society involvement with the federal government, housing financed through the Department of Housing and Urban Development (HUD), approval also had to come from government officials through the special corporations mandated when accepting HUD funds. By March 1997, the revisions had been approved and the Society's President could vote at Board meetings.[38] The Society made changes in its governance system because of new affiliations and acquisitions and because of federal and state mandates. Flexible when flexibility was demanded, the Good Samaritan Society continued to emphasize the religious ideals defined and practiced for three-quarters of a century.

Relations with the LHHS

A brief attempt to restore a fractured relationship from the past occurred in 1987. A proposal for a joint-venture with the Lutheran Hospital and Homes Society (Lutheran Health Systems) came from LHHS in early 1987.[39] A liaison committee, made up of representatives from the Society and LHHS, met on March 13. In late spring, via a conference call, the two health care organizations viewed areas of possible interest for a joint-venture. The list included 1) AIDS, 2) rural development, 3) a Center for Aging, and 4) insurance. Other matters took center stage in the late 80s and the proposed cooperative undertaking never materialized.

Leaders Relating to Others

During his 25-year tenure as head of the Good Samaritan Society, Augie Hoeger said he was fortunate to be surrounded by many good people. He related very well to these people and, in turn, the vast majority of them were loyal to the Good Samaritan Society. Augie combined the efficiency and expertise of many people. Corporate officers and Central Office personnel were given problems to solve. Collectively, they made decisions and brought them to the Executive Director for his approval and implementation or for referral to the Board of Directors. Using this system, the Good Samaritan Society continued to advance with intermittent periods of either rapid or slow growth. When he made his final report at the 1987 Annual Meeting, Augie noted that the average years of a regional director with the Society was just short of 19, with 12 of these years served as a regional director. The thing he hated worst about his position was having to release good hearted, hard working people, especially those who had been with him, who did an adequate job, but who could not quite keep up with the changes.[40] His greatest challenge had been to secure and to train personnel. He and the Central Office staff committed much time to securing skilled nurses, nurses aides, dietitians, social workers, and therapists.[41]

In addition to his administrative duties, August Hoeger, Jr., served on the Board of Directors of the American Health Care Association, the American Association of Homes for the Aging, and the National Geriatrics Society.[42] He received a brief respite from his regular tasks in 1983. In the previous year, the Board of Directors established a study leave program for the Executive Director and the Associate Director. The Society's executives could accumulate up to 16 weeks of leave with the final approval of the Board. The program provided reimbursement for salary, fringe benefits, travel, books, and some housing costs.[43] From August 20 to November 18, 1983, Augie and Betty Hoeger visited nursing homes, hostels, and independent living facilities in Australia and New Zealand. Between 1981-1983, three administrators from Australia had visited the Society's Central Office and several facilities, gaining knowledge of the Society's operations and returning to Australia to apply the information to their facilities.[44] In 1984, the Board of Directors approved a sabbatical study leave for John and Kathy Hoeger to visit care facilities in Germany, England, and Scandinavia.[45]

On December 12, 1986, with Dr. Charles Balcer presiding, Augie Hoeger announced to members of the Executive Committee of the Board of Directors his decision to retire in the forthcoming year. In a detailed memorandum, Hoeger asked for acceptance of his resignation as president of the Society at the 1987 annual meeting. He had served 25 years as Executive Director and President. He would be 60 years old in 1987, and he believed it was time to step down. Augie asked the Board not only to approve his resignation but to give its approval to plans that he and Betty had formulated for the next two years. They planned to visit all of the Society's centers, to do climate surveys, and to present programs on the roots, history, and philosophy of the Good Samaritan Society. They would remain in the Society's employ as consultants and archivists, proposing to gather all of the documents from the corporation's 65-year history and to organize them in the headquarters' archives. Augie recommended that his brother, John, be appointed president for a two or three year period, as John saw fit. Augie did not foresee the Society being run by co-directors in the future, and he proposed a governmental structure that included a president and several vice presidents — for Operations, Finance, Development, and

Human Relations.[46] After approving Augie's request to continue for two years as the Society's archivist and consultant, the Board's Executive Committee named John Hoeger President-elect, asking him to form his own management team.[47]

Augie and Betty Hoeger went on to visit the Society's facilities, listening to groups of people and discovering how the Society could improve its services. From their climate surveys, they drew several conclusions. They discovered that there were more state rules than federal; the Society operated in 26 states and had to contend with 26 sets of rules. Medicaid reimbursement continued to be a problem for many centers. The Society could be proud of its resident-centered environment. The Good Samaritan Society was doing what was expected of a Church home; Augie stated that "We are a Church Home." After visiting 69 centers, they stated that there were six basic needs for residents — independence, privacy, social interaction, spiritual fulfillment, recognition as an individual, and a supportive environment.[48]

There were several dramatic moments during the 1987 annual meeting. Six hundred Society administrators, their spouses and family members, and friends gathered to pay tribute to Augie Hoeger. They spoke of his dedicated, caring style of leadership and his personal display of faith and inspiration. At the evening banquet, honorary Doctor of Divinity degrees were conferred on August Hoeger, Jr., and John Hoeger by President Roger Fjeld of Wartburg Theological Seminary. The degrees had been formally awarded on May 10, 1987, at the Seminary's spring commencement exercise. With Dr. Charles Balcer, President of the Board of Directors and the Rev. Norman Eithreim, Bishop of the South Dakota District of the ALC, presiding, the evening events culminated with the installation of John Hoeger as the third President of the Good Samaritan Society.[49]

The Society's new President had a remarkable ability to create images through words. Leadership was synonymous with carrying a banner, proclaiming the mission. Upon his accession to his new role in the Society's work, he said that several years earlier he was:

> ...privileged to be a leader of a procession. Dozens of people were walking up the aisle of our church to the altar. It was Easter. I was carrying a banner proclaiming the reality of the resurrection. After the service, my very good friend, a

church janitor, told me, "John, I've never seen you
walk so tall." Even though I've shrunk a bit since
then, I have a feeling I'm going to break that
walking tall record. You've given me the honor of
carrying our Good Samaritan banner. I cannot
conceive of my receiving a greater honor. It's not
at all that I as an individual have earned or
deserved this honor more than you. It's just that
our Lord, through you, is placing the banner in
my hands with the order to march.[50]

John Hoeger was born at Arthur, North Dakota, on August 17,
1923. He made his first financial contribution to the Good
Samaritan Society with the "legendary quarter" given to help
prepare buildings of the old Fargo College for the Good
Samaritan Institute. John Hoeger graduated from Concordia
College (Moorhead, Minnesota) with a Bachelor of Arts degree in
1945. He received a Master of Divinity degree from Wartburg
Theological Seminary in 1948. John married Katherine Kauf-
man, a pastor's daughter, whom he met while serving as an
intern in Toledo, Ohio. Katherine had become a parish worker
after graduating from Capital University in Columbus, Ohio.
Three children were born to their marriage, two sons and a
daughter.

John was ordained on June 25, 1950, in Fargo, North Dakota,
by his father, the Reverend August Hoeger, Sr. The sermon was
delivered by Pastor A. L. C. Keller, a longtime friend and pastor
to the Hoeger family. By this time, lanky John Hoeger had
entered into the Society's work as administrator of the Parkston
Country Center between 1948-1950. After his ordination, he
became a parish pastor, serving congregations in Overland Park,
Kansas (1950-1957), and Ontario, California (1957-1966). Upon
returning to the Society in 1966, Hoeger became the administrator of the Good Samaritan Village, Hastings, Nebraska. The Village, at the time, had over 1,400 residents and a staff of 400.[51]
The Board of Directors called him to the Central Office as Associate Director in 1972.[52]

Shortly after being elected for a three-year term, Hoeger
appointed John Burkholder as Vice President for Finance,
Assets, and Expansion and Dr. Mark Jerstad as Vice President
for Facility Services. He proposed to name a Vice President for
Operations and to add a Maintenance Consultant to the staff.

The latter person would visit all of the facilities and initiate a preventative maintenance program.

During his 15 years as Associate Director, Pastor John Hoeger cast his own shadow on the Good Samaritan Society. He was deeply committed and unselfish in his devotion to the Good Samaritan Society. "His hand was firmer," wrote Michael Bice, "but never overbearing. He provides an effective counterpoint to Augie, and the end result is superb leadership for a large and diverse constituency."[53] John proposed an evaluation of the Central Office in the early spring of 1988. He believed that the decision-making process had become slower and more cumbersome due to a doubling of the staff over 12 years, technological changes, and increasing demands from governmental agencies. Insisting that the system be made more efficient, he recommended that the evaluation begin by examining the functions of the Operations Committee.[54] He was a fiscal conservative who urged good stewardship at both the Central Office and facility levels. Each dollar of dues should produce a dollar or more of value to the resident who provided it. Next to every member's loyalty to Christ was loyalty to the residents entrusted to the Society's care.[55] In his sermon at the 1989 Annual Meeting, John Hoeger told his audience that even with the Society's success it could lose it all. He retold Dad Hoeger's story of a very wealthy entrepreneur who farmed thousands of acres and owned many elevators in the Red River Valley. The successful businessman planned a trip to Europe, and he wanted the safest passage possible. He booked passage on the Titanic and drowned in the North Atlantic Ocean. His children proceeded to squander his wealth.[56]

As Augie's associate, John wrote many articles for periodicals such as the *Lutheran Standard*, *Lutheran Outlook*, and *The Good Samaritan*, relating the Society's achievements and mission. Humor and anecdotes, often relating to his personal experiences, were injected into his talks. Usually, there was a lesson in the anecdote. He recalled the dedication of a large, white frame house as a nursing home in Laurens, Iowa. Over the years, the Society had acquired several large, white houses. Some of them were dubbed "big, white elephants" by personnel at the Central Office.[57] At this particular white house, he delivered the dedicatory address to a crowd largely made up of older people, standing in the area between the house and a feed barn. His talk was much too long and many in the audience were reaching the point where their legs were about to give out. At that point, the Lord commanded a fly from the feed barn to make a kamikaze attack into Hoeger's mouth. He swallowed the fly, bringing his talk quickly to a conclusion.[58]

In discussing the importance of financial stewardship, President Hoeger told of how he always drove his car close to empty, believing that he would find cheaper gas down the road. His wife, Kathy, informed him that having faith does not mean you don't fill the tank. For the Good Samaritan Society, the net operating margin was the gas in the tank that enabled the Society to run.

For over two decades, the older Hoeger brother was an active leader in developing long-term care on the national scene. He had served as second vice president of the Nebraska Nursing Home Association, vice president at large of the American Health Care Association, a committee member for the American Association of Homes for the Aging (AAHA), and as vice president of the National Foundation for Long-Term Care.[59] On September 13, 1989, he was presented with the AAHA Prestigious Chairman Citation.[60]

Meeting with the Board of Directors in February 1989, President John Hoeger said that he planned to retire at the time of the 1989 Annual Meeting.[61] Having served only two years as President, he indicated that a multitude of factors pointed to his retirement being in the best interest of the Society and the Lord's will.[62] Except for his years as a parish pastor, most of his adult life had found him engaged in the Society's work.

The two brothers had guided the Good Samaritan Society with strong but gentle hands. Since 1963, the Society had continued its pioneering efforts in the nursing home industry, and it became a pioneer and national leader in residential apartments for independent living. The Society was in the vanguard of community outreach programs such as meals on wheels, telephone reassurance, senior companions, adult day care, partial care, respite care, hospice care, referrals and consulting service, and home health services. The Good Samaritan Society pioneered the concept of supervised care units, as well. Since 1963, the Society had experienced phenomenal growth. It had become a major force in the nursing home industry, adjusting to federal and state mandates and providing a superb service structure for its member facilities.

In stepping down as President, John Hoeger compared the Good Samaritan Society to a ship that had been completed and had experienced a shakedown cruise on stormy waters. The ship had come through with flying colors with much good being accomplished. It was now time to set sail and make others aware of the Society. Two years earlier, he had attributed the success of the Society to consistency. Hoeger wrote:

> We've avoided so many half-baked schemes and fads of the hour that have plagued so many organizations this past decade. We've stuck to our knitting. Even looking back with 20-20 vision, I can think of few things that could have been done differently, viewing the circumstances. So much of what has happened is impossible to explain on a purely human basis. What I am saying is each of these banner carriers were the Lord's person for that period.[63]

As he surrendered the reigns of leadership, he again made reference to carrying the banner. He urged the Society to select a new president who could hold the Society banner even higher — not for the sake of the Society but for the opportunity it would give for greater service. He concluded that Society members should "Be able to share the good we have received from our Lord and share it with many more than ever before."[64] Augie and John Hoeger had continued the fierce dedication to mission set forth by their father. The only thing that finally counted was that the Society's members remain in, with, and under the grace of God in Jesus Christ.[65]

Above: *Mark Jerstad and Sioux Falls Mayor Gary Hanson discuss plans for a campus for the National Center for Long Term Care, to be build on land adjacent to the present national headquarters of The Evangelical Lutheran Good Samaritan Society.*

Below: *A winter view of the north facade of the national headquarters of the Society in Sioux Falls, South Dakota.*

Chapter Fifteen
NEW VISIONS -
NEW REALITIES
1989-1997

"Unless a living organism changes,
it necessarily dies."
— William Barclay,
Daily Celebration.

"Where there is no vision, the people
perish." (KJV) — Proverbs 29:18

T he selection process for a new president who would raise the Society's banner to new heights and who would prepare the Society for the 21st century began shortly after John Hoeger announced his intention to resign. The Board of Directors, chaired by Dr. Charles Balcer, named a search committee, chaired by Board member Dr. Sandra Looney, to conduct a national quest for a new leader. In taking this action, authority passed from the Hoeger brothers to the Board of Directors. A professional search firm was employed to develop a profile of characteristics desired in a new president and to identify possible candidates for the position. The committee sought a person who was creative, intelligent, dynamic, energetic, and who shared the Society's strong sense of mission.[1] In a letter to Society members, outgoing President Hoeger wrote that a change in leadership marked the beginning of a new chapter for the Good Samaritan Society. The new president might differ as to means, he wrote, but "our end purpose must always be the fulfillment of our mission." He went on to say that the handwriting of the author [Jesus Christ] is clear.[2]

During the search process, Doctor Balcer completed his term of office in July 1989. In relinquishing his position as chairman of the Board of Directors to his successor, Charles Halberg, Balcer urged the search committee and the Board to trust the process. Following a nationwide search, the Board, on September 11, 1989, announced its selection of Dr. Mark A. Jerstad from the

six finalists.[3] Doctor Jerstad took over as president of the Good
Samaritan Society on October 1. Twelve days later, on October
13, 1989, he was formally installed at the Central Office by
Charles Halberg and Reverend Dean Hofstad. The liturgists
were John Hoeger and Greg Wilcox; Augie Hoeger delivered the
meditation.

The new chief executive was born at Bagley, Minnesota, on
May 6, 1942. At his birth, his father, the Reverend Jacob Jerstad,
concerned about finances, asked the attending physician, "Can
we have this on time, please?" The doctor replied, "Well, you have
already had nine months."[4] Time payments and time passed
swiftly. Because his father was a pastor, Mark grew up in Iowa,
Minnesota, and North Dakota before his family finally settled in
Minneapolis. He graduated from the Minneapolis Academy,
received his Bachelor of Arts degree from St. Olaf College in
Northfield, Minnesota, in 1964, and his Master of Divinity degree
from Luther Theological Seminary in May 1968. While a student
at the Seminary, he married Sandy Skustad at Virginia, Minnesota, on August 21, 1965. Three children, two daughters and a
son, were born to their union. Mark Jerstad was ordained at
Bethel Evangelical Lutheran Church, Minneapolis, Minnesota,
on November 2, 1969. He completed his formal education at
Union Theological Seminary, Richmond, Virginia, where he
received a Master of Theology degree in Biblical Studies and a
Doctor of Philosophy degree.

A person who was comfortable in many environments, Jerstad
was well equipped to become the president of the Good
Samaritan Society. He had served as pastor of Zion Lutheran
Church, International Falls, Minnesota, from 1969 to 1976. While
at International Falls, Reverend Jerstad had taught courses in
philosophy at Rainy River Community College, worked as a psy-
chologist and group facilitator in a program of spiritual growth
and development, and served as a lecturer and resource person
for various area nursing homes. At these nursing homes, he
helped staff members relate to people near death. Jerstad also
worked with delinquent boys in northern Minnesota and as a
resource counselor and speaker in the primary treatment program of the Arrowhead Center on Problem Drinking at International Falls. He joined the faculty of Augustana College in Sioux
Falls, South Dakota, as campus pastor and a professor in the
Department of Religion, Philosophy and Classics in 1976.

Doctor Jerstad's interest in the Good Samaritan Society dated back to the 1970s. Close acquaintances envisioned that he would be with the Society at some future date.[5] They became more convinced that this would be his future when, as part of a sabbatical leave in 1984, he became an administrative intern (AIT — an Administrator in Training) at the Society's Sioux Falls Center. Jerstad had entered the program because he was interested in developing a program in gerontology and long-term care at Augustana College. Under the tutelage of Norman Stordahl, the Center's administrator, Doctor Jerstad completed the requirements for licensure as a nursing home administrator.[6] Fellow interns believed that Mark would never be a center administrator but that he was destined for a different role in the Good Samaritan Society. When he gave devotions, they marveled at his story-telling ability.[7] Jerstad's ability to explain complex behavior and problems through stories became almost legendary in the Society. All AITs were required to spend two weeks as certified nursing assistants (CNA). It was a "life changing experience" for Mark Jerstad. Later, he wrote about the esteem he felt for CNAs, the work they performed, and what he had learned from them and the residents.[8]

Jerstad's uncles, Augie and John Hoeger, recognized his ability and interests and brought him into the Society as Director of Administrative Personnel and Education in 1985. He was charged with the recruitment, hiring, placement and training of interns and licensed administrators.[9] Joining the Good Samaritan Society was a significant career change for Doctor Jerstad. He had no knowledge that someday he would be president of the corporation. Two years later, Jerstad became Vice President for Facility Services, and when he was selected to be President, he was Vice President for Operations. Jerstad was the right person at the right time to be selected as President of the Good Samaritan Society. He had one foot in the past, his family relationship, and a fervent belief in the Society's mission, and a foot in the future, his belief that changes must take place in the Society because of a rapidly changing health care environment.

The Good Samaritan Society's new president was a very active person, physically, mentally, and spiritually. He followed a regimen of exercising and dieting. According to his own accounts, he did not need much sleep. Aside from conducting Society matters, he enjoyed traveling to distant places. These trips often coincided with trips made by his children. At the annual meeting in

1996, he showed a video of his bungee-jumping exploits while in New Zealand.

Intellectually, Jerstad was very bright, and he never lost his curiosity. He enjoyed reading new works in theology, finding some of the views of the authors fascinating. Two of his favorite authors, however, were Loren Eiseley and Gerhard Frost. He often quoted Frost's "It's not so important who we are but whose we are." President Jerstad loved residing beside a lake. He enjoyed the ambience and atmosphere of lake life. The family cabin beside Rainy Lake, near International Falls, often entered into his conversation. Being at the lake provided him with the opportunity to "sit back," read, relax and be with family.

From the pulpit, Jerstad primarily delivered talks, not sermons. He would take a text and relate a story to it. Listeners knew that he had a grasp of what the text was trying to say but he did not engage in an elucidation of the text or textual criticism. The stories he related were often emotional and poignant.[10] As chaplain at Augustana College, he gave devotions on such topics as "Hands" and "Feet." During one Christmas season, he raised the question: "What If It Had Been A Girl?"[11]

The new chief executive was a very political person. He had a sense of the hidden dynamics that go into organizations and between people. As a pastor he could see one's brokenness. Jerstad was not naive about people. He had a good sense of what they really were and he had a good sense of who he was.[12] According to David Horazdovsky, who became Chief Operating Officer (COO) of the Society, "Mark was always reading people," and as a result, their relationship grew with him. Because of his interest in a person, he was good at drawing that person out.[13] Doctor Jerstad knew how to use people's skills or talents, not along formal lines of authority, but as he needed them without regard to administrative structure.[14] He was confident in his leadership and decision making.

As Jerstad settled into his new position, colleagues discovered that he had an anticipatory sixth sense in a very spiritual way. He would see the intent of things that other people would not think of or miss, issues centered around human nature or human need. There would be meetings when after everyone else had exhausted their ideas, he would come up with a new approach. His colleagues would say, "Gee, why didn't we think of that?"[15]

By nature, President Jerstad was a very inclusive person. He lived the Society's mission, and he wanted others to do the same. In addressing members of the Society, he would say — "You people are awesome" or "You people need to understand" or "You people are wonderful." By using "You people," he was defining them as a distinct mission body; he was defining them as a congregation.[16]

Mark Jerstad was a multifaceted personality. He never let the Society's personnel forget that mission was central to the Society's work. He was without peer in articulating the uniqueness and importance of the Society's mission. He maintained the Christ-centeredness of the Good Samaritan Society during a time when it could easily have dissipated. He changed how the Society did things without changing its traditional mission. At the same time he lived out the mission, he enjoyed some of the accoutrements of leadership. He was always looking for the best, was very meticulous in his public attire, and enjoyed good cars, be it a DeLorean or a Lexus.

This interesting dichotomy in their leader's personality was never an issue for the Society's members and the residents in its facilities. He spoke from the heart when he said that the Good Samaritan Society's employees must continue to share Christ's love in word and deed. He provided inspired knowledgeable and visionary leadership. Jerstad called people to something larger than themselves. He excelled at encouraging people to do their best and to be their best.[17] In his short tenure as president, he successfully dealt with the necessity for change in many of the Society's operative functions.

Challenges and Opportunities

As his accession to office took place, the Board of Directors indicated a number of long-range challenges facing the Society and its new president. The Board's foremost goals were 1) seeking greater public visibility, outreach and leadership, being an example to other long-term care providers; 2) joining with the ELCA, the Society's new partner, in ministering to the sick, aged and infirm; and 3) establishing a presence and identity in the halls of city, state, and federal governments in seeking solutions to the problems facing the nursing home industry. President Jerstad, in turn, indicated some immediate problems that he would encounter. They included shortages of qualified staff, changing demographics, increasingly complex regulations, meager reimbursements, and the growing complexity of care for the Centers' residents.[18]

According to David Horazdovsky, the major challenge in meeting the rapidly changing health care environment of the 1990s "did not mean we [the Good Samaritan Society] change who we are or what we believe in but we need to change the way we go about caring for people."[19] Changes in the health care environment included new modes of care, competition and clientele, increasing self-interest among American workers, and diminishing reimbursement for services rendered.

In the health care marketplace, alternatives to traditional nursing home care mushroomed. The new options included home care, assisted living units, and independent living services. Simultaneously, the health care industry entered an era of managed care, an entrepreneurial system that emphasized outcomes, cost, and quality. How could the Society, a faith-based long-term care provider, go about controlling costs in competition with secular, proprietary health care systems?

The changed economic, political, and social environment raised new questions regarding reimbursement. Different states required different reimbursement procedures. The Omnibus Budget Reconciliation Act (OBRA) of 1987 became fully effective in 1990. The legislation had eliminated the distinction between skilled and intermediate care facilities, meaning that all nursing homes in the country needed to qualify for skilled nursing care. OBRA also required extensive upgrading of facilities, particularly the Society's buildings in North Dakota. The Good Samaritan Society agreed to upgrade its facilities, satisfying regulatory requirements, without imposing an unmanageable financial burden on current and future residents. OBRA became a challenge to balancing a budget. It was a fair system if reimbursement was based on operating costs, but that was not how the system was designed. In the mid-1990s, the fiscal policies of the federal government, and many state governments, became more conservative. What would be the future status of Medicaid and Medicare? As of 1996, the Society's revenue from Medicaid and Medicare was 60 percent of the corporation's income, an indication of how reliant it had become on this source of revenue. Ironically, the Good Samaritan Society had reluctantly entered the Medicare program. Certification of a facility was a laborious task. Caring for rehabilitation patients required new forms of care, including therapy and additional technology. Sub-acute care units began to resemble hospitals. By the 90s, Society facilities with these units were competing with home health care, assisted living facilities, and rural hospitals which used "swing beds" to capture Medicare funds.[21] The Society became a victim of its own circumstances. With its growing reliance on income from Medicaid and Medicare, the Society did not have to depend as much on community support. Community support was considered less important with the access to federal dollars that had emerged out of President Lyndon B. Johnson's "Great Society" program of the mid-1960s.[22] As the government dollars diminished, how could the Good Samaritan Society rekindle community support? Were there philanthropists and charity-minded groups that would support the Society? Should the Society seek more private pay residents to fill its facilities? If so, who would care for the medically indigent — people for whom Medicaid did not pay full price but who were in need? How could the Society understand its mission to serve all when it needed new sources of revenue to continue to give quality care?

The Good Samaritan Society likewise had to adapt to changes in demography and its labor force. The continued decline of the rural population necessitated a review of services that would be viable in rural areas. As the census declined in many of the Society's rural centers, Central Office personnel also had to consider what should be done with the buildings. In urban areas, consideration would have to be given to care for a more diverse population. Would changes have to be made in the Society's social and spiritual care to meet the needs of the growing number of non-white minority groups and non-Christian residents? Would the increased longevity of the general population necessitate new forms of care? Should the Society become involved in caring for persons with Alzheimer's Disease, Huntington's Disease, and other maladies that required long-term care?

Finding skilled and compassionate people to work in the Society's facilities was also becoming a problem. In a competitive market, finding personnel with a service mindset became more difficult. After being employed, how could these workers be inspired to embrace the Society's mission and find meaning in their work? In a culture where many workers were concerned only with wages, benefits, and furthering themselves professionally, what could be done to motivate people to provide compassionate, Christian care?

The Response

The Jerstad administration moved quickly to respond to the issues and questions raised in the preceding paragraphs. The great challenge was to accomplish needed changes without changing the Society's essence, its tradition of being a Christian nonprofit provider of services. People had to realize that the Good Samaritan Society was an organization that met people's needs and as these needs changed in the health care environment so the Society needed to change. The new president was up to the task. Until he became fatally ill in November 1996, Mark Jerstad dealt successfully with the need for change; he changed how the Society did things without changing its mission.

President Jerstad first proposed that long-term care providers develop alternate models of care delivery; expand staff development programs, including staff scholarship opportunities; work with both the private and public sectors to obtain adequate funding; and diversify services while maintaining high standards of care.[23] It was an ambitious agenda but much of it was accomplished between 1989 and 1996.

To order the concerns expressed, the Board of Directors, in 1990, had set in motion a process for organizational planning. Personnel from the Central Office, administrators from large and small facilities, and non-administrative Board members joined President Jerstad in developing a strategic plan. The plan would guide the Good Samaritan Society's ministry toward the 21st century. The goals included:

1. Renewing the Society's commitment to champion the Christ- centered focus in all of its activities.
2. Providing the highest quality health care and service for the whole person.
3. Achieving financial security to sustain and enhance the Society's mission through sound operations and resource development.
4. Developing and supporting effective leaders.
5. Providing the highest quality work environment to establish the Society as the employer of choice.
6. Establishing a plan for long-range growth while maintaining quality service.

7. Diversifying Society/Facility services based on community needs and Society/Facility potential.
8. Instituting a coordinated legislative advocacy effort linked to the Society's mission.
9. Developing collaborative, beneficial joint ventures.
10. Investigating the feasibility of developing the Good Samaritan Center (Institute) for long-term care.

At the annual meeting in 1991, the assembly adopted the ten long-range goals included in the strategic plan. These goals became a driving force as the Good Samaritan Society engaged in programs and planning during the 1990s. In the ensuing five and one-half years following their adoption, Mark Jerstad, in a capable and enthusiastic manner, led the Society toward fulfillment of the strategic plan. The ensuing pages relate how much was accomplished during his administration in successfully restructuring the Good Samaritan Society to be proactive in responding to a radically changing health care environment.

His various administrative and educational experiences enabled Doctor Jerstad to closely evaluate the Society's organizational structure and operations and relate them to the rapid changes taking place in the health care field. One of his goals became to ensure the success of the Good Samaritan Society within the evolving complexity of the health care reimbursement and regulatory system. Mark Jerstad realized that the Society had to go to a new level; the early years had served the Society well, but the economic, political, and social environment had changed. He believed that the administrative component of the Good Samaritan Society had to be restructured for a proper response to a changed health care environment.[24]

Leadership: The Executive Committee

President Jerstad's creation of a new executive structure was one of the several important changes that he introduced to help the Society's personnel begin to see what else they could be. He wanted to move the Good Samaritan Society ahead in a dramatic way, and the selection of several highly qualified and responsible individuals to assist him in governing the Society was a major step in that direction. In seeing the need for a management team of vice presidents, mirroring the structure of proprietary long-term care nursing home chains, he empowered others to be responsible for the affairs of The Evangelical Lutheran Good Samaritan Society.[25]

Bonnie Brown, who began her work with the Society as administrator of the Good Samaritan Center, Tyndall, South Dakota, in November 1971, was appointed Vice President for Operations in 1990. She was charged with day-to-day oversight of the Society's facilities with the regional directors reporting to her.[26] Brown was recognized by center administrators and regional directors as the person who kept them focused on their responsibilities — in terms of mission and service to residents and staff. Dan Holdhusen, the Chief Financial Officer, and Dean Mertz, who took charge of the new Human Resources Department on May 1, 1993, also were given vice presidential status. Mertz had joined the Society in 1978, and he had served as a center administrator and Regional Director before coming to the Central Office.

David Horazdovsky, who had joined the Good Samaritan Society in August 1978, and who had served as a Regional Director since 1989, became Vice President for Advancement, Support, and Planning on June 1, 1994. Horazdovsky would coordinate the activities of the New Development, Project Development, Resident and Community Services, and Resource Development Divisions. When Bonnie Brown announced that she would retire at the end of 1996, Horazdovsky was named the new Vice President for Operations. Dennis Beeman, a former center administrator and the Director of New Development and Expansion since April 1993, succeeded Horazdovsky as Vice President for Advancement, Development, and Planning.

Immediately after he became aware that he had terminal cancer, in November 1996, President Jerstad selected Horazdovsky to be the Society's Chief Operating Officer (COO). Bonnie Brown set aside her retirement plans and continued as Vice President for Operations. The vice presidents became members of a six-person Executive Committee which made crucial governing decisions for the Good Samaritan Society.

William (Bill) Kubat replaced Ed Kilen as Director for Resident and Community Services in the summer of 1995. Several months earlier, Kilen had asked for a reduced assignment because of failing health. His new role was that of Care and Services Regulatory Consultant until his retirement in April

1997. Kubat, a 1979 graduate of Marquette University, had been with the Society for 16 years, 15 of them as an administrator. He was Regional Director of the Eastern Region prior to succeeding Kilen. In December 1994, Jerstad named Dr. James Beddow, former president of Dakota Wesleyan University, Mitchell, South Dakota, to coordinate planning of a National Center for the Society and the Center's educational component, the National Institute for Long-Term Care.[27] Beddow holds a Ph.D. from the University of Oklahoma. In addition, he had completed post-doctoral studies at Harvard University's Institute of Educational Development.[28]

It was necessary for the Society to move towards greater centralization of decision making. At the same time, however, when he was establishing a new corporate executive structure, Mark Jerstad attempted to uphold the elbow room concept for administrators. In this regard, he walked a fine line very effectively. It would have been very easy to further consolidate decision making within the Central Office without paying homage to decision making at the local level. Certain functional matters were centralized but key operational matters were kept in the hands of the administrators.[29]

President Jerstad would be out of the Central Office more than he was in. He expected his vice presidents to run the Society in his absence. Nevertheless, he was always very interested in what they were about. He knew the importance of details but he left them to responsible people. He had the big picture in mind as he prepared the Good Samaritan Society to enter the 21st century.[30]

Jerstad's Administrative Style

As the Society's chief executive, Mark Jerstad was not a micro-manager. He had selected excellent people to surround him as advisers, and they were the ones who paid attention to the details. He gave the vice presidents, regional directors, department and division heads considerable latitude in carrying out their assigned responsibilities, but there were times when he would intercede if he believed an action or policy was not in the best interests of the Good Samaritan Society or of a particular individual.

Although President Jerstad was confident in his leadership and decision making, he found it difficult to see an employee dismissed from the Society. With his great personal warmth, he always had a strong desire to respond to an individual's problem. There were a few occasions when he interceded on behalf of an employee when the latter's supervisor had recommended dismissal.

The chief executive's interpersonal skills were superb. He controlled the dynamics of a meeting through relationships.[31] In meetings of the Executive Committee, he wanted all sides to be heard. Although Jerstad was not afraid of conflict, he listened carefully to discordant views and had a gentle way of correcting people if he felt their policies were not right. He always said that there should be "no secrets, no surprises, no subversion." Everything should be on the table, an overt signal that he did not want to be deceived or misled.[32] Doctor Jerstad lifted up the points people were trying to make, summarizing the key issues. Favoring consensus, he tried to let the group evolve toward its own conclusion. If no decision was forthcoming, he would make it later on. There were times when his decision was neither popular nor well accepted. However, he openly accepted criticism and was never defensive or protective of himself.

Although he was not into per diems and ratios, President Jerstad always understood the Society's financial situation. He understood what made the Society financially successful and where the Society was financially vulnerable. He knew the key performance numbers. When the President perceived there were problems with the so-called big picture, he sought experts to assist in dealing with the complexities of the Good Samaritan Society's operations and investments. He counseled for the bottom line, relying heavily on the Society's chief financial officer, Dan Holdhusen. He said that Society personnel should never forget where the dollars came from; they were provided by the residents. His expression "No margin, no mission" indicated the importance of good stewardship in using those dollars to carry out the Society's mission of quality care.

As the Society's chief administrator, Mark Jerstad never asked the people around him to do something for the Society that he did not truly believe in his heart was correct. He always expressed his gratefulness for the work they were doing for the Society. "Awesome" was the word he often used when recognizing individual or group accomplishments. Through his keen sense of the changing health care environment and the current trends of the culture, he described it as "holding a wet finger to the wind," through his remarkable leadership skills and vision, and through his selection of quality people, the Good Samaritan Society made remarkable strides toward readying itself to continue its mission of fulfilling people's needs into the next century.

Opening the Society to the World

Having ensured that the internal affairs of the Society would be administered properly, Mark Jerstad directed much of his attention to external affairs. His creation of a greater awareness of the Good Samaritan Society's strengths and unique qualities on the national scene was another of the major accomplishments of his administration. He opened the Society to the world, particularly to the health care world. In a very visible and articulate way, Jerstad opened the shutters to new relationships with non-profit health care associations, government agencies, and the Church. Through his efforts, the Society's story was brought to the attention of congressmen in Washington, D.C., of delegates to meetings of national long-term health care associations, and to representatives of the print media. His actions were infectious. They not only affected the Central Office but also motivated many administrators to become more knowledgeable and active and to take an active role in health care trade associations. This new proactive stance was healthy for all members of the Society.[33]

Very shortly after assuming leadership of the Society, Doctor Jerstad became involved in the work of national health care associations, striving to improve the conditions for long-term care. In 1990, he became chairman of the American Health Care Association's (AHCA) Consumer Relations Committee. With his intense focus on the resident and the quality of care, he brought a different perspective to the AHCA. He reaffirmed that the organization's quality initiatives were on the right track. It was Mark Jerstad who introduced the idea of an ethics agenda for the Association.[34] The Good Samaritan Society had its own formal Code of Ethics. The Central Office Ethics Committee met on a regular basis. In 1994, the Development Committee of the Board of Directors adopted its own Code of Ethics, believing that "as Christian people we are committed to personal and professional excellence in our service to the Society."[35] (Appendix D, Code of Ethics).

The president of the AHCA, Dale Thompson, said of Jerstad:

> His unwavering focus on the core mission of the long term care industry served as an ever-present "conscience." It's easy for us to get lost in the shuffle of reimbursement or the economics of what we do, or the regulation of what we do, at the expense of why we're here, which is to care for the elderly.... He [Jerstad] brought that, and it was always there. That shouldn't be so unique, but sometimes it is.[36]

Mark Jerstad became vice president of the American Health Care Association's Multifacility Steering Committee and a member of its Ethics Task Force, its Legislative Committee and its Nonproprietary Committee. He joined the House of Delegates of the American Association of Homes and Services for the Aging (AAHSA). Through these national affiliations, Mark represented the Good Samaritan Society in actively lobbying for adequate Medicaid and Medicare funding. In this role, he had contacts not only with South Dakota's congressional delegation but with the Vice President of the United States, Albert Gore, Jr., and former U. S. Senator George Mitchell of Maine. The Society's Chief Executive Officer also became an advisory board member of the ELCA's Division of the Church in Society and a member of the coalition of Executives of the ELCA's Social Ministries Organizations.

His effectiveness in relating to individuals and to large groups was based on his warm, outgoing personality and his insistence on personalizing every encounter, every relationship. David Horazdovsky said that Jerstad's "handshake in many ways depicted who he was as a person and how he saw his ministry to people — one handshake at a time." Mark's colleagues asserted that "at the core of his spiritual, professional, and personal mission was a constant focus on the individual."[37]

President Jerstad combined this personality trait with great energy, drive, intelligence, insight, and sensitivity to the aging in carrying out the Society's mission, in fulfilling his administrative responsibilities, and in being proactive on the national health care scene. He was an early riser, getting up well before dawn.

The tall and slender executive would set aside time for devotions before coming to the office. When greeting a person in or out of the office there was the familiar handshake. Mark would put his hand out at a certain angle, stand very erect, and grasp his or her hand in a powerful handshake, always in a warm way. It was always a very welcoming and inviting greeting. The accompanying smile was contagious.

He was very effective in the use of body language. In intimate conversations, Jerstad would sit down, cross his long legs and lean in. He leaned intentionally into the conversation, showing genuine interest in what the other person had to say. The same body language was present if he was concerned or distraught about some issue. On these occasions, the Society's Chief Executive would sit back, look off in the distance, and heave a sigh, indicating that he was not happy with the situation.[38]

In addressing a group, Doctor Jerstad again used body language to gather people in. He had an ability to project himself to any of the people who were in the listening audience. He moved around a lot, using his hands to make a point. He fixed people with his gaze. Listeners felt that his eyes were on them when he spoke to a large audience. He would look at a person as if he or she were the only one in the room. Mark had a wonderful ability to match names and faces which he used in referring to people by name in a large group. He possessed a certain presence that commanded attention, even among those individuals who did not know him well. What he said and how he carried himself made him a leader among leaders.[39]

He captivated audiences with his stories, and he had a story for every occasion. There was usually a smile and a twinkle in his eyes as he related the tale. Some of the stories involved his children and his wife, Sandy. Through his ability to orally describe a situation and through his mastery of detail, President Jerstad articulated persuasively the healing power of love. In an address to the Ohio Health Care Society, he stressed that great health care givers share in words their love, compassion, and care for residents. At the heart of the matter, he concluded, is "our faith in our Lord Jesus Christ." He said it was at the heart of the mission of the Good Samaritan Society. Jerstad informed his audience that Christ's love takes on flesh as employees care for residents.[40]

Visiting Facilities

One of President Jerstad's favorite expressions was "People helping people helping people." He saw the Central Office as a service to administrators who, in turn, enabled their staffs to serve residents. The two jobs that meant everything to him were the administrator and the nursing assistant; he constantly talked about their role in the Society's mission. By extension, he was talking about housekeepers, laundresses, and other employees of the Society's facilities, as well. In the winter of 1992-1993, President Jerstad completed 70 hours of training to become a certified nursing assistant (CNA). The two weeks that he spent as a CNA made an indelible impression on him. In the June 1995 issue of the *Provider*, a publication of the American Health Care Association, Mark described his training to be a certified nursing assistant and the esteem that he developed for CNAs and the work that they do. He believed that CNA training would be invaluable for any health care executive. He wrote, "Spending a day with a CNA ... offered humbling reminders of how easy it is for those of us in executive positions to lose touch with the essential nature of our work." He concluded the article by stating, "My hope is that this experience will reawaken our sense of mission in action and help make us better servant leaders."[41]

Part of his being an external president was to try and visit every facility once a year. He saw this as a calling, not work. The constant travel meant absence from family, and he dearly valued his family. He emphasized to the Society's employees that they must take care of their families. People should be right with Christ and their families.[42] In addition to regular visits to facilities, Jerstad was present for the observance of a center's anniversary and for week-end open houses. In visiting a facility, he would say how special that place was, that he felt like he should take his shoes off because "I am on holy ground."[43] Asserting that the common denominator in all that the Society did was the residents, he always met with several of them when visiting a center. It was common for him to kneel or hunker down before an elderly woman in a wheelchair, take her hand, and say "Oh, be still my heart." He would talk to the elderly men and women about what was going on in their lives. His ability to remember residents' names and the names of their relatives often came into play in these conversations. Discussions might involve a new great grandchild, the crops, the weather, an old car, or some aspect of faith. He had a way of knowing if someone was in pain. Jerstad could sense when people were grieving, "like a missile to a heat source."[44]

In visiting the many centers of the Society, Mark Jerstad always asked "Who is the best care giver here?" Usually, one name would come up at each Center. He shared some of his findings during a post-luncheon address to the Ohio Health Care Society. He had discovered that:

1. Great care givers treat each person as someone who is real.
2. Great care givers share in words their love, compassion and care for the residents.
3. Great care givers enter into relationships with the residents, learning from the interaction.
4. Great care givers learn through listening as well as by giving, and
5. Great care givers are team builders. They engage in their work with joy.[45]

A woman from Ross Products Division of Abbott Laboratories had heard Jerstad list the criteria for an excellent care giver. When her firm heard that he was ill, its officers decided to sponsor an annual award to one certified nursing assistant in the Good Samaritan Society, the award to be given at the annual meeting. Using the characteristics that President Jerstad had determined from his inquiries, the Central Office sent nomination forms to the various nursing facilities. The replies were evaluated by a Central Office committee and one CNA was selected to receive the award, in honor of Mark Jerstad, at the 1997 annual meeting of the Society.[46]

Educating and Sustaining Administrators

The emphasis on the training and education of the Society's staff increased during Jerstad's administration. The quality of care continued to depend on well-educated, well-trained, and committed administrators. The Administrator-in-Training (AIT) program was further developed and refined during his tenure as chief executive. New administrators and interns attended week-long orientation, financial, and spiritual leadership workshops, an important part of the AIT curriculum. Improvements were made as well in the Second Level Internship Program, designed to prepare experienced administrators for leadership positions in multi-level facilities. According to Dean Mertz, the Vice President for Human Resources, administrators who completed this program knew what it really meant to be a multi-level administrator.

In 1995, the Society-sponsored Master's degree program was terminated due to the difficulties and expense of having administrators travel for classes at the University of North Texas in Denton and Luther Northwestern Seminary in St. Paul, Minnesota. In this program's stead, administrators were given the opportunity to work with other universities which offered graduate programs that could be applied toward long-term care. This change enabled administrators to pursue Master's degrees closer to their sites of service.

As the education of the Society's work force increased, so did their income. President Jerstad stressed that competitive salaries and benefit packages would be provided for staff members. He said, "One of my goals is to make sure staff can have a decent living wage."[47] The care and nurturing of administrators paid dividends; the Society's turnover rate for administrators continued to be between 6 and 7 percent, one of the lowest turnover rates in the long-term care profession.[48] Nationwide, the turnover of administrators in the early 1990s was 26.4 percent.[49]

New Growth — New Services

With client needs becoming more complex and building costs increasing, the Central Office assigned construction and design consultants to specific geographical areas. They would ensure that standards were met, that expansion possibilities were taken into account and that construction timetables were followed. Using master construction plans at the national headquarters ensured continuity, maximized resources, and contributed to the most functional environment for resident services.[50]

As part of a plan for long-range growth, Mark Jerstad challenged the relevant Society divisions to prepare models of financing, construction-design, and possible joint-venturing to provide senior housing and assisted living models in a wide variety of Society communities. In conjunction with the challenge, Jerstad authorized a $25 million initiative for the development of assisted living and congregate housing projects. The first of the new congregate living facilities, at Pine River, Minnesota, was completed in May 1993.

The creation of a Growth Task Force was a key element in the planning process. The Growth Task Force met periodically at the Central Office. Growth plans, however, continued to be tempered by a decline in census and the uncertain future of the Medicaid and Medicare programs. In 1994, 50 percent of the revenue at the Society's nursing facilities came from Medicaid, another 7 percent from Medicare. The Society continued to expand Medicare certification. By 1995, 172 facilities were certified and Medicare use increased 36 percent. The long-term care market was expected to grow from $111 billion in 1995 to $287 billion in 2005. Most of the population over age 85 was projected to be in the Prairie Plains, from Oklahoma to the Dakotas and from Montana eastward through the Old Middle West to New England.[51]

The Growth Task Force considered the implications of managed care options, including the future role of health management organizations (HMOs), as they related to future revenues for long-term care centers.

Managed care implied a move away from a sense of ownership by the staff in the Society's facilities and the communities in which the facilities were located. Managed care required a greater need for centralization of decision making. It required coordinated and planned activities from the top down, a procedure that generally had not been a part of the Society's governing practices.[20] How could the Society alter its decision-making process to quicken the response time to financial and market issues while keeping administrators involved in monetary decisions?

As part of the further diversification of Society services based on community needs, a specialized Huntington's Disease Care Unit was opened at the University Good Samaritan Center, Minneapolis, Minnesota, in 1993. One of the few of its kind in the United States, the unit was soon operating at full capacity. A program to serve persons with traumatic brain injury was established at the University Good Samaritan Center in Minneapolis. The Good Samaritan Center in Anoka, Minnesota, began providing kidney dialysis treatments for community members. The Society continued to construct special care units for victims of Alzheimer's Disease and related disorders as well as quarters for physical therapy at several locations. Throughout the 90s, the Good Samaritan Society added home health care, hospice, assisted living, outpatient rehabilitation, and other therapy services at facilities in various parts of the country.

The Society initiated contacts with other health care providers to see if they would be interested in beneficial joint-ventures for care and research. The Good Samaritan Society announced that its services could help other long-term care facilities.

Overriding the plan for new growth and services was the Society's commitment to the highest quality health care and services for the whole person. A new quality assurance program, introduced in 1995, affirmed the Society's Number One goal — "To champion the Christ-centered focus in all of its activities" and the Society's Number Two goal — "To provide the highest quality health care and service to the whole person." The Central Office suggested that staff members approach quality improvement from Scriptural perspectives. In particular, the following perspectives were recommended:

1. Christ's teaching that "Whatever you did for these my brothers and sisters, you did for me." (Matthew 25:40).
2. Christ's challenge to "Love your neighbor as you love yourself." (Mark 12:31).
3. Christ's inspiring example of servant leadership as seen in the washing of the disciples' feet. (John 13:15).[52]

Striving for Financial Security

The Good Samaritan Society advanced several new initiatives to promote the financial security of the organization. Realizing that continued government support at its present level was tenuous, the Central Office asked each facility to inaugurate resource development programs, either in the form of annual fund drives or capital campaigns. Planned gifts would be a major source for building endowment funds. Beginning in 1992, Central Office staff provided fund raising training for administrators and local advisory boards at 70 Society facilities. The development program was expanded to include almost every Society facility in 1994.[53] The original thought, proposed by Mark Jerstad, was that each facility could achieve a million dollar endowment, ensuring financial stability and continued quality care even if government support decreased.

One criticism of the Good Samaritan Society was that it had always been very innovative in caring for those in need but not in the handling of its surplus funds. This shortcoming was remedied with the creation of the "Helping Hands Fund" in 1991. It was designed to provide facilities with a safe and convenient method of investing monies and maximizing the return on investments. President Jerstad reminded administrators that they and the Society at large were entrusted with the meager funds of the elderly and that it would be good stewardship to properly invest these monies. Facilities owned by The Evangelical Lutheran Good Samaritan Society began investing in the pooled fund in January 1992.

The Helping Hands Fund was a professionally managed investment portfolio consisting of high quality stocks, bonds, annuities, and other market investments. Within two years, the fund had experienced substantial growth while providing shareholders with an excellent combination of return on investment and protection of capital. Since its inception, the Helping Hand Fund has had an average annual return of 8 percent.[54]

The centralized control of investments initially created a significant community public relations problem for several facility administrators. For many years, a facility's surplus funds had been invested in local banks. It took time to convince local citizens that the Helping Hands Fund would give their facility a better return on its money. Through a greater sophistication of the investment program, centers increased their capacity to offer additional services, to buy equipment and furniture, and to implement new technology.

A major change in the Helping Hands Fund took place in 1995. A money market fund called the Short-Term Asset Management Fund (SAM) was established. Investors in SAM could maximize their cash positions while safeguarding their principal. Operating cash was more accessible to administrators through this fund.

The Board of Directors exercised fiduciary responsibility over the Helping Hands Fund and other Society assets. The fund forced the Board to be more policy conscious in the allocation of funds, determining what percentages should be in assets, in the equity market, and in the bond market.[55]

Gender and Leadership

The gender issue proved frustrating for the Society's chief executive. He recognized that the great majority of employees in

Good Samaritan facilities were women, as were an even larger percentage of residents. In 1997, approximately 40 percent of the administrators were female. Jerstad was very interested in providing leadership opportunities for women. He stated that women in the same roles as men, with the same experience and qualifications, should receive the same salary. Female employees said that the Society had been very fair to them. The problem was finding qualified women who were willing to accept leadership positions in the Central Office.

During the Jerstad presidency, only one woman, Bonnie Brown, Vice President for Operations, was a member of the Executive Committee. At one time there were four female regional directors, three of them appointed by Brown, who was instrumental in providing leadership opportunities for women. Only one woman had served as a Division Director. Women had been offered positions as regional and divisional directors but they were reluctant to accept them because of the amount of travel required with the position. A regional director could be away from his or her family four out of five days of the work week.

Women have served as chair of the Society's Board of Directors. Dr. Joyce Nelson, Professor of Nursing at Augustana College (Sioux Falls), elected to the Board in 1987, became the first female to preside over the policy-making body in June 1991. It was during her tenure as chair that the Society purchased the Good Neighbor nursing home facilities. Her successor, Dr. Marilyn Stember, the Dean and Director for the Center of Nursing Research at the University of Colorado, was instrumental in restructuring the Board of Directors, assigning specific committee duties to the members.

The Good Neighbor Acquisition

In the third year of Mark Jerstad's administration, the Good Samaritan Society markedly increased its number of facilities with the purchase of the Minnesota-based Good Neighbor Corporation. The association of the two health care organizations began a few years earlier when Jerstad met Bill Hargis of the Good Neighbor organization at a meeting in Arizona. The two men became friends and when Good Neighbor made a decision to sell its facilities, the Good Samaritan Society was given the opportunity to acquire the for profit corporation. At first, the Society backed away from purchasing Good Neighbor, believing that the asking price was above real market value.[56] Negotiations continued and, on October 30, 1992, the acquisition of Good Neighbor Affiliated Groups was completed for $66.3 million.[57] Many of the long-term care facilities acquired in the transaction had interesting legal histories and an additional $1.8 million was expended in legal fees to bring these legal histories up to date.[58]

Good Neighbor, as the second largest Minnesota operator and owner of nursing homes, operated 26 long-term care facilities, a senior housing complex, and four personal care locations. A nursing services pool and two affiliated management and medical supply companies were included in the transaction. With 13 facilities in the Minneapolis-St. Paul metropolitan area and 14 homes in greater Minnesota, Good Neighbor employed some 3,500 staff and served approximately 2,780 residents.[59] Already operating and managing 23 nursing homes, serving 2,147 residents in Minnesota, the Good Samaritan Society decided to continue operating the former Good Neighbor headquarters as a regional service center in St. Paul. Charles Halberg was named president and chief executive officer of The Evangelical Lutheran Good Samaritan Society of Minnesota, a subsidiary of the Good Samaritan Society.[60] Halberg was a classmate of Mark Jerstad at St. Olaf College, and had later earned a law degree from William Mitchell College of Law, St. Paul. When President Jerstad first began restructuring the executive leadership of the Society, Halberg had been appointed Senior Vice President and Chief Financial Officer, beginning June 1, 1991. In this role, he had charge of financial operations, coordinated legal and governmental activities, and supervised the work of the Central Office department directors.[61] As Jerstad created his new Executive Committee, Halberg's role shifted. For a time, he served as head of Society Advancement, Director of the Society's Purchasing Department, and as the Society's General Counsel.[62] As the Society's legal counsel, Halberg handled the legal problems involved in acquiring the Good Neighbor facilities. Ultimately, Halberg assumed leadership of Good Samaritan Supply Services, Inc.

President Jerstad took a bold step in favoring the acquisition of the Good Neighbor facilities. The Board of Directors engaged in lengthy discussions on how to finance the venture without endangering the financial standing of the Good Samaritan Society. Jerstad favored the acquisition for several reasons. He saw it as a mission opportunity, as an evangelical act. He saw potential in learning from their systems. By incorporating the experienced people of Good Neighbor into the Society, Jerstad believed that the management personnel could gain new insights and expertise into operation of facilities in metropolitan markets.[63] The Society's chief executive viewed the purchase as an opportunity for expansion of the ministry, as well. This was an opportunity to increase the number of Good Samaritan licenses in Minnesota. In Jerstad's view, the opportunities for growth outweighed the potential problems of leveraging a large amount of money to make the purchase.[64]

All staff members of Good Neighbor became employees of the Good Samaritan Society. The Society's Board of Directors governed both entities. The Board and the personnel of the Central Office believed that the nonprofit and for-profit providers could be successfully integrated over a three to five year period. President Jerstad felt that the transition would occur smoothly. David Horazdovsky commented that the Society wanted to be a welcoming, inclusive body. He went on to say that "There was the hidden expectation that they [Good Neighbor personnel] would be like us, that when they saw us they would like us."[65] It did not always play out that way.

A major difference between the two organizations was the Society's Christ-centered emphasis. Some people in Good Neighbor appeared anxious over the Good Samaritan Society's irrevocable application of the Gospel in care for those in need.[66] Society officials reasoned that just because the former owners of Good Neighbor were motivated to make a profit did not mean that same motivation applied to the employees. The latter group, hopefully, would accept the Christian mission of the Society.[67]

In retrospect, the creation of The Evangelical Lutheran Good Samaritan Society of Minnesota was not a wise move. It increased the belief of a number of former Good Neighbor personnel that they could continue with many of their policies and practices and that the Society would also follow these policies. It became a test of wills because they believed that their model was sound and that they would change the Good Samaritan Society. The division between the two corporate cultures ran much deeper than had been expected.

A Transition Retreat was held at the Central Office in early April 1993 to further facilitate the integration of the Good Samaritan Society of Minnesota into the larger Good Samaritan

Society. Retreat members took a proactive stance, stating that the Society's mission statement and the spiritual component of the Good Samaritan Society's ministry would be implemented in all former Good Neighbor facilities. By this time, Central Office personnel had recognized that the Society could not have two different systems operating in South Dakota and Minnesota. As a practical matter, the data from *all* of the Society's facilities needed to be aggregated in one central office.[68] There were also problems with reimbursement; the recently acquired Good Neighbor homes needed to be integrated into the Good Samaritan Society's accounting system. The decision was made to dissolve the transition entity, legally known as The Evangelical Lutheran Good Samaritan Society of Minnesota, on December 31, 1994. The Society would continue to maintain a significant presence in the Twin Cities area through a regional service center.[69]

The acquisition of the Good Neighbor facilities was an expensive venture, both monetarily and in the time directed towards solving the cultural differences and overcoming the challenges experienced by people in both organizations. It was a learning experience for Society personnel. Buying Good Neighbor was an extension and test of the mission statement. From the beginning, the Central Office should have been more directive in assimilating the for profit corporation. By mid-1997, many of the upper-echelon people, formerly with Good Neighbor, had left the Society.[70] A staff of approximately 80 former members of Good Neighbor in the Twin Cities had been reduced to a staff of 25 by June 1997. The turnover of administrators in the former Good Neighbor facilities was much less. Most of the remaining administrators possessed the same goals as the Good Samaritan Society. Several of their facilities, however, posed a problem as they were aging, older buildings.[71]

Although the Good Neighbor acquisition continued to be a difficult chapter in the Society's history, significant strides toward reconciliation took place in 1996-1997. Nevertheless, significant differences of opinion continued to be expressed. Some members of the Board of Directors considered the purchase of Good Neighbor to be one of the crowning achievements of Mark Jerstad's administration. They praised the successful integration of a proprietary bottom line organization with the nonprofit Good Samaritan Society. In the long run, they have argued, one should consider how many residents in these former Good Neighbor facilities will benefit from the Society's Christ-centered mission and quality care.[72]

The Institute for Long-Term Care

For several years, the Society's Board of Directors and its executive officers had discussed a center for the study of long-term care. In a 1986 memorandum, Albert Erickson and Elliot Thoreson, proposing a joint-venture with Augustana College, had suggested a Lutheran Center for the Study of Aging.[73] In the following year, the Board proposed that such a center should include education, research, and resource and professional development as the main points of concentration.

President Jerstad zealously took up the cause of establishing a national institute for long-term care. For a period of time, he was almost alone in attempting to fulfill the vision of a national center for long term care. He saw the creation of an institute as a means for the Society to do things for the entire health care industry. Seeming obstacles were overcome as he pressed forward, revising and remodeling the details of his vision for a national institute. The Society's strategic goal of "Investigating the feasibility of developing the Good Samaritan Center (Institute) for Long-Term Care" was only a stepping stone to developing a full-blown campus for the Good Samaritan Society.

Having adequate space was one of the problems that had to be solved if the National Center was to become a reality. The Central Office had continued to encounter space problems at its location on West Avenue North in Sioux Falls. On January 1, 1990, the Society had acquired a building directly south of the national headquarters, at 908 West Avenue North. A Board action to fund a 7,000 foot expansion of the Central Office proved unnecessary with the acquisition of the 30,000 square foot, "908" location. Accounting and data processing functions were housed in the newly acquired structure. The two locations accommodated 108 Central Office personnel.

When the building which housed the former Bank of New York credit card center became available in 1993, the Good Samaritan Society took action to acquire it. Located in southwestern Sioux Falls, at 4800 West 57th Street, the building accommodated 200 employees, with room for expansion. A purchase agreement was signed on December 30, 1993, with the expectation that the sale would be completed the following February.[74] The Board of Directors stipulated that no more than $3,300,000 should be expended in the purchase of the structure. The building was purchased for 40-50 cents on the dollar.[75]

President Jerstad cited several reasons for the purchase. The building's size allowed the Society's Central Office staff to work together under one roof. From this one location, supportive services could be provided for more than 240 Good Samaritan facilities, serving 28,000 residents in 26 states. The new quarters had areas for staff training besides housing the Good Samaritan Federal Credit Union, Senior Companions Program and, for a short time, Good Samaritan Supply Services, Inc.[76] There was adequate parking space for staff and visitors, something lacking at the old quarters on West Avenue North. Having everyone housed under a single roof was good for staff morale. It had been difficult to get together for devotions in two different buildings. Having been the site of a credit card operation, the building contained much of the wiring needed for future technology.[77]

Most important was the location of the building. The Good Samaritan Society already owned 40 adjacent acres on West 57th Street, which, with the new corporate headquarters area, brought the Society's campus to more than 65 acres. The site would provide adequate space for the National Center for Long-Term Care.

One component of the national center, the National Institute, had already been approved by the Board of Directors prior to the purchase of the Bank of New York building. At its December 1993 meeting, the Board approved funds for further investigation into the need for a Center for Long-Term Care and possible means for financing the project.

With the acquisition of the Bank of New York property, Strategic Goal Number Ten was rewritten in 1994 as the first phase of development — investigating the feasibility of a National Center — had been successfully completed. At this time, Dr. James Beddow was employed to coordinate future planning of the National Center and its educational component, the National Institute for Long-Term Care.[78] The Board of Directors, in December 1994, authorized funds for a master plan of the National Center campus and its necessary infrastructure. The Institute was located in the Society's new national headquarters following the move from the old Central Office in late October 1994.

Proposed for the campus was a state-of-the-art nursing home, a retirement community where elderly people could live independently or with some assistance, a wellness and therapy center designed for the elderly, a geriatric clinic to be used for care teaching and research, a worship and life center, and a National Institute that would include offices, classrooms and a library. Following his retirement from Augustana College (Sioux Falls) in May 1996, Dr. Charles Balcer was named director of research, working under the supervision of Doctor Beddow. Balcer had been president of Augustana College from 1965 to 1980 and Distinguished Professor of Speech at the school until his retirement. He served a record-setting 13 years on the Society's Board of Directors.

The Institute's personnel would coordinate research and concentrate on resources, education, training, advocacy of and the image of the elderly, and ethics. Priorities for Jerstad included advocacy, studying ethics at the edge of life, and reshaping methods of care. The proposed center would be linked by satellite with the Society's facilities, providing one-way video and two-way audio communication for on-site training. The total campus project, costing an estimated $50 million, would be undertaken only if its financing did not detract from the services the Good Samaritan Society already provided.[79]

One source of funds for the National Institute was Good Samaritan Supply Services, Inc. When the Society purchased the Good Neighbor Affiliate Group in 1993, it acquired a medical supply company. The acquisition prompted Society officials to establish a separate for-profit corporation, Good Samaritan Supply Services, Inc. Charles Halberg was named president of this corporation on January 1, 1996. The new Good Samaritan entity sold and marketed pharmaceutical supplies and other medical materials in product areas such as enterals, perenterals, nutrition, urologicals, ostomy, and tracheostomy. In 1994, the for-profit corporation began a national distribution of its medical supply products. As a single-source supplier, the new corporation enabled Good Samaritan facilities to purchase products at reduced costs. These reductions were passed on to residents.[80]

Good Samaritan Supply Services expanded its services in mid-1994 with the acquisition of an institutional pharmacy. The pharmacy provided for the cost-effective delivery of pharmaceutical supplies for residents of facilities located in the Twin Cities metropolitan area and in other Minnesota facilities where demand existed and local market conditions permitted. Good Samaritan Supply Services and the National Institute were both owned and operated by the Good Samaritan Foundation, a 501 (c) (3) non-profit entity, according to the Internal Revenue Code. The Foundation had been formally incorporated on September 18, 1992.[81] The net income, after taxes, from the Supply Services, Inc., was used to fund the charitable, religious and educational purposes of the Foundation, including the advancement of the goals of the National Center for Long-Term Care.[82]

The National Institute, with funds made available through the for-profit Good Samaritan Supply Services, Inc., had several projects underway by July 1996. Two research projects had been funded and steps taken to develop a satellite television network that would link every facility in the Society with the Central Office, providing access to e-mail, use of CD-ROM, the Internet, and video conferencing. The Board of Directors of the Supply Services, having declared a dividend, provided a check for $500,000 to the Foundation at the Society's annual meeting in July 1996.

A scaled back version of the expanded campus was prepared in the spring of 1997. The national campus planners decided to abandon, for the time being, plans for long-term care nursing facilities. Approval of the Board of Directors, however, was sought for a Retreat Center which would contain sleeping rooms for 40 people. The Retreat Center would be located alongside a man-made lake. The proposal provided as well for the linking to the Retreat Center of a building housing the Institute for Long-Term Care and a Conference Center. The new expansion would house the dining facilities formerly located in the national headquarters building. The new structures would be connected to the present Central Office building by a skyway. The entrance to the national headquarters would be enlarged and become a Welcome Center. Changes within the Central Office building would include making offices out of the present Board and Archives Storage Rooms and transforming the dining room into a Board Room.[83]

Under Mark Jerstad's leadership, the Good Samaritan Society had made great strides toward fulfilling the strategic goals adopted by its membership in 1991. The Society was likewise positioned to meet the new challenges constantly emerging from ongoing changes in the health care industry. Although the Society made major changes in how it went about caring for people, President Jerstad never permitted the organization to forget its mission. Like his grandfather, August Hoeger, Sr., and his two uncles, August Hoeger, Jr., and John Hoeger, he proclaimed and maintained the Society's commitment to its Christian mission, first established in 1922.

Chapter Sixteen
THE MISSION GOES FORWARD

*"Whatever your task, work hearti-
ly....as you are serving the Lord."* —
Colossians 3:23-24.

*"Therefore, my beloved brethren, be
ye steadfast, unmoveable, always
abounding in the work of the Lord,..."*
— *I Corinthians 15:58.*

Renewing the Society's commitment to champion the
Christ-centered focus in all of its activities had been the
first goal of the strategic plan adopted by the Good
Samaritan Society in 1991. Five years later, the Christian
emphasis in all of the Society's work was declared in even
stronger terms. When the ten strategic goals were further
refined and reduced to five in 1996, Goal # 1 was to "Preserve and
enhance the Society's ongoing commitment to its Christian mission." Designed to describe what the Society would be in the year
2005, four of the five goals included the word Christian. The four
remaining goals were:

2. Provide the highest quality health care and services for the whole person within a supportive,
   Christian environment.

3. Create and maintain a quality Christian work
   environment that encourages fulfillment of each
   individual's potential; identifies and develops
   leadership potential; and results in co-workers
   who feel valued, are motivated, demonstrate safe
   work practices, and are committed to the mission
   of the Society.

4. Establish a plan for long range growth which
   emphasizes the enhancement of existing operations; the development of new service and mission opportunities (both center-based and
   Society-wide); and provides encouragement to
   seek collaborative, beneficial strategic alliances.

5. Achieve financial security to sustain and enhance our Christian mission through sound operations and resource development.

The greatest achievement of Mark Jerstad's administration was his keeping the Christ-centeredness of the Society intact during a time of great change, when its traditional mission could easily have been diminished. He lifted the mission banner higher; he kept the mission flame burning brightly. Jerstad's favorite Bible verse, 1 John 4: 7-8, permeated the Society's work. He often quoted this Scriptural passage by heart: "Beloved, let us love one another; for love is of God, and he who loves is born of God and knows God. He who does not love does not know God; for God is love."[1]

Through the Society's spiritual ministry program, the mission remained strong in the Society's facilities. The strength of the mission was documented in the minutes of the various centers and the periodic surveys that solicited the views of staff, residents, and the families of residents.[2] Workshops continued to play a vital role in enhancing the Society's mission among the employees in its facilities. The first phase of the STAR workshops was completed in all regions in 1993, including what was the Good Samaritan Society of Minnesota. Shortly thereafter, a second phase of one-day cluster workshops, centering on pastoral care techniques, appropriate for all staff, began.

A key element of the Society's renewed commitment to a Christ-centered focus was the establishment of a Clinical Pastoral Education (CPE) program, emphasizing the special needs of long-term residents. The Society's CPE program had its beginnings in the Good Neighbor system. Good Neighbor's Spiritual Care Committee, under the leadership of Professor Melvin Kimble of Luther Northwestern Seminary, envisioned and began the preliminary work to implement a Clinical Pastoral Education program in long-term care. Reverend Mark Anderson, a CPE supervisor, was asked to facilitate the candidacy accreditation process, and the program was accredited as a candidacy center by the Association for Clinical Pastoral Education (ACPE) in the spring of 1992, just as the Good Samaritan Society purchased the Good Neighbor homes.

The program was placed on hold for a year as the assimilation of the Good Neighbor facilities into the Society took place. In June 1993, Reverend Gary Sartain was called to implement the program. The program began the following September with three stipend resident chaplains and several additional students. In the following winter, when University Good Samaritan in Minneapolis, experienced a chaplaincy vacancy, a second CPE supervisor, Rock Stack, was hired. Since 1993, the program has grown rapidly. In 1996, it was the largest program in the North Central Region of ACPE (Illinois, Iowa, Minnesota, North and South Dakota and Wisconsin). It involved 43 students in 58 units of training. During the year, 11,600 hours of pastoral care was provided to residents in 19 Good Samaritan facilities and sister institutions.

The Society's CPE program received full accreditation from ACPE. A reviewer, representing the site visit team, wrote:

> There is so much uniqueness and excitement about the program [that] I have a strong feeling that there is within this center a deep, genuine concern, an active pastoral love and a breadth of integrity .... It sounds like a wonderfully rich theological and educational center."[3]

The Good Samaritan Society recognized the needs of other charitable organizations when disposing of its old national headquarters buildings. The former Central Office building at 1000 West Avenue North was renovated to meet code requirements for multiple tenants and leased to several nonprofit agencies, providing them with office space at lower rental rates.[4] In announcing the Society's action, Mark Jerstad said, "It has been a dream of ours ... that the building where we once worked could be put into a benevolent use." Minnehaha County purchased the "908" building for use as a juvenile center.

Adapting to change is necessary for the success of any organization, but timely reminders of its roots, past culture, and direction are essential to keeping it on course. With this in mind, the entire Central Office staff journeyed to Arthur, North Dakota, in the spring of 1992, to capture some of the spirit of the Society's past. They spent the day at the Arthur Center, visiting with residents, worshipping together, and listening to Augie and Betty Hoeger recount the early days of the Society. Staff members returned to Sioux Falls renewed, having been inspired by the selfless, loving character of Dad Hoeger and other committed, caring Society workers.[5] Similar visits to Arthur were planned for newer staff members as part of the Central Office's 75th Anniversary Celebration in 1997.

Mark Jerstad's remarkable efforts to move the Society forward came to an end shortly after he learned, in November 1996, that he had an advanced stage of aggressive colon cancer. Despite his steadily weakening condition, he continued to go to his office in the national headquarters building for several weeks, making decisions, inspiring the staff and meeting with the Executive Committee. His wisdom in creating an executive structure was demonstrated during this critical time in the Society's history. He selected one of his vice presidents, David Horazdovsky, to be chief operating officer. Overall, President Jerstad had done an excellent job of ensuring the future success of the Good Samaritan Society.

Jerstad faced death without resentment, anger, or bitterness. His lack of anger he attributed to a gift. "The gift of faith," he said. "Maybe I'm not angry because I'm so hopeful for the life beyond this life."[6] Up until the end, he was concerned about other people. As he gave to the Society, he was giving to those who were around him in his final days. He died on March 29, 1997. Shortly after his death, the Bishop of the South Dakota District of the Evangelical Lutheran Church of America, Andrea DeGroot-Nesdahl, said of him, "He found God and found Gospel in the everyday. He was secure in his faith."[7] At an executive session of the Board of Directors on April 21, 1997, Dr. Charles Balcer, former chairman of the Board of Directors and the present director of education and research for the Institute, was named Interim President of the Society, effective May 1, 1997.[8]

Mark Jerstad often referred to the Good Samaritan Society as a treasure or jewel when speaking to the Board of Directors or the leadership staff. In his last few months, he often raised up this statement, and he said the Society should be treated and handled as such.[9] From its humble origins at Arthur, North Dakota, in 1922, this treasure had become, by 1995, the nation's largest nonprofit provider of long-term health care and retirement living services. It was the fourth largest nursing home corporation in the United States. The Society owned and leased 206 facilities, managed 16 others, and administered 14 HUD-related corporations. More than 22,000 Good Samaritan employees served over 27,000 residents in 26 states.[10]

During the 1980s, the intrinsic nature of the Good Samaritan Society as it accomplished its mission was summarized under the following foci: the Society is Christ-centered, Resident-centered, Staff-centered, and Community-centered. In 1995, President Jerstad reaffirmed that the Society, first and foremost, continued to be Christ-centered. He declared, "In union with Christ we are empowered and strengthened to share comfort and care."[11] The Society's foremost priority remains to provide care for the whole person — body, mind, and soul.[12] The question must continue to be asked, "Lord, what do you want of me today?" It is not so important to know what the future holds, but to recognize that God holds the future, working through His faithful servants in contemporary society.

Dad Hoeger, at an earlier date, drafted a memo entitled "Would You Like To Be A Real Good Samaritan?" He wrote:

> Do you consider it an honor, yes, a great privilege to care for the aged? To look upon them as Christ's mother and brothers? "Inasmuch as ye have done it unto one of these my brethren, ye have done it unto me." (Matthew 25:40).
>
> What do you expect for your work? Is it enough, that you are privileged to serve in His name? Or do you expect to get rich, to receive much honor?
>
> Are you too good for this work? Think of Christ as He put the towel about Himself and kneeled down to wash His disciples' feet. He is God and Lord of all. Who are you? Wouldn't you like to take Him as your example and follow His steps? He would like to have you as His examples: You are to take His place.[13]

Keys to the Good Samaritan Society's success during the past 75 years have been discipleship and leadership. Starting as a bootstrap operation, the Society grew from town to town and city to city to its present position of being in the vanguard in care for the elderly because of its leaders, Dad Hoeger, his sons August, Jr., and John, and his grandson, Mark Jerstad. They possessed a unique combination of faith, determination, communication, and management skills, and adaptability.

In the latter half of 1997, the Good Samaritan Society stood on the results of great change. It needed another leader, like Mark

Jerstad, who would change its functions, as necessary, but never its mission. The promise of tomorrow for this jewel, the Good Samaritan Society, would be fulfilled only with the selection of a skilled new leader who would keep the flame of mission burning. The Society's past standard bearers had strong convictions, and they selected men and women who answered the call for a radical response to discipleship. Thousands of people were willing to give their labor and financial support "to older persons and others in need" because they believed and continue to believe that "In Christ's Love, Everyone Is Someone."

A NOTE ABOUT THE AUTHOR

Lynwood E. Oyos was born in North Dakota in 1927 and received his Ph.D. from the University of Nebraska in 1958. He was a Professor of History at Augustana College (Sioux Falls) from 1957-1994. His published works include: *The Little Church That Grew and Grew* (1971), (Co-author) *Prairie Faith, Pioneering People, A History of the Lutheran Church in South Dakota* (1981), *Over A Century of Leadership: South Dakota's Territorial and State Governors* (1987), and *The Noble Calling* (1990). He is currently working on *A History of the South Dakota Farmers Union, Guardians of the Family Farm, 1914-1997*.

Professor Oyos was appointed a Danforth Associate in 1981, and he received a Burlington Northern Faculty Achievement Award in 1987. He held the Orin M. Lofthus Distinguished Professorship at Augustana from 1992-1994.

Notes

Chapter One

1 The store was also called the "Racket Store" or the "ten cents store."

2 Box 5, DAD HOEGER, Good Samaritan Society Archives. With a few designated exceptions, all documentation for the text of this history is found in the Good Samaritan Society Archives.(GSSA).

3 *The Little Blue Book*, translated by Dr. Gerhard Schmutterer, Professor Emeritus, Augustana College, Sioux Falls, South Dakota. DAD HOEGER'S WRITINGS.

4 Reminiscences of Maria Hoeger, Box 5, DAD HOEGER.

5 Ibid.

6 A part of Rev. August Hoeger, Jr.'s response on receiving a Doctor of Divinity degree from Wartburg Seminary, 10 May 1987. AUGIE HOEGER, Box 4. GSSA.

7 Reminiscences of Maria Hoeger, Box 5, DAD HOEGER. August Hoeger's older brother, John, also resided in Sterling. He worked in a department store, and he played the organ at the local ALC church. — Henry Christline, Sterling, Nebraska, interview by Ken Halvorsrude, 1974, Tape # 44 (GSSA). Future citations using material from interviews by Ken Halvorsrude will begin with (KH).

8 Maria Hoeflinger Hoeger's letters to August John Hoeger. Translation by Dr. Gerhard Schmutterer, Sioux Falls, South Dakota.

9 Letter to Ken Halvorsrud, Sioux Falls, South Dakota, from Robert C. Wiederaenders, Archivist, the ALC, dated 27 November 1974.

10 (KH) Dr. Erwin Fritschel, Fort Collins, Colorado, 1974, Tape No. 39.

11 Box — DAD HOEGER'S WRITINGS.

12 (KH) Reverend William Kraushaar, Seguin, Texas, 1974, Tape # 49.

13 (KH) Reverend George Unruh, Bismarck, North Dakota, 1974, Tape # 19.

14 Reverend John Hoeger, "Reflections of `Dad.'" *The Good Samaritan*, Vol. 3, No. 4 (December 1970).

15 Most sources state that the homestead was in Kidder County but there is a record indicating that August filed for land in Section 24, Township 142, Range 75 in Burleigh County, North Dakota.

16 (KH) Mr. and Mrs. Fred Heidt, Wing, North Dakota, 1974, Tape # 31.

17 Unpublished manuscript of Dolores Harrington, Sioux Falls, South Dakota, 1966 — "Dad Hoeger — Man in Motion." Box 3, DAD HOEGER, AWARDS, WRITINGS, NEWSCLIPPINGS, MAGAZINE FEATURES, ETC.

18 Box 4, DAD HOEGER, HIS INTERESTS, MISCELLANEOUS PAMPHLETS.

19 Amelia Aden was the niece of Tjade Ehmen, Maria Hoeger's good friend at Sterling, Nebraska.

20 Agnes Hoeger and Irma T. Person, *Ever Forward!*, The Story of Dad Hoeger. (Sioux Falls: The Ev. Lutheran GSS, 1981) 13.

21 (KH) Mr. and Mrs. Fred Heidt, Tape # 31.

22 (KH) Mrs. Jacob Dockler, Bismarck, North Dakota, 1974, Tape # 41.

23 (KH) Hilda Hinkle, Jamestown, North Dakota, 1974, Tape # 18.

24 (KH) Mrs. Jacob Dockler, Tape # 41.

25 (KH) Mr. and Mrs. Fred Heidt, Tape # 31.

26 (KH) Mrs. W. C. Sweeney, Fargo, North Dakota, 1974, Tape # 43.

27 Archival Tidbits, The Administrator.

28 Box 3, DAD HOEGER, AWARDS, WRITINGS, NEWSCLIPPINGS, MAGAZINE FEATURES, ETC.

29 The GSS archives contain copies of *Die Mission Stunde* from January 1913 to November 1916.

30 Box 3, DAD HOEGER, AWARDS, WRITINGS, NEWSCLIPPINGS, MAGA-ZINE FEATURES, ETC.; (KH) Rev. J. H. Groth, Knoxville, Tennessee, 1974, Tape # 49.

31 The success of his appeal for funds for the saw mill is not known.

32 Box 4, DAD HOEGER, HIS WRITINGS, MISCELLANEOUS PAMPHLETS.

Chapter Two

1 Letter from Johannes Heinrich (Hans) Grothe, Knoxville, Tennessee, to August Hoeger, Jr., 17 July 1966.

2 (KH) Reverend George Unruh, Bismarck, North Dakota, 1974, Tape # 19.

3 Letter from Johannes H. Groth, 17 July 1966.

4 "Archival Tidbits," August and Betty Hoeger, *The Administrator*.

5 (KH) Frank Kuehn, Arthur, North Dakota, 1974, Tape 24B.

6 History of the First Dakota District of the Evangelical Lutheran Synod of Iowa, 1982.

7 Booklet — *100th Anniversary of St. John's Lutheran Church, Arthur, North Dakota, 1888-1988*.

8 In 1949, the cornerstone for a new St. John's Lutheran Church at Arthur was laid. St. Martin's Church burned the following year after being struck by lightning. Its members joined Arthur and Amenia in a one-point parish at Arthur. — Booklet — *St. John's Lutheran Church, 75th Anniversary, 1963*.

9 (KH) Bertha Wolf, Arthur, North Dakota, 1974, Tape # 16; Box 3, DAD HOEGER — AWARDS, WRITINGS, NEWSCLIPPINGS, MAGAZINE FEA-TURES, ETC.

10 (KH) Mr. and Mrs. Howard Pueppke, Arthur, North Dakota, 1974, Tape #23.

11 *Ibid.*

12 *100th Anniversary of St. John's Lutheran Church, Arthur, North Dakota, 1888-1988*.

13 DAD HOEGER, "DAD'S REMINISCENCES."

14 Minutes of the Conference of the Laity, Arthur, North Dakota, 27 June 1922, GSS HISTORY AND ADULT SERVICES; *The Sunshine*, Vol. XIX, No. 4 (July-August 1941).

15 Minutes of the Conference of the Laity, Arthur, North Dakota, to Found a Home for Cripples and Feeble Minded, 27 June 1922, GSS HISTORY AND ADULT SERVICES.

16 Minutes of the GSS, 29 September 1922, GSS HISTORY AND ADULT SER-VICES.

17 *Ibid.*

18 Letter from Professor H. J. Arnold, Waverly, Iowa, to August J. Hoeger, Sr., 3 August 1922. GSS HISTORY AND ADULT SERVICES.

19 Article written by August J. Hoeger, Sr., in *Kirchen-Blatt*, 9 September 1922. Found in the Neuendettelsau Archives.

20 Letter to Dorothy Fowler, Arthur, North Dakota, from Minnie Hermina Hove, Minneapolis, Minnesota, 18 August 1972. DAD HOEGER'S WRITINGS.

21 DAD'S REMINISCENCES, DAD HOEGER.

22 (KH) Augusta Priewe, Fargo, North Dakota, 1974, Tape #14.

23 *Ibid.*

24 Bertha Bosch Christian on the Occasion of Dad's Death," October 1970. DOC-UMENTS, MOTHER AND DAD HOEGER.

25 *Sunshine*, Vol. III, No. 1 (January-February 1925).

26 Fargo Forum, 4 July 1966.

27 "DAD'S REMINISCENCES," DAD HOEGER.

28 Minutes of the GSS, 18 December 1923.

29 *Sunshine,* Vol. III, No. 1 (January-February, 1925).

30 Note of Secretary Pro-tem, Sister Sena Hestad, 18 November 1925.

31 *Ibid.*

32 *Sunshine*, Vol. III, No. 4 (July-August 1925).

33 *Sunshine*, Vol. IV, No. 3 (May-June 1926).

34 Minutes of the GSS, 6 June 1926.

35 Minutes of the GSS, 18 November 1925.

36 *Ibid.*

37 *Sunshine*, Vol. IV, No. 3 (May-June, 1926).

38 *Sunshine*, Vol. II, No. 3 (May-June 1924). The first Holstein cow came to the Home courtesy of Dr. Herman Seifkes. This cow was the beginning of a registered Holstein herd for the Good Samaritan Home at Arthur.

39 *Sunshine*, Vol. IV, No. 3 (May-June 1926).

40 *Sunshine*, Vol. IV, No. 5 (September-October 1926).

41 Minutes of the GSS, 18 November 1925; *Sunshine*, Vol. III, No. 6 (November-December 1925).

42 Box — DAD HOEGER AND OTHERS.

43 *Sunshine*, Vol. IV, No. 3 (May-June 1926).

44 GSS PUBLICATIONS. GSSA.

Chapter Three

1 Minutes of the GSS, 1 August 1932.

2 Lois Phillips Hudson, *Reapers of the Dust, A Prairie Chronicle*. (Boston: Little Brown and Company, 1951), 3.

3 Written comments addressed to his siblings by Lauren Haacke, 6 June 1990.

4 Letter from August Hoeger, Sr., to Mrs. Hattie Hoeger, Santa Monica, California, 12 November 1932. MOTHER AND DAD HOEGER, PERSONAL.

5 *Ibid.*

6 (KH) Reverend George Unruh, Tape # 19. Some members of the Arthur community were very critical of the epileptics from the Home who had seizures on the streets or on the floors of main street stores.

7 Burgum's brother, Lee, married Ruth Hoeger. Lee Burgum became the principal of the Good Samaritan Institute at Fargo in the 1930s.

8 (KH) Al Burgum, Arthur, North Dakota, 1974, Tape # 24A.

9 Burgum saw his own father in Hoeger when it came to finances. They both kept their financial dealings in their heads. — *Ibid.*

10 *Sunshine*, Vol. V, No. 3 (May-June 1927).

11 *Sunshine*, Vol. VII, No. 7 (August 1929).

12 Rev. Hoeger's newsletter to Good Samaritan workers, Vol. 1, No. 3, 23-24 December 1932.

13 *Ibid.*

14 *The Administrator*, Vol. I, No. 33 (26 October 1989).

15 *Sunshine*, Vol. X, No. 7 (October-November 1933).

16 *Ibid.*

17 Etta Jensen, who came to the Arthur Home in 1925, served as administrator for twenty-six years.

18 Bertha Bosch Christian entered Society work in 1928; Viola Baugatz and Bertha Halvorson Holstein began their employment in 1931; Marie Schugaan

Bosch started her career with the GSS in 1937 at the Harvey, North Dakota Hospital.

19 Viola Baugatz, Video of the Heritage Celebration, 1985.

20 (KH) Mr. and Mrs. Clark Lincoln, Arthur, Nor Dakota, 1974, Tape # 20.

21 (KH) Bertha Bosch Christian, Hastings, Nebraska, 1974, Tape # 46.

22 Letter from Lauren D. Haacke, Sioux Falls, South Dakota, Reverend Haacke's son, to Rev. John Hoeger, 30 October 1991.

23 Written comments addressed to his siblings by Lauren Haacke, 6 June 1990.

24 *Sunshine*, Vol. XIII, No. 6 (January-February 1937).

25 Minutes of the GSS, 1 April 1930.

26 "Tribute to Dad Hoeger at the Time of His Death," October 1970.

27 "Dad's Reminiscences," DAD HOEGER.

28 Minutes of the GSS, 5 November 1924.

29 Letter to Ken Halvorsrude from Richard Fruehling, 5 November 1974. "Martin Luther Home," OTHER RELATED ORGANIZATIONS.

30 "Dad's Reminscences," DAD HOEGER.

31 *Sunshine*, Vol. V., No. 3 (May-June 1927).

32 (KH) Minnie Hove, Minneapolis, Minnesota, 1974. Tape # 50.

33 Minutes of the GSS, 6 March 1929.

34 *Sunshine*, Vol. VII, No. 7 (August 1929).

35 *Sunshine*, Vol. VII, No. 2 (February 1929).

36 Minutes of the GSS, 28 August 1929.

37 *Sunshine*, Vol. VII, No. 7 (August 1929). The Valley City facility was taken over by the Lutheran Hospital and Homes Society in 1940.

38 Minutes of the GSS, 1 April 1930.

39 Hoeger's salary was set at $1,400 per year.

40 *Sunshine*, Vol. IX, No. 5 (July-August-September 1932).

41 Cited in HISTORY AND PERSONNEL, Inter-office Memo, 7 May 1987.

42 *Sunshine*, Vol. VIII, No. 7 (May-June 1931).

43 A formal agreement was not signed until 14 November 1932.

44 Minutes of the GSS, 6 November 1931.

45 (KH) Wallace Franke, Kansas City, Missouri, 1974, Tape # 46.

46 *Ibid*.

47 (KH) Mrs. Fred Knautz, Fargo, North Dakota, 1974, Tape # 24A.

Chapter Four

1 (KH) Dr. Anne Carlsen, Jamestown, North Dakota, 1974, Tape # 52.

2 (KH) Rev. Wilko Schoenbohm, Minneapolis, Minnesota, 1974, Tape # 50.

3 Minutes of the GSS, 20 June 1932.

4 The cornerstone of the Library was laid by Theodore Roosevelt.

5 Minutes of the GSS, 1 August 1932.

6 *Sunshine*, Vol. XIII, No. 4 (July-August 1936).

7 *Sunshine*, Vol. IX, No.5 (July-August-September 1932).

8 Rev. John Hoeger, "Reflections of Dad," Good Samaritan, Vol. III, No. 4 (December 1970).

9 Later, Augsburg Business College associated with GSI and shared space in the Library Building.

10 Leland S. Burgum, "From Obscurity to Security, An Historical and Statistical Analysis of the Movement to Aid Physically Handicapped Children and Disabled Adults in North Dakota." (Fargo: Good Samaritan Press, 1937).

11 *GSI Yearbook*, 1937.

12 (KH) Mrs. Harold Axen (Dorothea Olson), Fargo, North Dakota, 1974, Tape # 48; Emma Eide, Hastings, Nebraska, 1974, Tape # 9; Lucille Wedge, Hill City, South Dakota, 1974, Tape # 52.

13 Lucille Greer Wedge, "I Knew Rev. Hoeger."

14 *Ibid.*

15 (KH) Dr. Anne Carlsen, Tape # 52.

16 *Sunshine*, Vol. XIII, No. 10 (September-October 1937).

17 (KH) Mrs. Ray Anderson, Fargo, North Dakota, 1974, Tape # 52.

18 (KH) Dr. Anne Carlsen, Tape # 52.

19 *Sunshine*, Vol. XIII, No. 2 (April 1936).

20 Ruth Erickson, 1974, Tape # 30.

21 Burgum, "From Obscurity to Security."

22 *Sunshine*, Vol. XIII, No. 6 (January-February 1937).

23 (KH) Wilko Schoenbohm, Tape # 50.

24 *GSI Yearbook*, 1937.

25 *Sunshine*, Vol. XIII, No. 9 (July-August 1937).

26 Burgum, "From Obscurity to Security."

27 Minutes of the GSS, 2 April 1934.

28 *Ibid.*, 17 January 1935.

29 *Sunshine*, Vol. XIII, No. 7 (March-April 1937).

30 Information Booklet for Prospective Students, Lutheran Good Samaritan Bible and Training School, Fargo, North Dakota.

31 Lutheran Good Samaritan Bible and Training School, 1939, Allen Memorial Hospital, Waterloo, Iowa.

32 Silver Jubilee, First Evangelical Lutheran Church, Waterloo, Iowa. ALLEN MEMORIAL HOSPITAL, WATERLOO, IOWA.

33 *Waterloo Daily Courier*, 11 December 1938. ALLEN MEMORIAL HOSPITAL, WATERLOO, IOWA. The Allen Memorial Hospital Association contributed $25 per month for the Good Samaritan Society's home office to defray office expenses for services rendered by Hoeger. The Society had no financial or other obligations to the Association. — Minutes of the GSS, 13 January 1939.

34 *Waterloo Daily Courier*, 30 June 1939. ALLEN MEMORIAL HOSPITAL, WATERLOO, IOWA. *Sunshine*, Vol. XIV, No. 5 (September-October 1939). The Good Samaritan Bookstore was also transferred to the Allen Memorial Hospital, with Sister Sena Hestad in charge.

35 *Sunshine*, Vol. XVI, No. 2 (March-April 1941).

36 Letter from H. H. Diers, Secretary, Allen Memorial Hospital Corporation, Waterloo, Iowa, to August Hoeger, Sr., 18 October 1944. ALLEN MEMORIAL HOSPITAL ASSOCIATION.

37 *The Good Samaritan*, Vol. IV, No.3 (December 1971).

38 (KH) Mrs. Fred Knautz, Fargo, North Dakota, 1974, Tape # 24A; Emma Eide, Tape # 9.

39 *Sunshine*, Vol. XIII, No. 4 (July-August 1938).

40 *Sunshine*, Vol. XIV, No. 5 (September-October 1939).

41 Minutes of the GSS, 8 November 1937.

42 Minutes of the GSS, 6 December 1937, 19 April 1938, 8 August 1938.

43 Minutes of the GSS, 23 May 1938; (KH) Wilko Schoenbohm, Tape # 50.

44 *Ibid.*

45 Carlsen's salary at GSI was room and board and $25 per month.

46 Letter to the Board of Directors, the GSS, from Frederick R. Knautz, early 1938.

47 Minutes of the GSS, 7 November 1939.

48 Minutes of the GSS, 1 May 1939.

49 *Ibid.*, 15 November 1938.

50 Minutes of the LHHS, Fargo, North Dakota, 3 January 1938.

51 Minutes of the GSS, 7 November 1939.

52 *Ibid.*

53 Minutes of the Commission on Charities, ALC, 31 October 1939.

54 Minutes of the Commission on Charites, ALC, 12 December 1939.

55 Minutes of the LHHS and GSS, 9 April 1940 and 9 August 1940.

56 *Ibid.*

57 Minutes of the LHHS, 30 April 1940.

58 Brochure, Dedication of the School for Crippled Children, Jamestown, North Dakota, 21 September 1941.

59 *Lutheran Hospitals and Homes Advocate*, Vol. V., No. 3 (July-August 1949).

60 (KH) Rev. John Hoeger, 1974, Tape # 32.

61 (KH) Anne Carlsen, Tape # 52.

62 (KH) Rev. H. S. Froiland, Northfield, Minnesota, 1974, Tape # 41.

63 (KH) Rev. Wilko Schoenbohm, Tape # 50.

64 "Dad Hoeger's Account of the Move to Fargo College.'

Chapter Five

1 Tweton, D. Jerome and Rylance, Daniel F. *The Years of Despair, North Dakota in the Depression.* (Grand Forks, North Dakota: The Oxcart Press, 1973), 2.

2 *Sunshine*, Vol. XIII, No. 4 (July-August 1936).

3 Tweton and Rylance, *Years of Despair*, 13.

4 *Ibid.*

5 *Sunshine*, Vol. XIII, No. 4 (July-August 1936).

6 Minutes of the GSS, August 1932.

7 *Ibid.*, 1 April 1934.

8 Minutes of the GSS, 17 January 1935.

9 (KH) Rev. August Hoeger, Jr., 19 August 1974; Rev. John Hoeger, Tape # 32; Rev. Wilko Schoenbohm, Minneapolis, Minnesota, 1974, Tape # 50.

10 Minutes of the GSS, 2 April 1934; 15 March 1935.

11 Minutes of the Committee on Charities, ALC, Chicago, Illinois, 27 February 1940.

12 Frederick R. Knautz's letter to the Chairman and Members of the Board of Directors, GSS, 14 January 1938.

13 *Ibid.*

14 August Hoeger, Sr., A Typewritten Memorandum prepared before the split of 1938-1940. LUTHERAN HOSPITAL AND HOMES SOCIETY.

15 Minutes of the GSS, 8 November 1937; 6 December 1937.

16 August Hoeger, Jr., and Betty Hoeger, "Archival Tidbits," *The Administrator*.

17 Minutes of the GSS, 3 January 1938; Minutes of the LHHS, 3 January 1938.

18 F. R. Knautz to Chairman and Members of the Board of Directors (GSS/LHHS), 14 January 1938.

19 *Ibid.*

20 Minutes of the Committee on Charities, ALC, 27 February 1940.

21 Letter from Dr. Agnes Hoeger, M.D., London, England, to August Hoeger, Sr., dated 12 June 1938; *The Good Samaritan*, Vol. 1, No. 12 (13 April 1989).

22 *Ibid.*

23 Minutes of the GSS, 8 August 1938.

24 *Ibid.*, 13 January 1939.

25 F. R. Knautz's Report to the LHHS Board of Directors, October 1939.

26 *Ibid.*

27 Minutes of the Commission on Charities, ALC, Chicago, Illinois, 11-12 April 1939.

28 *Ibid.* 31 October 1939.

29 *Ibid.*

30 (KH) Eugene Hackler, Olathe, Kansas, 1974, Tape # 45.

31 Minutes of the Commission on Charities, ALC, 12 December 1939.

32 *Ibid.*, 27 February 1940.

33 *Ibid.*

34 *Ibid.*

35 *Sunshine*, Vol. XV, No. 1 (January-February 1940).

36 Minutes of the GSS, 13 December 1939.

37 Minutes of the GSS, 9 April 1940.

38 Commission on Charities, ALC, Report to the Board of Trustees, ALC, 2 June 1940.

39 *Ibid.* The minutes for the Board of the LHHS for 6 December 1940 stated that the GSS had a bad reputation throughout the Church.

40 Letter from Rev. W.W.A. Keller, Jamestown, North Dakota, to Rev. August Hoeger, Sr., 15 June 1940.

41 Letter from Rev. August Hoeger, Sr., Fargo, North Dakota, to Rev. W.W.A. Keller, Jamestown, North Dakota, 24 June 1940.

42 *Ibid.*

43 *Ibid.* Keller did resign from the GSS Board.

44 *Sunshine*, Vol. XV, No. 4 (July-August 1940).

45 Minutes of the GSS, 25 September 1940; 16 October 1940.

46 *Sunshine*, Vol. XVIII, No. 6 (November-December 1940).

47 (KH) Bertha Bosch Christian, Tape # 46.

48 Rev. Hoeger's General Christmas Letter for 1940. DAD HOEGER, BOX 2.

49 F. R. Knautz letter to Rev. J. F. Graepp after the LHHS Board meeting of 9 October 1943.

50 (KH) August Hoeger, Jr., 19 August 1974.

51 John Hoeger's "Reflections."

52 Comment of Ken Halvorsrude following an interview with Erwin Chell, 1974.

53 (KH) Verne Pangborne, Lincoln, Nebraska, 1974, Tape # 13; Blanche Jackson, a confidant of Knautz said that he always played to win.

54 (KH) Clarence Austad, Bemidji, Minnesota, 1974, Tape # 22.

Chapter Six

1 John T. Flanagan, Theodore C. Blegen, A Memoir. (Northfield, Minn: The Norwegian-American Historical Association, 1971), 1.

2 *Sunshine*, Vol. XXXI, No.1 (January-March 1954).

3 *Sunshine*, Vol. XXI, No. 2 (March-April 1943).

4 *Sunshine*, Vol. XXI, No. 1 (January-February 1943).

5 Rev. August Hoeger, Jr., Annual Meeting of the GSS, 10-13 August 1983.

6 Annual Report of the GSS, 1974. AUGIE HOEGER, BOX 4.

7 (KH) Bertha Bosch Christian, Tape # 46.

8 David Brewer, "Administrator's Desk," *Bonell Torch*, Bonell GS Center, Greeley, Colorado (December 1970), 2.

9 Rev. William Goldbeck's comments following the death of August Hoeger, Sr., 12 October 1970.

10 (KH) Eugene Hackler, Olathe Kansas, Tape # 45.

11 (KH) Rev. Hugo Schwartz, Independence, Iowa, 1974. Tape # 43.

12 *The Good Samaritan*, Vol. 6, No. 2 (2 June 1973).

13 (KH) Elizabeth and Gilbert Lindgren, Hastings, Nebraska, 1974, Tape #5.

14 (KH) Rev. Hugo Schwartz, Independence, Iowa, Tape # 43.

15 *Ibid.*

16 (KH) Rev. August Hoeger, Jr., 19 August 1974.

17 Newsletter to GSS Workers, Vol. 1, No. 2, 3 November 1932.

18 Rev. Hoeger's letter to Co-Workers, 15 December 1969, Hastings, Nebraska. DAD HOEGER, BOX 2.

19 (KH) Rev. John Hoeger, Tape # 32; Rev. August Hoeger, Jr., 19 August 1974.

20 August Hoeger, Jr., Annual Meeting of the GSS, 10-13 August 1983.

21 (KH) Rev. William Goldbeck, Hastings, Nebraska, Tape # 6.

22 (KH) Eugene Hackler, Olathe, Kansas, Tape # 45.

23 Rev. William Goldbeck's comments on Hoeger's character following Rev. Hoeger's death in 1970.

24 (KH) Jeruel Tangen, Fargo, North Dakota, Tape # 2.

25 (KH) Mrs. Beryl Jensen, Hastings, Nebraska, Tape # 7.

26 Lucille Greer Wedge, "I Knew Rev. Hoeger."

27 Letter from Mrs. Lyle A. Jensen, Howard, Nebraska, to August Hoeger, Jr., n.d.

28 Lucille Greer Wedge, "I Knew Rev. Hoeger."

29 (KH) Rev. John Hoeger, Tape # 32.

30 (KH) Erv and Betty Chell, Sioux Falls, South Dakota, 1974, Tape # 41.

31 Rev. William Goldbeck's tribute to Dad Hoeger, Chaplain's Corner, 1970.

32 (KH) Erv and Betty Chell, Sioux Falls, South Dakota, Tape # 41.

33 "Dad Hoeger — Man in Motion," unpublished manuscript of Dolores Harrington, Sioux Falls, South Dakota, circa. 1966.

34 (KH) Rev. William Goldbeck, Tape # 6.

35 (KH) Jeruel Tangen, Tape # 2.

36 (KH) Eugene Hackler, Tape # 45.

37 Notes of a conversation with John Bosch, 9 September 1991.

38 GSS Newsletter, 28 April 1960.

39 (KH) Col. Charles Peterson, Sioux Falls, South Dakota, Tape # 46.

40 (KH) Verne Pangborne, Lincoln, Nebraska, Tape # 13.

41 (KH) Rev. George Unruh, Bismarck, North Dakota, Tape # 19.

42 (KH) Bertha and James Holstein, Devils Lake, North Dakota, Tape # 24B.

43 Annual Report of the GSS, 1974. AUGIE HOEGER, BOX 4.

44 (KH) Clarence Austad, Bemidji, Minnesota, Tape # 22.

45 (KH) Rev. William Goldbeck, Tape # 6.

46 (KH) Clarence Austad, Tape # 22.

47 *Ibid.*

48 Letter from Dr. Agnes Hoeger, Hastings, Nebraska, to her sisters, October 1970.

49 David C. Cook, *Sunday Digest*, 23 March 1958.

50 (KH) Bertha and James Holstein, Tape # 24B; (KH) Lillian Whitely, Wymore, Nebraska, Tape # 12.

51 (KH) Eugene Hackler, Tape # 45.

52 (KH) Rev. John Hoeger, Tape # 32.

53 (KH) Ray Conlon, Beresford, South Dakota, 1974, Tape #40.

54 (KH) Rev. Jacob Jerstad and Laura Jerstad, Tape # 3.

55 (KH) Rev. John Hoeger, Tape # 32.

56 Observations by Ken Halvorsrude, 1974.

57 *Sunshine*, Vol. XXIX, No. 1 (January-February 1951).

58 (KH) Col. Charles Peterson, Tape # 46.

59 Rev. August Hoeger, Sr., Tape # 35.

60 Rev. Jacob Jerstad and Laura Jerstad, Tape # 3.

61 Rev. August Hoeger, Sr., Tape # 38.

62 Rev. August Hoeger, Sr., Tape # 36.

63 (KH) Mrs. Dorothy Fowler, Arthur, North Dakota, 1974, Tape # 24B.

64 Rev. August Hoeger, Sr., Tape # 38.

65 (KH) Woody Jorgenson, Daytona Beach, Florida, Tape # 47.

66 (KH) Rev. August Hoeger, Jr., 19 August 1974.

67 *Ibid.* Rev. John Hoeger recalled his father's non-confrontational style. The senior Hoeger went into a store to pick up a radio that he had had repaired. Driving away from the store, Dad Hoeger looked at the bill and complained — "Imagine charging $10 for one tube." John told him, "Why don't you ask for the manager and have him evaluate it?" Dad replied, "No, if that is the way they want to do it, I will never go back there again." Rev. John Hoeger, "Reflections of `Dad.'" *The Good Samaritan*, Vol. 3, No. 4 (December 1970).

68 (KH) Rev, August Hoeger, Jr., 19 August 1974. When Clarence Austad asked Hoeger where the money was coming from to pay contractors, the Superintendent told him not to worry. "While I sleep," he said, "He [God] can take care of it for eight hours and after that, I'll see if He won't help me through the others." — (KH) Clarence Austad, Tape # 22.

69 Rev. John Hoeger, "Comments on His Mother."

70 (KH) Orvis Okerland, Greeley, Colorado, Tape # 39.

71 (KH) Mrs. Henry Foege, Lincoln, Nebraska, Tape # 44.

72 Hoeger had established a close relationship with Andy Johnson, an Osnabrock resident, and through their perseverance, the Board had reversed its decision. Johnson became the first administrator of the Osnabrock Home.

73 (KH) Eugene Hackler, Tape # 45.

74 Rev. August Hoeger, Sr.'s letter to the membership, 1957. DAD HOEGER, BOX 2.

75 (KH) Dr. Erwin Fritschel, Tape # 39.

76 *Ibid.*

77 August Hoeger, Sr.'s response to letter from the Seminary on 8 November 1955.

78 *The Good Samaritan*, Vol. 26, No. 1 (Spring 1993).

79 Letter from Mrs. Lyle A. Jensen, Howard, Nebraska, to Rev. August Hoeger, Jr., n.d.

80 *American Health Care Association Journal*, Vol. 4, No. 1 (January 1978) 5-18.

81 Minutes of the GSS, 17-18 September 1957.

Chapter Seven

1 Minutes of the GSS, September 1947.

2 Minutes of the GSS, 21 September 1949.

3 Minutes of Annual Meeting Reports, 1922-1980, Wallingford, Iowa, 23-25 August 1955.

4 GSS Annual Report, 1952.

5 Adams also supervised single Homes in Oklahoma and Texas.

6 Minutes of the GSS, 14 October 1957.

7 Minutes of the GSS, 17-18 September 1957.

8 Minutes of the GSS, 23 August 1959.

9 Minutes of the GSS, 14 October 1957.

10 Letter from Dr. Albert J. Chesley, Minnesota Department of Health, St. Paul, Minnesota, to August Hoeger, Sr., 10 December 1953.

11 Minutes of the GSS, 4 August 1952; 7-8 October 1952.

12 Minutes of the GSS, 4 August 1952.

13 Minutes of the GSS, 21-22 September 1954; 22-25 August 1955; 17-18 September 1957.

14 Minutes of the GSS, 24 July 1956.

15 Minutes of the GSS, 17-18 September 1957.

16 Minutes of the GSS, 23 August 1959.

17 (KH) Eugene Hackler, Tape # 45.

18 Minutes of the GSS, 21-22 September 1954.

19 Minutes of the GSS, 13 December 1939.

20 Minutes of the GSS, 21-22 September 1954.

21 (KH) Rev. Hugo Schwartz, Independence, Iowa, 1974, Tape # 43.

22 *Sunshine*, Vol. XIX, No. 3 (May-June 1941).

23 *Sunshine*, Vol. XIX, No. 5 (September-October 1941).

24 *Sunshine*, Vol. XV, No. 3 (May-June 1940).

25 *Sunshine*, Vol. XX, No. 1 (January-February 1942; *Sunshine*, Vol. XX, No. 4 (July-August 1942).

26 In the late 1950s, proceeds from the sale of rugs were placed in a special fund to buy items for the Home — a canary, tropical fish and an aquarium, a croquet set and a redwood picnic table set. — *Smoke Signals*, 12 July 1965.

27 *The Sunshine*, first published in English and German in 1923, was printed at the Arthur Home until 1930, when the GSI print shop in Fargo assumed this task. Publication resumed at Arthur in 1948 with the construction of the Industrial Building; it was printed there until 1954, when publication ceased for 19 years. The Arthur Center revived publication of its press outlet in December 1973, but it was now printed at the Cass County Reporter office in Fargo.

28 Newsclipping from the *Fargo Forum*, 1965.

29 *Smoke Signals*, 20 November 1964; Christmas letter from Dorothy Fowler, administrator of the Arthur Home, 8 December 1964.

30 (KH) Ed and Esther Schur, Arthur, North Dakota, 1974, Tape # 30.

31 *The Good Samaritan*, Vol. 10, No. 1 (April 1977).

32 *Sunshine*, Vol. XVIII, No. 5 (September-October 1940).

33 Minutes of the GSS, 1941.

34 (KH) Rev. George Unruh, Tape # 19.

35 During the 1930s, over 2,000 people came to Arthur for the annual Home Day. In 1934, the morning sermon was delivered by Rev. F. Schaffnit, the superintendent and founder of Wartburg Hospice, Minneapolis, Minnesota. At the afternoon session, neighboring congregations presented a sacred choir concert. The presentation by the massed choirs was followed by the Society's annual business meeting. Choral music was featured at most Home Days. On June 14, 1939, choirs from Valley City and Davenport, North Dakota and a massed Luther League choir presented a spirited concert. The 1939 event also featured two speakers and a program by students from GSI.

36 *The Good Samaritan*, Vol. 3, No. 1 (Christmas 1969).

37 "Rest Home Residents to Thresh Own Wheat," Newsclipping from the *Fargo Forum*, undated but post-1974.

38 (KH) Mrs. Dorothy Fowler, Arthur, North Dakota, 1974, Tape # 24B.

39 Developed by the activity director, the choir, made up of staff and residents, provided background for the program.

40 *Sunshine*, Vol. XV, No. 1 (January-February 1940); *Sunshine*, Vol. XIX, No. 1 (January-February 1941); (KH) Mrs. Joanne Iwen, Arthur, North Dakota, 1974, Tape # 16.

41 *Fargo Forum*, 3 September 1967.
42 Lucille Greer Wedge, "I Knew Reverend Hoeger."
43 Letter to Reverend August Hoeger, Sr., Fargo, North Dakota, from the State Department of Health, 31 December 1952.
44 (KH) Mr. and Mrs. Bill Zimmerman, Arthur, North Dakota, 1974, Tape #25; (KH) Rev. George Unruh, Tape # 19.
45 (KH) Mr. and Mrs. Frank Kuehn, Arthur, North Dakota, 1974, Tape # 24B.
46 (KH) Bertha and James Holstein, Devils Lake, North Dakota, 1974, Tape # 24B.
47 *Fargo Forum*, 4 September 1962; (KH) Mrs. Dorothy Fowler, Arthur, North Dakota, 1974, Tape # 24B.
48 *Fargo Forum*, 3 September 1967.
49 (KH) Joyce Zewicki, Nurses Aide, Arthur, North Dakota, 1974, Tape # 21.
50 One Hundred Years With Arthur, 1882-1982.
51 *Sunshine*, Vol II, No. 2 (May 1974).
52 In 1976, Dorothy Fowler became a member of the Society's Board of Directors. She was the only woman in the 15-person body. — Dorothy Fowler's Christmas Letter, December 1976.
53 *Smoke Signals*, June 1974.
54 *Sunshine*, Vol. IV, No. 1 (May 1976).
55 "Cass Senior Citizens A Progressive Community," *Fargo Forum*, 14 February 1980.
56 Minutes of the GSS, 25 September 1940.
57 *Sunshine*, Vol. XX, No. 2 (March-April 1942).
58 *Sunshine*, Vol. XXVII, No. 3 (May-June 1949).
59 *Ranch News from the GS Ranch*, Vol. I, No. 1 (June 1949).
60 *Sunshine*, Vol. XXVII, No. 6 (November-December 1949).
61 *Sunshine*, Vol. XXVII, No. 3 (May-June 1949).
62 *The Good Samaritan*, Vol. I, No. 31 (27 September 1989).
63 *Sunshine*, Vol. XXIV, No. 5 (September-October 1946).
64 *Sunshine*, Vol. XXV, No. 4 (July-August 1947). On October 27, 1948, the Doerings sold the remainder of their farm to the GSS.
65 File 1, 1978, JOHN HOEGER.
66 File 1, 1985, JOHN HOEGER.
67 Parkston, South Dakota., Papers, Records, Documents. Jim River Ranch.
68 Rita and Nikolais Reinfelds, Records of Retired Personnel of the GSS.
69 (KH) Rita and Nikolais Reinfelds, Olathe, Kansas, 1974, Tape # 43.
70 Author's interview with Opal and Glen Maggert, Sioux Falls, South Dakota, 22 July 1996.
71 *Parkston Advance*, 10 August 1988; Minutes of the GSS, 17 November 1972.
72 Parkston, South Dakota, Papers, Records, Documents; Jim River Ranch.
73 Minutes of the GSS, 15-18 June 1975.
74 Newsclipping — "Jim River Ranch Aids Youth, Needs Support," Jim River Ranch. For a while, the Jim River Ranch was called Fun on the Farm Camp. — *The Administrator*, Vol. 1, No. 33 (26 October 1989).
75 "Jim River Ranch Provides Camping Experience for Youth," *Parkston Daily Republic*, 1971.
76 Camp Meeting Minutes, 23 March 1972. James River Ranch.
77 Parkston, South Dakota, Papers, Records, Documents.
78 Letter to John and Augie Hoeger and Col. Peterson from Jeanette Wudel, Parkston, South Dakota, 9 March 1987.

79 Minutes of the GSS, 6-8 June 1988. The Board of Directors originally wanted to sell the Parkston facilities for no less than $100,000. — Minutes of the GSS, 17 October 1988; *Parkston Advance*, 10 August 1988.

80 Minutes of the GSS, 7-8 October 1952, History and Adult Services.

81 (KH) Dr. Erwin Fritschel, Tape # 39.

82 Luther Lodge, Estes Park, Colorado.

83 Minutes of the GSS, 5-6 October 1953, History and Adult Services.

84 Minutes of the GSS, 19-21 June 1967.

85 *The Good Samaritan*, Vol. V, No. 3 (19 January 1993); Guest Books, Luther Lodge, Estes Park, Colorado.

86 Minutes of the GSS, 19-20 November 1970.

87 Minutes of the GSS, 11-14 June 1974.

Chapter Eight

1 *Life-Time*, A 50th anniversary publication of the GSS, 1972.

2 Minutes of the GSS, 15 March 1936; *The Good Samaritan*, Vol. 3, No. 2 (Easter 1970); Comments of Marie Bosch at the 60th anniversary celebration of the GSS, 3 October 1982, indicating that the Society took over the Parker residence in 1936. Irma Person, a co-author of *Ever Forward*, said that Dad Hoeger purchased the former Parker home on 28 May 1935. — *The Good Samaritan*, Vol. 28, No. 3 (Fall 1995.)

3 *Monitor, Journal of the South Dakota Health Care Professionals*, Vol. IV, No. 5 (September-October 1989).

4 Minutes of the LHHS, 27 May 1940; a 1938 newsclipping from the Sioux Falls Argus Leader.

5 Minutes of the GSS, 13 December 1939.

6 Notes of a conversation with Viola Baugatz and John and Marie Bosch, 9 September 1991.

7 (KH) Bertha Boasch Christian, Tape # 46.

8 Irma Person, *History of the Sioux Falls Good Samaritan Center*, 31 December 1984.

9 Marie Bosch's comments on the Sioux Falls Good Samaritan Center, *The Good Samaritan*, Vol. 15, No. 4 (Winter 1982).

10 Letter from Bertha Bosch to August Hoeger, Sr., 26 April 1944. Sioux Falls Home.

11 Irma Person, *History of the Sioux Falls Good Samaritan Center*.

12 Presentation by Marie Bosch, 3 October 1982, Sioux Falls, South Dakota.

13 Minutes of the GSS, 5-9 August 1973.

14 Carson Walker, "Good Samaritan Center to Add Space," Sioux Falls *Argus Leader*, 19 March 1966.

15 Excerpts from a letter August Hoeger, Sr., wrote to His Co-Workers in the GSS, December 1937.

16 (KH) Dr. Erwin Fritschel, Tape #39; *Sunshine*, Vol. XXXI, No. 2 (April-June 1953).

17 (KH) Dr. Erwin Fritschel, Tape # 39.

18 *The Good Samaritan*, Vol. 3, No. 3, August 1970.

19 (KH) Dr. Erwin Fritschel, Tape # 39.

20 *The Good Samaritan*, Vol. 3, No. 3, August 1970.

21 (KH) Dr. Erwin Fritschel, Tape # 39.

22 *Sunshine*, Vol. XV, No. 4 (July-August 1940).

23 *Bonell Family News*, Vol. II, No.3 (10 June 1980).

24 (KH) Mrs. Marie Walz, Volla Park, California, 1974, Tape # 49.

25 *Sunshine*, Vol. XXXI, No. 2 (April-June 1953).

26 (KH) Dr. Erwin Fritschel, Tape # 39.

27 *The Good Samaritan*, Vol. 12, No. 1 (Winter 1979).

28 (KH), Dr. Erwin Fritschel, Tape # 39.

29 GSS Personnel Records, Betty and Erv Chell.

30 *The Good Samaritan*, Vol. 3, No. 3 (August 1970).

31 *Ibid.*

32 Remembrances of Affairs in Iowa and Kansas, 1965, DAD HOEGER.

33 *Sunshine*, Vol. XXIX, No. 1 (January-February 1951).

34 (KH) - Rita and Nikolais Reinfelds, Olathe, Kansas, 1974, Tape # 43.

35 *Ibid.*

36 Olathe File, KANSAS.

37 *Ibid.*

38 Olathe File, KANSAS.

39 (KH) — Rita and Nikolais Reinfelds, Tape # 43.

40 Olathe File, KANSAS.

41 Olathe File, KANSAS.

42 Remembrances of Affairs in Iowa and Kansas, 1965, DAD HOEGER.

43 Olathe File, KANSAS.

44 *Buffalo Tales*, Vol. 16, No.1 (January-February 1993), Buffalo County, Nebraska, Historical Society.

45 On the Occasion of the 25th Anniversary of St. Luke's Home, 1979.

46 *Buffalo Tales* (January-February 1993).

47 An Account of St. Luke's Home and Center, 3 September 1963.

48 *Buffalo Tales* (January-February 1993).

49 "83 Years of History, St. Luke's Home and Center," *Kearney Daily Hub*, 1973.

50 *Buffalo Tales* (January-February 1993).

51 St. Luke's Home, NEBRASKA.

52 St. Luke's Home, NEBRASKA.

53 St. Luke's Home and Center, 3 September 1963.

54 The new construction cost $269,000.

55 On the Occasion of the 25th Anniversary of St. Luke's Home, 28 January 1979.

56 "83 Years of History, St.Luke's Home and Center," *Kearney Daily Hub*, 1973.

57 On the Occasion of the 25th Anniversary of St. Luke's Home, 28 January 1979. Because Cochran Hall had no elevator, the day care center was not permitted to use the two upper stories of the building. — *Buffalo Tales* (January-February 1993).

58 50th Anniversary, West Union, Iowa, GSS Center, 1991. IOWA HOMES.

59 *Ibid.*

60 West Union, Iowa, Groundbreaking and Dedication brochures, 24 October 1965 and 9 October 1966.

61 50th Anniversary, West Union, Iowa, GSS Center, 1991.

62 *Ibid.*

63 Contract of Sale, Palmer Memorial Hospital, 30 June 1975.

64 50th Anniversary, West Union, Iowa, GSS Center, 1991.

65 The Hilltop Review, West Union GSS Center, West Union, Iowa.

66 GSS Center, Clearbrook, Minnesota. BOX 2. MINNESOTA.

Chapter Nine

1 "Fargo Man Marks 50 Years as Pastor: Feted at Dinner," *Fargo Forum*, 1958.

2 *Smoke Signals*, 20 November 1963.

3 Annual Report of the GSS for 1971.

4 "Dad Hoeger — Man in Motion," Unpublished manuscript of Dolores Harrington, Sioux Falls, South Dakota, circa. 1966. Box 3 of Dad Hoeger Papers.

5 Author's interview with Rev. August Hoeger, Jr., Sioux Falls, South Dakota, 13 October 1994.

6 (KH) Eugene Hackler, Tape #45.

7 *Ibid.*

8 *Ibid.*

9 Minutes of the GSS, 2 November 1962.

10 Minutes of the GSS, 11 May 1962.

11 *Ibid.* (KH) Bertha Bosch Christian, Hastings, Nebraska, Tape #46.

12 Minutes of the GSS, 25 January 1962.

13 *Good Samaritan Village, the First 25 Years.* Hoeger Memorial Library, Good Samaritan Village, Hastings, Nebraska, 1983.

14 *Good Samaritan Society Newsletter*, 17 May 1957, 19 March 1958.

15 *The Good Samaritan*, Vol. 19, No. 2 (Spring 1986).

16 (KH) Reverend William Goldbeck, Hastings, Nebraska, Tape #6.

17 (KH) Rev. William Goldbeck, Tape # 6.

18 Rev. Hoeger's letter to the membership, 1957. DAD HOEGER, BOX 2.

19 *Ibid.*; Minutes of the GSS, 28 August 1958.

20 *Good Samaritan Village, First 25 Years*, Hastings, Nebraska, 1983.

21 Minutes of the GSS, 28 August 1958.

22 *Hastings Tribune*, 12 September 1992.

23 (KH) Viola Baugatz, Hastings, Nebraska, 1974, Tape # 10.

24 Hastings Nebraska, *Daily Tribune*, April 1972.

25 *Good Samaritan Village, First 25 Years*, Hastings, Nebraska, 1983.

26 Minutes of the GSS, 24 November 1969.

27 Author's interview with Augie Hoeger, 13 October 1994.

28 *Ibid.*

29 (KH) Ray Brown, Broken Bow, Nebraska, 1974, Tape # 40.

30 Dad Hoeger's Reminiscences.

31 Interview with Augie Hoeger, 13 October 1994.

32 Interview with Augie Hoeger, 13 October 1994.

33 (KH) Ray Brown, Tape # 40.

34 Letter to August Hoeger, Sr., from the U. S. Treasury Department, Washington, D.C., 24 May 1955. DAD HOEGER'S WRITINGS.

35 Minutes of the GSS, 12 May 1961.

36 Eugene T. Hackler, GSS PERSONNEL - RETIRED.

37 *The Good Samaritan*, Vol. 1, No. 1 (14 August 1967).

38 *Ibid.*

39 Author's interview with August Hoeger, Jr., 13 October 1994.

40 *The Union*, West Union, Iowa, 4 May 1978.

41 *Vital Signs*, May 1978.

42 (KH) Eugene Hackler, Tape # 45.

43 *Body and Soul* (Summer 1965).

44 Central Office Staff Meeting, 3 August 1964.

45 *Body and Soul* (Summer 1967).

46 *Body and Soul* (1965).

47 *The Good Samaritan*, Vol. 9, No. 1 (April 1976).

48 *Ibid.*

49 Minutes of the GSS, 26-27 February 1965.

50 Minutes of the GSS, 15-18 August 1965.

51 *Smoke Signals* (November 1970).

52 (KH) William Goldbeck, Tape #6.

53 Minutes of the GSS, 19-21 June 1967; (KH) William Goldbeck, Tape # 6.

54 (KH) Eugene Hackler, Tape #45.

Chapter Ten

1 Elie Wiesel, Memoirs, *All Rivers Run to the Sea*. New York: Alfred A. Knopf, 1995), 416.

2 *Good Samaritan Newsletter*, 18 November 1959.

3 Minutes of the GSS, 23 August 1959.

4 (KH) Eugene Hackler, Olathe, Kansas, 1974, Tape # 45.

5 (KH) Bertha Bosch Christian, Hastings, Nebraska, 1974, Tape # 46.

6 Good Friday Letter, March 1960. BOX 2, DAD HOEGER.

7 Christmas Letter, 1960. BOX 2, DAD HOEGER.

8 Newsletter from Dad Hoeger, 27 December 1960.

9 (KH) Mrs. Alberta Haferman, Junction City, Kansas, 1974, Tape # 49.

10 *Ibid.*

11 (KH) Jim Wunderlich, Osceola, Nebraska, 1974, Tape # 48.

12 Letter to August Hoeger, Jr., from Denver, Colorado, 2 February 1959. BOX 1, AUGIE HOEGER.

13 Interview with August Hoeger, Jr., 13 October 1994.

14 Minutes of the GSS, 22-24 August 1962.

15 *Ibid.*

16 Minutes of the GSS, 19 December 1962.

17 (KH) Bertha Bosch Christian, Tape # 46.

18 Inteview with August Hoeger, Jr., 13 October 1994.

19 Interview with August Hoeger, Jr., 13 October 1994.

20 Interview with August Hoeger, Jr., 13 October 1994.

21 *The Cynosure*, Fargo Senior High School, 27 April 1945; John Hoeger's 1987 Annual Report.

22 (KH) Reverend Jacob and Laura Jerstad, Tape #3.

23 *The Good Samaritan*, Vol. 20, No. 4 (Fall 1987).

24 A non-credible story is told of Augie and Betty coming home after a summer rainstorm and finding the basement office flooded. Augie shouted down to Betty — "How are the files?" She replied, "Soaking wet." "How are my books?" asked Augie. Betty said, "They are soaked too." Augie then asked Betty, "How are my old lectures?" She quickly replied, "They're just as dry as the day you delivered them." — FILE 4, AUGIE HOEGER.

25 (KH) Hugh Adams, Salina, Kansas, 1974, Tape # 49.

26 (KH) Jeris Tangen, Tape # 50.

27 Interview with August Hoeger, Jr., 13 October 1994.

28 Minutes of the GSS, 24-27 August 1964.

29 There were subsequent but infrequent complaints about administrative behavior reported at Central Office meetings. One administrator did not provide adequate food for his residents, and he did not bring them to chapel. In 1970, another administrator had failed to comply with Society standards after being given one more chance. He was given a "pink slip."— Central Office Staff Meeting, 19 May 1966; Staff retreat, 30 November-1 December 1970. CALENDAR OF EVENTS AND STAFF MEETINGS.

30 Wayne Lee Bute's interview with Richard Gorsuch, Sioux Falls, South Dakota, 2 February 1973.

31 (KH) Ray Conlon, Beresford, South Dakota, 1974, Tape #40.

32 John Hoeger's Annual Report, 1987; (KH) Erv and Betty Chell, Sioux Falls, South Dakota, 1974, Tape # 41.

33 John Hoeger's Annual Report, 1987; Steve Rogers, "Carrying on the Good Samaritan Tradition," *Contemporary Long Term Care* (October 1986).

34 John Hoeger's Annual Report, 1987.

35 *The Good Samaritan*, Vol. 18, No. 3 (Summer 1985).

36 Video, Heritage Celebration, Annual Meeting, 1985.

37 File and transcript of Col. Charles Peterson.

38 File and Transcript of Col. Charles Peterson.

39 Col. Charles Peterson's written responses to the author's questions, August 1996.

40 Foege, a longtime friend of Dad Hoeger had been a missionary to New Guinea for seven years. He had associated with the GSS in 1947. Besides serving as regional director for Kansas and Oklahoma (1964-1965), Foege assumed a similar role for Nebraska in 1966. In October 1973, he was named Director of New Development for the Society. Two months later, in December 1973, he died of a heart attack.

41 Gloria Whitson, GSS PERSONNEL - RETIRED.

42 Steve Rogers, "Carrying on the Good Samaritan Tradition."

43 John Hoeger's Annual Report, 1987. In a memo dated 29 September 1965, the Executive Director reminded administrators that they should never be absent from their duties without leaving someone in charge of the Home and notifying the regional director. He noted that some administrators came to work at 9:00 or 9:30 A.M., such tardiness was detrimental to the morale of the other employees.— Memo of the Executive Director, 29 September 1965. FILE 1, AUGIE HOEGER.

44 FILE 1, AUGIE HOEGER.

45 Philosophy Committee, Central Office Staff, 27 March 1966.

46 File and Transcript, Colonel Charles Peterson.

47 Col. Peterson's written responses to the author's questions, August 1996.

48 Steve Rogers, "Carrying on the Good Samaritan Tradition."

49 Minutes of the GSS, 19-21 June 1967.

50 *Ibid*.

51 Minutes of the GSS, 19 December 1962; 23-24 February 1967.

52 *The Good Samaritan*, Vol. 16, No. 2 (Summer 1983). Nordiss Winge retired on April 30, 1983. Mrs. Phyliis Day replaced her as Assistant to the President. She had joined the Central Office staff in July 1970 as receptionist and secretary.

53 Minutes of the GSS, 3 May 1965. Tompkin returned to private architectural practice in June 1968. — Minutes of the GSS, 22 June 1968. Ray Dirks assumed Foege's role in Kansas.In his report for 1968, the Executive Director listed the regional director's primary duties. They included:

    1. Assist, guide and supervise the administrators in their region.

    2. Visit most Centers at least four times a year.

    3. Hold one area meeting with administrators plus workshops, seminars and association meetings.

    4. The goal of the regional director should be the same as that of the administrator.

        a. To increase quality care of the resident — spiritually, mentally, emotionally and physically.

        b. Attend educational and training seminars, workshops and read geriatric research literature.

5. Other responsibilities:
   a. Influence nursing home legislation
   b. Cooperate in legal tax matters
   c. Ask to speak to all types of organizations
   d. Secure financing for new projects
   e. Meet with state, county and city welfare officials and with health and fire departments to discuss rates, standards and expansion requirements.
   — Minutes of the GSS, 15 November 1968.

54 Minutes of the GSS, 30 March 1969.

55 (KH) Ray Conlon, Beresford, South Dakota, 1974, Tape # 40.

56 August Hoeger, Jr., Annual Report, 1968.

57 Minutes of the GSS, 15 May 1968; 22 June 1968.

58 Minutes of the GSS, 15 June 1969.

59 In a paper he delivered at a conference in San Francisco, California, on 21 November 1968, August Hoeger, Jr., listed some of the qualifications of a good Center administrator. Society administrators 1) should have a prior successful employment record; 2) must demonstrate competence in the areas of nursing care and administration; 3) must believe that a Center is a place of "joy, compassion, dignity, activity and opportunity for spiritual growth rather than a sterile, professional atmosphere" and 4) should engage in necessary in-service education, not necessarily toward a degree. — Minutes of the GSS, 15 November 1968.

60 Minutes of the GSS, 15 November 1968.

61 *The Good Samaritan*, Vol. 2, No. 2 (December 1968).

62 Minutes of the GSS, 27 February 1969.

63 Minutes of the GSS, 17-20 August 1969.

64 Minutes of the GSS, 23-26 June 1970.

65 Minutes of the GSS, 23-26 June 1970; 12-15 June 1977.

66 Minutes of the GSS, 16 April 1969; 15 June 1969. FILE 2, AUGIE HOEGER.

67 Minutes of the GSS, 22 February 1969.

68 Minutes of the GSS, 16 April 1969.

69 Minutes of the GSS, 16 May 1969.

70 Minutes of the GSS, 18 August 1969.

71 Minutes of the GSS, 16-19 August 1970.

72 The symbol, designed by Thomsen, was approved by the Society's membership at the annual meeting, August 17-20, 1969. — Minutes of the GSS, 17-20 August 1969.

73 John Hoeger, "What Do You See?" *The Good Samaritan*, Vol. 9, No. 1 (April 1976).

74 Annual Report of the General Superintendent, 1968.

75 Minutes of the GSS, 13 August 1968.

76 Prior to building the chapel at Hastings, Colonel Peterson and Dad Hoeger had stopped at a little roadside chapel near New Underwood, South Dakota, to secure possible measurements for the proposed structure at Hastings. Pete used a dollar bill (six inches long) to measure the windows of the small chapel. — (KH) Col. Charles Peterson, Sioux Falls, South Dakota, 1974, Tape # 46.

77 John Hoeger, "What Is the Society's Greatest Concern?" *The Good Samaritan*, Vol. 15, No. 3 (Fall 1982).

78 Letter from Agnes Hoeger, Hastings, Nebraska, to her sisters, October 1970.

79 (KH) Col. Charles Peterson, Sioux Falls, South Dakota, 1974, Tape # 46.

80 Letter from Agnes Hoeger, Hastings, Nebraska, to her sisters, October 1970.

81 *Sioux Smoke Signals*, November 1970.

82 Brochure — "Introducing the Ev. Luth. GSS."

83 Russell Cox, "One Man's Opinion," Sunday, 13 February 1972.

84 *Ibid.*

Chapter Eleven

1 John Montgomery Bell, "We Give Thee But Thine Own," Lutheran Service Book and Hymnal. (Minneapolis: Augsburg Publishing House, 1965), 544.

2 *Body and Soul*, Summer 1965.

3 Letter from Paul Beidler to Rev. A. J. Hoeger, Jr., 31 March 1966; Letter from Sen. George McGovern to Rev. A. J. Hoeger, Jr., 30 March 1966. PROJECT VIETNAM.

4 Letter from Rev. A. J. Hoeger, Jr., to Sen. George McGovern, 21 April 1966.

5 PROJECT VIETNAM.

6 Minutes of the GSS, 19-21 June 1967.

7 PROJECT VIETNAM.

8 Minutes of the GSS, 20 November 1967.

9 Col. Charles Peterson's written responses to the author's questions, August 1996.

10 Letter from Dr. August Hoeger, Sr., to Center Administrators, Ash Wednesday, 1968. DAD HOEGER.

11 *Ibid.*

12 Project Vietnam Report to the 1970 Convention of the GSS. PROJECT VIETNAM.

13 Minutes of the GSS, 15 November 1968.

14 Project Vietnam Report to the 1970 GSS Convention. PROJECT VIETNAM.

15 Brochure of the World Relief Commission. PROJECT VIETNAM.

16 Letter from John D. Constable, M.D., to Hans G. Keitel, M.D., New York City, New York, 12 June 1973. PROJECT VIETNAM.

17 Christmas Letter to the GSS from Everett D. Graffam, 11 December 1972.

18 Letter to John Hoeger from Everett S. Graffam, Executive Vice President, WRC, 11 June 1974. PROJECT VIETNAM.

19 *Smoke Signals*, October 1972.

20 Project Vietnam's Annual Report to the 1972 Annual Meeting. PROJECT VIETNAM.

21 Letter to Mrs. W. H. Barclay, Boulder, Colorado, from Everett S. Graffam, WRC, 7 January 1975. PROJECT VIETNAM.

22 Letter from John Hoeger, to Dr. Everett Graffam, WRC, 26 March 1975.

23 Telegram to John Hoeger from WRC, 20 March 1975.

24 Letter to John Hoeger from Everett Graffam, WRC, 6 May 1975.

25 Telegram to John Hoeger from WRC, 20 March 1975.

26 Minutes of the GSS, 9-12 August 1974, Annual Meeting.

27 Financial Report, 31 July 1971. PROJECT VIETNAM.

28 Minutes of the GSS, 9-13 August 1974.

29 *The Good Samaritan*, Vol. 8, No. 1 (May 1975).

30 Minutes of the GSS, 15-18 June 1975; 10-13 August 1975.

31 Letter from Rev. John Hoeger to Dr. Everett S. Graffam, World Relief Commission, 11 September 1975. PROJECT VIETNAM.

32 Minutes of the GSS, 10-13 August 1975.

33 *The Good Samaritan*, Vol. 8, No. 2 (October 1975).

34 *Ibid.*, Vol. 8, No. 1 (May 1975).

35 *Ibid.*, Vol. 10, No. 2 (Fall 1977).

36 *Ibid.*, Vol. 2, No. 3 (Fall 1978); Vol. 12, No. 4 (Fall 1979).

37 Minutes of the GSS, 12-15 August 1984.

38 Minutes of the GSS, Annual Meeting, 9-12 August 1987.

39 At the 1996 annual meeting, the offering from the opening worship service, $3,536.90, went to the LAMB Project. The offering from the closing prayer luncheon, $3,645.60, was directed towards the support of John and Cathy Larson, missionaries in Cameroon, a Russian orphanage and World Hunger Relief. — *The Administrator*, 1 August 1996.

40 Rev. Greg Wilcox, Report on Project Outreach, Annual Meeting of the GSS, Sioux Falls, South Dakota, 21-24 July 1996.

41 Minutes of the GSS, 17 August 1970; 13-16 June 1971.

42 Letter from David E. Walters, Regional Director, GSS, to Rev. Rudolph A. Martin, Christ Church, Kansas City, Missouri. CHRISTIAN ACTION MINISTRY.

43 "CAMs Come Along Way, 10 Years of Action, 1965-1975," Christian Action Ministry brochure; *The Good Samaritan*, Vol. 3, No. 4, December 1970.

44 Minutes of the GSS, 5 March 1971.

45 Christian Action Ministry, ILLINOIS.

46 Christian Action Ministry, ILLINOIS.

47 Minutes of the GSS, 11-14 June 1974.

48 Minutes of the GSS, 13-16 June 1976.

49 Minutes of the GSS, 6 April 1977.

50 Management Agreements, 19 November 1976 and 3 March 1977, Christian Action Ministry, ILLINOIS.

51 Mary Nelson's letter to Rev. John Hoeger, 20 April 1978, Christian Action Ministry, ILLINOIS.

52 Author's interview with Rev. John Hoeger, 25 October 1995.

53 Christian Action Ministry, ILLINOIS.

54 Dedication brochure, Center for Human Development, 4 November 1979, Christian Action Ministry, ILLINOIS.

55 Author's interview with Rev. John Hoeger, 25 October 1995.

56 Letter to Al Brown and Rev. August Hoeger, Jr., 1 July 1981, CAM, ILLINOIS.

57 Release Agreement, 11 February 1983. CAM, ILLINOIS.

58 Minutes of the GSS, 18-19 February 1983.

59 *Chicago Tribune*, August-September 1983.

60 *Ibid.*

61 Minutes of the GSS, 22 June 1968; 11-14 August 1968 (Annual Meeting).

62 *The Good Samaritan*, Vol. 4, No. 1 (April 1971).

63 Minutes of the GSS, 9 August 1971; *The Good Samaritan*, Vol. 2, No. 3 (April 1969).

64 *The Good Samaritan*, Vol. 4, No. 1 (April 1971).

65 Minutes of the GSS, 5-9 August 1973; 21-22 February 1974.

66 *The Good Samaritan*, Vol. 10, No. 2 (Fall 1977).

67 Minutes of the GSS, 20 April 1979.

68 Minutes of the GSS, 7 October 1979.

69 Minutes of the GSS, 22-23 February 1980.

70 Minutes of the GSS, 22-23 February 1980.

71 Minutes of the GSS, 24 April 1981.

72 Minutes of the GSS, 8 December 1982.

73 Minutes of the GSS, 10 December 1982.

74 Minutes of the GSS, 18-19 February 1983.

75 Minutes of the GSS, 5-8 June 1983.

76 Annual Report of the GSS for 1970s; Minutes of the GSS, 18-19 August 1970.

77 Author's interview with Eduard Kilen, 29 May 1996.

78 *Ibid.*

79 *Ibid.*

80 *The Good Samaritan*, Vol. 12, No. 1 (Winter 1979).

81 *The Good Samaritan*, Vol. 20, No. 2 (Spring 1987); Senior Companion Brochure. The Good Samaritan Center at Fontanelle, Iowa, had established an Outreach Program to the elderly in 1970. The Center was staffed and prepared to provide grooming, assistance with toilet needs, laundry, light housekeeping, food preparation, delivery of prepared meals, and companionship and/or supervision to the community elderly in their own homes or apartments. — *The Good Samaritan*, Vol. 4, No. 1 (April 1971).

82 Author's interview with Eduard Kilen, 29 May 1996.

83 John Montgomery Bell, "We Give Thee But Thine Own."

Chapter Twelve

1 Minutes of the GSS, Board of Directors in Executive Session, 12 December 1986.

2 *The Good Samaritan*, Vol. 20, No. 4 (Fall 1987).

3 Minutes of the GSS, 23 November 1969.

4 DAD HOEGER'S REMEMBRANCES OF AFFAIRS IN IOWA AND KANSAS, 1965.

5 Rev. John Hoeger, "Reflections of Dad," *The Good Samaritan*, Vol. 3, No. 4 (December 1970).

6 Walter Pfeffer, Mason City, Iowa, 16 August 1972. OTHER RELATED ORGANIZATIONS.

7 Augie Hoeger said that his father and Reverend Mueller were both doers. In his words, they were "stubborn German pastors;" they were individualists and builders who, unfortunately, could not work together. It was Rev. Mueller who handpicked the Board of Directors for the Mason City and Spokane Homes. — Author's interview with Rev. August Hoeger, Jr., Sioux Falls, South Dakota, 13 October 1994.

8 Mason City, Iowa, 28 February, 9 April and 25 May 1958. OTHER RELATED ORGANIZATIONS.

9 Mason City. RECORDS OF INDIVIDUAL HOMES, IOWA.

10 Mason City, Iowa, 7 April 1962; 7 December 1962. OTHER RELATED ORGANIZATIONS.

11 Minutes of the GSS, 23 November 1969.

12 (KH) Eugene Hackler, Tape # 45; Mason City, Iowa. RECORD OF INDIVIDUAL HOMES.

13 Minutes of the GSS, 23-26 June 1970.

14 Minutes of the GSS, 15 June 1969.

15 Calendar of Events at the Central Office and Staff Meetings, 20 July 1973.

16 *The Good Samaritan*, Vol. 8, No. 2 (October 1975); 1977 Mission Statement.

17 Calendar of Events at the Central Office and Staff Meetings, 5 February 1973.

18 *The Good Samaritan*, Vol. 8, No. 2 (October 1975).

19 *Ibid.*, Vol. 11, No. 1 (May 1977).

20 21 July 1978. AUGIE HOEGER.

21 *The Good Samaritan*, Vol. 11, No. 1 (Winter 1978).

22 Minutes of the GSS, 5 September 1978; 2 October 1978.

23 The Society was exempt from the federal income tax under Section 501(c) (3) of the Internal Revenue Code.

24 *The Good Samaritan*, Vol. 12, No. 3 (Summer 1979); John Hoeger's letter to Senator Rex Haberman, Nebraska Legislator, 4 August 1980. JOHN HOEGER FILE.

25 *The Good Samaritan*, Vol. 14, No. 2 (Fall 1981); Minutes of the GSS, 9 August 1981.

26 Annual Report of the GSS, 1981.

27 The financial position of the GSS over forty years, from 1955 to 1995, is shown in the following table:

YEAR	ASSETS	LIABILITIES	EQUITY
1955	$ 3,133,000	$ 844,000	$ 2,289,000
1965	28,930,000	6,145,000	12,785,000
1975	111,639,000	82,228,000	28,411,000
1985	372,564,943	249,510,535	123,054,408
1990	445,149,464	254,624,273	190,525,191
1994	691,695,000	396,836,000	294,859,000
1995	722,720,000	398,398,000	324,322,000

— Annual Report of the GSS, 1995

28 Annual Report of the GSS, 1982.

29 Annual Report of the GSS, 1987.

30 Annual Report of the GSS, 1988.

31 Annual Report of the GSS, 1989.

32 *The Administrator*, Vol. 1, No. 10, 29 March 1989.

33 *Ibid.*, Vol. 1, No. 28, 8 September 1989.

34 Minutes of the GSS, 21-22 April 1989.

35 *The Administrator*, Vol. 2, No. 16, 1 June 1990.

36 At a Financial Statement Seminar in Denver, Colorado, on November 28, 1972, one of the participants asked Ray Conlon, a member of the Central Office staff, if the Good Samaritan Society was the largest corporation in geriatric care. Conlon responded, "We don't know and we're really not interested in that. Our concern is about the quality of care we provide." — Financial Statement Seminar, CHCA, Denver, Colorado, 28 November 1972.

37 (KH) Interview with Ray Conlon, 1974, Tape No. 40, GSS Archives.

38 *Ibid.*

39 Michael O. Bice, President of Lutheran Health Systems, Fargo, North Dakota, 1986. AUGIE HOEGER, BOX 2.

40 A Report on August Hoeger, Jr., Selection Research, Inc., 31 August 1981. AUGIE HOEGER, BOX 1.

41 Evaluation of August Hoeger, Jr., by the Board of Directors, Administrators and Central Office Staff of the GSS. AUGIE HOEGER, BOX 1; Selection Research Inc. Report on August Hoeger, Jr., 31 August 1981. AUGIE HOEGER, BOX 1.

42 Augie Hoeger's Final Report at the 1987 Annual Meeting. AUGIE HOEGER, BOX 4.

43 *Ibid.*

44 Minutes of the GSS, 11 February 1972.

45 (KH) Ray Conlon, Beresford, South Dakota, 1974, Tape # 40.

46 Final Report of August Hoeger, Jr., Annual Meeting, 1987. AUGIE HOEGER, BOX 4.

47 AUGIE HOEGER, 1986, BOX 2.

48 *Sioux Smoke Signals*, December 1972.

49 *The Good Samaritan*, Vol. 10, No. 1 (April 1977).

50 *Ibid.*, Vol. 5, No. 2 (August 1972).

51 Calendar of Events at the Central Office and Staff Meetings, 5 February 1973.

52 *Vital Signs*, 1 July 1977.

53 *The Good Samaritan*, Vol. 2, No.3 (Fall 1978).

54 Annual Report of the President, 1987. AUGIE HOEGER, BOX 4.

55 *The Good Samaritan*, Vol. 25, No. 3 (Fall 1972). Dr. Agnes Hoeger died on June 23, 1992, at Kissimmee, Florida. She was 82 years old.

56 Hoeger completed the study leave during the winter of 1974-1975. Minutes of the GSS, 21 February 1975.

57 Retreat, Parkston Country Center, 12-13 October 1976. REORGANIZATION, 1976-1978.

58 Minutes of the Reorganization Meeting, 8 March 1978. REORGANIZATION, 1976-1978.

59 Calendar of Events of the Central Office and Staff Meetings, 30 November 1983 and 22 May 1985.

60 *The Good Samaritan*, Vol 2, No. 3 (Fall 1978).

61 John Hoeger, Annual Report of the GSS, 1986.

62 *Smoke Signals*, published between 1963 and 1980.

63 Minutes of the GSS, 19-20 November 1970.

64 Minutes of the GSS, 16 November 1971.

65 Minutes of the GSS, Annual Meeting, 9-13 August 1974.

66 Minutes of the GSS, 21 February 1975, 14 August 1976, 23-27 July 1977 (Annual Meeting), 24 April 1981.

67 Minutes of the GSS, 20 February 1976.

68 When he retired to Hastings, one of August Hoeger Sr.'s first projects was to plan, to purchase and to plant a lovely prayer garden. A life-size crucifix was placed at the head of the garden.

69 *The Good Samaritan*, Vol. 9, No. 2 (October 1976); Eight thousand dollars of memorial gifts were given over to the publication of *Ever Forward*. Three thousand books at $3.00 per copy were printed. — Minutes of the GSS, 24 April 1981. Cost of the prayer garden was estimated at $12,000. — *The Good Samaritan*, Vol. 9, No. 1 (April 1976).

70 Minutes of the GSS, 20 February 1976.

71 *The Good Samaritan*, Vol. 9, No. 1 (April 1976). Dr. Thomsen, a native of Denmark and head of the Art Department at Dana College, Blair, Nebraska, died on January 6, 1991, at age 84.

72 Annual Report of the GSS, 1984. JOHN HOEGER, BOX 1.

73 Revised Administrators Manual and Procedures, 1 May 1987.

74 Instructions to Administrators, Area Meetings for 1986. AUGIE HOEGER, BOX 3.

75 Author's interview with August Hoeger, Jr., Sioux Falls, South Dakota, 13 October 1994.

76 Bertha Christian, Good Samaritan Society Prairie Center, Miller, South Dakota. *The Administrator*, Vol. III, No. 24, 8 August 1991.

77 In 1993, the local board of the Metropolis Center elected not to renew its contract with the Good Samaritan Society. — Annual Report of the GSS, 1993.

78 *The Good Samaritan*, Vol. 3 (April 1970).

79 Minutes of the GSS, 7-10 June 1987.

80 *Ibid.*, 25-28 February 1988.

81 Minutes of the GSS, 11-14 June 1974. The Laniolu facility was sold in 1992. Annual Report of the GSS, 1992. In April 1990, the Society made arrangements for the sale of the Laniolu Center, constructed by the ALC in 1962. The sale of the building was prompted by continued urbanization of downtown Honolulu, making it a less desirable site for a retirement residence. The agreement stipulated that the Good Samaritan Society continue to operate the Laniolu GS Center until May 1994. — Annual Report of the GSS, 1994.

82 Minutes of the GSS, 22-23 February 1980, 10-13 August 1980, 25 November 1980.

83 Minutes of the GSS, 4 August 1979; *The Good Samaritan*, Vol. 12, No. 4 (Fall 1979).

84 For many years, Dad Hoeger had remodeled large old houses, hospitals and hotels as nursing homes. In the summer of 1970, fire marshals ruled against further use of frame structures as nursing homes. — Minutes of the GSS, 19-20 November 1970.

85 Minutes of the GSS, 23 November 1969.

86 Minutes of the GSS, 19-20 November 1970.

87 Calendar of Events at the Central Office and Staff Meetings, 25-26 January 1984.

88 *The Good Samaritan*, Vol. 12, No. 2 (Spring 1979).

89 Annual Report of the GSS, 1986.

90 *The Good Samaritan*, Vol. 17, No. 1 (Winter 1984).

91 *Ibid*.

92 Minutes of the GSS, 15 June 1969.

93 GS CENTRAL OFFICE; *The Good Samaritan*, Vol. 15, No. 3 (Fall 1982). The first addition was dedicated on 24 July 1977.

94 Minutes of the GSS, 24 April 1981.

95 Minutes of the GSS, 4-7 June 1989.

96 *The Good Samaritan*, Vol. 25, No. 1 (Spring 1992).

97 Albert Erickson, Presentation at the GSS Heritage Celebration, Annual Meeting, 1985.

Chapter Thirteen

1 According to one administrator, government regulations made it more difficult for residents to feel that the nursing home was their home. Beryl Jensen believed people should be allowed to do some of the things they did in their own homes. — (KH) Mrs. Beryl Jensen, Hastings, Nebraska, 1974, Tape # 7.

2 Col. Peterson's written responses to the author's questions, August 1996.

3 *Ibid*.

4 Author's meeting with retired Good Samaritan Society administrators, Sioux Falls, South Dakota, 22 July 1996.

5 Col. Peterson's written responses to the author's questions, August 1996.

6 *The Good Samaritan*, Vol.18, No. 4 (Fall 1985).

7 Dad Hoeger's letter to administrators, 29 November 1968. DAD HOEGER, BOX 2.

8 (KH) Erv and Betty Chell, Sioux Falls, South Dakota, 1974, Tape # 41.

9 Rev. John Hoeger, 1985. JOHN HOEGER.

10 Minutes of the GSS, 14-18 August 1976.

11 Rev. August Hoeger, Jr.'s memo to administrators, 24 November 1976. AUGIE HOEGER, BOX 1.

12 *Good Samaritan Society Newsletter*, 7 December 1962.

13 *Smoke Signals*, September 1968.

14 Minutes of the GSS, 10 February 1972.

15 August Hoeger, Jr., Annual report for 1971.

16 *The Good Samaritan*, Vol. 4, No. 3 (December 1971).

17 Minutes of the GSS, 5-9 August 1973.

18 Minutes of the GSS, 11-14 June 1974; 15 November 1974.

19 *The Good Samaritan*, Vol. 9, No. 1 (April 1976).

20 *The Good Samaritan*, Vol. 2, No. 2 (Spring 1978).

21 *The Good Samaritan*, Vol. 19, No. 2 (Spring 1986).

22 Annual Report of the GSS for 1974.

23 Annual Report of the GSS for 1981; Staff Meetings, 2 May 1972; 21 December 1973. CALENDAR OF EVENTS AND STAFF MEETINGS.

24 Annual Report of the GSS for 1983.

25 Annual Report of the GSS for 1983.

26 *The Good Samaritan*, Vol. 22, No. 2 (Summer 1989).

27 *Ibid.*

28 Memorandum of 17 March 1986 Proposing a Joint Venture between Augustana College and the Good Samaritan Society.

29 Letter from Thomas J. Fairchild, Director, Center for Studies in Aging, University of North Texas, Denton, Texas, 9 September 1988. AUGIE HOEGER.

30 *The Administrator*, Vol. 7, No. 5, 15 February 1989.

31 Annual Report of the GSS for 1988.

32 *The Good Samaritan*, Vol. 24, No. 1 (Spring 1991).

33 *The Good Samaritan*, Vol. 23, No. 4 (Winter 1990-1991).

34 Annual Report of the GSS for 1992.

35 Minutes of the GSS, 15-18 June 1975.

36 A Recapitulation of the Elbow Room Rap Session of South Dakota Administrators, February 1984.

37 Author's interview with August Hoeger, Jr., 13 October 1994.

38 Steve Rogers, "Carrying on the Good Samaritan Tradition," Contemporary LTC (October 1986).

39 Speech by August Hoeger, Jr., Racine, Wisconsin, 24 February 1974.

40 GSS Newsletter, Summer 1963.

41 Author's interview with Kilen, 29 May 1996.

42 *The Good Samaritan*, Vol. 12, No.1 (Winter 1979).

43 *Ibid.*, Vol. 2, No. 2 (Spring 1978).

44 *Ibid.*, Vol. 15, No. 3 (Fall 1982); Minutes of the GSS, 9-12 August 1981 (Annual Meeting).

45 Author's interview with Kilen, 29 May 1966.

46 *Ibid.*

47 Annual Report of the GSS for 1974; Minutes of the GSS, 1978 Annual Meeting. ANNUAL MEETINGS FILE, 1976-1982.

48 *The Good Samaritan*, Vol. 6, No. 1 (April 1973).

49 *The Good Samaritan*, Vol. 4, No. 2 (August 1971).

50 *Ibid.*, Vol. 2, No. 2 (Spring 1978); Minutes of the GSS, 18 February 1977.

51 Author's interview with Kilen, 29 May 1996.

52 Eduard B. Kilen, "Family Discussion Group Meetings," *American Health Care Association Journal*, Vol. 4, No.1 (January 1978) 5-18.

53 Letter to the author from Don and Florence Toft, Sioux Falls, South Dakota, 29 July 1996.

54 *The Good Samaritan*, Vol. 12, No. 3 (Summer 1979).

55 *Ibid.*, Vol. 18, No. 2 (Spring 1985).

56 *Ibid.*, Vol. 15, No. 2 (Summer 1982).

57 *Ibid.*

58 *Ibid.*, Vol. 16, No. 1 (Spring 1983).

59 *Ibid.*, Vol. 19, No. 3 (Summer 1986).

60 AUGIE HOEGER, FILE 4, 1983.

61 *The Good Samaritan*, Vol. 22, No. 2 (Summer 1989).

62 *Ibid.*, Vol. 23, No. 3 (Fall 1990).

63 *Ibid.*, Vol. 5, No. 2 (August 1972).

64 Minutes of the GSS, Annual Meeting, 9-12 August 1981.

65 Minutes of the GSS, Annual Meeting, 24-28 July 1988; Alzheimer's Disease is a clinical disorder causing pathological changes in the brain. The disease was discovered by Dr. Louis Alzheimer in 1906 when he was doing an autopsy of the brain of a 51-year-old man. He found tangles and plaques on diseased brain tissue. — *Smoke Signals*, January 1985.

66 *The Good Samaritan*, Vol. 22, No. 4 (Winter 1989-1990).

67 *Smoke Signals*, September 1993; Huntington's Disease, a degenerative brain condition which affects the body and mind, is inherited. It does not skip generations. Each offspring of a Huntington affected patient has a 50 percent chance of inheriting the disease. It is a rare disease, affecting approximately 25,000 people in the United States.

68 *The Good Samaritan*, Vol. 27, No. 4 (Winter 1994-1995).

69 Hearing of the activities and quality of care, many prospective residents looked forward to a new life at the Centers. For example, Tony was scheduled to come to Northern Pines GS Center, Blackduck, Minnesota, on a Tuesday. He showed up the preceding day with all of his belongings. He was anxious to check-in, and he soon called the Center a resort. — Letter to the author from Don and Florence Toft, Sioux Falls, South Dakota, 29 July 1996.

Chapter Fourteen

1 Minutes of the GSS, 13 September 1974.

2 August Hoeger, Jr., Report to the Annual Meeting, 1978.

3 John Hoeger's Address at a Regional Meeting, 1970. JOHN HOEGER, BOX 1.

4 *Ibid.*

5 Annual Report of the GSS, 1986. JOHN HOEGER, BOX 1.

6 Dad Hoeger's letter of 29 November 1968. DAD HOEGER, BOX 2.

7 *The Good Samaritan*, Vol. 2, No. 2 (December 1968).

8 Rev. Jacob B. Jerstad was born 3 September 1913 at Fergus Falls, Minnesota. Ordained in 1941, he spent forty years in active ministry, retiring in December 1981. He died at Kissimmee, Florida, on 26 June 1994 at age eighty. — *The Good Samaritan*, Vol. 27, No. 3 (Fall 1994).

9 *The Good Samaritan*, Vol. 11, No. 1 (Winter 1978); *The Good Samaritan*, Vol. 13, No. 1 (Spring 1980).

10 Frank Wilcox was born on 18 June 1922. While an assistant pastor of a congregation in Seattle, Washington, he met "Billie" Hoeger, a member of the congregation. Prior to his death on 20 October 1993, he served as part-time chaplain at the Good Samaritan Society facility at Kissimmee, Florida. Committal services were held at Arthur, North Dakota on 27 October 1993. — *The Good Samaritan*, Vol. 26, No. 4 (Winter 1993-1994); Genealogical data in a letter written by Dr. Agnes Hoeger, February 1985.

11 Annual Report of the GSS, 1982; Minutes of the GSS, 5-8 June 1983.

12 Memorandum from Reverend John Hoeger to Good Samaritan Society administrators, 10 May 1988. GS SPIRITUAL DIRECTORS AND CHAPLAINS.

13 *The Administrator*, Vol. 4, No. 37 (10 September 1992).

14 Reverend Gregory Wilcox, *The Administrator*, Vol. 1, No. 20 (15 June 1989).

15 *The Administrator*, Vol. 4, No. 10 (24 March 1992).

16 *The Good Samaritan*, Vol. 26, No. 1 (Spring 1993).

17 Author's telephone conversation with Rev. John Hoeger, 26 October 1995.

18 No documentation can be found that the hierarchy of the American Lutheran Church proposed to censure August Hoeger, Sr., at a meeting in Waterloo, Iowa, in the mid-1930s. The Society's former legal counsel, Eugene Hackler, alludes to a censure motion in his interview with Ken Halvorsrude in 1974 (Tape # 45).

19 *Good Samaritan Society Newsletter*, 15 July 1958.

20 "God Had a Plan and A Man," *Lutheran Standard*, Vol. II, No. 8 (20 April 1971).

21 Letter from John M. Mason, Director, Services for Aging, ALC, to August Hoeger, Jr., 16 March 1973. Mason said that the Good Samaritan Society had failed to meet certain conditions stipulated by the ALC.

22 Letter from August Hoeger, Jr., to Dr. David W. Preus, Acting President of the ALC, 12 May 1973.

23 Author's interview with Rev. John Hoeger, 25 October 1995).

24 Letter from August Hoeger, Jr., to Dr. David W. Preus, Acting President of the ALC, 12 May 1973.

25 Minutes of the GSS, 20 February 1976.

26 Annual Report of the GSS, 1986.

27 Affiliation with the ALC and LCA, August 1986. Annual Report of the GSS, 1986; MISCELLANEOUS FILE.

28 *Ibid.*

29 *The Good Samaritan*, Vol. 20, No.1 (Winter 1987).

30 Lutheran Church-Missouri Synod to President Mark Jerstad, Good Samaritan Society, 25 September 1990.

31 Society News Items, 1994.

32 *The ALSMO Times*, June 1996.

33 Minutes of the GSS, 5 March 1970.

34 Minutes of the GSS, 12 August 1971; 9 August 1978.

35 Annual Report of the GSS, 1984.

36 Minutes of the GSS, 9-12 August 1987. Prior to the Society's affiliation with the ALC, it had not been possible for non-Lutheran Christians to serve as Board and Executive Staff members because of tax restrictions. — *The Good Samaritan*, Vol. 20, No. 1 (Winter 1987).

37 Members of the Society began receiving only summaries of Board meetings in 1992. The summaries included all reports presented and all resolutions projected and approved. Detailed minutes of Board meetings, essential for historical perspective and accuracy, would still be recorded and members, if interested, could request an official copy from the Secretary of the Society. As of 1993, in addition to the Executive Committee, the Board of Directors had three standing committees — Planning, Financial and Board Development. There were two special committees — the Audit Committee and the Nominating Committee.

38 Author's interview with Sylvia Gause, Secretary to the Board of Directors, 10 July 1997.

39 Minutes of the GSS, 21 February 1987.

40 Author's interview with August Hoeger, Jr., 13 October 1994.

41 *Ibid.*

42 31 May 1987. AUGIE HOEGER, BOX 2.

43 Study Leave Program, 1 July 1982. AUGIE HOEGER, BOX 2.

44 *The Good Samaritan*, Vol. 17, No. 2 (Spring 1984).

45 Minutes of the GSS, 12 August 1984.

46 Minutes of the GSS, Executive Session, 12 December 1986. AUGIE HOEGER, BOX 2.

47 Minutes of the GSS, Executive Session, 12 December 1986.

48 Climate Survey Results, 9 May 1988. AUGIE HOEGER, BOX 3.

49 Although his title was General Superintendent, Dad Hoeger may be considered the first president of the Good Samaritan Society. Minutes of the GSS, 9-12 August 1987.

50 Rev. John Hoeger, Annual Report, 1987.

51 1986. AUGIE HOEGER, BOX 2; 1987, JOHN HOEGER, BOX 1.

52 When the Society's Articles of Incorporation were revised in 1987, Augie and John Hoeger's title were changed to President and Executive Vice President respectively.

53 Michael Bice, President, Lutheran Hospital and Homes Society. AUGIE HOEGER, BOX 2.

54 Proposal to Evaluate the Central Office, 23 March 1988. AUGIE HOEGER, BOX 4.

55 JOHN HOEGER, BOX 1.

56 Rev. John Hoeger's Sermon at the 1989 Annual Meeting. JOHN HOEGER, BOX 1.

57 Author's conversation with Rev. John Hoeger, 25 October 1995.

58 Author's interview with Rev. John Hoeger, 25 October 1995.

59 *The Good Samaritan*, Vol. 22, No. 4 (Winter 1989-1990).

60 13 September 1989. JOHN HOEGER, BOX 1. Earlier, in 1974, the Good Samaritan Society had received the Meritorious Service Award at the 12th annual conference of the American Association of Homes for the Aging in Philadelphia. Eugene Hackler was president of the AAHA at that time. — *The Good Samaritan*, Vol. 7, No. 1 (February 1974).

61 Minutes of the GSS, 16-18 February 1989; *The Good Samaritan*, Vol. 22, No. 24 (Winter 1989-1990). Hoeger did not step down as president until October 1, 1989.

62 Rev. John Hoeger's Retirement Speech, 1989. JOHN HOEGER, BOX 1.

63 Rev. John Hoeger, Annual Report, 1987.

64 Rev. John Hoeger's Retirement Speech, 1989. JOHN HOEGER, BOX 1.

65 Sermon by Rev. John Hoeger, Annual Meeting, 1989. JOHN HOEGER, BOX 1.

Chapter Fifteen

1 Annual Report of the GSS, 1989.

2 Letter from Rev. John Hoeger to members of the GSS, 15 August 1988.

3 Letter from Charles C. Halberg, Chairman, Board of Directors, to all members of the GSS, 11 September 1989.

4 Laura Hoeger Jerstad, Mark Jerstad's mother, 22 July 1996, Sioux Falls, South Dakota.

5 Author's interview with Dr. Elliot Thoreson, Member of the Board of Directors, GSS, 4 June 1997.

6 *Ibid.*

7 Author's interview with Cynthia Moegenburg, GSS Regional Director for southern Minnesota, 3 June 1997.

8 Lynn Wagner, "Editor's Desk," Provider, (June 1997).

9 PERSONNEL — MARK JERSTAD FILE. In the first two weeks of his internship, Jerstad served as a nursing aide. He received word that he had passed his State and National Board of Nursing Home Administrator exams on his 42nd birthday, 6 May 1984.

10 Author's interview with Greg Wilcox, Director of Spiritual Ministries, GSS, 27 May 1997.

11 Dr. Charles Balcer, former president of Augustana College, Video of the Family Service for Mark Jerstad, 2 May 1997.

12 Greg Wilcox, 27 May 1997.

13 Author's interview with David Horazdovsky, COO, GSS, 29 May 1997.

14 Author's interview with Dennis Beeman, Vice President for Advancement, Development and Planning, GSS, 29 May 1997.

15 Horazdovsky, 29 May 1997.

16 Beeman, 29 May 1997.

17 Dr. Charles Balcer, Sioux Falls *Argus Leader*, 30 March 1997.

18 Annual Report of the GSS, 1989.

19 Author's interview with David Horazdovsky, Chief Operating Officer, GSS, 29 May 1997.

20 Author's interview with William (Bill) Kubat, Director for Resident and Community Services, GSS, 27 May 1997.

21 Author's interview with Joe Herdina, Accounting Department, GSS, 28 May 1997.

22 Horazdovsky, 29 May 1997.

23 *The Good Samaritan*, Vol. 27, No. 4 (Winter 1994-1995).

24 Horazdovsky, 29 May 1997.

25 Author's interview with Joe Herdina, Accounting Department, GSS, 28 May 1997.

26 *The Administrator*, Vol. 4, No. 10 (24 March 1992).

27 *The Good Samaritan*, Vol. 25, No. 1 (Spring 1992); *The Administrator*, Vol. 5, No. 42 (November 1993).

28 *The Administrator* (7 April 1995).

29 Beeman, 29 May 1997.

30 Horazdovsky, 29 May 1997.

31 William Kubat, Director for Resident and Community Services, GSS, 27 May 1997.

32 Horazdovsky, 29 May 1997.

33 Moegenburg, 3 June 1997.

34 "One Handshake At A Time," *Provider* (June 1997), 31.

35 Code of Ethics for the Board of Directors, GSS, revised on 3 May 1997.

36 *Ibid.*

37 "One Handshake At A Time," *Provider* (June 1997), 30.

38 Horazdovsky, 29 May 1997.

39 Beeman, 29 May 1997.

40 Keynote Address by Dr. Mark Jerstad to the Ohio Health Care Association — Observing Its 50th Anniversary, "At the Heart of the Matter, It's A Matter of the Heart," Video Tape, GSS Archives, 1997.

41 Lynn Wagner, "Editor's Desk," *Provider*, (June 1997), 6.

42 Beeman, 29 May 1997.

43 Horazdovsky, 29 May 1997.

44 Author's interview with Dr. Joyce Nelson, former chair of the Board of Directors, GSS, 29 May 1997.

45 "At the Heart of the Matter, It's a Matter of the Heart," Video Tape, GSS Archives, 1997.

46 Author's interview with Sonia Bury, Executive Secretary, GSS, 3 June 1997.

47 Marla Fern Gold, "A Portrait of Long-Term Care," *Provider*, Vol. 19, No. 1 (January 1993), 24.

48 Annual Reports of the GSS, 1993, 1994.

49 Marla Fern Gold, "A Portrait of Long-Term Care," 24.

50 *The Good Samaritan*, Vol. 24, No. 2 (Summer 1991).

51 Advancement, Support and Planning Session, 1996 Annual Meeting, 23 July 1996, Sioux Falls, South Dakota.

52 Annual Report of the GSS, 1995.

53 Minutes of the GSS, 19 October 1991; Annual Report of the GSS, 1994.

54 1995 Annual Report of the Ev. Luth. GSS and Related Corporations.

55 Elliot Thoreson, 4 June 1997.

56 CENTRAL OFFICE STAFF MEETINGS, Expanded Staff Meeting, 20 May 1992.

57 Minutes of the GSS, 4 June 1992.

58 Dr. Joyce Nelson, 29 May 1997.

59 Annual Report of the GSS, 1992.

60 *The Administrator*, Vol. IV, No. 47 (3 November 1992). The Good Neighbor Homes, being a part of a for profit corporation, paid local taxes in Minnesota. Although the Society realized the importance of this source of revenue for small communities, the GSS did not want to start paying taxes. Steps would be taken to remove the Society from the tax rolls while seeking other means to gain acceptance in the affected communities. — CENTRAL OFFICE STAFF MEETINGS, Expanded Staff Meeting, 20 May 1992.

61 Letter from Mark Jerstad to Co-Workers, 25 February 1991. PERSONNEL — MARK JERSTAD.

62 *The Administrator*, Vol. 5, No. 10 (24 March 1992); Vol. 6, No. 16 (1 April 1994).

63 Bill Kubat, 27 May 1997.

64 Dr. Joyce Nelson, 29 May 1997.

65 Horazdovsky, 29 May 1997.

66 Annual Report of the GSS, 1992.

67 Minutes of the GSS, 4 June 1992.

68 Bonnie Brown, 28 May 1997.

69 CENTRAL OFFICE STAFF MEETINGS, Expanded Staff Meeting, 20 May 1992.

70 Author's interview with Dean Mertz, Vice President for Human Resources, GSS, 27 May 1997.

71 Author's interview with Bonnie Brown, Vice President for Operations, 28 May 1997; Cynthia Moegenburg, 3 June 1997.

72 Elliot Thoreson, 4 June 1997; Joyce Nelson, 29 May 1997.

73 Proposed Joint Venture Between Augustana College and the GSS, Memorandum, 17 March 1986.

74 *The Administrator*, Vol. VI, No. 1 (4 January 1994).

75 Dr. Joyce Nelson, 29 May 1997.

76 *The Good Samaritan*, Vol. 27, No. 4 (Winter 1994-95).

77 Dr. Joyce Nelson, 29 May 1997.

78 *The Good Samaritan*, Vol. 25, No. 1 (Spring 1992); *The Administrator*, Vol. 5, No. 42 (November 1993).

79 Brenda Wade Schmidt, "Big Plans for Good Sam," Sioux Falls *Argus Leader*, 30 October 1994.

80 Annual Reports of the GSS, 1994. In July 1996, President Jerstad announced that Good Samaritan Supply Services, Inc., operated three pharmacies. — Report of the President of the GSS, July 1996.

81 Data secured from Sylvia Gause, Secretary to the Board of Directors, 10 July 1997.

82 Annual Report of the GSS, 1994.

83 Sonia Bury, 3 June 1997; National Campus Proposal, 19 May 1997.

Chapter Sixteen

1 Letter from Sandy Jerstad, Sioux Falls, South Dakota, to author dated 30 June 1997.

2 Cynthia Moegenburg, 3 June 1997.

3 Statement from Rev. Gary Sartain forwarded by Dean Mertz, Vice President for Human Resources, GSS, to author on 10 June 1997.

4 The Good Samaritan Society rented office space for $9.50 a square foot, including utilities.

5 *The Good Samaritan*, Vol. 25, No. 1 (Spring 1992).

6 Steve Young, "CEO Who Counseled the Dying Faces His Own Death with Faith." Sioux Falls *Argus Leader*, 4 February 1997.

7 Sioux Falls *Argus Leader*, 30 March 1997.

8 Data secured from Sylvia Gause, Secretary to the Board of Directors, GSS, 10 July 1997.

9 David Horazdovsky, 29 May 1997.

10 Annual Report of the GSS, 1995; *Metro Lutheran*, Vol. 9, No. 2 (February 1994).

11 Annual Report of the GSS, 1995.

12 *The Biggest Challenge Facing the GSS*, Prepared by NRECA Market Research, May 1993; *The Good Samaritan*, Vol. 27, No. 4 (Winter 1994-95).

13 Memorandum from Rev. August Hoeger, Sr., to GSS members, undated.

APPENDIX A

PRESIDENTS/CHAIRPERSONS
OF THE GOOD SAMARITAN SOCIETY
BOARD OF DIRECTORS, 1959-1997

1959 - 1963 DR. ERWIN G. FRITSCHEL
   GREELEY, COLORADO

1963 - 1965 WALLACE ESTENSON
   LUVERNE, MINNESOTA

1965 - 1970 FRED FRIEDRICHSEN
   OMAHA, NEBRASKA/ GLENVILLE, MIN-
   NESOTA.

1970 - 1972 REV. REINHARD BECKMAN
   SYRACUSE, NEBRASKA

1972 - 1974 REV. ORVAL K. NOREM
   DULUTH, MINNESOTA

1974 - 1978 JOHN M. LUNDBLAD
   JACKSON, MINNESOTA

1978 - 1980 MAURICE NELSON
   FORT COLLINS, COLORADO

1980 - 1982 DR. ELLIOT THORESON
   SIOUX FALLS, SOUTH DAKOTA

1982 - 1984 A. ROBERT LANGEMO
   ALBERT LEA, MINNESOTA

1984 - 1989 DR. CHARLES L. BALCER
   SIOUX FALLS, SOUTH DAKOTA

1989 - 1991 CHARLES C. HALBERG
   BURNSVILLE, MINNESOTA

1991 - 1993 DR. JOYCE I. NELSON
   SIOUX FALLS, SOUTH DAKOTA

1993 - 1995 DR. MARILYN STEMBER
   DENVER, COLORADO

1995 - 1997 CURTIS HAGE
   SIOUX FALLS, SOUTH DAKOTA

APPENDIX B

THE GROWTH OF THE GOOD SAMARITAN SOCIETY
1955 - 1995 *

YEAR	NO. OF STATES WHERE LOCATED	NO. OF FACILITIES	RESIDENT CAPACITY
1955		47	1,200
1960		68	3,000
1965 **		101	6,800
1966		106	7,800
1967		112	9,200
1968	17	122	9,168
1969	16	136	10,560
1970	17	145	11,500
1971	20	154	12,480
1972	21	160	13,414
1973	24	165	14,374
1974	24	168	15,885
1975	25	172	16,288
1976 ***			
1977	26	181	17,641
1978	26	188	18,224
1979	26	192	20,496
1980	26	201	22,776
1981	26	196	22,486
1982	26	196	20,725
1983	25	197	20,608
1984	25	196	23,000
1985	25	198	23,637
1986	25	200	23,943
1987	25	201	24,250
1988	25	201	24,201
1989	26	205	24,449
1990	26	208	24,736
1991	26	208	25,140
1992	26	241	28,448
1993	26	241	28,214
1994	26	236	27,431
1995	26	236	27,350

* Annual Reports of the GSS.
** Includes Centers owned and leased or managed by the GSS. The first Center managed by the Society, beginning in 1965, was at Metropolis, Illinois. Facilities under the aegis of the Good Samaritan Society, Inc. (the related HUD Corporations) are included as of 1980 with the opening of a HUD facility complex at El Paso, Texas in December 1980.
*** Annual Report Data for 1976 is missing.

APPENDIX C

FINANCIAL POSITION
GOOD SAMARITAN SOCIETY
1955 - 1995 *

YEAR	ASSETS	LIABILITIES	EQUITY
1955	$3,133,000	$ 844,339	$ 2,288,661
1960	10,700,000		6,900,000
1965	28,930,193	16,144,860	12,785,333
1966	35,600,000		14,500,000
1967	43,300,000		17,200,000
1968	50,000,000	31,400,000	19,800,000
1969	55,200,000	34,000,000	22,400,000
1970	61,330,608	35,802,558	25,500,000
1971	68,339,500	44,492,197	23,847,300
1972	73,839,074	46,594,373	27,244,701
1973	86,463,014	58,245,191	28,217,823
1974	97,153,931	66,392,336	30,761,595
1975	111,639,000	82,883,989	28,411,000
1976	120,727,099	86,847,291	33,879,808
1977	30,884,412	91,618,479	39,265,933
1978	146,658,370	101,481,261	45,177,109
1979	175,983,903	123,641,561	52,267,762
1980	195,602,870	134,302,262	58,738,316
1981	216,314,119	153,175,966	63,138,153
1982	248,074,000	170,852,000	77,222,000
1983	264,448,917	176,080,323	88,368,594
1984	315,737,950	211,775,806	103,962,144
1985	372,564,943	233,505,746	123,054,408
1986	392,979,509	253,055,931	139,923,578
1987	405,907,348	256,487,564	149,419,785
1988	408,511,944	247,742,027	160,769,917
1989	426,554,205	249,956,593	176,597,612
1990	445,149,464	254,624,273	190,525,191
1991	479,883,581	279,994,780	206,888,801
1992	596,500,000	303,377,867	234,861,000
1993	665,283,000	396,972,000	268,311,000
1994	697,814,000	396,836,000	293,517,000
1995	722,720,000	398,398,000	324,332,000

*   Annual Reports of the GSS.

APPENDIX D

CODE OF ETHICS FOR BOARD OF DIRECTORS

The National Board of Directors of the Evangelical Lutheran Good Samaritan Society (hereafter referred to as the Society) endorses the Code of Ethics currently in use throughout the Society. We believe that as Christian people we are committed to personal and professional excellence in our service to the Society.

AS A BOARD MEMBER:

● I will be informed of the culture, history, philosophy and mission of the Society.

● I will recognize my primary obligation and responsibility to serve the Society - residents, staff, members and other constituencies.

● I will uphold the integrity of the Society by exhibiting dedicated service through active participation, regular attendance and sound judgment. Honesty, commitment and loyalty are critical to the decisions made by the Board.

● I will with dignity, recognize, support and respect Board members in our efforts to govern and serve the Society.

● I will strive to advance my knowledge and skills as a Board member, participating in education and training opportunities.

● I will recognize and maintain confidentiality with respect to issues where discretion is indicated.

AS A BOARD:

● We will dedicate our work to upholding the mission of The Evangelical Lutheran Good Samaritan Society:

"To share God's love in word and deed by providing shelter and supportive services to older persons and others in need, believing that `In Christ's Love, Everyone Is Someone.'"

● We will recognize that it is our primary obligation and responsibility to serve the Society - residents, staff, members and other constituencies.

● We will uphold the integrity of the Society by promoting Christian service, health care excellence and fiscal responsibility.

● We will with dignity recognize, support, respect and empower Society employees in their efforts of professional growth and development.

● We will set strategic direction for the Society and support all organizational strategic planning goals and the efforts necessary to achieve these goals.

● We will promote the utmost professionalism in all Society employees and will act on behalf of the Society when breeches of conduct

● I will act in the best interest of the Society and refrain from using my position to secure special privilege, gain or benefit for myself through my actions or influence.

● I will uphold all laws and regulations relating to business activities and decision making policies of the Society.

are presented to Board for deliberation or direction.

● We will act in a responsible manner when faced with ethical, legal, corporate or organizational problems that could potentially violate the integrity of the Society.

● We will govern with fundamental honesty in adherence to the law and the decision-making policies of the Society.

The Code of Ethics was revised on May 3, 1997.

BIBLIOGRAPHY

Most of the research material used in this endeavor is housed in the archives of the Good Samaritan Society at the Society's national headquarters in Sioux Falls, South Dakota. The archives are a collection of collections — consisting of the personal papers of the Society's leadership, financial and personnel records, the various programs and policies of the Society since its beginning in 1922, books, periodicals, cassette tapes, video tapes, still photographs, and information on the 240 plus facilities of the Good Samaritan Society.

FILES CITED:

Allen Memorial Hospital, Waterloo, Iowa
Annual Meetings
Annual Reports of the Good Samaritan Society, 1952-1995
Arthur Home
Arthur Home and Residents - Early Years
Arthur Home File
Articles of Incorporation and Other Documents
Central Office Calendar of Events - Staff Meetings
Central Office - 1970 Construction
Christian Action Ministry
Colorado - Homes
Crippled Children's Homes
Dad Hoeger
   Dad Hoeger- Awards, Writings, Newsclippings, Magazine Features
   Dad Hoeger - Correspondence, 1905-1970s
   Dad Hoeger - "Dad's Reminiscences"
   Dad Hoeger - His Interests, Miscellaneous Pamphlets
   Dad Hoeger - Mother and Father
   Dad Hoeger - Personal
   Dad Hoeger and Others
   Dad Hoeger's Writings
   Documents - Mother and Dad Hoeger
   Mother and Dad Hoeger - Personal
DOAS - Development of Adult Services
Expansion Reports, 1970-1984
Good Neighbor
Good Samaritan Society - History and Adult Services
Good Samaritan Society - Personnel Records
Good Samaritan Society - Spiritual Directors and Chaplains
Hastings

Helpers Club
History and Personnel
August (Augie) Hoeger, Jr., Executive Director (2 boxes)
John Hoeger
Illinois - Homes
Iowa - Homes
Mark Jerstad
Jim River Ranch
Kansas Homes
Luther Lodge
Lutheran Good Samaritan Training School
Minnesota - Homes
Minutes of Annual Meeting Reports, 1922-1980s
Minutes of the Commission on Charities, ALC, 1939-1940
Minutes of the Conferences of the Laity, Arthur, ND, 1922
Minutes of the Good Samaritan Society, 1922-1995
Minutes of the Lutheran Hospital and Homes Society, 1938-1940
Miscellaneous
Mission Statements
Nebraska - Homes
North Dakota - Homes
Other Related Organizations
Parkston, SD - Papers, Records, Documents
Personnel
Colonel Charles Peterson
Project Vietnam
Records of Retired Personnel
Reorganization, 1976-1978
Seventieth Anniversary Celebration
Sixtieth Anniversary Celebration
Society Goals
Society News Items
South Dakota - Homes

GOOD SAMARITAN SOCIETY PERIODICAL FILES CITED:

The Administrator, 1989-1996
Body and Soul, 1965-1967
Bonell Family News, 1980
Die Mission Stunde, 1913-1918
Good Samaritan, 1969-1996
Good Samaritan Newsletter, 1955-1963
Ranch News from the GSS Ranch, 1949
Smoke Signals, 1963-1980
Sunshine, 1923-1954

Vital Signs, 1971-1984

UNPUBLISHED MANUSCRIPTS:

Dad Hoeger's Account of the Move to Fargo College.
Haacke, Lauren, "Comments to His Siblings," 6 June 1990.
Harrington, Dolores, "Dad Hoeger - Man In Motion."
Krause, Herbert, "Incomplete Literary Biography of Dad Hoeger."
"Notes of a Conversation with John Bosch," 9 September 1991.
Person, Irma, "History of the Sioux Falls Good Samaritan Center," 31 December 1984.
Wedge, Lucille Greer, "I Knew Reverend Hoeger."

ORAL INTERVIEWS:

By author:

Dennis Beeman
Bonnie Brown
Sonia Bury
Sylvia Gause
Joe Herdina
Rev. August Hoeger, Jr.
Rev. John Hoeger
David Horazdovsky
Eduard Kilen
William Kubat
Opal and Glen Maggert
Patrice Meier
Dean Mertz
Cynthia Moegenburg
Dr. Joyce Nelson
Col. Charles Peterson
Retired GSS Administrators
Dr. Elliot Thoreson
Gregory Wilcox

By Ken Halvorsrude:

Assembling data for a biography of Dad Hoeger, Ken Halvorsrude, in 1974, conducted interviews with over eighty people, who at one time or another, had been associated with the Good Samaritan Society. Typed transcripts of all of these interviews are housed in the Good Samaritan Society Archives. For each of the interviews the author used, the number of the tape is indicated in parentheses beside the name of the person interviewed.

Hugh Adams (49), Mrs. Ray Anderson (52), Clarence Austad (22), Mrs. Harold Axen -Dorothea Olson (48), Viola Baugatz (10), Ray Brown (40), Al Burgum (24A), Dr. Anne Carlsen (52), Erv and Betty Chell (41), Bertha Bosch Christian (46), Henry Christline (44),

Ray Conlon (40), Mrs. Jacob Dockler (41), Emma Eide (9), Ruth Erickson (30), Mrs. Henry Foege (44), Mrs. Dorothy Fowler (24B), Wallace Franke (46), Dr. Erwin Fritschel (39), Rev. H. S. Froiland (41), Rev. William Goldback (6), Rev. J. H. Groth (49), Eugene Hackler (45), Mrs. Albert Haferman (49), Mr. and Mrs. Fred Heidt (31), Hilda Hinkle (18), Rev. August Hoeger, Jr.(nn), Rev. August Hoeger, Sr. (35,36,38), Rev. John Hoeger (32), Bertha and James Holstein (24B), Minnie Hove (50), Mrs. Joanne Iwen (16), Mrs. Beryl Jensen (7), Rev. Jacob and Laura Jerstad (3), Woody Jorgenson (47), Mrs. Fred Knautz (24A), Rev. William Kraushaar (49), Frank Kuehn (24B), Mr. and Mrs. Clark Lincoln (20), Elizabeth and Gilbert Lindgren (5), Orvis Okerland (39), Rev. Hugo Schwartz (43), Col. Charles Peterson (46), Augusta Priewe (14), Mr. and Mrs. Howard Pueppke (23), Rita and Nikolais Reinfelds (43), Rev. Wilko Schoenbohm (50), Ed and Esther Schur (30), Rev. Hugo Schwartz (43), Mrs. W. C. Sweeney (43), Jeris Tangen (50), Jeruel Tangen (2), Rev. George Unruh (19), Mrs. Marie Walz (49), Lucille Wedge (52), Lillian Whitely (12), Bertha Wolf (16), Jim Wunderlich (48), Joyce Zewicki (21), Mr. and Mrs. Bill Zimmerman (25).

VIDEO TAPES:

Heritage Celebration, 1985.
"At the Heart of the Matter, It's A Matter of the Heart."
Family Service for Mark Jerstad, 2 May 1997.
"Origins of the Good Samaritan Society, Arthur," 1992.

LIST OF PUBLISHED WORKS CITED:

ALSMO Times (June 1966).

American Health Care Association Journal. (January 1978).

Brewer, David, "Administrator's Desk." Bonell Torch (December 1970).

Burgum, Leland S., "From Obscurity to Security. An Historical and Statistical Analysis of the Movement to Aid Physically Handicapped and Disabled Adults in North Dakota." (1937).

Cook, David C., *Sunday Digest.* (22 March 1958).

Cox, Russell, "One Man's Opinion," *Sunday*. (13 February 1972).

Flanagan, John T., *Theodore C. Blegen, A Memoir*. Northfield, MN: Norwegian American Historical Association, 1971.

GSI Yearbook.

"God Had a Plan and A Man," *Lutheran Standard*. Vol. 2, No. 8 (20 April 1971).

Gold, Marla Fern, "A Portrait of Long-Term Care," *Provider*. Vol. 19, No. 1 (January 1993).

History of the First District of the Ev. Luth, Synod of Iowa, 1982.

Hoeger, Agnes and Person. Irma T. *Ever Forward! The Story of Dad Hoeger*. Sioux Falls: Ev. Luth. Good Samaritan Society, 1981.

Hudson, Lois Phillips. *Reapers of the Dust, A Prairie Chronicle*. Boston: Little, Brown and Company, 1951.

Kilen, Eduard B. "Family Discussion Group Meetings," *American Health Care Association Journal*. (January 1978).

Life-time, 50th Anniversary of the Good Samaritan Society. 1972.

Monitor, Journal of the South Dakota Health Care Professionals. (September-October 1989).

"One Handshake At A Time," *Provider*. (June 1997).

One Hundred Years With Arthur [North Dakota]. 1882-1982.

Rogers, Steve, "Carrying On the Good Samaritan Tradition," *Contemporary Long-Term Care*. (October 1986).

St. John's Lutheran Church, Arthur, ND, 75th Anniversary. (1963).

St. John's Lutheran Church, Arthur, ND, 100th Anniversary. (1888-1988).

Tweton, D. Jerome and Rylance, Daniel F. *The Years of Despair, North Dakota In the Depression*. Grand Forks: The Oxcart Press, 1973.

Wagner, Lynn, "Editor's Desk," *Provider*. (June 1997).

Wiesel, Elie. *Memoirs, All Rivers Run to the Sea.* New York: Alfred A. Knopf, 1995.

NEWSPAPERS:

Chicago Tribune, 1983.
Fargo Forum, 1958, 1962, 1965, 1967, 1980.
Metro Lutheran, 1994.
Parkston Advance, 1988.
Sioux Falls Argus Leader, 1938, 1966, 1994, 1997.